中国书法

THE ART OF CHINESE CALLIGRAPHY

Zhou Kexi

Better Link Press

This book is edited and designed by the Editorial Committee of *Cultural China* series

Managing Directors: Wang Youbu, Xu Naiqing
Editorial Director: Wu Ying
Editor: Daniel Clutton
Assistant Editor: Zou Jueping

Text by Zhou Kexi
Translation by Yawtsong Lee

Cover Design: Wang Wei
Interior Design: Yuan Yinchang, Li Jing, Hu Bin
Cover Image: Getty Images

ISBN: 978-1-60220-117-0

Address any comments about *The Art of Chinese Calligraphy* to:

Better Link Press
99 Park Ave
New York, NY 10016
USA
or
Shanghai Press and Publishing Development Company
F 7 Donghu Road, Shanghai, China (200031)
Email: comments_betterlinkpress@hotmail.com

Computer typeset by Yuan Yinchang Design Studio, Shanghai
Printed in China by Shanghai Donnelley Printing Co. Ltd.

1 2 3 4 5 6 7 8 9 10

CONTENTS

Preface

Seal script (篆 *zhuan*), clerical script (隶 *li*), regular script (楷 *kai*), running script (行 *xing*) and cursive script (草 *cao*), commonly referred to as the five styles of Chinese calligraphy, are actually a combination of script types and writing modes, which are two different concepts.

There are only three calligraphic styles if we consider script types only, they are: seal script (篆书 *zhuan shu*), clerical script (隶书 *li shu*) and regular script (楷书 *kai shu*). There are also only three calligraphic styles as far as writing modes are concerned: standard hand (正书 *zheng shu*), running hand (行书 *xing shu*) and cursive hand (草书 *cao shu*). Nowadays, regular script is commonly referred to as standard script, while regular script written in an abbreviated fashion is called cursive script and regular script written in a way that is not quite as formal as standard script and not quite as informal as cursive script, is called running script. In fact, the script types seal script and clerical script can be written in a neat hand with distinct strokes as in standard hand, in an expedient, abbreviated fashion with linked strokes as in cursive hand, or alternatively in running hand. Thus, the so-called cursive seal script (草篆 *cao zhuan*) is seal script written in the cursive style, and early cursive script (章草 *zhang cao*) is clerical script written in the cursive style.

An examination of the evolution of modes of writing in the history of Chinese calligraphy reveals an interesting phenomenon, i.e. increasing complexity and personalization of writing styles against a backdrop of increasing simplification and conventionalization of script types. Before the Wei and Jin dynasties, calligraphic evolution is mainly reflected in changes in script types, from oracle bone writing to greater seal script, to lesser seal script, to clerical script, as the structure of words became increasingly simplified and standardized. As calligraphic works in those times predominantly took the form of engravings, the modes of writing, through the evolution from oracle bone writing to clerical script, were relatively simple, with lines of uniform thickness. Even in clerical script, the only variations were found in the endings of diagonal strokes. No doubt this lack of variation was linked to the limitations of engraving with a cutting tool.

Things began to change in the Wei and Jin dynasties. For one thing, the evolution of script types had finally run its course with the advent of regular script, and calligraphers naturally turned their attention to writing styles for more possibilities of artistic expression. Paper and fabric were becoming in that period a worthy rival to bronze and stone as calligraphic medium and eventually supplanted stone as the main medium for calligraphy in the Song dynasty. Free of the limitations of engraving, the writing brush saw its potential fully deployed in showcasing the magic of brush technique, movement and spirit.

Unlike in the past, when there was no need to make a special distinction between the running hand and cursive hand in the writing of seal and clerical scripts (predominantly written in standard hand, with running hand and cursive hand a second choice), a clear distinction had to be made in the Wei and Jin dynasties between regular, running and cursive scripts because regular script was being written in the standard, running and cursive hand by calligraphers and all three styles were building a large following.

Therefore the categorization of seal script, clerical script, regular script, running script and cursive script is a result of the addition of the running and cursive writing modes (of regular script) to the three script types of seal script, clerical script and regular script.

The word 篆 (*zhuan*: seal script) has an archaic meaning of "inscribing or engraving." Seal script is further divided between greater seal script (大篆 *da zhuan*) and lesser seal script (小篆 *xiao zhuan*). Greater seal script is sometimes referred to as zhou writing (籀文 *zhou wen*) because its invention was attributed to a grand scribe named "Zhou." It is also called bronze or metal writing (金文 *jin wen*) or bell and pot writing (钟鼎文 *zhong ding wen*) because it was often engraved on bronze vessels. Stone drum writing (石鼓文 *shi gu wen*) is a standardized version of bronze writing, and can be considered the standard of greater seal script. Lesser seal script is also called Qin seal script (秦篆 *qin zhuan*), reputedly invented by Li Si, Grand Councilor of the Qin dynasty. Every word had a number of variants in greater seal script but only one in lesser seal script. Canonical works in seal script include *Inscriptions on Bronze Plate of the San Tribe* (散氏盘铭文 *san shi pan ming wen*), *Stone Drum Inscriptions* (石鼓文 *shi gu wen*), *Stone Tablet of Mount Yi* (峄山刻石 *yi shan ke shi*), *Divine Prophecy Tablet* (天发神谶碑 *tian fa shen chen bei*) and *Tombs of Ancestors* (栖先茔记 *qi xian ying ji*).

According to historical chronicles, clerical script was invented by Cheng Miao 程邈, a prison official of the Qin period. This script, being easier to work with than seal script, was first used in official correspondence and communications. The script came to be known as clerical script (*li shu*) because the low-ranking officials responsible for official correspondence were called "*tu li*" (徒隶). The Han dynasty was the golden age of clerical script. The majority of surviving works in the clerical script of the Han dynasty are inscriptions on memorial steles. It was little used from the Wei and Jin dynasties to the Ming dynasty. The few calligraphers who wrote in this style did not achieve any great artistic fame. It is only with the rise of the stele school in the Qing dynasty that the clerical script form reached another peak of artistic achievement. Canonical works in clerical script include *Ode to Stone Gate* (石门颂 *shi men song*), *Yi Ying Tablet* (乙瑛碑 *yi ying bei*), *Ritual Vessels Tablet* (礼器碑 *li qi bei*), *Mount Hua Tablet* (华山碑 *hua shan bei*), *Shi Chen Tablet* (史晨碑 *shi chen bei*), *Zhang Qian Tablet* (张迁碑 *zhang qian bei*), *Cao Quan Tablet* (曹全碑 *cao quan bei*), *Ode to Xixia* (西狭颂 *xi xia song*) and *Ode to Fuge* (郙阁颂 *fu ge song*).

Regular script is also called true script, and in more ancient times, regular clerical script (楷隶 *kai li*) or contemporary clerical script (今隶 *jin li*). According to historical records, regular script was adapted from clerical script by Wang Cizhong 王次仲 of the Qin dynasty. But regular script did not become popular until the Western Jin, and its evolution into a major form of calligraphic art had much to do with the pioneering efforts of the great calligraphic masters Zhong You 钟繇 and Wang Xizhi 王羲之. The expression "regular script" connotes "codes," "example" or "orthography." From the Wei and Jin dynasties onward, two styles of regular script evolved, with the northern school represented by the stele tradition and the southern school by Wang Xizhi and his son Wang Xianzhi 王献之, commonly referred to as the two Wangs. The Tang regular script style evolved from the southern school but merged the virility of the Wei stele inscriptions with the grace of the Southern tradition. The codes and conventions established for the Tang regular script by master calligraphers including Ouyang Xun 欧阳询, Yu Shinan 虞世南 and Chu Suiliang 褚遂良 have become the canon for the study of regular script writing. Canonical works in regular script include *Memorial to the Emperor for the Acceptance of Other's Surrender* (宣示表 *xuan shi biao*), *Memorial to the Emperor for Recommending Ji Zhi* (荐季直表 *jian ji zhi biao*), *Essay on Yue Yi* (乐毅论 *yue yi lun*), *Rhapsody on the Luo River Goddess* (洛神赋 *luo shen fu*), *Cuan Bao Zi Tablet* (爨宝子碑 *cuan bao zi bei*), *Cuan Long Yan Tablet* (爨龙颜碑 *cuan long yan bei*), *In Memory of a Buried Crane* (瘗鹤铭 *yi he ming*), *Zhang Meng Long Tablet* (张猛龙

碑 *zhang meng long bei*), *Epitaph for Zhang Hei Nü* (张黑女墓志 *zhang hei nü mu zhi*), *Long Cang Temple Tablet* (龙藏寺碑 *long cang si bei*), *Sweet Spring at Jiucheng Palace* (九成宫醴泉铭 *jiu cheng gong li quan ming*), *Monk Daoyin Tablet* (道因法师碑 *dao yin fa shi bei*), *Confucius Temple Tablet* (孔子庙堂碑 *kong zi miao tang bei*), *Monk Meng Tablet* (孟法师碑 *meng fa shi bei*), *Preface to Buddha's Teachings at Goose Pavilion* (雁塔圣教序 *yan ta sheng jiao xu*), *Zen Master Xinxing Tablet* (信行禅师碑 *xin xing chan shi bei*), *Preface to the Inscription of Officials' Name* (郎官石柱记序 *lang guan shi zhu ji xu*), *Prabhutaratna Buddha Pagoda Tablet* (多宝塔碑 *duo bao ta bei*), *Altar to an Immortal on Mount Magu* (麻姑仙坛记 *ma gu xian tan ji*), *Letter of Attorney* (自书告身 *zi shu gao shen*), *Tablet of the Xuanmi Pagoda* (玄秘塔碑 *xuan mi ta bei*), *Imperial Guard Tablet* (神策军碑 *shen ce jun bei*) and *Miaoyan Temple Chronicle* (妙严寺记 *miao yan si ji*).

Running script was, according to popular belief, invented by Liu Desheng 刘德升 in the late Eastern Han dynasty. It is easier to write than regular script and more legible than cursive script. It is called running script because it soon "runs" to every corner of the realm by virtue of its many practical uses. Unlike seal, clerical, regular and cursive script, running script does not have a rigid set of codes and rules for its execution. Running script written in a neat fashion is called running regular script (行楷 *xing kai*) and if it is written in a freer manner, it is called running cursive script (行草 *xing cao*). There is no shortage of running script works "contaminated" by regular or cursive script words. Running script has been a favorite among calligraphers through the ages because its ease of use and flexibility facilitate self-expression. *Orchid Pavilion Preface* (兰亭序 *lan ting xu*) by Wang Xizhi of the Eastern Jin dynasty, *Draft Eulogy for a Nephew* (祭侄文稿 *ji zhi wen gao*) by Yan Zhenqing 颜真卿 of the Tang dynasty and *Poem to Express Melancholy after Demotion* (黄州寒食诗卷 *huang zhou han shi shi juan*) by Su Shi 苏轼 of the Song dynasty are considered by later generations to be the foremost, the second best and the third best running script works in history. These exquisite masterpieces are excellent examples of self-expression through the brush. Other canonical works in running script include *Letter to Express Worries and Indignation towards the Destruction of an Ancestral Tomb* (丧乱帖 *sang luan tie*), *Letter to Say Thanks Again* (二谢帖 *er xie tie*), *Letter to Express Happiness and Greetings* (快雪时晴帖 *kuai xue shi qing tie*), *Letter about Duck's Head Pill* (鸭头丸帖 *ya tou wan tie*), *Mid-Autumn Scroll* (中秋帖 *zhong qiu tie*), *Letter to a Relative* (伯远帖 *bo yuan tie*), *Confucius Dreams of His Death* (仲尼梦

奠帖 *zhong ni meng dian tie*), *Epitaph for Princess Ru'nan* (汝南公主墓志 *ru nan gong zhu mu zhi*), *Rhyme Prose* (文赋 *wen fu*), *Preface to Buddha's Teachings Made by Pasting Together Ideograms from Wang Xizhi's Calligraphic Oeuvre* (集王圣教序 *ji wang sheng jiao xu*), *Yunhui General Li Xiu Tablet* (云麾将军李秀碑 *yun hui jiang jun li xiu bei*), *Letter to Guo Criticizing the Arrangement of the Seats* (争座位稿 *zheng zuo wei gao*), *Letter to Show Relief towards the Surrender of Rebels* (刘中使帖 *liu zhong shi tie*), *Letter about Huzhou* (湖州帖 *hu zhou tie*), *Pine Pavilion* (松风阁诗 song feng ge shi), *Poems Written on Sichuan Silk* (蜀素帖 *shu su tie*) and *Poems to Share with Friends before Leaving for Tiaoxi* (苕溪帖 *tiao xi tie*).

The first use of cursive script as an abbreviated mode of writing was associated with the writing of clerical script and the style was called early cursive script. Cursive script used in writing regular script in later eras is called new or contemporary cursive script (今草 *jin cao*). Contemporary cursive script written with less abandon is called small cursive script (小草 *xiao cao*) and if it is written with more abandon, it is called large cursive script (大草 *da cao*) or crazy or mad cursive (狂草 *kuang cao*). Chinese calligraphy gives great weight to the esthetics of brushwork and this finds a perfect vehicle in cursive script. One might say that in terms of "writing the words" the degree of complexity in descending order is highest for standard script, followed by running script, then by cursive script. But in terms of the "manipulation of the brush" the order is reversed, with standard script being the easiest to execute, running script not so easy and cursive script hardest of all. Canonical works in cursive script include *Literacy Textbook* (急就章 *ji jiu zhang*), *Greeting Note* (平复帖 *ping fu tie*), Zhi Yong's 智永 *Thousand Character Reader in Regular and Cursive Scripts* (真草千字文 *zhen cao qian zi wen*), *Discourse on Calligraphy* (书谱 *shu pu*), Zhang Xu's 张旭 *Four Ancient Poems* (古诗四帖 *gu shi si tie*), *Autobiographical Notes* (自叙帖 *zi xu tie*), *The Practical Way to Immortality* (神仙起居法 *shen xian qi ju fa*) and *Speech of Monks with High Moral Integrity* (诸上座帖 *zhu shang zuo tie*).

The solemnity of seal script, the elegance of clerical script, the neatness of regular script, the grace of running script and the undulation of cursive script are some of the distinguishing marks of the various script types. But the different script types interact closely with one another, and their distinctive forms and the charm conveyed by these forms interpenetrate. The entire rich history of Chinese calligraphy is a chronicle of the genesis and evolution of the various calligraphic styles and their cross-pollination and mutual influence.

Zhou and Qin Dynasties

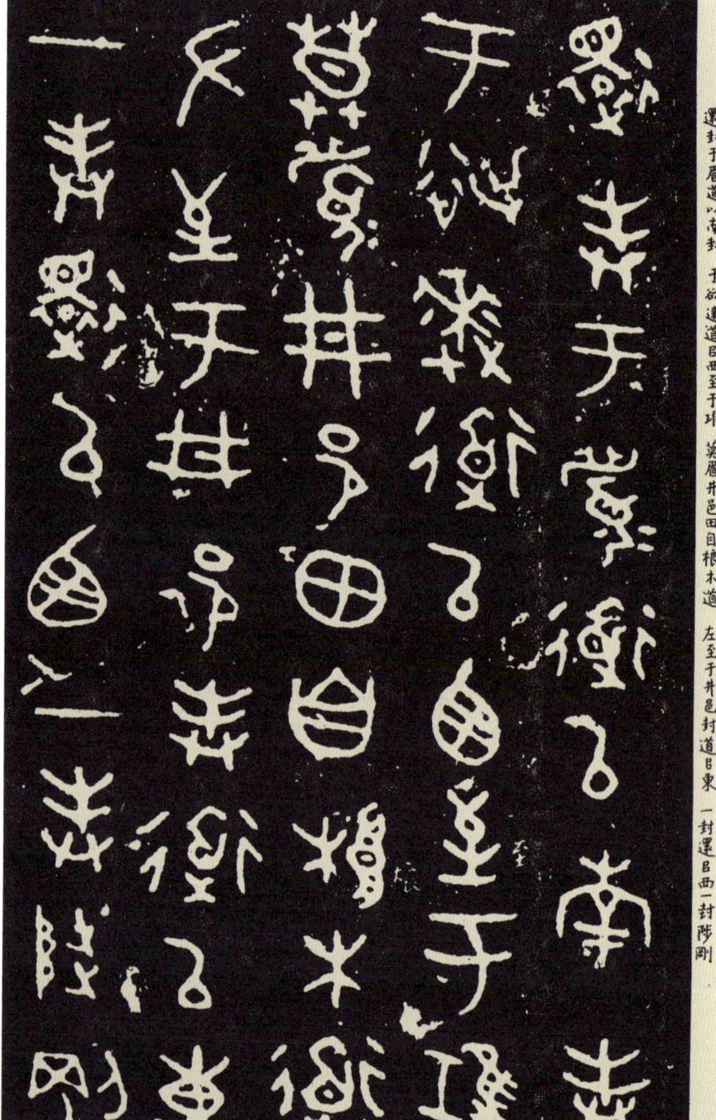

Rubbing from *Bronze Plate of the San Tribe* (散氏盘 *San Shi Pan*)

Unknown calligrapher, Western Zhou dynasty
Bronze writing (*jin wen*)
Palace Museum, Taipei

Bronze utensils made of an alloy of copper and tin in use in the Xia, Shang and Zhou dynasties often bear inscriptions, known as "jin wen," literally "metal or bronze writing," in addition to ornamental, pictorial elements. This inscription on the bronze vessel called *Bronze Plate of the San Tribe* dates to the reign of King Li of the Western Zhou. It exhibits a free-flowing, uninhibited style characterized by bold strokes, creating lines that, though not strictly horizontal or vertical, form a visually balanced whole, and surprise the reader with some charming twists and turns. This kind of expressive style has left a major imprint on later Chinese calligraphy.

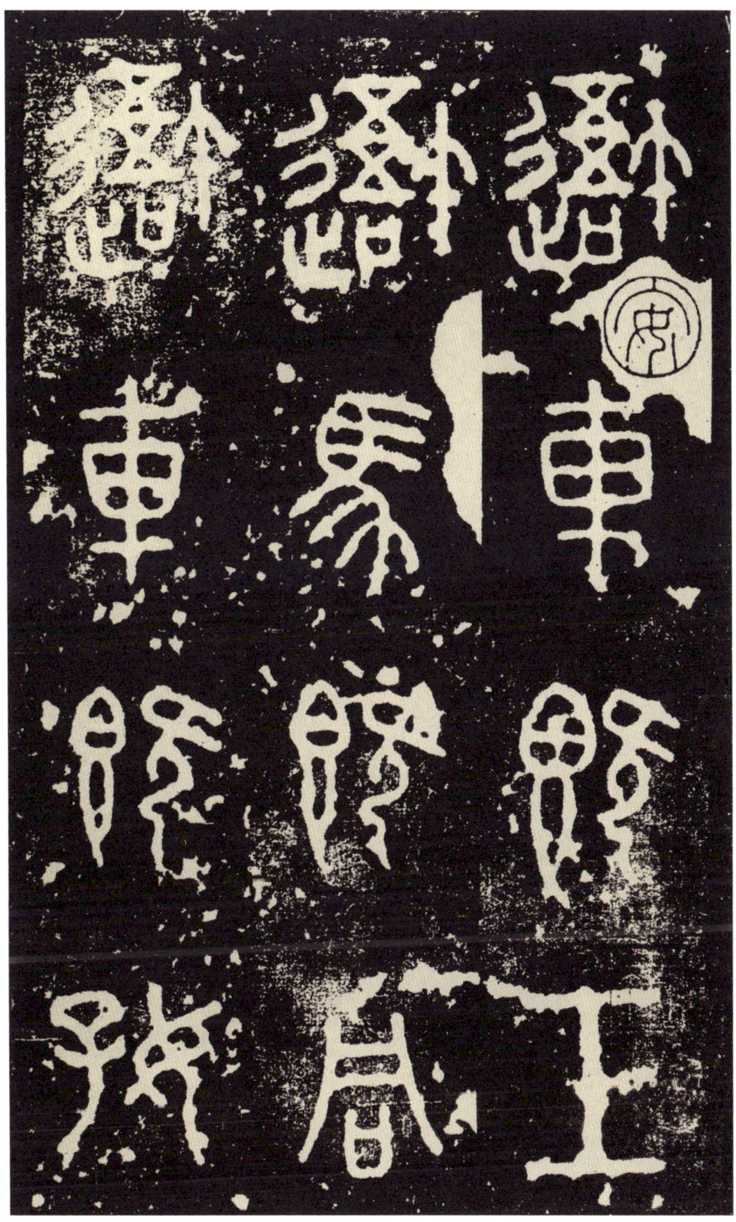

Rubbing from *Stone Drum Inscriptions* (石鼓文 *Shi Gu Wen*)

Unknown calligrapher, Warring States period
4th century BC (carving)
Seal script (*zhuan shu*)
23 cm in height
Mitsui Memorial Museum, Tokyo, Japan

The script and calligraphic style of Stone Drum Inscriptions evolved from the bronze ware inscriptions of the late Western Zhou but abandoned the "fat" stroke of the bronze writing and instead adopted lines that were of uniform thickness from start to finish and rounded at the corners, facilitating the flow of the brush and enhancing the ease of ink writing. In structure, the characters are composed of soft, fluid lines, with a bulge in the midsection, and peripheral lines curving outward. The style of *Stone Drum Inscriptions* is said to be representative of the expansive (外拓 *wai tuo*) style of calligraphy because of this "expansive," as opposed to a contractive (内擫 *nei ye*), quality of the writing. The renowned calligraphers Yan Zhenqing 颜真卿 (708–784, Tang dynasty), with his running script, and Huai Su 怀素 (725–785, Tang dynasty), with his cursive script works, are both adherents to the expansive style exemplified by the stone drum writing. In this sense, wrote Kang Youwei 康有为 (1858–1927, Qing dynasty), "the stone drums are the premier cultural relic of China and the writing on them embodies the premier principle that guides Chinese calligraphers."

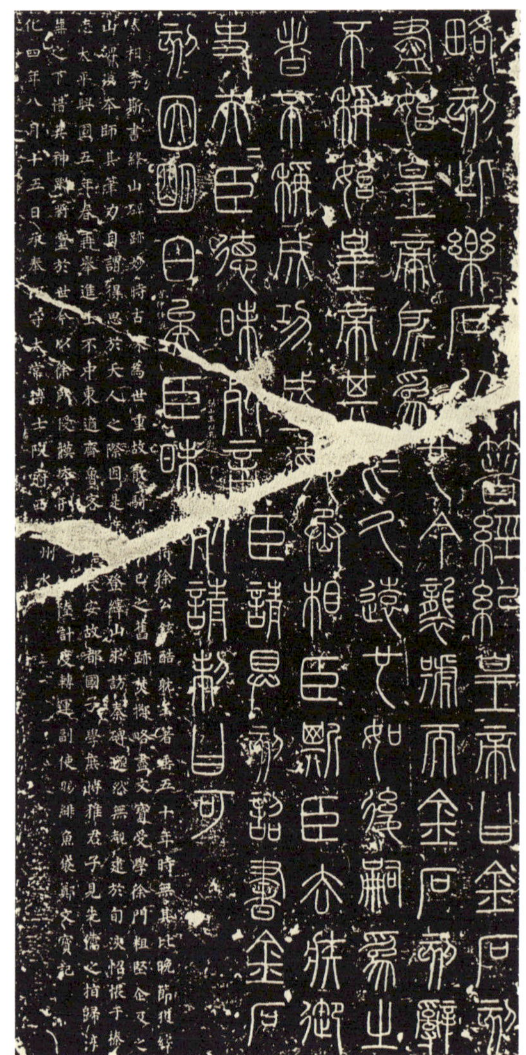

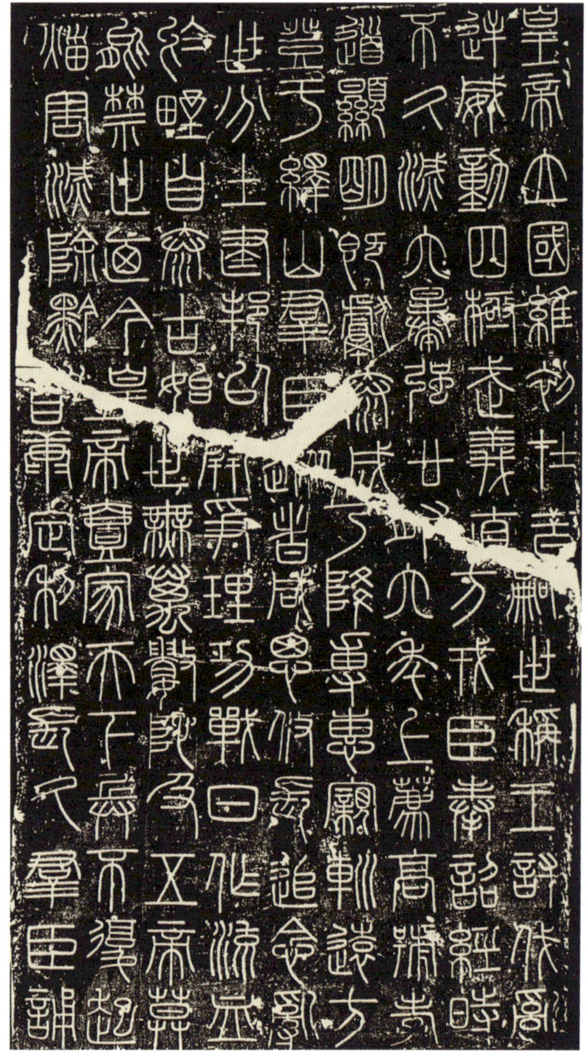

Rubbing from a Song dynasty re-creation of *Stone Tablet of Mount Yi* (峄山刻石 *Yi Shan Ke Shi*)

Li Si 李斯 (?-208 BC, Qin dynasty)
219 BC (carving)
Seal script (*zhuan shu*)
218 cm × 84 cm
Xi'an Beilin Museum, China (Song Tablet)

Following the unification of China by Qin Shi Huang, a unified written language was created, based on previous scripts, with the more formal script standardized into the lesser seal script (小篆 *xiao zhuan*) and the less formal script standardized into the clerical script (隶书 *li shu*). The original *Stone Tablet of Mount Yi*, one of numerous monuments to the great deeds of Emperor Qin Shi Huang, was erected in his honor as he toured Mount Zouyi (in present-day Shandong Province). The laudatory inscription on the tablet is attributed to the Chief Minister Li Si both as author and calligrapher. This Qin carving shows that the lines in lesser seal script remain of uniform thickness. The structure of characters in lesser seal script is characterized by: 1) a rectangular shape, dictated by a preponderance of horizontal strokes over vertical ones in the written Han language, and 2) level horizontal strokes and plumb vertical strokes, to ensure an esthetic distribution of the characters in the writing space.

Han, Wei, Jin and Southern and Northern Dynasties

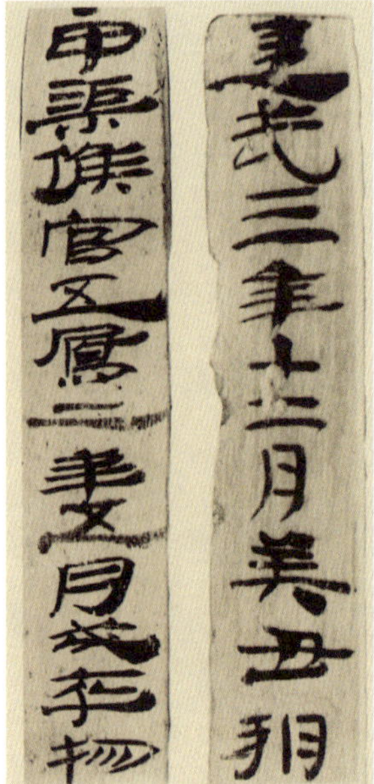

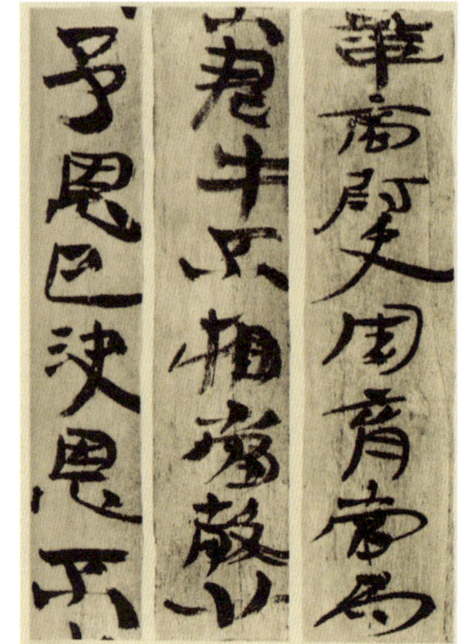

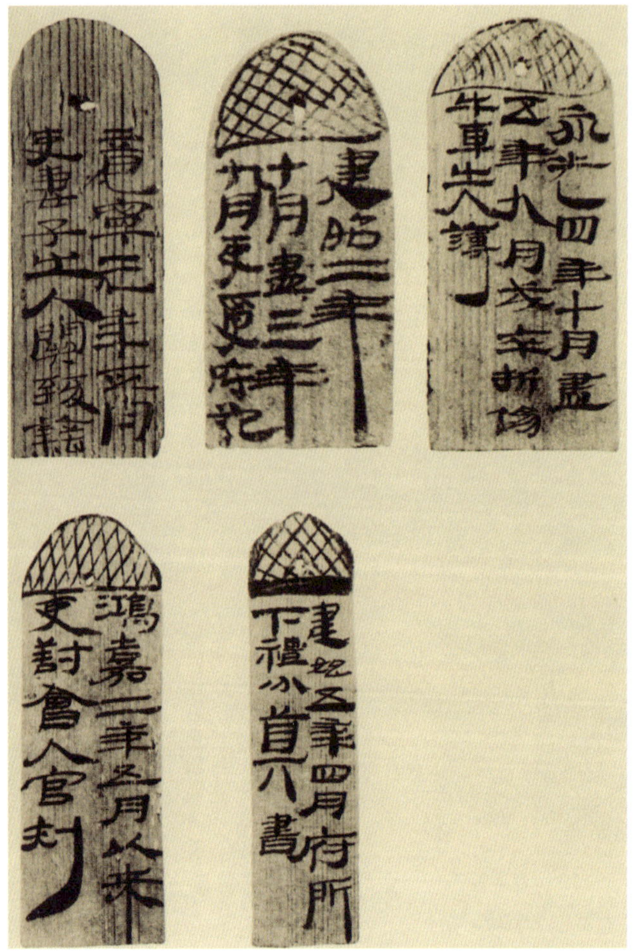

Han dynasty *Wooden Tablets of Juyan* (居延汉简 *Ju Yan Han Jian*)

Unknown calligrapher, Han dynasty
Clerical script (*li shu*)
Gansu Provincial Museum

From the Warring States period through the later years of the Eastern Han dynasty, writing was done mostly on enlaced wooden or bamboo slips. *Wooden Tablets of Juyan*, a register of weapons, are dated to the fifth year (93 AD) of the Yongyuan Era of Emperor He of the Eastern Han, were discovered in the ruins of a beacon tower of the Han dynasty in the Ejina river basin of Inner Mongolia. The record-keeper was doing a routine inventory of weapons and miscellaneous items in a relaxed state of mind. One can easily imagine, from the fluent ink writing, the clerk leaning on a desk or standing, with his left hand holding the wooden slats and his right hand wielding a brush. He stretched all the strokes sideways, apparently to flatten the characters to squeeze as many as possible into the exiguous space of the strips, adapting the shape of the characters to the writing material.

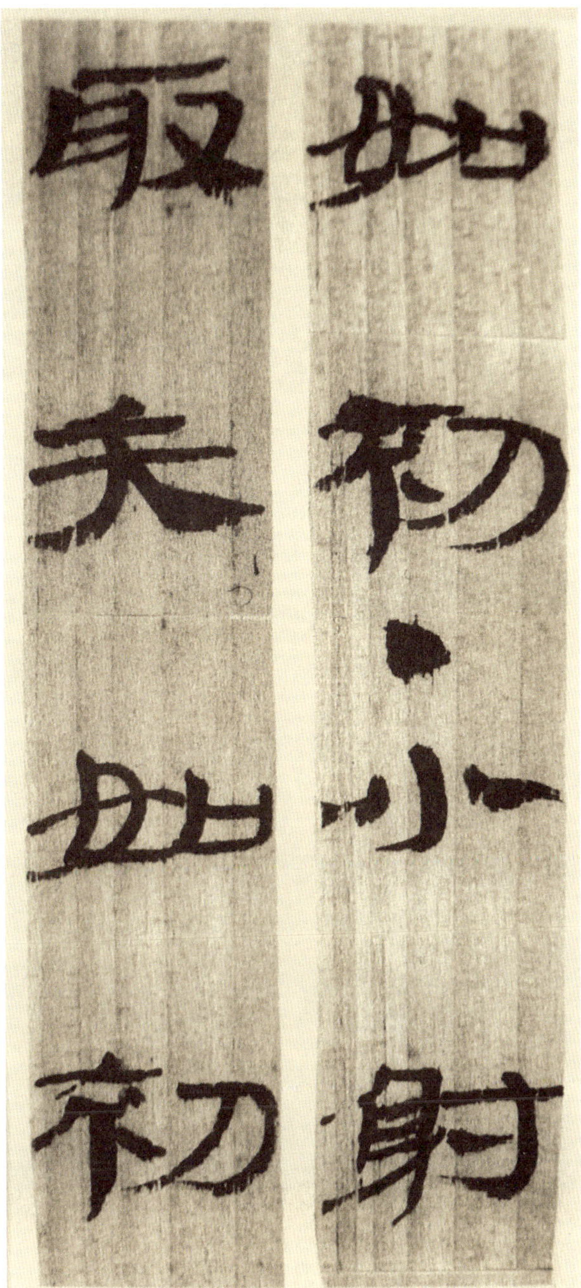

Wooden and Bamboo Slips Bearing Partial Contents of the Confucian Classics on Rites and Etiquette Unearthed in Wuwei (武威礼仪简 *Wu Wei Li Yi Jian*)

Unknown calligrapher, Han dynasty
Clerical script (*li shu*)
Municipal Museum of Wuwei, Gansu Province

As the calligraphic style underwent a transition from the seal script to the clerical script, the brushwork characterized by uniformity of stroke speed, roundness and even thickness of lines began to give way to a greater freedom in the use of the brush. As a result, a major shift occurred in the shape and form of calligraphy and its esthetic values. The variability in stroke speed imparted a stronger sense of rhythm; the emergence of the "square" stroke added to the diversity of character shapes; and the alternation between different widths of the lines provided a new vehicle for conveying the emotions of the calligrapher. Because of the faster speed of the brushwork employed in these Wuwei wooden slats, the quick lifting of the brush at the completion of a stroke created features peculiar to the regular script (楷书 *kai shu*) style of later periods. This appears to be a corroboration of the theory that the regular script evolved as a quickened version of the clerical script.

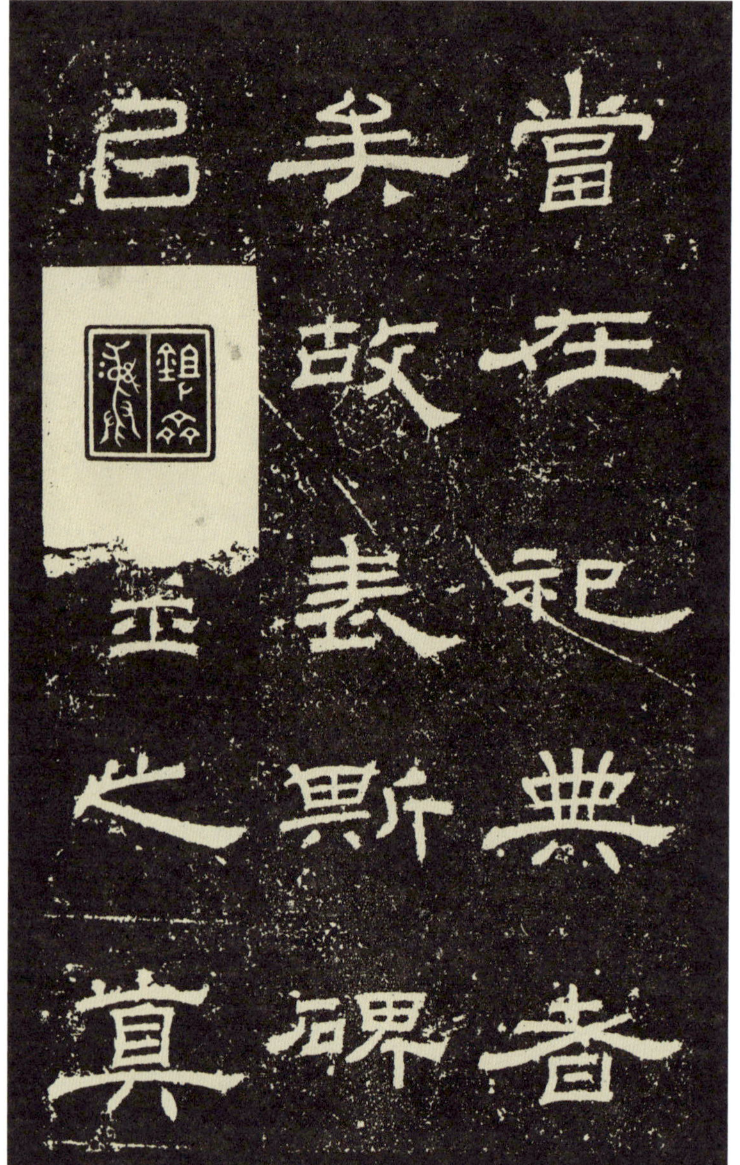

Fragment of *Stone Inscription of a Biographical Note* (朝侯小子残碑 *Chao Hou Xiao Zi Can Bei*)

Unknown calligrapher, Han dynasty
Clerical script (*li shu*)
Palace Museum, Beijing

This stone tablet, was unearthed in Xi'an, Shaanxi Province in 1911. The partially damaged tablet, discovered much later than other Han steles, is given the name of "*Chao Hou Xiao Zi*" because these characters appear in the first line of the inscription. The brushwork is characterized by round strokes (圆笔 *yuan bi*) with minimal variation in line thickness, apparently following the seal script style. Because of the presence of more than one "swallow tail" (燕尾 *yan wei*: the up-tilt ending of a horizontal stroke) in a single character in several ideograms containing multiple horizontal strokes, for instance, " 在 " and " 真 ", it bears greater similarity to the clerical script style used on wooden and bamboo slips in the latter period of the Western Han than to the many stone inscriptions of the Eastern Han, for which the rule of "no paired swallows" (燕不双飞 *yan bu shuang fei*) was the norm.

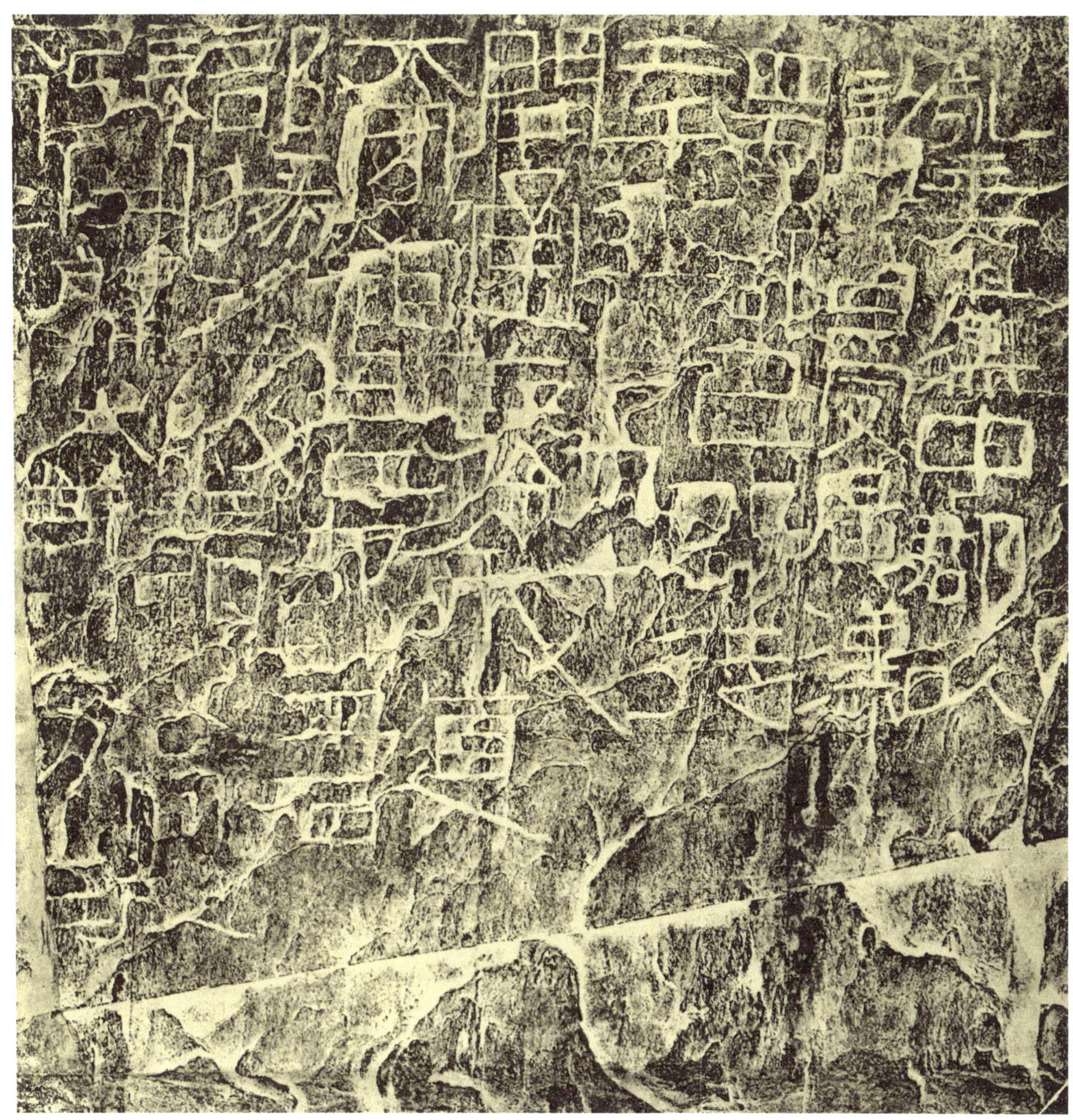

Cliff Carving on Rock Celebrating the Opening of a Suspended Plank Trail in Baocheng (开通褒斜道刻石 *Kai Tong Bao Xie Dao Ke Shi*)

Unknown calligrapher, Han dynasty
63 AD
Clerical script (*li shu*)
Baocheng (present-day Mian County), Shaanxi Province

This earliest example of cliff carvings of the Eastern Han dynasty was discovered in the Song dynasty. The annotations incised on its margins by the Song discoverers, soon obscured by moss, would not see the light of day again until they were rediscovered six centuries later in the Qing dynasty. The inscription exudes a compelling energy, with huge characters of unusual, bold structures, a rare treasure among stone carvings in the Han clerical script style. The shape of the characters is square; all lines are kept inside the confines of the character's structure, with minimal overflow. Characters and columns are spaced close together with little blank space, creating a coherent, balanced whole, compact yet grandiose.

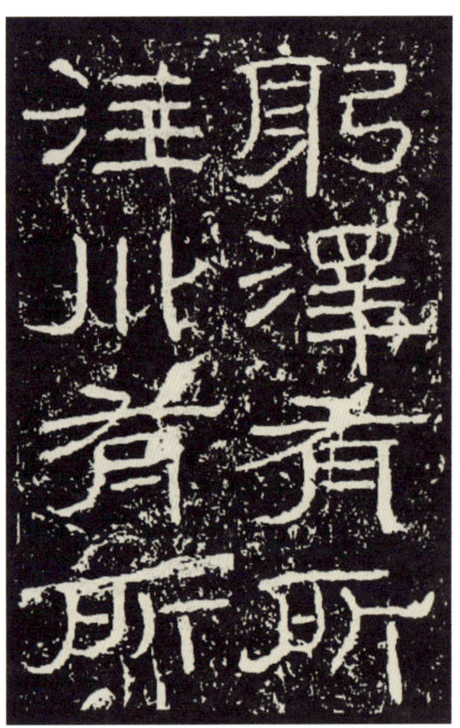

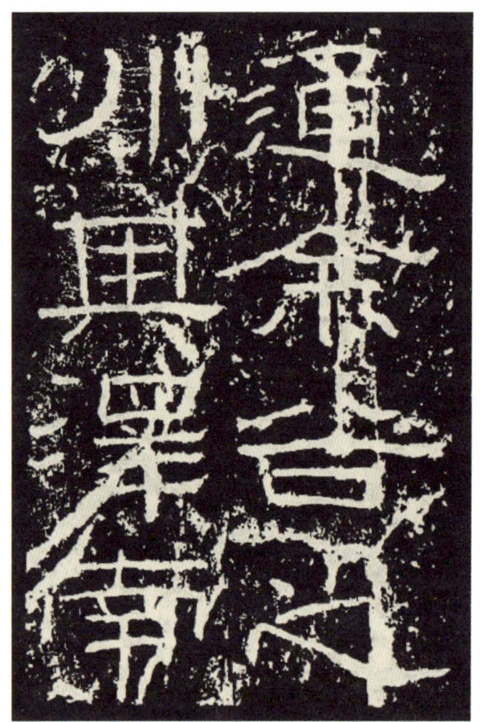

Rubbing from *Ode to Stone Gate* (石门颂 *Shi Men Song*)

Unknown calligrapher, **Han dynasty**
148 AD (carving)
Clerical script (*li shu*)
Cliff carving
Hanzhong Museum, Shaanxi Province
(the carving removed from cliff face)

Stone carvings flourished in the Han dynasty, especially inscriptions in clerical script on stone tablets. The calligraphic styles exhibited on Han tablets are multifarious, exemplified by the grace of *Cao Quan Tablet* (曹全碑 *cao quan bei*), *Yi Ying Tablet* (乙瑛碑 *yi ying bei*), *Ritual Vessels Tablet* (礼器碑 *li qi bei*) and *Shi Chen Tablet* (史晨碑 *shi chen bei*); the robustness of *Zhang Qian Tablet* (张迁碑 *zhang qian bei*) and *Heng Fang Tablet* (衡方碑 *heng fang bei*); and the free-spirited, carefree *Ode to Stone Gate* (石门颂 *shi men song*) and *Mount Fenglong Tablet* (封龙山碑 *feng long shan bei*).

There is an antique simplicity and spontaneity to the calligraphy in this stone inscription, which makes it so much more interesting. The reversed-brush tip technique (逆锋 *ni feng*: brush slanted and moved in the direction of the tip of the brush) used to start the strokes imparts a tone of understatement; the grace with which the brush then travels on gives the characters a down-to-earth, solid feel; and the back brush-tip technique (回锋 *hui feng*: brush folded back into the body of the stroke) used to end a brushstroke creates a fluid look. The piece displays an easy virtuosity and is full of delights and surprises. The calligrapher writes as the spirit takes him and there is no trace of any conscious attempt at achieving an excessively ornate effect. Kang Youwei rightly observed that this artist's style, packed with power and irrepressible spirit, would deter any emulators who are "faint of heart or weak of energy."

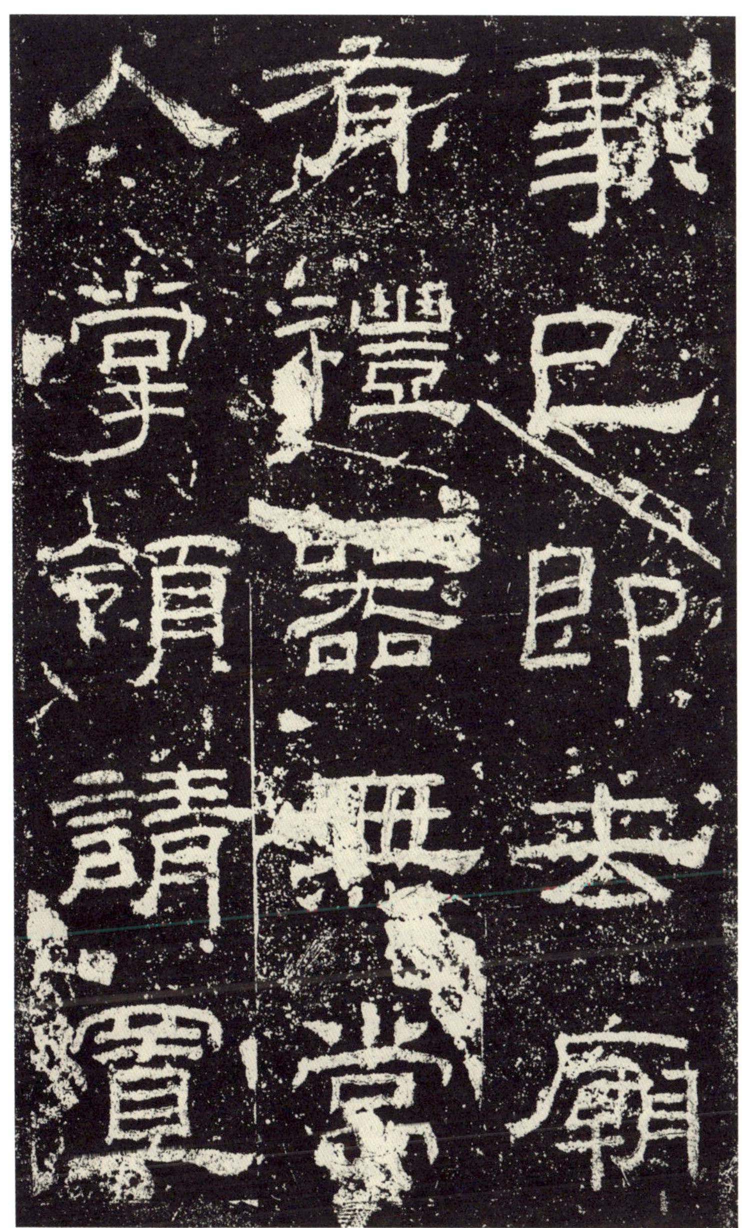

Rubbing made in the Ming dynasty from *Yi Ying Tablet* (乙瑛碑 *Yi Ying Bei*)

Unknown calligrapher, Han dynasty
153 AD (carving)
Clerical script (*li shu*)
Confucius Temple in Qufu, Shandong Province

Yi Ying Tablet, like *Shi Chen Tablet* and *Ritual Vessels Tablet* is preserved in the Confucius Temple of Qufu, Shandong Province. The features of "silkworm head and swallow tail" (蚕头雁尾 *can tou yan wei*) characterizing the beginning and ending of strokes in clerical script, and the diagonal strokes (波磔 *bo zhe*) to the right and to the left (new features in clerical script not previously found in seal script) are already clearly in evidence in the inscription. The brushwork is neat and nimble throughout. There is great variability in stroke transitions and the character structures are smart and trim. The piece exhibits a virile grace and an airy elegance. Later critics saw in this work "proper balance of bone and flesh, and fluency of content and calligraphic style."

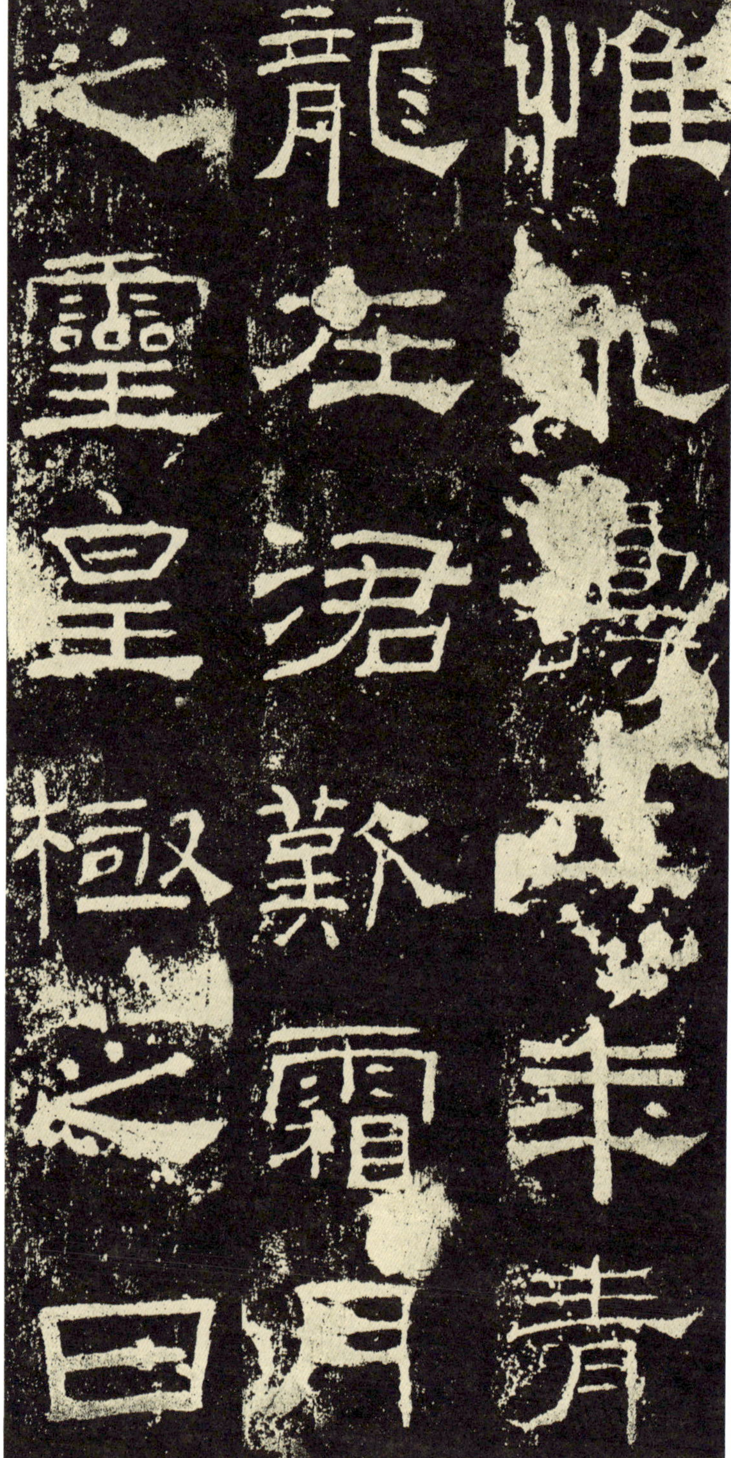

Rubbing made in the Ming dynasty from *Ritual Vessels Tablet* (礼器碑 *Li Qi Bei*)

Unknown calligrapher, Han dynasty
156 AD (carving)
Clerical script (*li shu*)
Confucius Temple in Qufu, Shandong Province

The inscriptions in clerical script on tablets of the Han dynasty best embody the artistic achievement of clerical script calligraphy. The numerous Han tablets that have survived shine in their own unique, inimitable ways. *Ritual Vessels Tablet* is renowned for its uncommon grace. At first glance, the structure of the characters may appear neatly executed strictly in accordance with calligraphic codes; but a closer scrutiny will uncover unconventional touches. Take for instance the character "歎" in the inscription: whereas the longer left half appears unremarkable, the short left and right diagonal strokes at the top of the right half "欠" are quite interesting. The long, left diagonal in "欠" appears undecided between staying upright and leaning to one side, and the long, right diagonal ends with a perfectly sized "swallow tail" tilted at just the right angle.

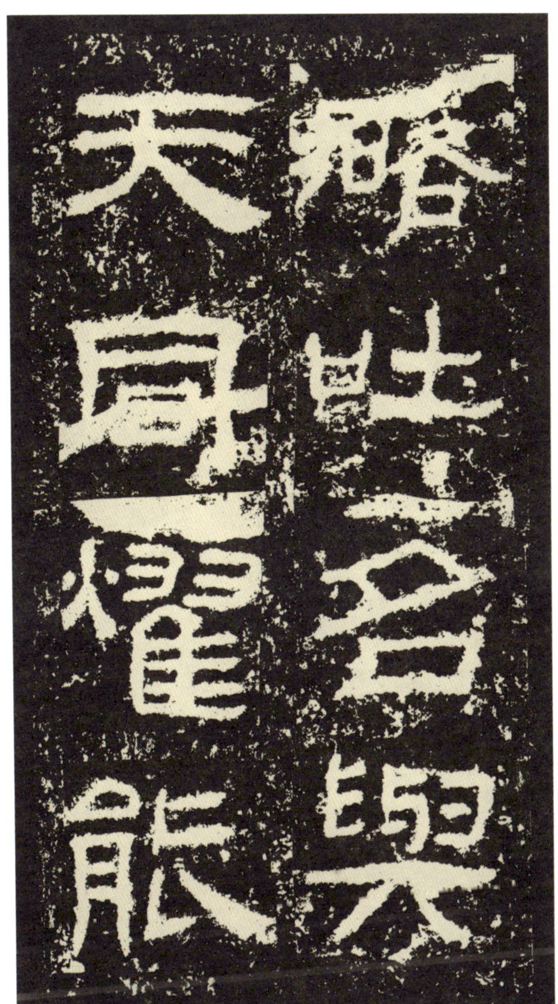

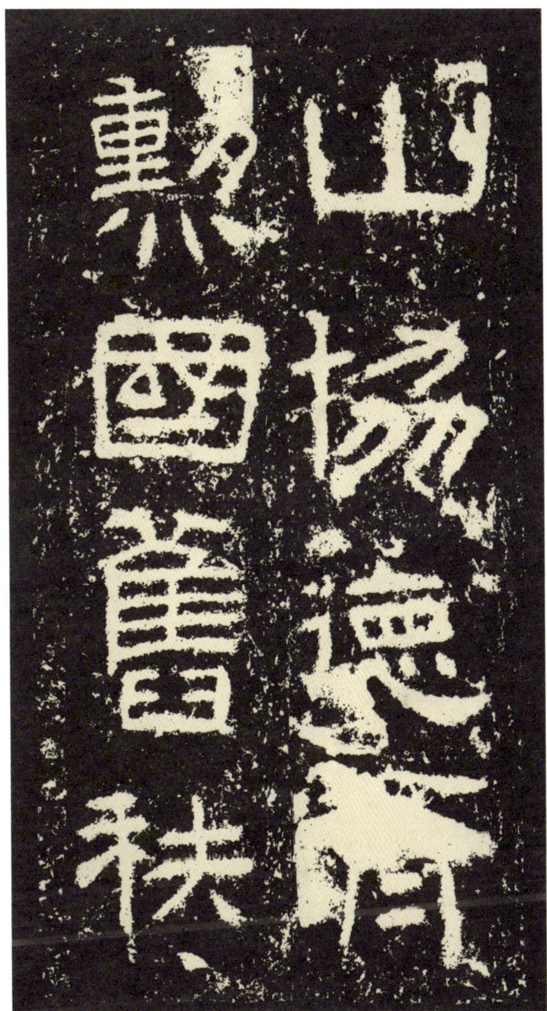

Mount Fenglong Tablet (封龙山碑 *Feng Long Shan Bei*) of the Han dynasty

164 AD (carving)
Clerical script (*li shu*)

The inscription on *Mount Fenglong Tablet* is characterized by a neat, airy composition and variable, unconventional character structures. In the character " 燿 " for example, the left radical " 火 " is squeezed upward to almost the level of the upper part " 羽 " of the right radical " 翟 ", all without giving the character a lopsided, right-heavy appearance. Or take for instance the character " 旧 ", at almost double the height of other characters in the inscription, it is still very much part of a harmonious whole. The boldness of the writing makes this tablet stand out among the clerical script style Han tablet inscriptions.

Rubbing from *Mount Hua Tablet* (华山碑 *Hua Shan Bei*)

Guo Xiangcha 郭香察 (years of birth/death unknown, Han dynasty)
165 AD (carving)
Clerical script (*li shu*)
Palace Museum, Beijing (rubbing)

The original stone tablet was destroyed in a 1555 earthquake. Only the original rubbing has survived. The inscription has a strong emphasis on features of "one wave, three reversals" (一波三折 *yi bo san zhe*: starting a horizontal stroke by first moving the brush-tip left, secondly turning the brush around to move to the right, and thirdly folding the brush left, back into the body of the stroke to complete it) and "silkworm head and swallow tail." The character structure is tight in the center and loose in the periphery, with diagonal strokes overflowing the invisible character grid, creating an ornate effect. Later calligraphers are divided in their opinion of the inscription on this tablet. In the early period of the revival of the stele school of calligraphy in the Qing dynasty, the taste leaned toward the graceful and delicate style of writing, and *Mount Hua Tablet* became a favorite among calligraphers. According to Zhu Yizun 朱彝尊 (1629–1709, Qing dynasty), its penmanship was a rare combination of neatness, fluent grace and quaint antiquity, and arguably "the premier masterpiece of Han tablet inscriptions." In the latter part of the renaissance, however, excessively ornate pieces fell out of vogue as a more archaically clumsy style came back into favor. Thus, Kang Youwei denigrated *Mount Hua Tablet* as "an inferior piece, having lost all flavor of antique simplicity." These two strikingly different esthetic judgements by contemporaries of the same historical period serve to illustrate two different aspects of the calligraphic style of *Mount Hua Tablet*.

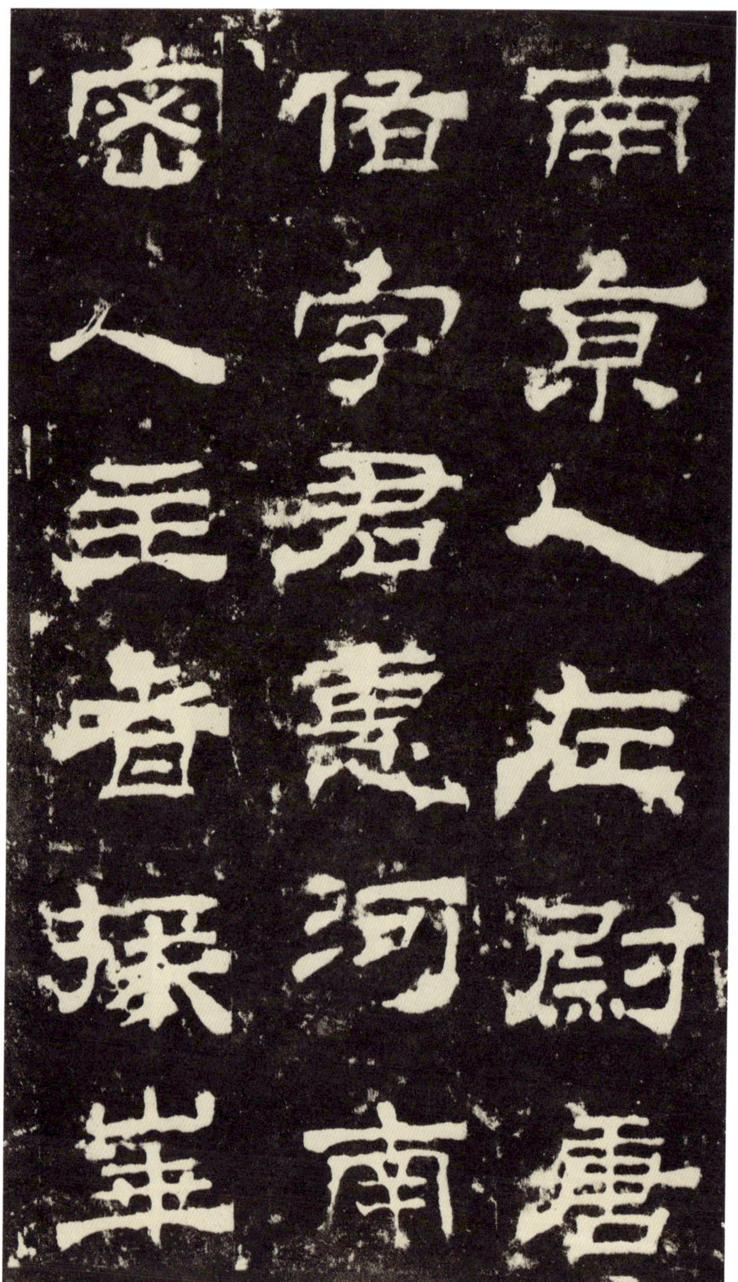

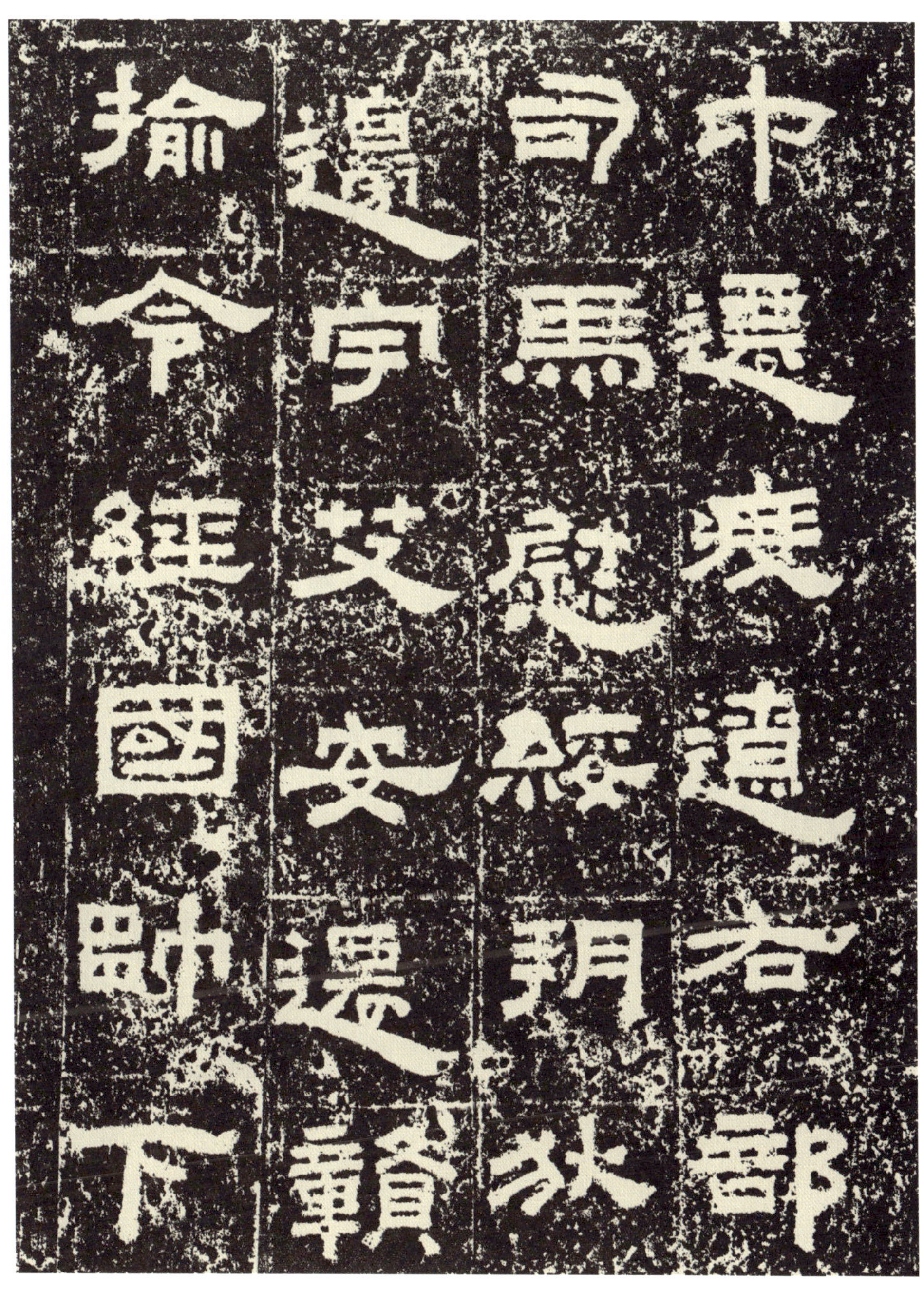

Xian Yu Huang Tablet (鲜于璜碑 *Xian Yu Huang Bei*)

Unknown calligrapher, Han dynasty
165 AD (carving)
Clerical script (*li shu*)
Tianjin Municipal Museum of History

Like *Zhang Qian Tablet* which it preceded by 21 years, this piece is also a Han tablet in the square stroke (方笔 *fang bi*) style. It was arguably a trendsetter for the style on Han tablets. The carefully penned brushstrokes form compact characters arranged judiciously into an organic whole. The archaically clumsy postures of the characters foreshadow the sharply articulated, squarish corners found in regular script, often thought to have their origins in *Zhang Qian Tablet* and *Xian Yu Huang Tablet*.

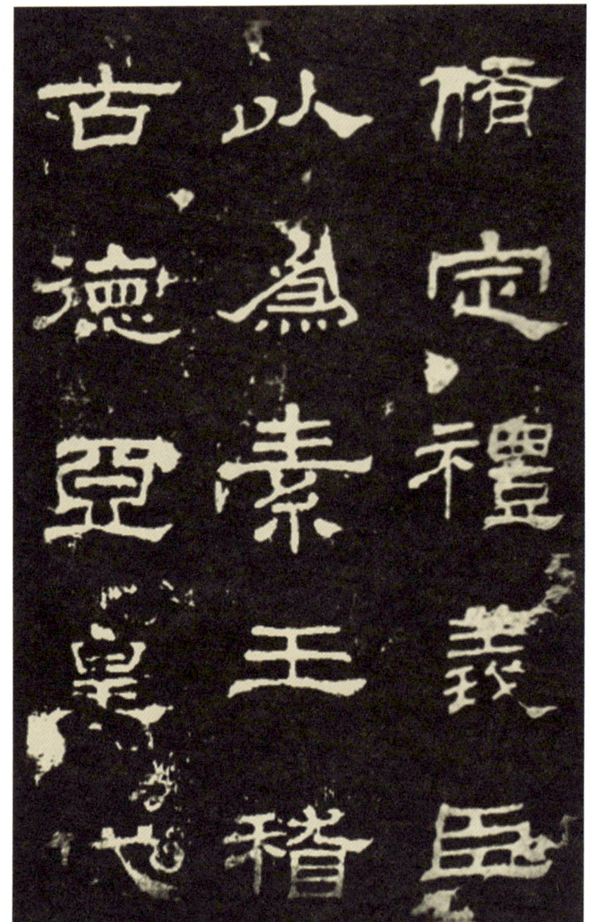

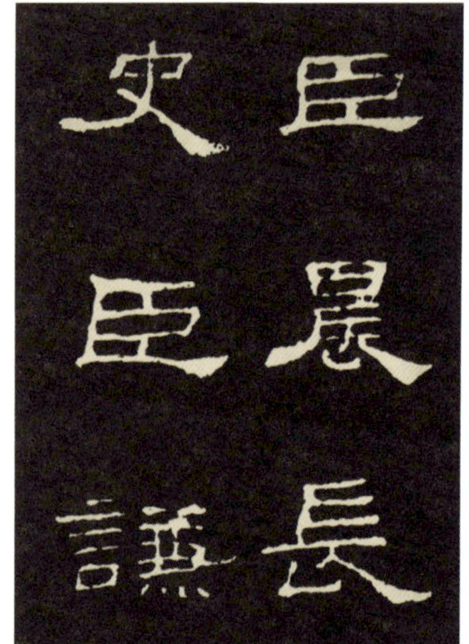

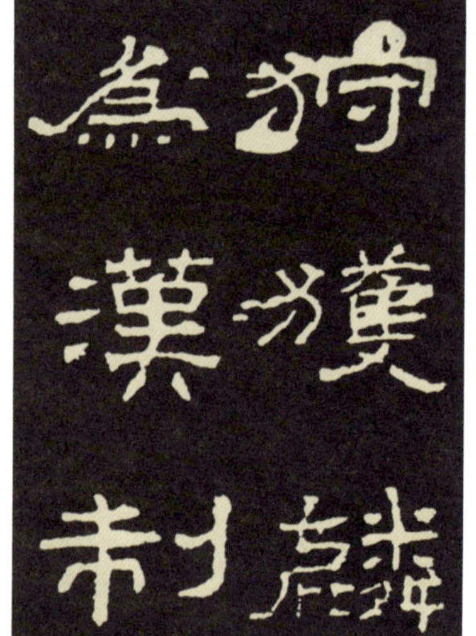

Rubbing made in the Ming dynasty from *Shi Chen Tablet* (史晨碑 *Shi Chen Bei*)

Unknown calligrapher, Han dynasty
169 AD (carving)
Clerical script (*li shu*)
Confucius Temple in Qufu, Shandong Province

This tablet is one of the renowned "Three Masterpieces of the Confucius Temple," the other two being *Yi Ying Tablet* and *Ritual Vessels Tablet*. The brushwork carefully follows the codes, with regular, neatly structured characters and meticulously executed strokes. It typifies those clerical script inscriptions of the Han dynasty that adhered to the Confucian esthetic principle of "beauty in balance." The spatial composition of the inscription emphasizes equidistance, composure and serenity. Absent is any exaggerated contraction or distension of the characters, although some brushstrokes in individual characters have been skillfully extended to create an overall effect of balanced proportion and lively rhythm.

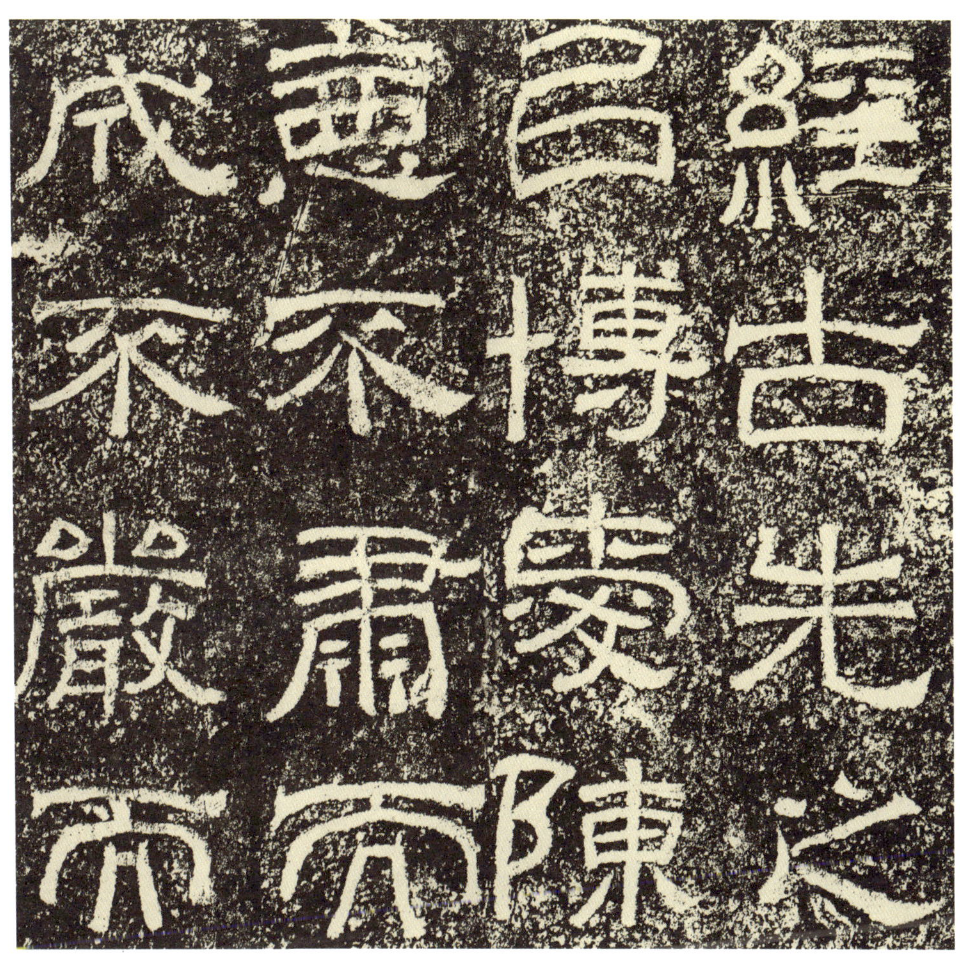

Ode to Xixia (西狭颂 *Xi Xia Song*)

Unknown calligrapher, Han dynasty
171 AD (carving)
Clerical script (*li shu*)
Cliff carving

The calligraphic style of the cliff carving *Ode to Xixia* sets it apart from the many other stone inscriptions of the Eastern Han dynasty in two respects. The first distinguishing mark is its merging of square and round strokes. Most straight lines have rounded ends to temper the hard edge and avoid a rigid look, while curved lines are given vigorous square ends to compensate for the softness of a curve. The second distinguishing mark is the openness of the character structure. Unlike in other clerical script style inscriptions, where the character structure tends to be squat, the strokes in this piece gravitate toward the periphery of the square or elongated character frame, leaving "enough interior space to accommodate a trotting horse."

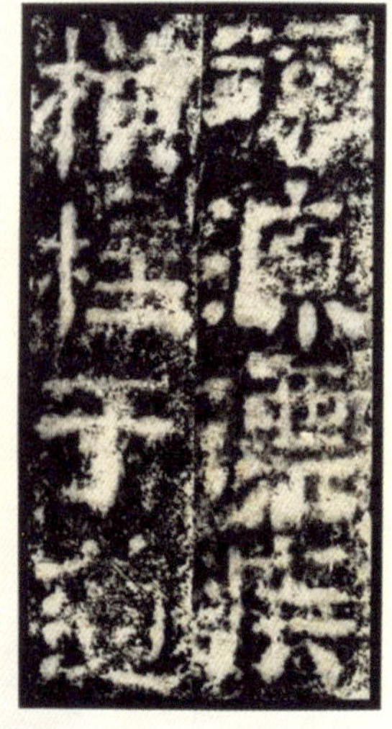

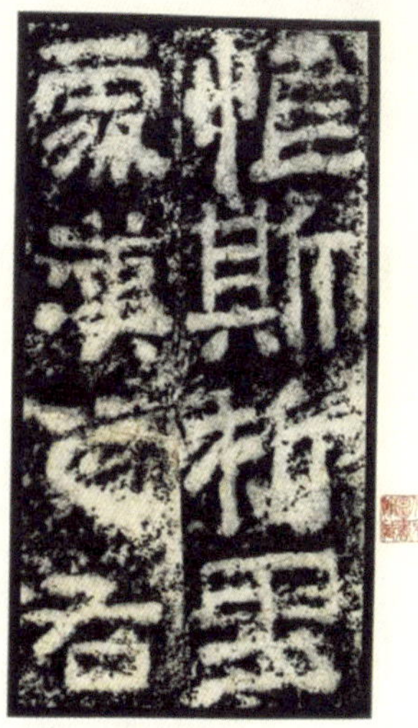

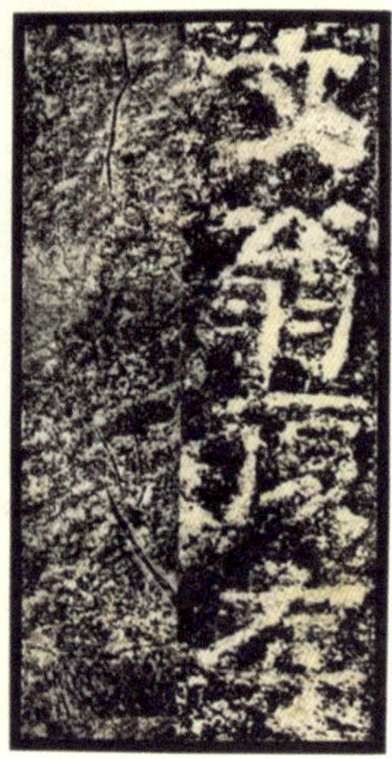

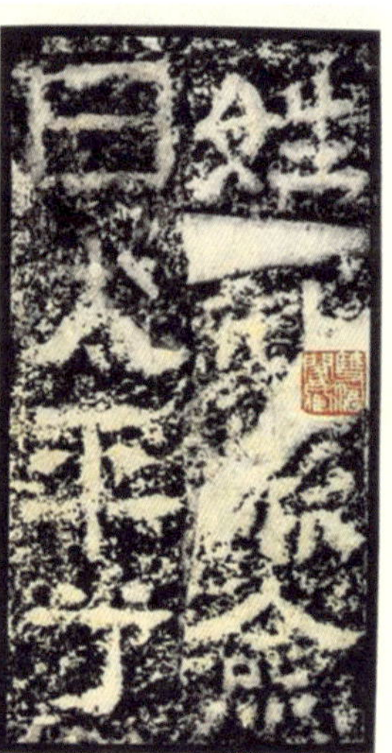

Ode to Fuge (郙阁颂 *Fu Ge Song*)

Unknown calligrapher, Han dynasty
172 AD (carving)
Clerical script (*li shu*)
Cliff carving

The brushwork in *Ode to Fuge* is full-bodied and eschews excess. Its diagonal strokes do not have a pronounced "swallow tail," ending instead with only a subtle tilt upward, giving the flavor without overstating it. The character structure is gracefully expansive, unfolding horizontally and vertically, creating a spacious interior inside the character form and a neat, noble profile. The spatial composition of the piece and its distinctive character structure bring to mind the regular script inscription on *Tablet of the Ancestral Shrine of the Yan Clan* (颜家庙碑 *yan jia miao bei*) written by Yan Zhenqing in a later age.

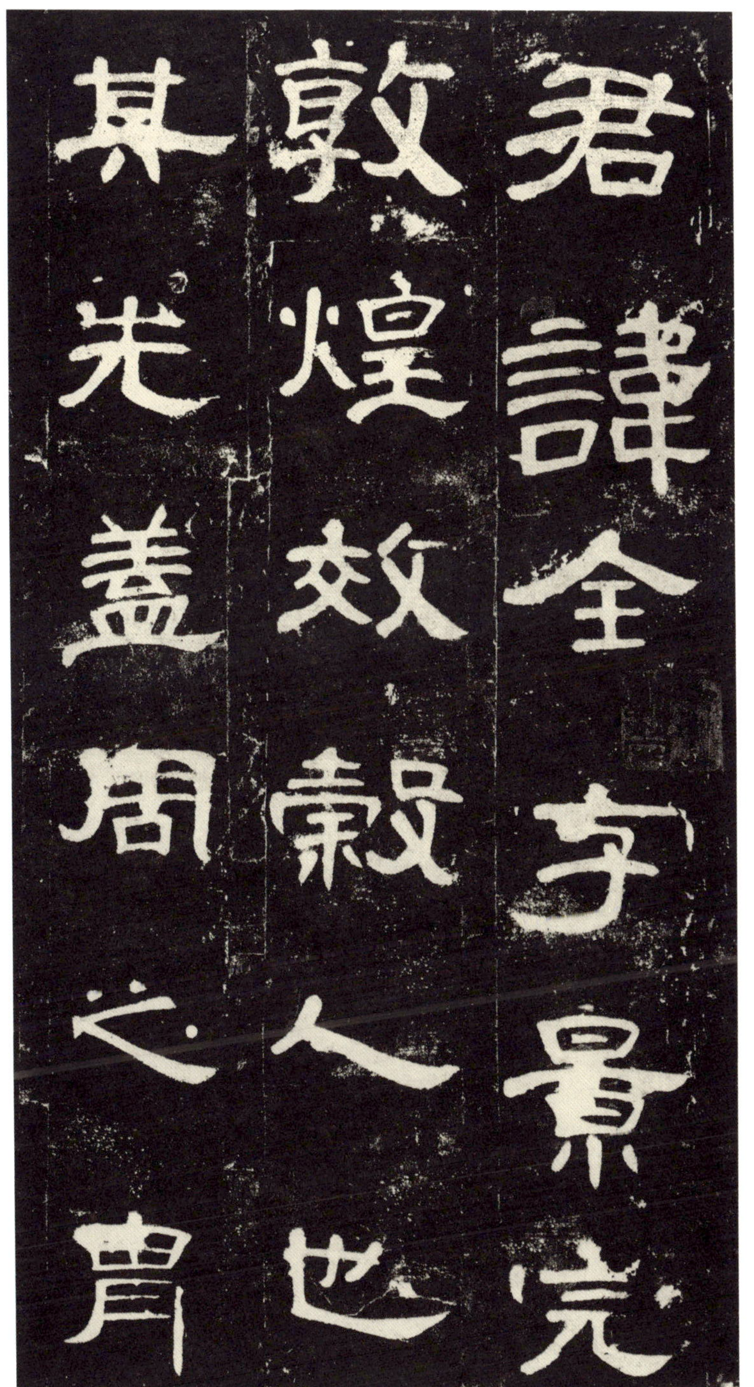

Cao Quan Tablet (曹全碑 *Cao Quan Bei*)

Unknown calligrapher, Han dynasty
185 AD
Clerical script (*li shu*)
Beilin Museum in Xi'an, Shaanxi Province

Among the Han dynasty tablet inscriptions in clerical script, *Cao Quan Tablet* and *Ritual Vessels Tablet* are two shining gems of the "delicate beauty" category. In elegance and grace, *Cao Quan Tablet* brought to the clerical script style of calligraphy what Zhao Mengfu 赵孟頫 (1254-1322, Yuan dynasty) and Dong Qichang 董其昌 (1555-1636, Ming dynasty) of a later age brought to the style of running script with similarities to the regular script. The strokes in the inscription are generally shorter and closer together, while the diagonal strokes are longer and spaced wider apart. Some characters feature a charming vertical stroke that hangs down like a needle (e.g. the right vertical of " 月 ", the lower component of the character " 胄 "). Elements of regular script can already be detected in the brushwork if one takes a closer look. The shape of the dots and the shorter diagonals to the lower right in characters such as " 全 " and " 效 " bear similarities to the regular script that evolved in a later period.

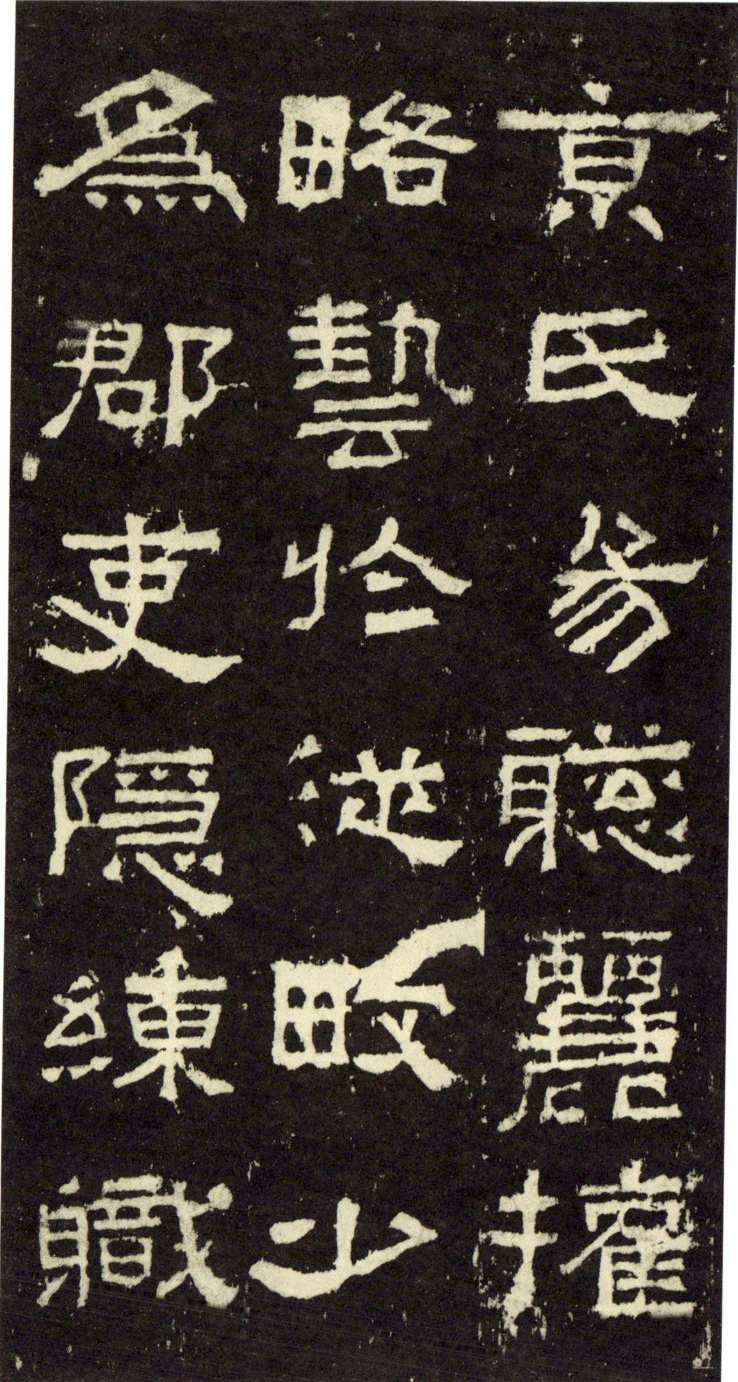

Rubbing made in the Ming dynasty from *Zhang Qian Tablet* (张迁碑 *Zhang Qian Bei*)

Unknown calligrapher, Han dynasty
186 AD (carving)
Clerical script (*li shu*)

Zhang Qian Tablet of the late Han dynasty, in a departure from the "one wave, three reversals" and "silkworm head and swallow tail" brushwork features prominent in other clerical script style inscriptions, employed strokes with square starts and endings, short, thick lines and a style characterized by "levelness, hardness, mass and heft." In character structure, it also abandoned the convention of "compact, smaller upper part and looser, larger lower part" to adopt exactly the opposite principle. Another of its innovations was deliberately making the columns slightly skewed, resulting in a naïve, crude and simple style reminiscent of antiquity. This transition in the artistic style of the Han tablets from ornate to simple was in the same vein of the "pendulum swinging back to an ancient writing style from the extreme of an ornate style (骈体 *pian ti*)" in Chinese literature.

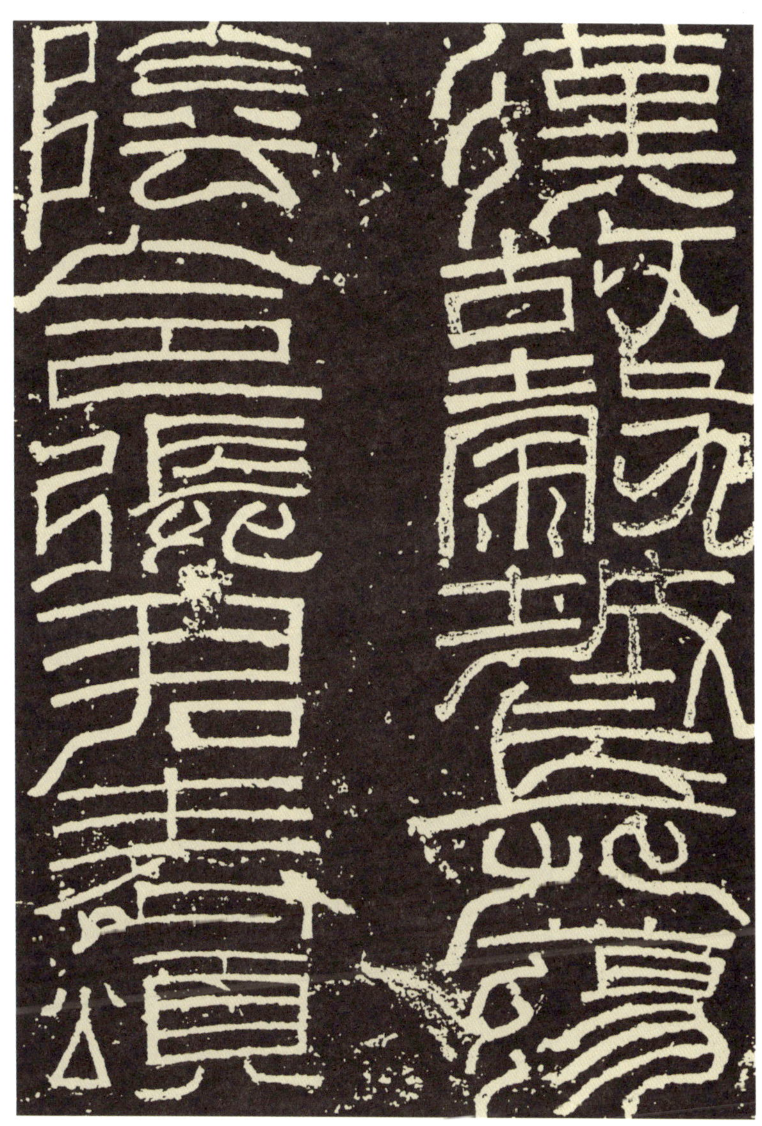

Rubbing made in the Ming dynasty of an *Inscription across the Top of the Zhang Qian Tablet* (张迁碑额 *Zhang Qian Bei E*)

Unknown calligrapher, Han dynasty
186 AD (carving)
Seal script (*zhuan shu*)

As the clerical script matured toward the latter part of the Eastern Han dynasty, the seal script ceded its place as the contemporary official writing style and was no longer used except on rare occasions, such as on the brow of stone tablets. Even there, the seal script had shed the solemn, serious air of former times to display an uninhibited, childlike exuberance. To take full advantage of the limited space for the inscription on the brow of the tablet, the seal script characters there are arranged with a high degree of freedom and variation.

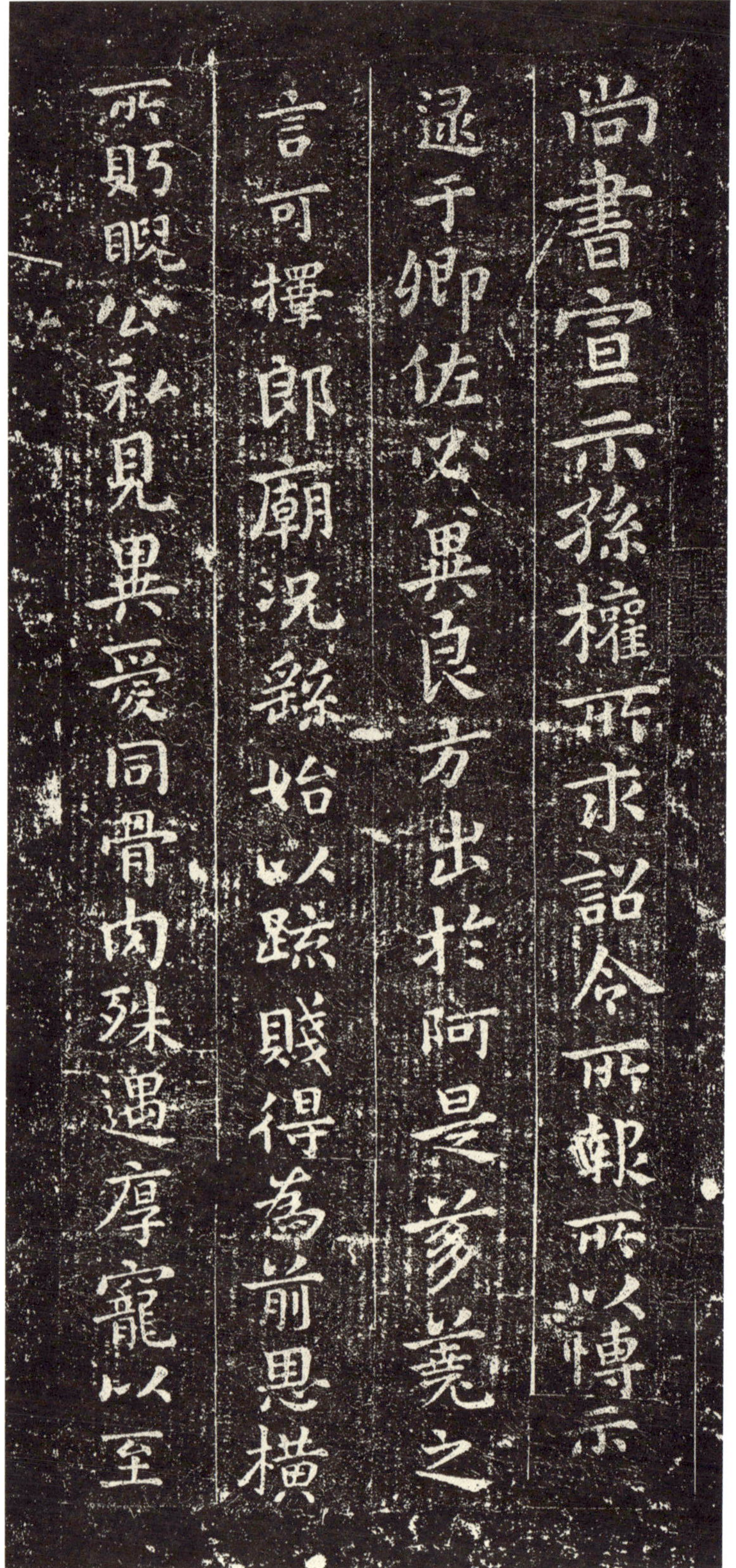

Rubbing from *Memorial to the Emperor for the Acceptance of Other's Surrender* (宣示表 *Xuan Shi Biao*)

Zhong You 钟繇 **(151-230, Wei, Three Kingdoms)**
Regular script (*kai shu*)

In the Three Kingdoms, regular script gradually freed itself from the influence of the clerical script and matured into a style of its own. Zhong You was the first calligrapher renowned for his mastery of the style and is revered as the "father of regular script." In brushwork and structure, *Memorial to the Emperor for the Acceptance of Other's Surrender* demonstrated its maturity; its dots and strokes were simple and robust and its characters squat and robust. Not being tied down by a convention yet to be established for the regular script style, the brushwork here is untrammeled and unrestrained, spontaneous and archaically clumsy, and full of variation. In the words of later critics "In Zhong's calligraphy, spontaneity trumps virtuosity."

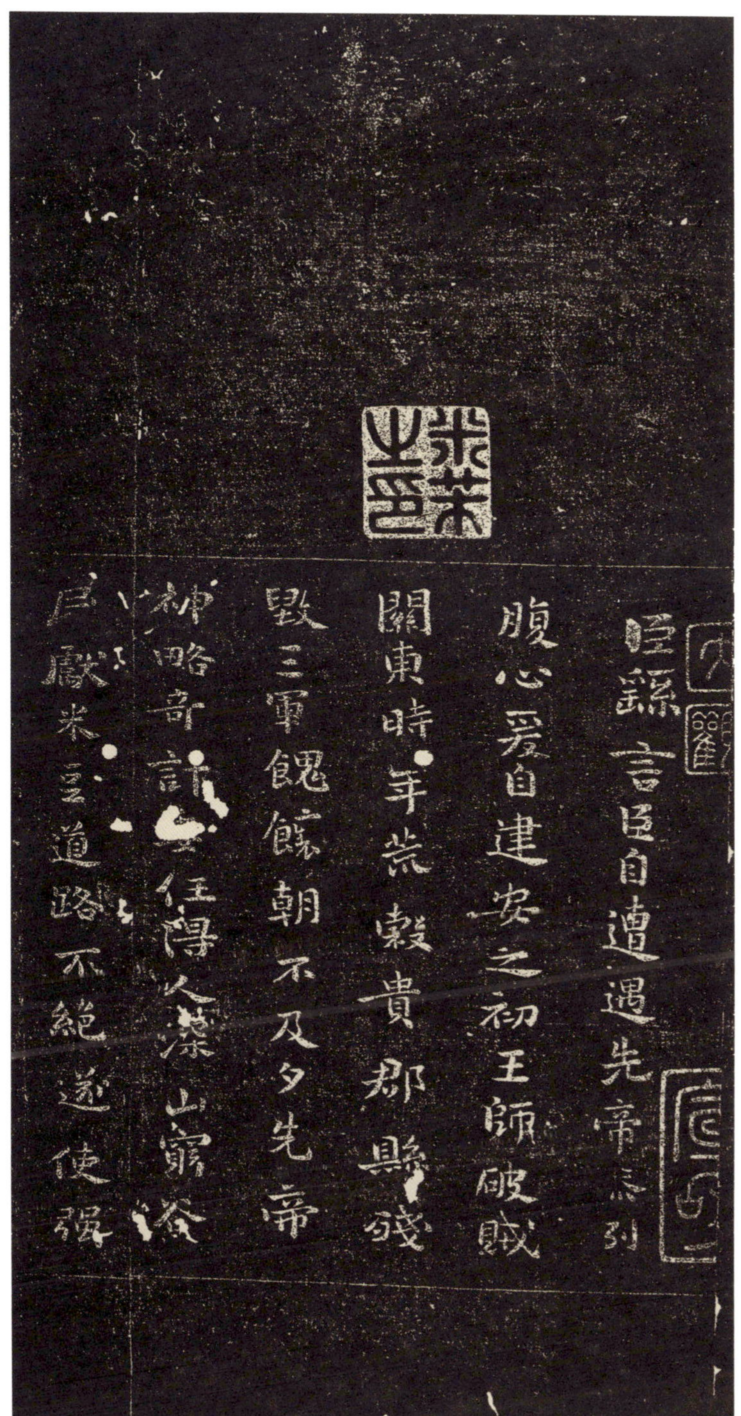

Rubbing from *Memorial to the Emperor for Recommending Ji Zhi* (荐季直表 *Jian Ji Zhi Biao*)

Zhong You 钟繇 (151–230, Wei, Three Kingdoms)
Regular script (*kai shu*)

The squat shape of the characters is clearly a borrowing from clerical script. The simplistic, stocky verticals and the unhurried, flowing horizontals are distinctive. In all single-component characters, a prominent role is played by the stabilizing effect of the central strokes, which are sometimes exaggerated for that purpose. An open, spacious character structure is accomplished by compensating with long horizontals, or big diagonals to the lower right or lower left. In compound characters with a right and a left component, the two parts are often kept some distance apart, in a posture of "mutual admiration," with a stroke or two acting as go-between. In characters composed of an upper and a lower component, the structure is generally top-heavy, giving the characters a spontaneous, unaffected charm.

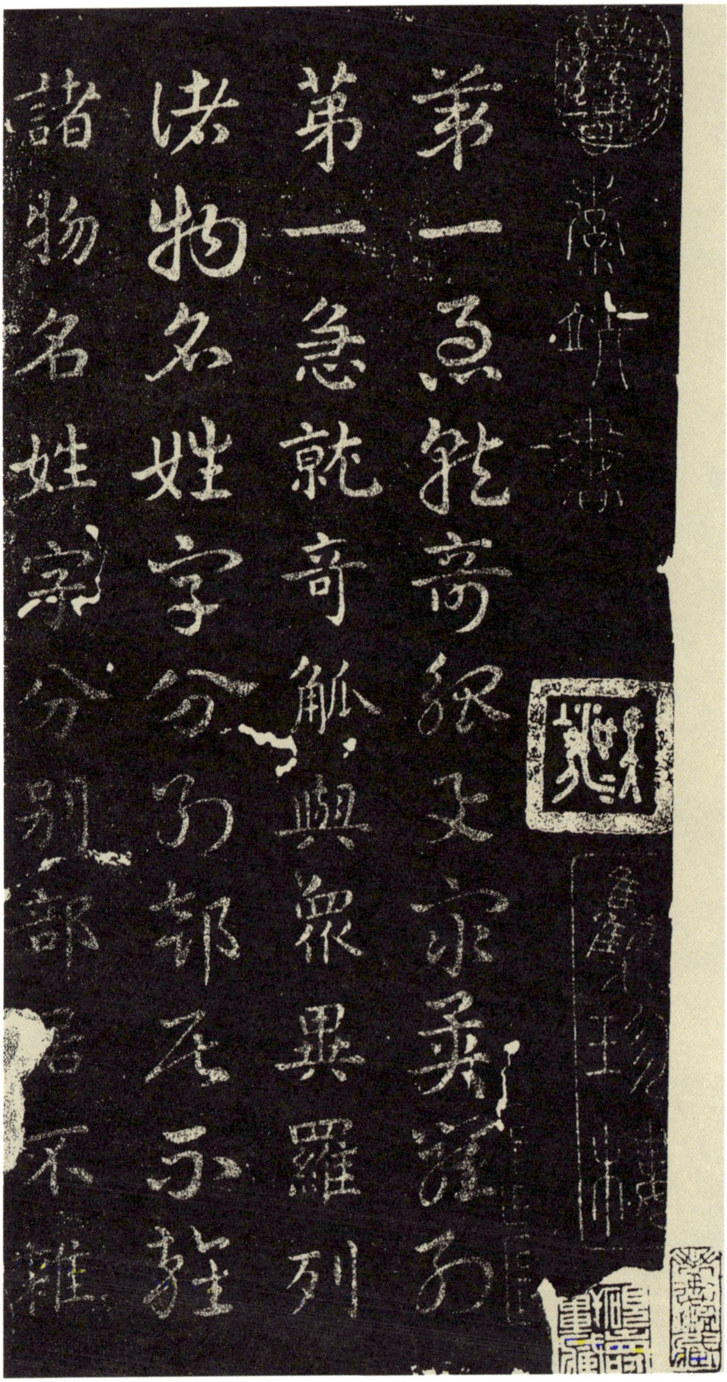

Rubbing from *Literacy Textbook* (急就章 *Ji Jiu Zhang)*

Huang Xiang 皇象 (years of birth/death unknown, Wu, Three Kingdoms)
Early cursive script (*zhang cao*)
24.2 cm × 13.5 cm
Private collection of Qi Gong

Literacy Textbook is a work in early cursive script (as opposed to contemporary cursive script 今草 *jin cao*). Early cursive script is actually a simplified, streamlined version of clerical script. The strokes employed in the piece recall the clerical script style because of their spareness, solemnity and subtlety. The characters are structurally restrained, but with horizontal and diagonal strokes to the lower right ending in "swallow tails," overstepping the invisible character grid to the right or slightly tilting upward to modulate the rhythm. The spatial composition is meticulously neat and disciplined, conveying a simple honesty and a solemn mood.

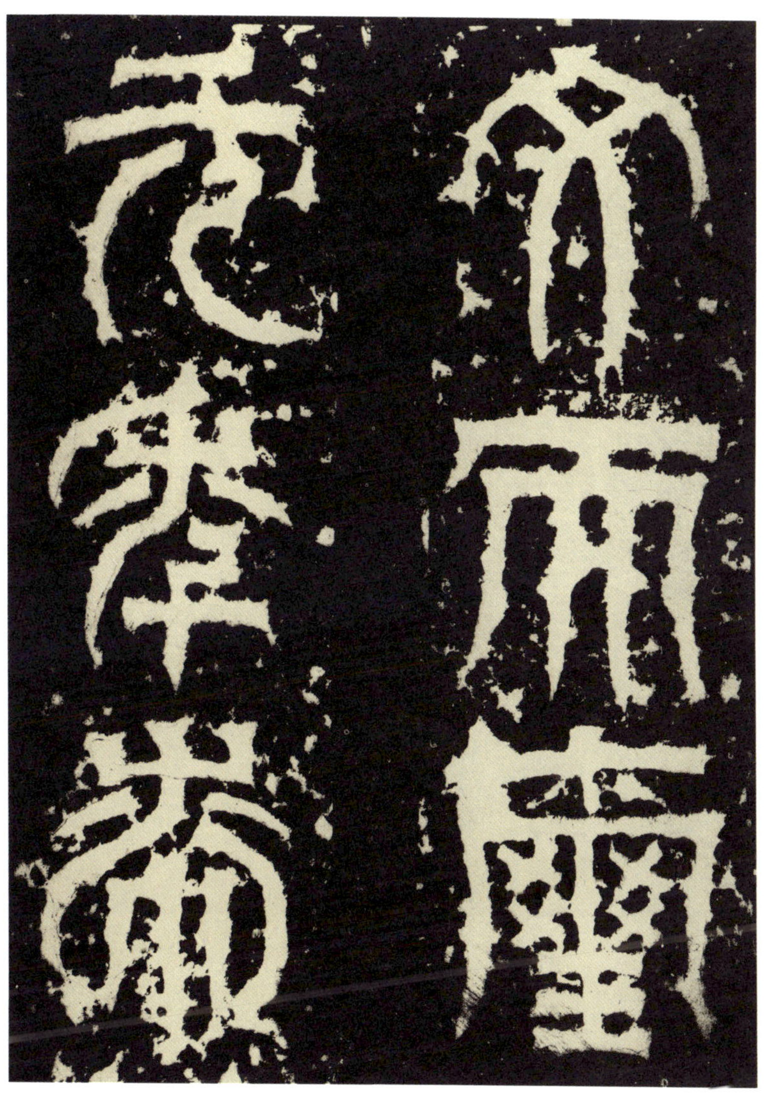

Rubbing made in the Ming dynasty from *Divine Prophecy Tablet* (天发神谶碑 *Tian Fa Shen Chen Bei*)

Unknown calligrapher, Wu, Three Kingdoms
276 AD (carving)
Seal script (*zhuan shu*)
Palace Museum, Beijing

Divine Prophecy Tablet is a very unique piece in seal script. Strokes typically have "square" starts and endings, forming lines that are thicker at the two ends and thinner in the middle, seemingly folded back upon themselves. The character structure tends to have angular instead of rounded corners, giving the characters an aura of vigor and energy. The most distinctive feature is the vertical stroke that tapers downward, resembling a lethal sword with its tip pointing down. The calligraphic style, displayed in this work, of "using clerical script brushwork to execute a seal script piece" represents a radical departure from the traditional seal script, characterized by a more rounded, expansive character structure. In the words of one critic in a later age, this piece is "a sensational masterpiece of uncommon grandeur."

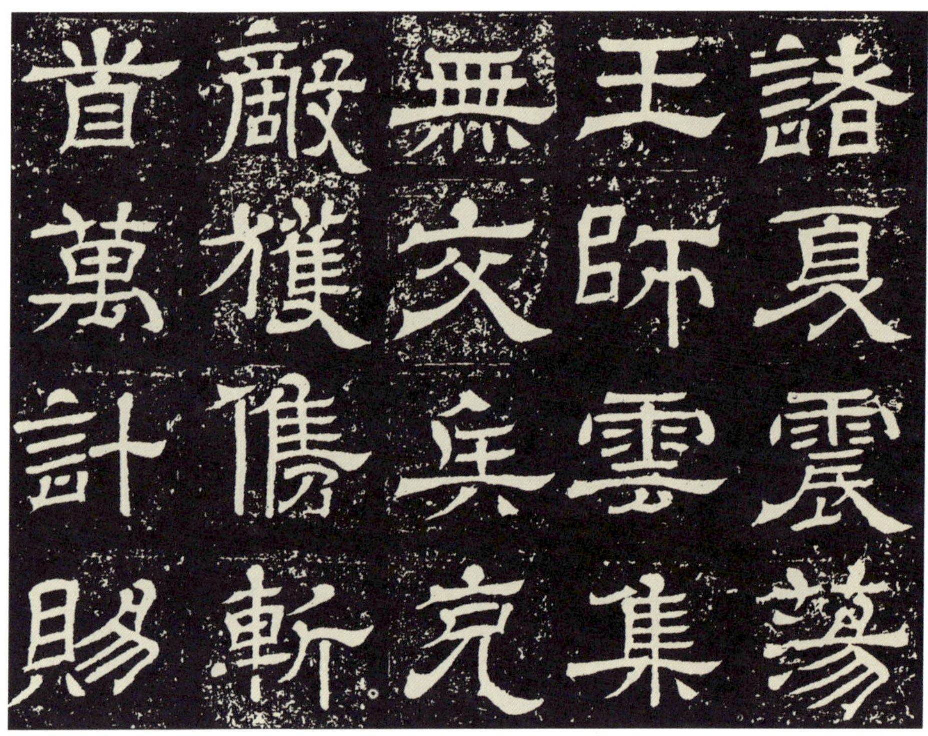

Rubbing from *Wang Ji Tablet* (王基碑 *Wang Ji Bei*)

Unknown calligrapher, Wei, Three Kingdoms
261 AD (carving)
Clerical script (*li shu*)

In the Wei and Jin dynasties, the clerical script style of calligraphy gradually went into decline as regular script came into its own. *Wang Ji Tablet* features level horizontals and plumb verticals, and characters rigidly structured "like abacus beads" in a sharp departure from the clerical script style of the Han dynasty. But the strokes employed in the piece already foreshadow, in a significant way, the regular script style, characterized by a freer flow and faster pace in the brushwork. This clerical script style transformed by the regular script had a major influence on later calligraphic development. Through the Jin, Tang, Song, Yuan and Ming dynasties, up to the early period of the rise of the stele school of calligraphy in the Qing dynasty, it dominated the field of clerical script style calligraphy.

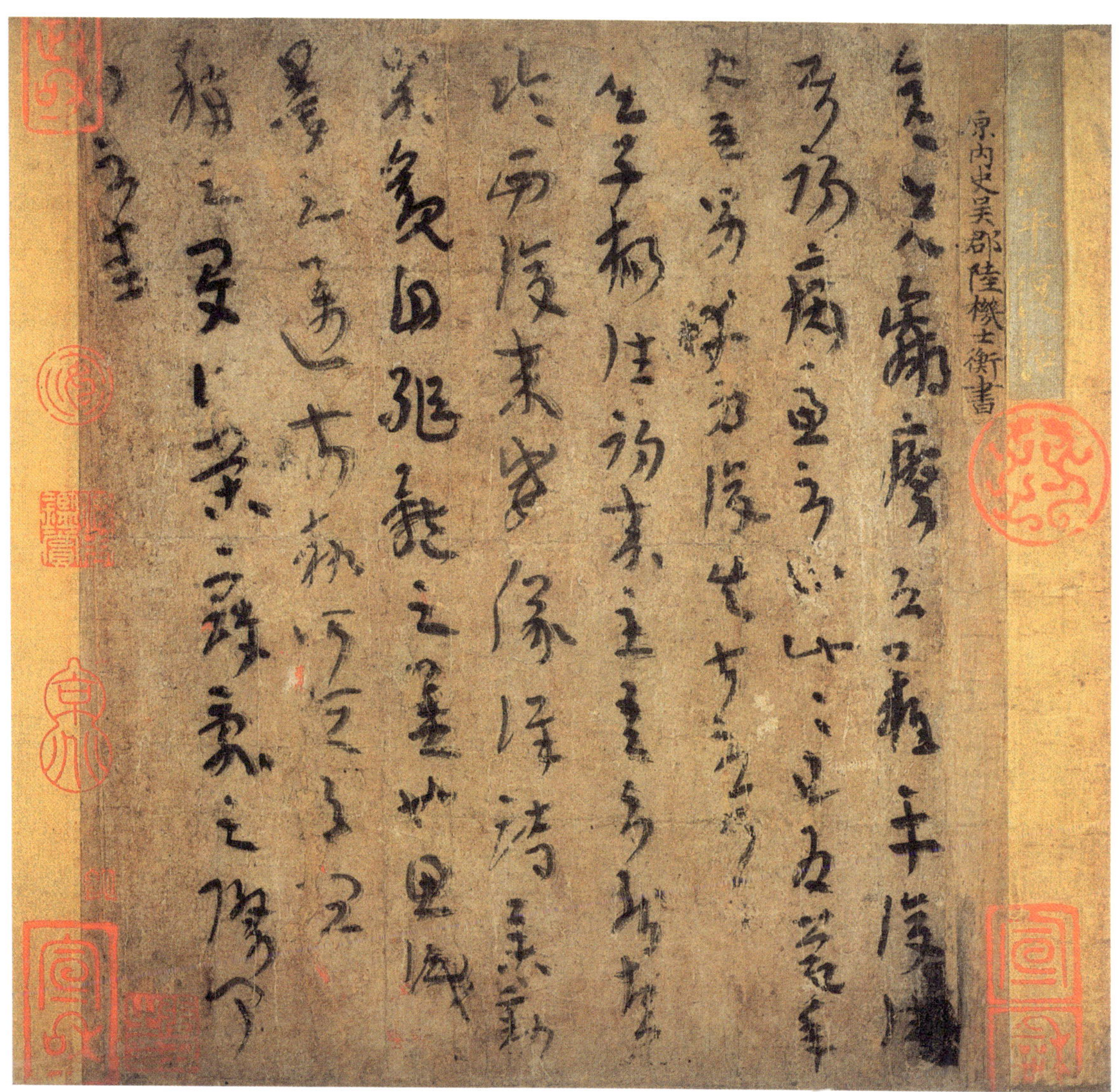

Greeting Note (平复帖 *Ping Fu Tie*)

Lu Ji 陆机 (261-303, Jin dynasty)
Cursive script (*cao shu*)
23.8 cm × 20.5 cm
Palace Museum, Beijing

Dating back seventeen hundred years, this is the earliest surviving Chinese calligraphic work written on paper and is often referred to as the "father of all calligraphic exemplars." Its script falls somewhere between early cursive script and contemporary cursive script. Its brushwork, done with a "dry" brush (秃笔 *tu bi*), exhibits a stocky roundness that brims with latent energy. Because it was written on paper, nature has left its mark on the piece: discoloration (blurring and fading caused by repeated folding, handling and moisture stains) has added to the feel of antiquity. Age-induced coarseness of the paper support also makes the lines appear grave and remote. The piece has, as it were, been re-created by the hand of nature.

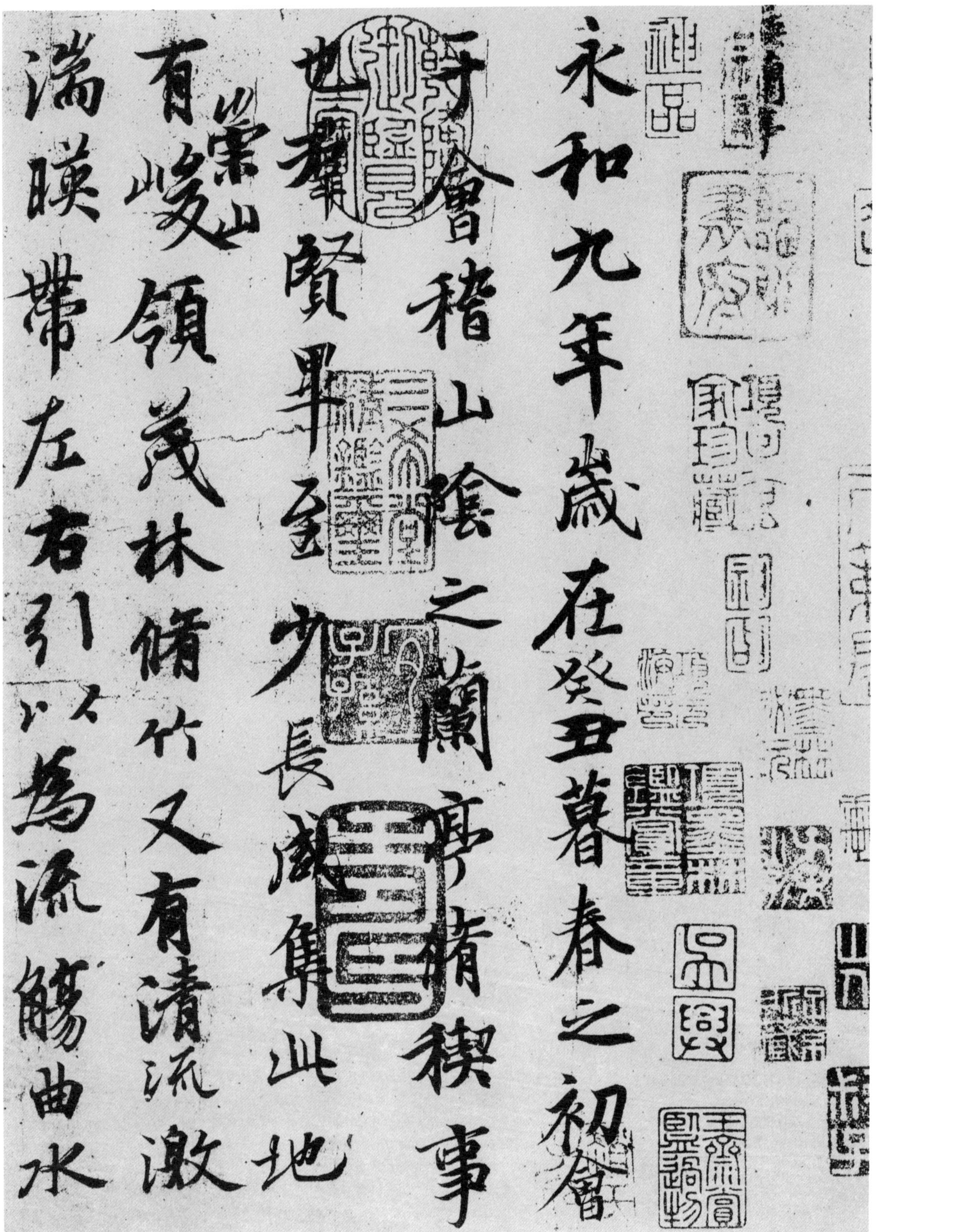

永和九年歲在癸丑暮春之初會
于會稽山陰之蘭亭脩稧事
也羣賢畢至少長咸集此地
有崇山峻領茂林脩竹又有清流激
湍暎帶左右引以為流觴曲水

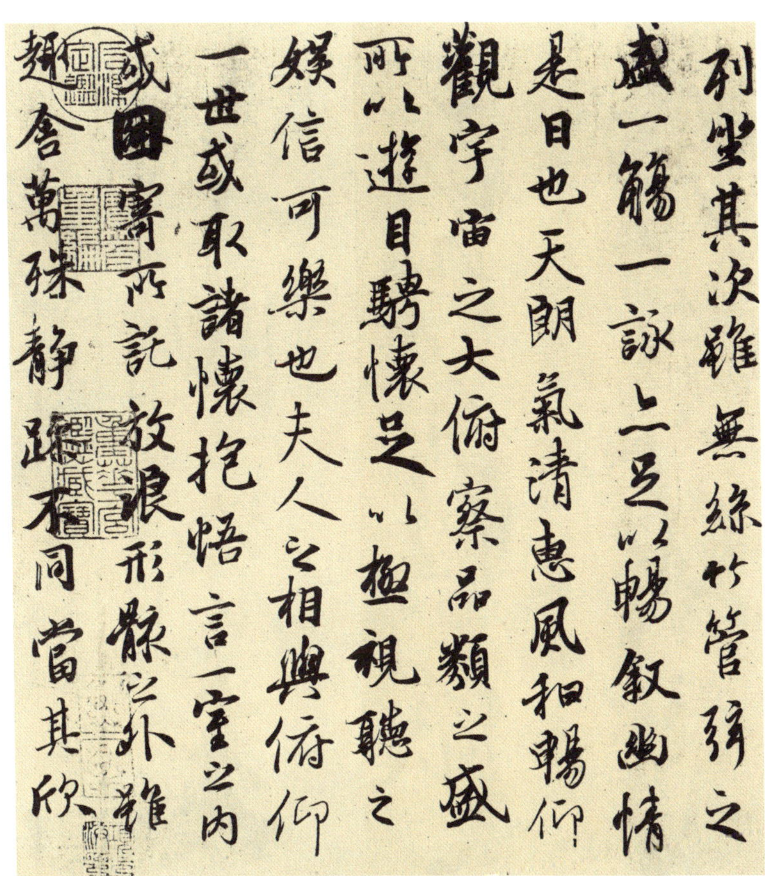

Copy by Feng Chengsu 冯承素 (Tang dynasty) of *Orchid Pavilion Preface* (兰亭序 *Lan Ting Xu*)

Wang Xizhi 王羲之 (303-361, or 321-379 according to some sources, Eastern Jin dynasty)
Running script (*xing shu*)
24.5 cm × 69.9 cm
Palace Museum, Beijing

Chinese calligraphy attained a peak of splendor in the Eastern Jin dynasty. Wang Xizhi, often referred to as the "sage of calligraphy," was also known as "Wang You Jun" because of his title of General of the Right Army (*you jun*). He was born in Linyi, Shandong Province, but he retired to Shanyin in Shaoxing, Zhejiang Province. There he lived a simple, charmed life, insulated from worldly cares in the company of the literati and enjoying the beauties of nature. His calligraphy excels in the use of the rounded brushwork to convey the carefree spirit of his literary contemporaries. His mellow and graceful style was in line with the esthetic taste of his time.

Orchid Pavilion Preface, a signature work of Wang Xizhi, is often referred to as the "premier work in running script." In this work, characters are often made to interact with each other to produce a charming effect. Thus, of the two characters " 流 " and " 觴 ", the former leans toward the upper left while the latter leans toward the upper right, creating a pleasing sense of rhythm. One noteworthy feature in the brushwork of *Orchid Pavilion Preface* is the way the brush-tip is turned inside a stroke. Thus, interestingly, in the two identical left and right elements of the upper part of the character " 乐 ", as the brush-tip comes to the end of the diagonal stroke to the lower left, it is lifted and turned toward the upper left, away from the horizontal stroke to follow, in the process, crossing and re-crossing parts of the diagonal and the horizontal strokes. The hidden overlapping brushstrokes caused by the turnings of the brush-tip create crisp, robust lines; to make a musical analogy: one could almost hear the tintinnabulation of metal or jade objects clinking together. The way the columns, none of which stay on a strictly vertical axis, slightly undulate in an interesting array of variations enlivens the composition. This esthetic artifice also greatly influenced later calligraphers.

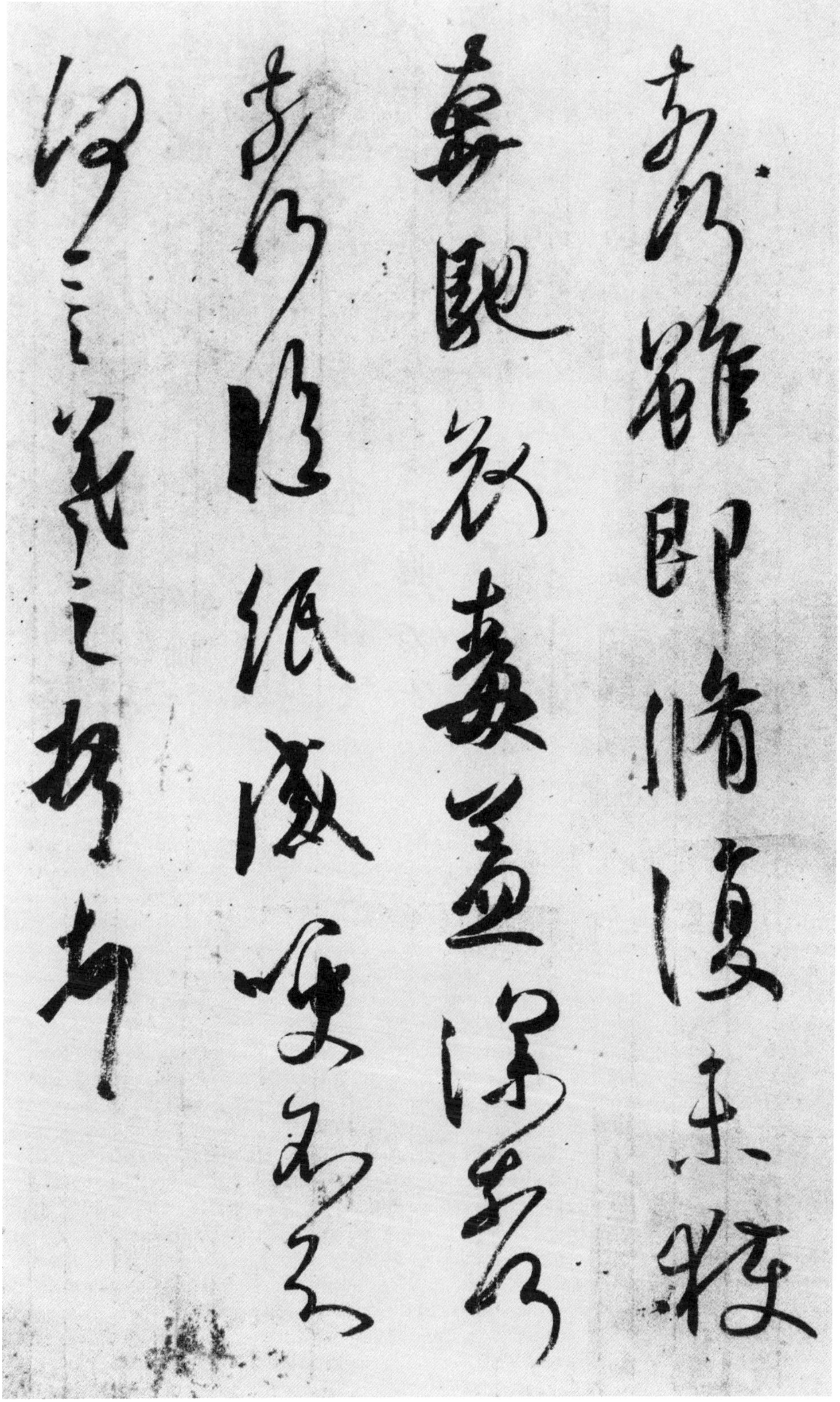

奉別雖即漸復來晤
奉聽欲盡無深歎
奉別悵恨感慨無已
何之羲之頓首

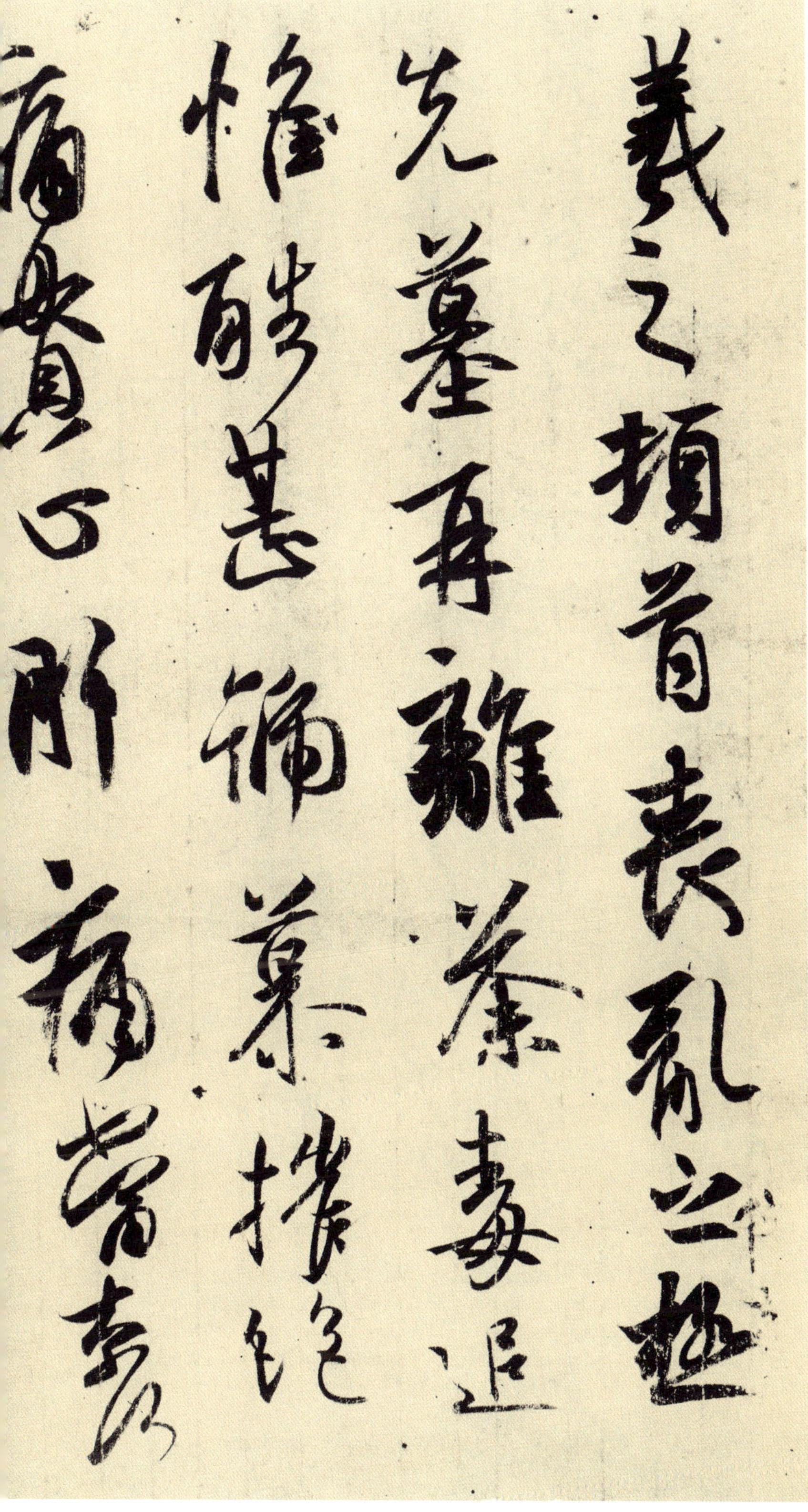

Copy from the Tang dynasty of *Letter to Express Worries and Indignation towards the Destruction of an Ancestral Tomb* (丧乱帖 *Sang Luan Tie*)

Wang Xizhi 王羲之 (303–361, or 321–379 according to some sources, Eastern Jin dynasty)
Running script (*xing shu*)
26.2 cm × 58.4 cm
Sannomaru-Shozokan (Museum of the Imperial Collections) of the Imperial Household Agency of Japan

Letter to Express Worries and Indignation towards the Destruction of an Ancestral Tomb is a brief letter written by Wang Xizhi to a friend. Wang's ancestral tomb was desecrated in the ravages of war, and all his worries and indignation found expression at the tip of his brush, adding an emotional tone to the brushwork. The piece has made a clean break with the clerical script style in brushwork; in character structure, it sets aside the frontal, regular posture of the *Orchid Pavilion Preface*, and adopts instead a slightly inclined posture. The first two columns display a virile charisma, and the last six columns a forlorn beauty, revealing the author's mood swings.
The writing makes a transition from the running script to the cursive script as the author's mood changes from the grief of "heartrending pain" (痛贯心肝 *tong guan xin gan*) to the remorse of "inability to run to its aid" (未獲奔馳 *wei huo ben chi*), turning to all cursive when he swallows hard to suppress his sobbing (臨纸感哽 *lin zhi gan geng*). The cohabitation of two different scripts in the same work does not disturb in any way the overall harmony and coherence of the piece, because the transition from one to the other appears so natural and uncontrived. The spatial composition also appears very natural, with the character "喪" in the first column, "離" in the second, "肝痛" in the fourth and "毒" in the sixth written large, thick and dark, for an eye-catching effect. In contrast, other characters are smaller, with thinner lines and lighter ink tone, and still other characters act as a transition between the two. The graded shading contributes to a strong sense of rhythm.

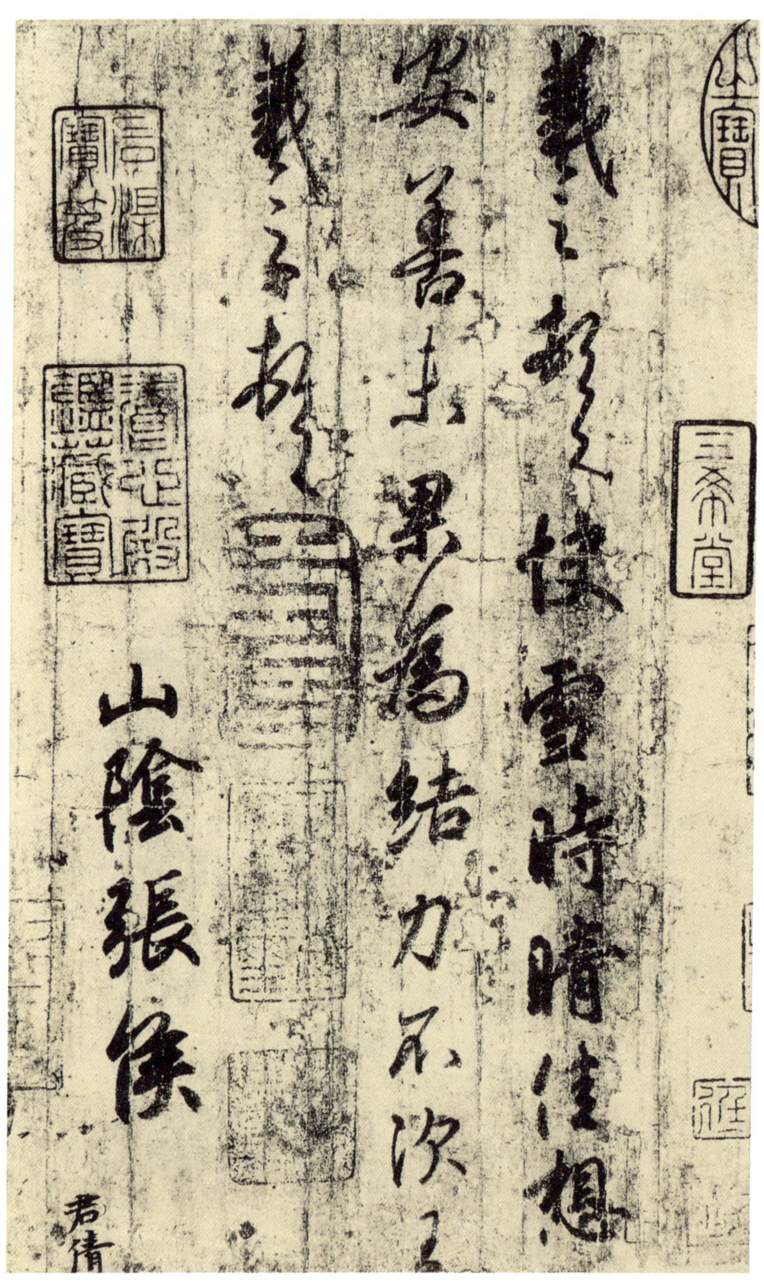

Copy from the Tang dynasty of *Letter to Express Happiness and Greetings* (快雪时晴帖 *Kuai Xue Shi Qing Tie*)

Wang Xizhi 王羲之 (303-361, or 321-379 according to some sources, Eastern Jin dynasty)
Running script (*xing shu*)
32 cm × 14.8 cm
Palace Museum, Taipei

Comprising a total of only 28 characters, *Letter to Express Happiness and Greetings* boasts "virile characters, fluid brushwork, brilliance of traveling clouds and the agility of an awakened dragon." The Qianlong emperor of the Qing dynasty praised the work as "a string of 28 black pearls" and set aside a special hall called Hall of Three Rarities (三希堂 *san xi tang*) as repository of this work by Wang Xizhi, *Letter to a Relative* (伯远帖 *bo yuan tie*) by Wang Xun 王珣 (349-400, Eastern Jin dynasty) and *Mid-Autumn Scroll* (中秋帖 *zhong qiu tie*) by Wang Xianzhi 王献之 (344-386, Eastern Jin dynasty).

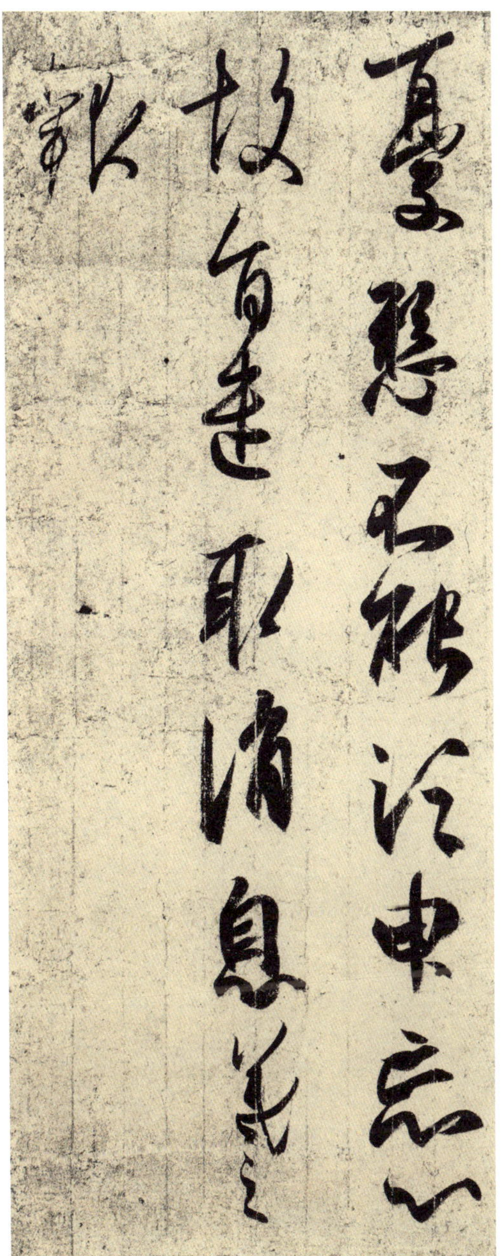

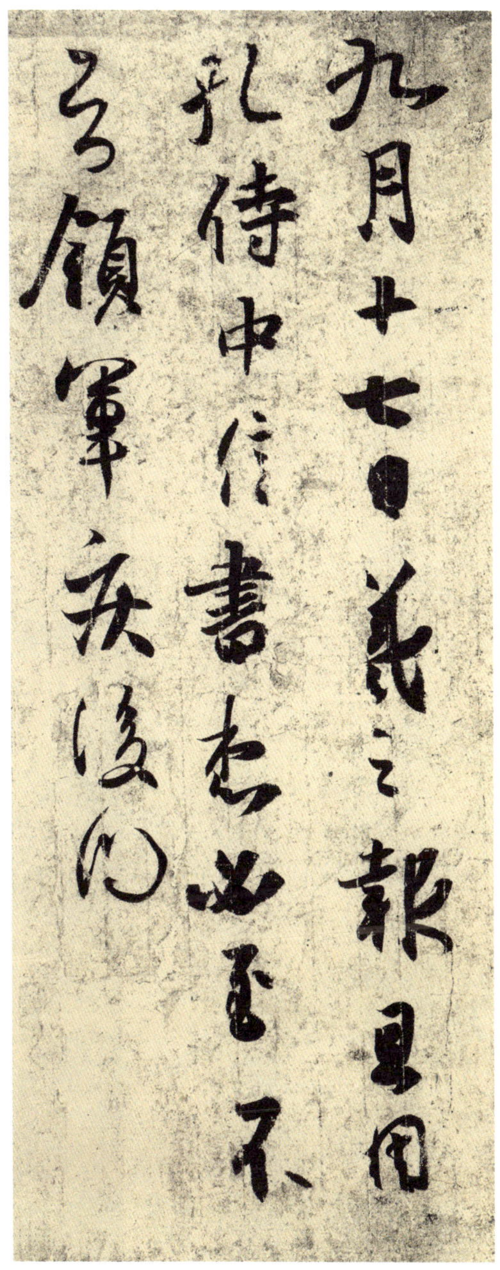

Copy from the Tang dynasty of *Letter to Kong* (孔侍中帖 *Kong Shi Zhong Tie*)

Wang Xizhi 王羲之 (303-361, or 321-379 according to some sources, Eastern Jin dynasty)
Running script (*xing shu*)
24.8 cm × 42.8 cm
Maeda ikutoku kai, Tokyo, Japan

The use of the side-brush (侧锋 *ce feng*) technique, the square strokes and the oscillation of lines adds energy to the piece. The square strokes executed with the side-brush technique stand in sharp contrast to characters written in center-brush (中锋 *zhong feng*) round strokes, e.g. "孔" and "報". The merging of lines at certain points creates darker characters without causing blurring or running. This piece was brought to Japan by a Japanese emissary to the Tang court in the Nara period.

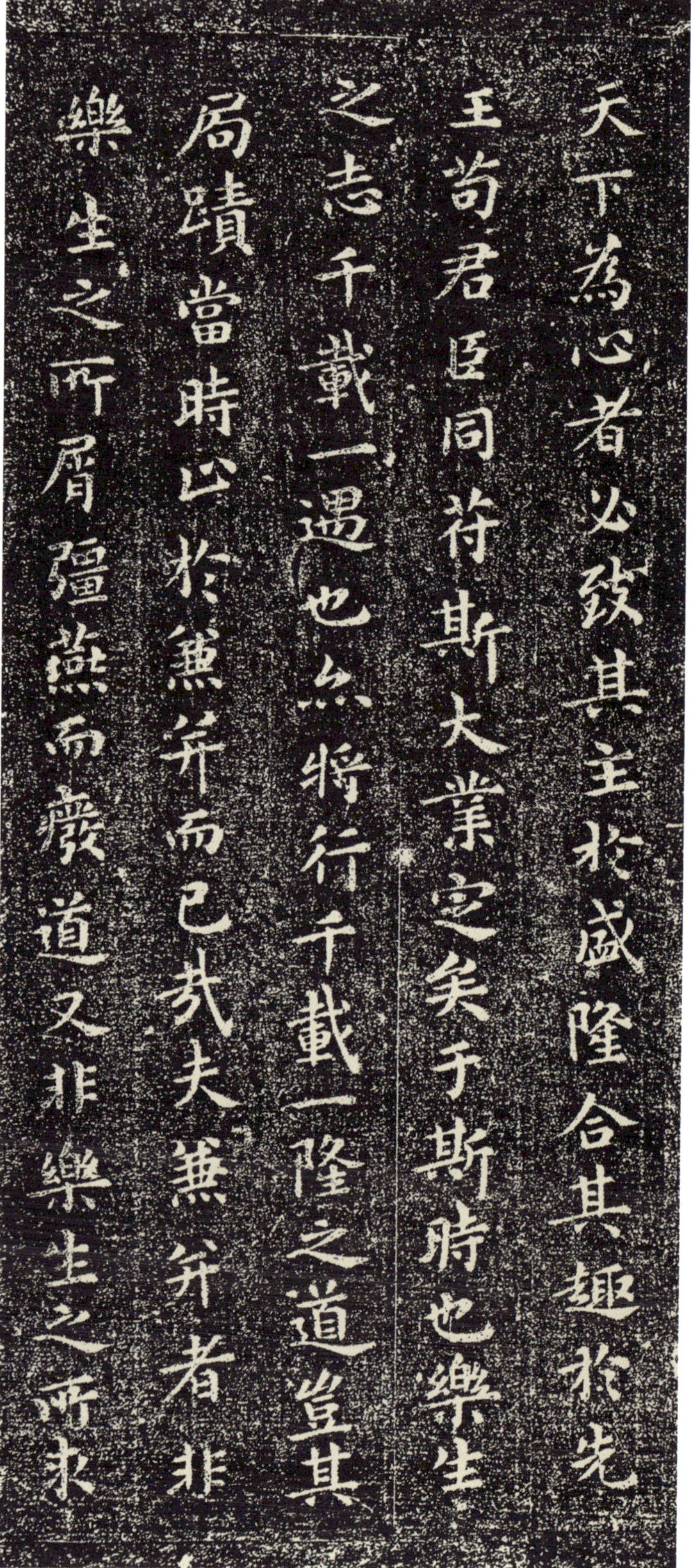

Rubbing from *Essay on Yue Yi* (乐毅论 *Yue Yi Lun*)

Wang Xizhi 王羲之 (303-361, or 321-379 according to some sources, Eastern Jin dynasty)
Regular script (*kai shu*)
5 pages, each 23.4 cm × 11.9 cm
Palace Museum, Beijing

The small regular script (小楷 *xiao kai*) of Wang Xizhi exudes a serene beauty without the aid of ornamentation. An aura of effortless elegance emanates from its dispassionate rationality. His small regular script style is characterized by a rounded brushwork, characters with a full midsection, a posture that is level without sacrificing charm, and a structure that allows each character to assume its natural shape. Wang achieves a style and greatness unmatched by others, without having to strain for the new and the startling.

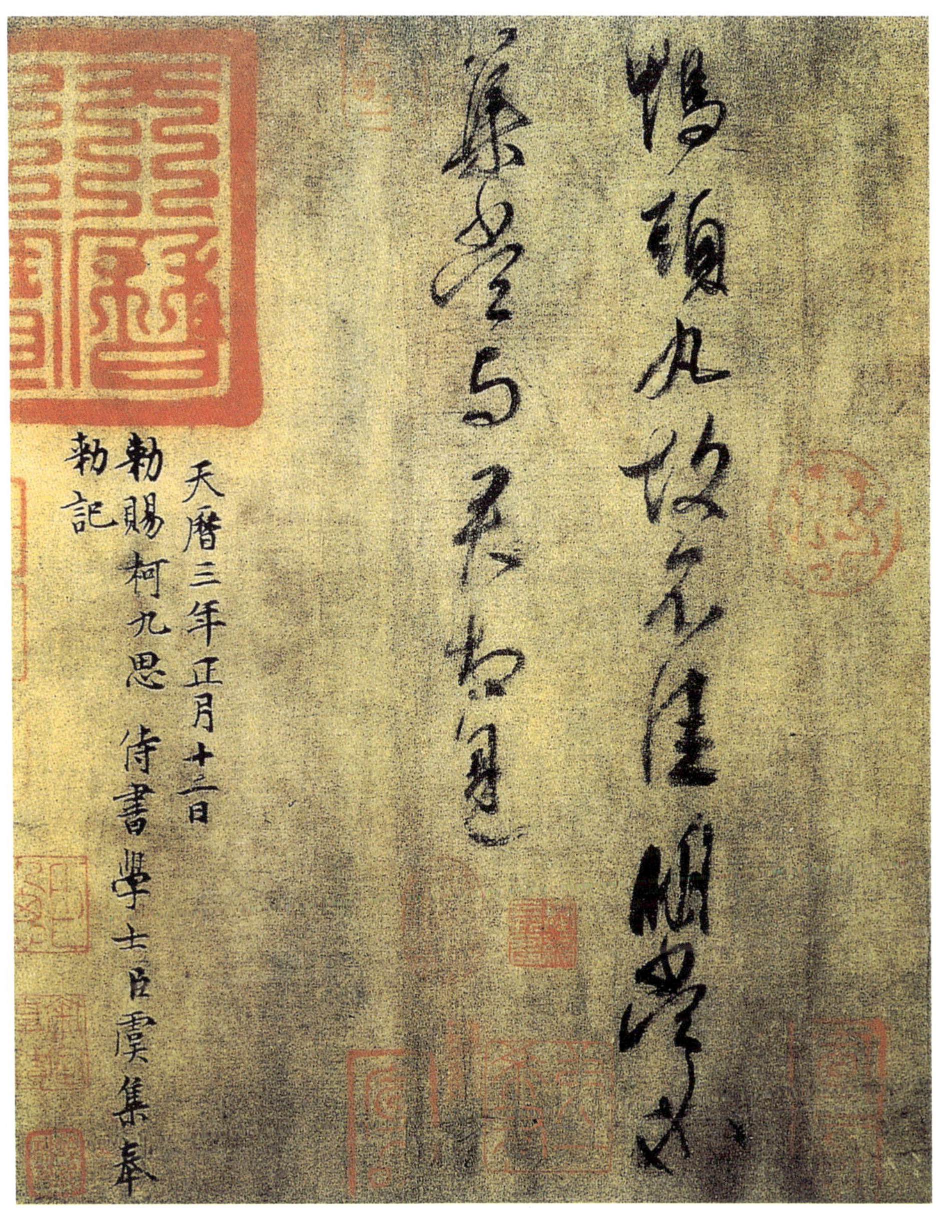

Copy from the Tang dynasty of *Letter about Duck's Head Pill* (鸭头丸帖 *Ya Tou Wan Tie*)

Wang Xianzhi 王献之 **(344-386, Eastern Jin Dynasty)**
Running script (*xing shu*)
26.1 cm × 26.9 cm
Shanghai Museum

Wang Xianzhi, seventh son of Wang Xizhi, was also known as "Wang Da Ling" because of the official position of Secretariat Director (中书令 *zhong shu ling*) he once held. Father and son were known as the "Two Wangs." He was greatly influenced by his father's calligraphic style but added his own innovations. The key word about *Letter about Duck's Head Pill* is "curve." There is not a single straight line in the piece: the horizontals are sloped, the verticals dance around the plumb line, all in the shape of curves. In compound characters formed by an upper and a lower component, the two parts are not centered along the same axis. In spatial composition, the characters also undulate about the center line of the columns. This kind of "rolling" arrangement of the strokes and lines, the character structure and the spatial composition heralded the expansive style of running cursive script (行草 *xing cao*) calligraphy, in contrast to the contractive style of Wang Xizhi.

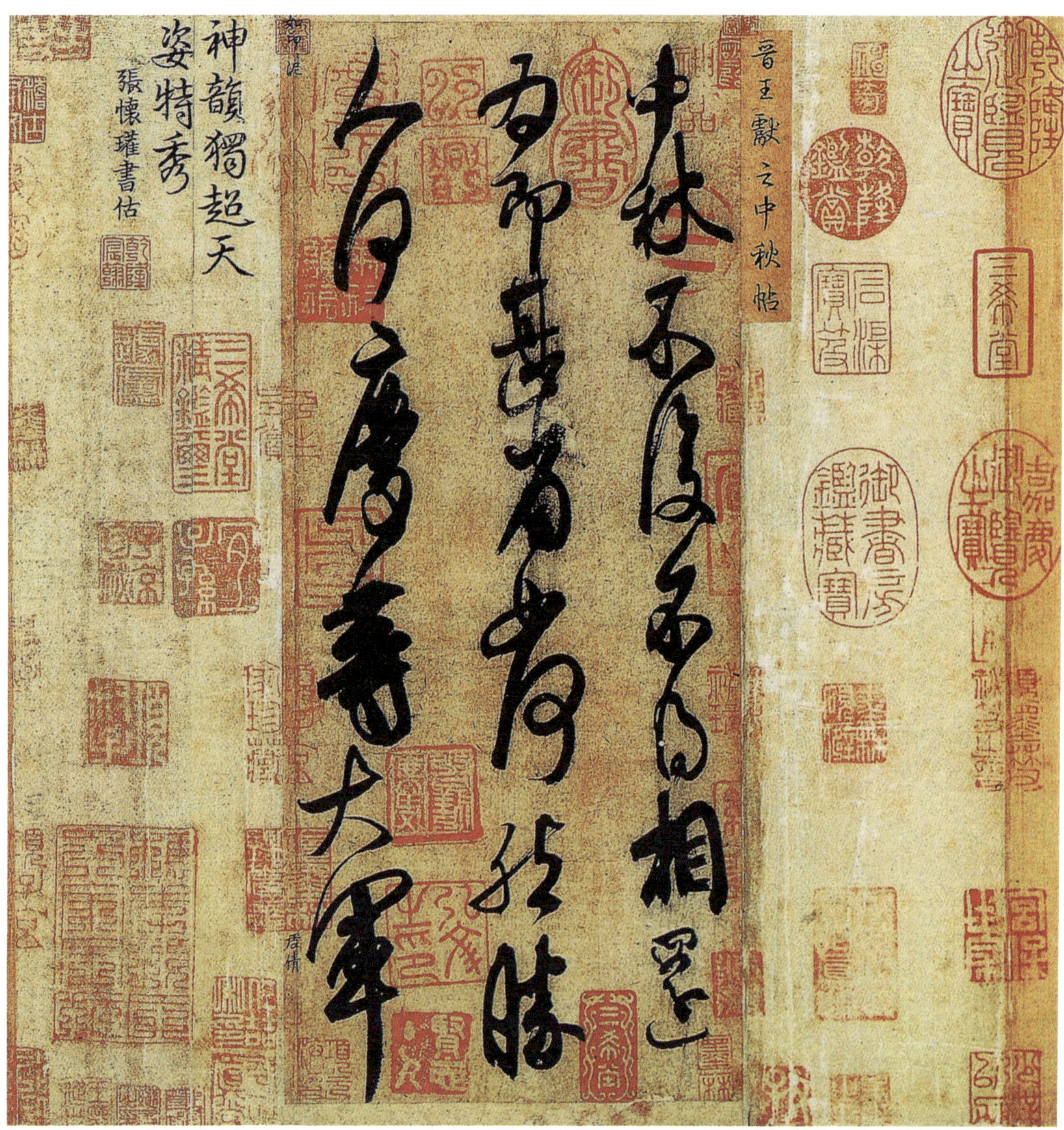

Copy from the Tang dynasty of *Mid-Autumn Scroll* (中秋帖 *Zhong Qiu Tie*)

Wang Xianzhi 王献之 (344-386, Eastern Jin dynasty)
Running script (*xing shu*)
27 cm × 11.9 cm
Palace Museum, Beijing

In this piece of 28 characters there are only eight points at which the brush is lifted off the writing support (not counting changes of columns). The brushwork swooshes along without pause. The power and energy of the six characters " 中秋不复不得 ", completed in one unbroken stroke, is particularly awe-inspiring. Wang Xianzhi's calligraphic style is more romantic, unconventional and iconoclastic than his father's.

Rubbing from a stone inscription, carved in the Song dynasty, of *Rhapsody on the Luo River Goddess* (洛神赋 *Luo Shen Fu*)

Wang Xianzhi 王献之 (344–386, Eastern Jin dynasty)
Regular script (*kai shu*)
4 pages, each 13.4 cm × 6.1 cm
Palace Museum, Beijing (Song dynasty stone inscription)

A notable distinction in style between *Rhapsody on the Luo River Goddess* of Wang Xianzhi and *Memorial to the Emperor for Recommending Ji Zhi* of Zhong You is found in the phrase "plumper in antiquity and slimmer today" (古肥而今瘦 *gu fei er jin shou*). *Rhapsody on the Luo River Goddess* is a signature work of Wang Xianzhi in the small regular script style. It is not unduly restrained by requirements of horizontal or vertical alignment and the brush enjoys wide latitude as it turns out characters of varying postures and sizes. The work with its clean, crisp lines conveying a sense of laisser-aller is considered a "premier model of the small regular script style." *Rhapsody on the Luo River Goddess* epitomizes the esthetic of the Eastern Jin literati, which stemmed from their commitment to shedding worldly attachments.

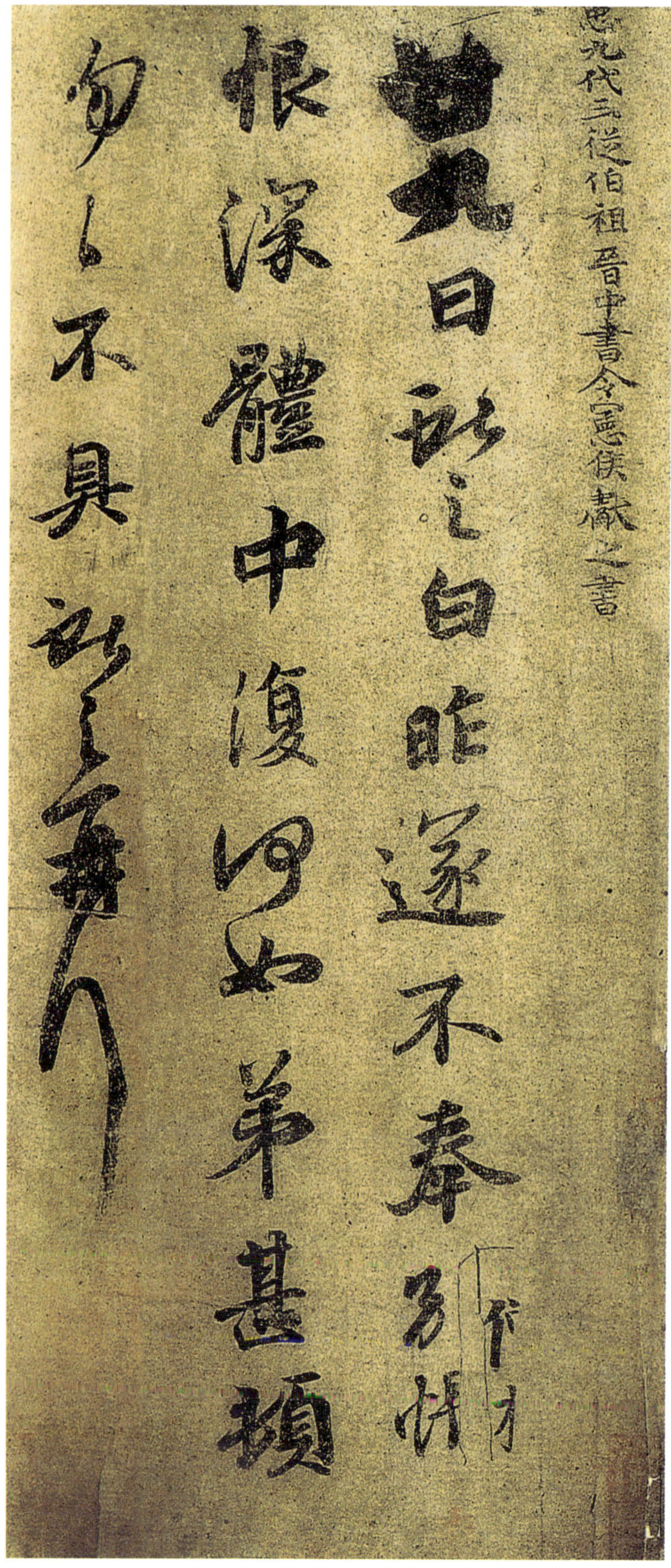

Copy from the Tang dynasty of *On the Twenty-ninth Day*, a Letter (廿九日帖 *Er Shi Jiu Ri Tie*)

Wang Xianzhi 王献之 **(344–386, Eastern Jin dynasty)**
Running regular script (*xing kai*)
26 cm × 11 cm
Palace Museum, Beijing

The brushwork of *On the Twenty-ninth Day* is steady and free-flowing. The characters have a carefree elegance, their serenity belying rich variations in posture inclinations, structural contraction and distension, height and length, giving the brushwork a strong sense of movement and rhythm. The occasional appearance of cursive script style characters in the midst of a running regular script paragraph, in defiance of the homogeneity of style, reflects the uninhibited creative style of the Jin literati.

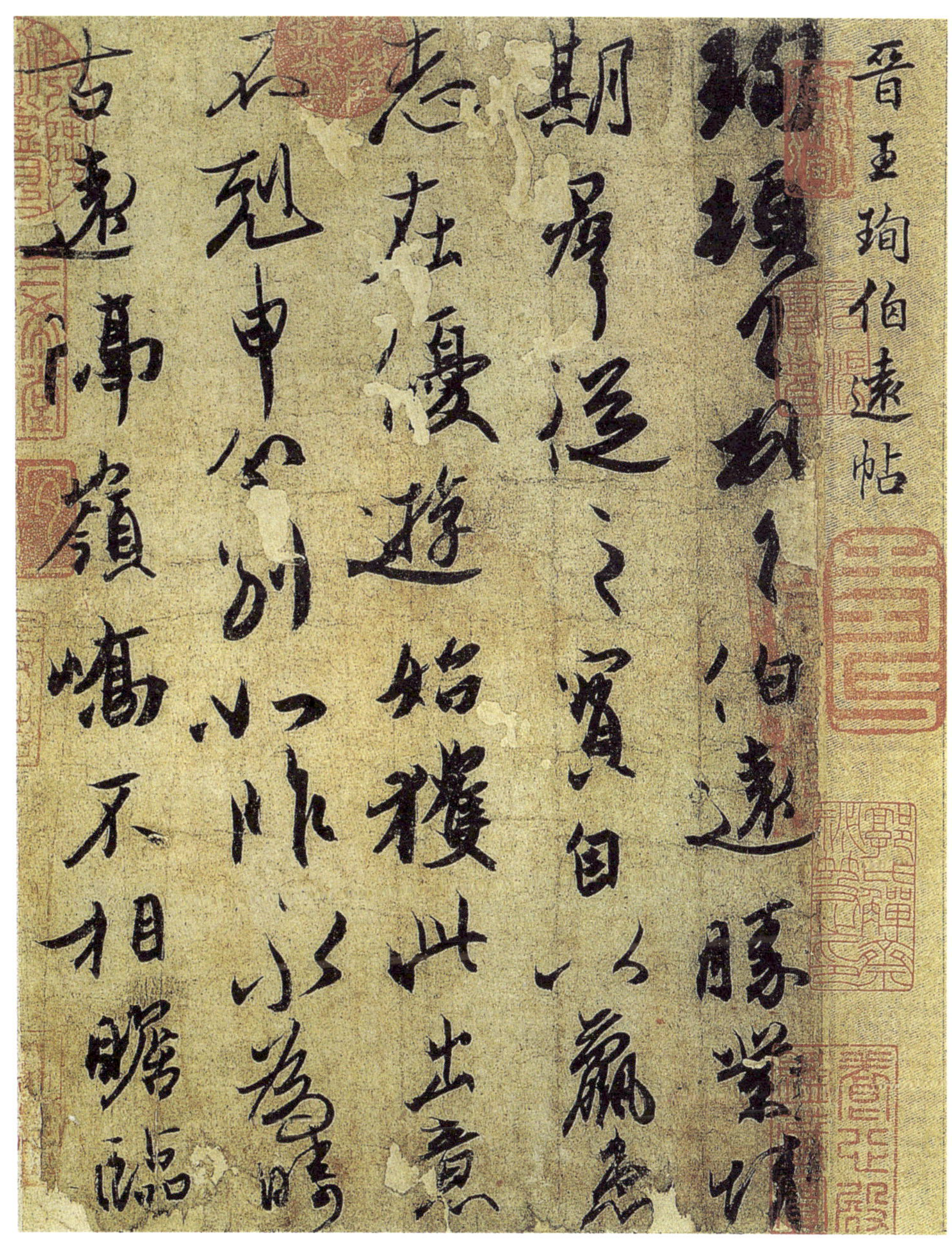

Letter to a Relative (伯远帖 *Bo Yuan Tie*)

Wang Xun 王珣 **(349-400, Eastern Jin dynasty)**
Running script (*xing shu*)
25.1 cm × 17.2 cm
Palace Museum, Beijing

Wang Xun was a paternal cousin of Wang Xianzhi's. *Letter to a Relative* exhibits a leisurely, fluid style, with an airy spatial composition and shapely characters, some of which, such as " 志在 ", " 不剋 " and " 瞻臨 ", are written in center-brush with lines that seem to lift off the writing support in keeping with the convention of running script from the Sui and Tang dynasties onwards. Others, such as " 别如 ", are written in a completely different fashion: with no discernible pressing at the beginning of the strokes, or lifting at the end, and no contrasting brush movements; only straightforward, simple lines. The coexistence in the same work of contrasting brush techniques reflects the transition in calligraphic scripts and styles occurring in the Wei, Jin and Southern and Northern dynasties and the eclectic tastes peculiar to those dynasties.

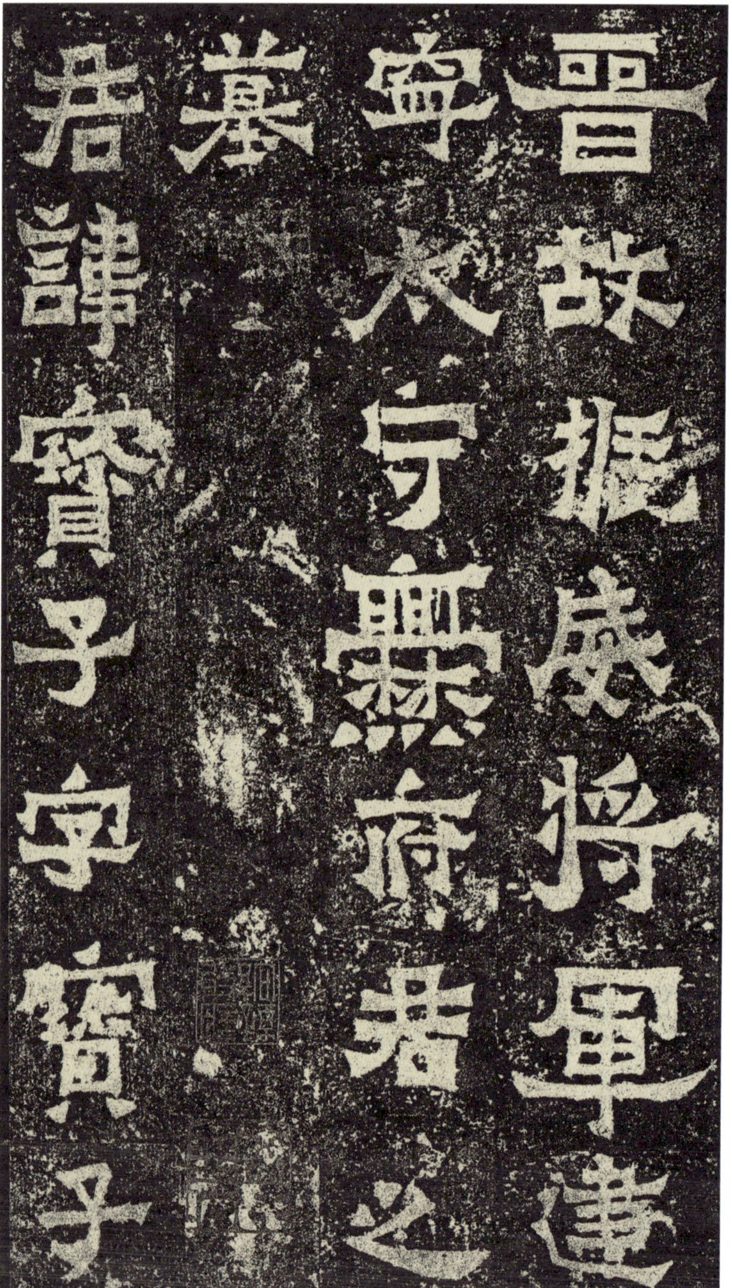

Cuan Bao Zi Tablet (爨宝子碑 *Cuan Bao Zi Bei*)

Unknown calligrapher, Eastern Jin dynasty
405 AD (carving)
Regular script (*kai shu*)

A renowned tablet of the Southern dynasties, this work together with *Cuan Long Yan Tablet* (爨龙颜碑 *cuan long yan bei*), also unearthed in Yunnan, constituted the so-called "Twin Cuans of Yunnan." Following the move of the Jin capital to the east, the Southern dynasties of Song, Qi, Liang and Chen lasted another 169 years. Due to a ban on the erection of tablets in the Southern dynasties, there were far fewer stone tablets in the South than in the Northern dynasties and as a consequence very few stone inscriptions have survived from the Southern dynasties. At the time of the carving of *Cuan Bao Zi Tablet*, the clerical script style had not completely ceded its place to the emerging regular script, as shown in this inscription, which is in regular script but heavily flavored by the clerical script style. The horizontal strokes ending in "swallow tails," the use of square strokes and the mixing of characters in varying postures and sizes give the piece a quaintly clumsy and antique feel.

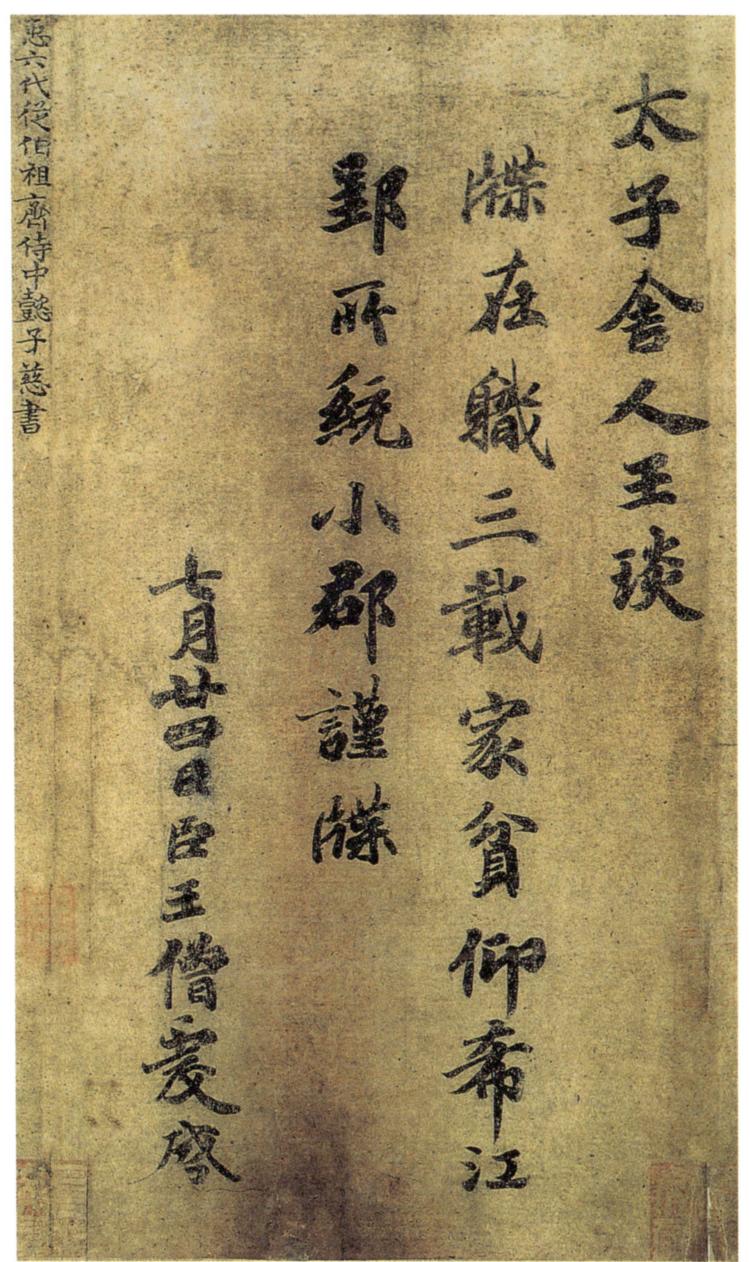

太子舍人王琰
牒在職三載家貧仰希江
郢所統小郡謹牒
七月廿四日臣王僧虔啓

Letter about Wang Yan (太子舍人帖 *Tai Zi She Ren Tie*)

Wang Sengqian 王僧虔 **(426-485, Qi of the Southern dynasties)**
Running regular script (*xing kai*)
Provincial Museum of Liaoning

Wang Sengqian, fourth-generation grandson of Wang Xizhi, specialized in regular script and running script calligraphy. His calligraphic style, heavily influenced by family tradition, was solid and down to earth but lacked eye-catching beauty, as shown in this critique "it is like a stream carrying floating ice, hills covered by snow, clean and spare but bland." In this work, the space is well managed and the strokes are expertly executed, giving a sense of serene beauty; but an excess of care in execution may have prevented the calligrapher from giving full rein to his talent, and it shows.

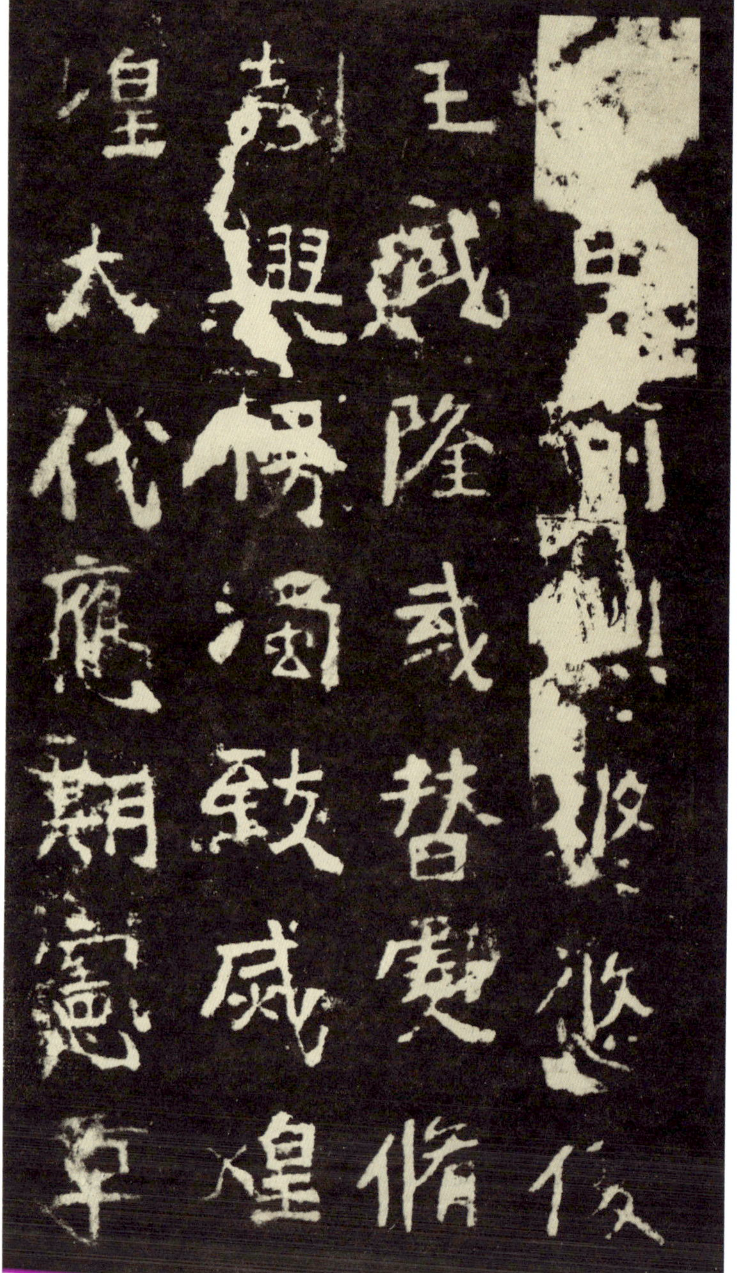

Rubbing made in the Ming dynasty from *Song Gao Ling Miao Tablet* (嵩高灵庙碑 *Song Gao Ling Miao Bei*)

Unknown calligrapher, Northern Wei of the Northern dynasties
456 AD (carving)
Regular script (*kai shu*)
Palace Museum, Beijing

The "swallow tail" endings of dots and strokes in this inscription are a borrowing from clerical script, whereas the "close left and open right," the "lower left and higher right" and the "staggered lengths" rules are clearly characteristics of the regular script style. Clearly, disparate stylistic elements were freely mixed together when old conventions were in decline and new ones had yet to be established. Without any extant model to follow, this inscription had to rely entirely on an exploratory spirit and the will to innovate. The resulting new script, later known as the Northern Wei style, elicited an initial response of surprise, followed by the relief of comprehension, and finally delight, with its rich mix of varied strokes and character structures. This work has won high praise for its ability to make use of all available stylistic elements and esthetic artifices.

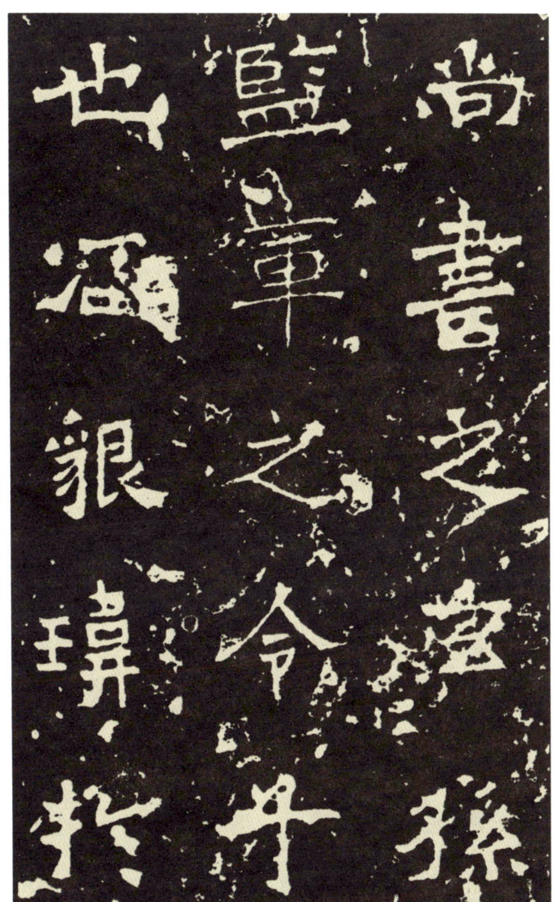

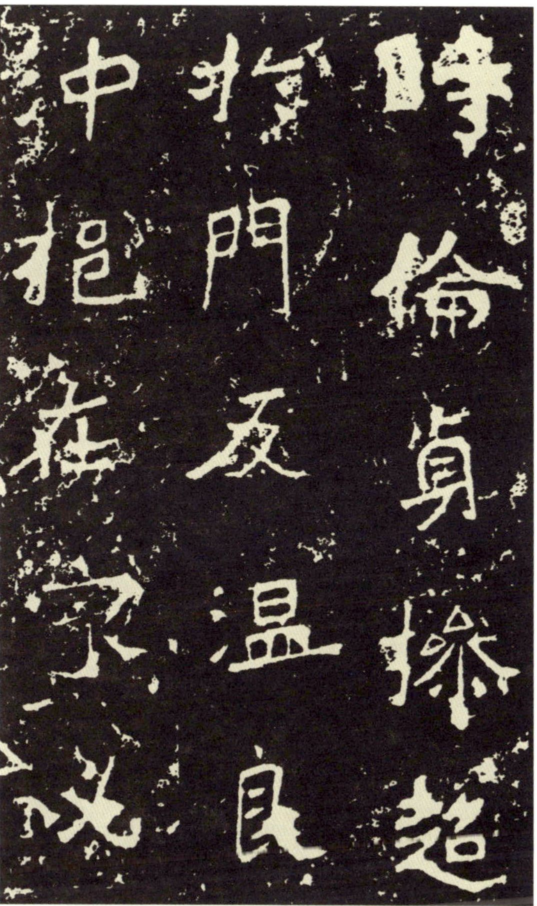

Rubbing from *Cuan Long Yan Tablet*
(爨龙颜碑 *Cuan Long Yan Bei*)

Unknown calligrapher, Song of the Southern dynasties
458 AD (carving)
Regular script (*kai shu*)

In the inscription on the *Cuan Long Yan Tablet*, emphasis is placed on moving the brush-tip at right angles to the stroke being made, both when starting and when ending the stroke. The resulting angular corners give the characters a masculine structure and aura. A strong visual effect is created by treating some short strokes as dots, spreading the brush as it moves on to form a sharp-looking triangle. The character structure tends to be open, and consistent with the "lower left and higher right" rule of character posture. The composition is solid and stable but not without an unconventional charm.

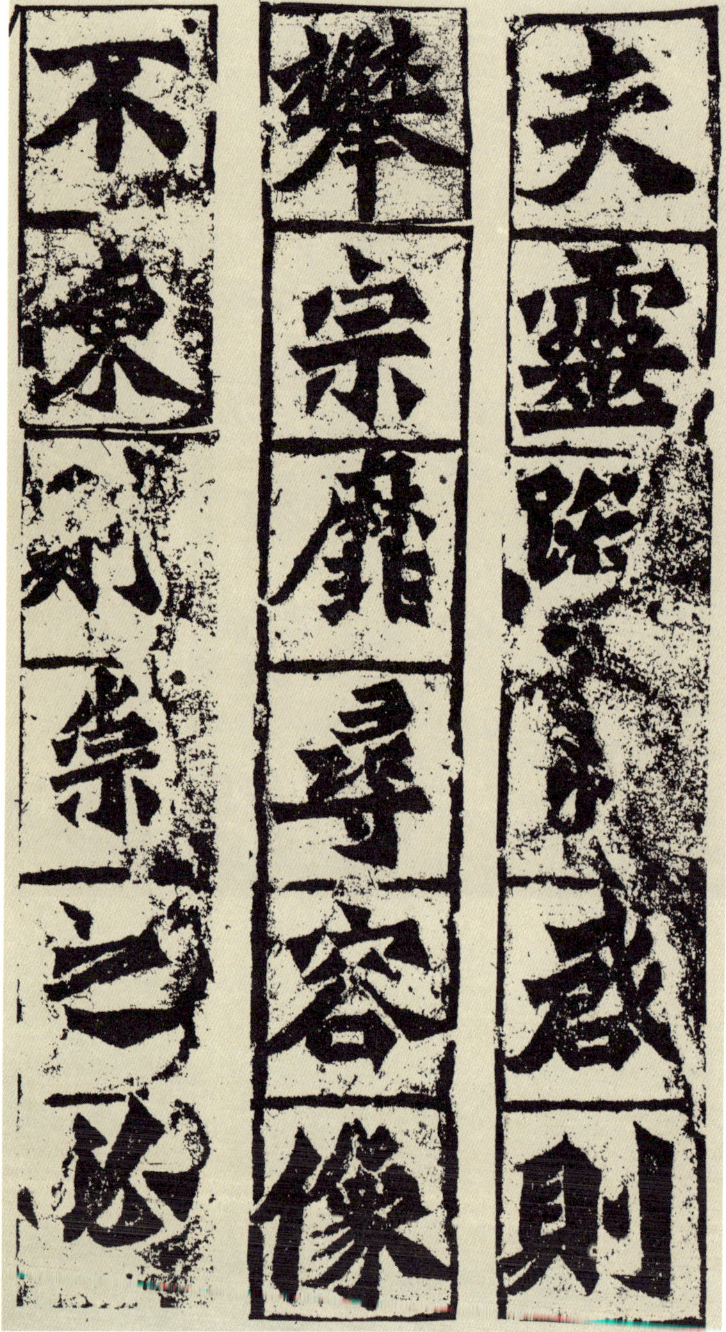

Rubbing from *Chronicle of the Building of the Buddha Image by Shi Pinggong* (始平公造像记 *Shi Ping Gong Zao Xiang Ji*)

Unknown calligrapher, Northern Wei of the Northern dynasties
489 AD (carving)
Regular script (*kai shu*)

Building Buddhist niches and sculpting Buddha images was in vogue during the Southern and Northern dynasties. The inscriptions accompanying the images were called *Chronicle of the Building of the Image* (造像记 *zao xiang ji*). The construction of Buddha images reached a peak at the Longmen Caves near Luoyang during the Northern Wei dynasty. The "Longmen 20" is a famous example of the high achievement in this area. *Chronicle of the Building of the Buddha Image by Shi Pinggong*, one of the "Longmen 20," embodies, with its solid, energetic brushwork and stocky character structures, the tough, untamed and straight-as-an-arrow temperament of the northern peoples. The strokes start with the side-brush technique; the dots are formed into triangles; the verticals are made into suspended needles; the right-falling strokes end in a distinctive fashion; corners are handsomely angular; the character structure adheres to the "lower left and higher right" rule, with sharp left and right leanings of the character components. The entire inscription radiates a virile quality.

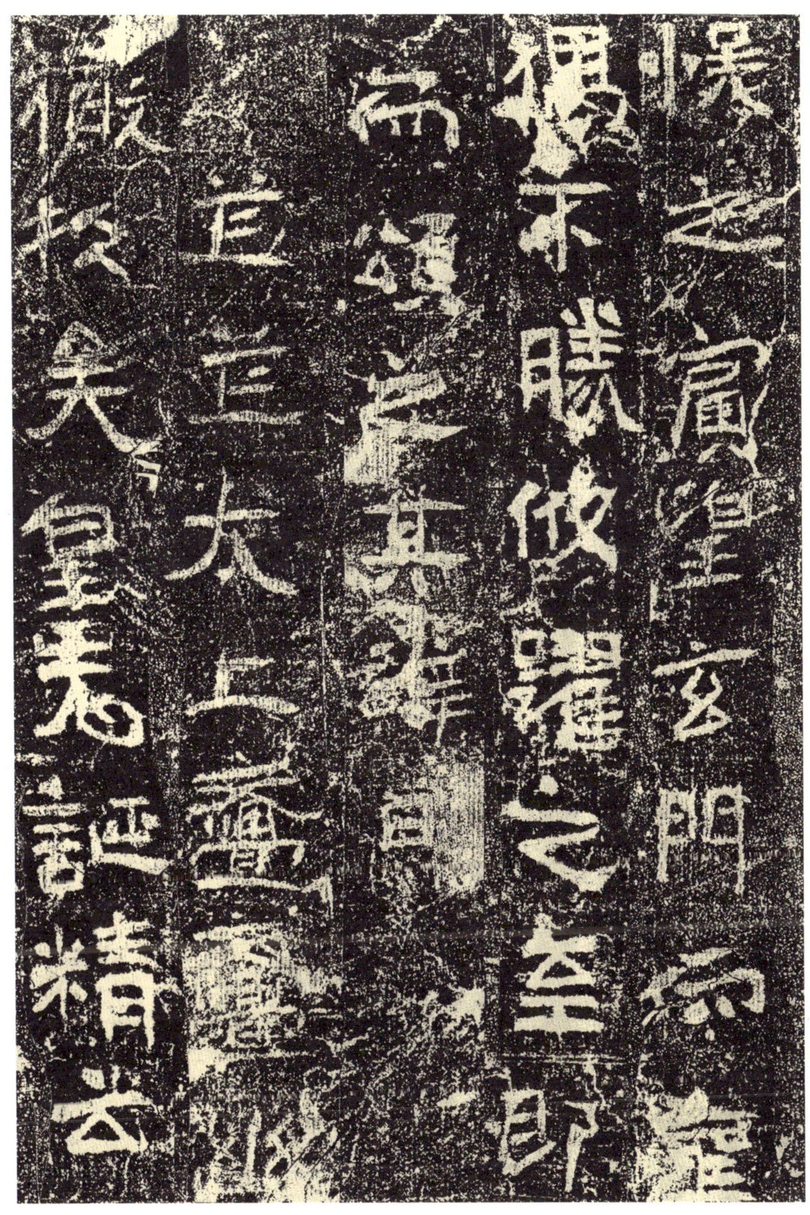

Rubbing from *Chronicle of the Building of the Buddha Image by Yao Boduo and His Brothers* (姚伯多兄弟造像记 *Yao Bo Duo Xiong Di Zao Xiang Ji*)

Unknown calligrapher, Northern Wei of the Northern dynasties
496 AD (carving)
Regular script (*kai shu*)

A Chronicle of the Building of an Image was carved by a sculptor based on the writing traced in cinnabar by a calligrapher. There were inscriptions directly carved into the stone without the aid of a calligrapher's tracing. *Chronicle of the Building of the Buddha Image by Yao Boduo and His Brothers* was one such work. Besides exhibiting a rough-hewn look, inscriptions falling in this category often display a carefree spontaneity and are rich in visual surprises. Reflecting the transition from the clerical (隶 *li*) to the regular (楷 *kai*) script happening in that period, *Chronicle of the Building of the Buddha Image by Yao Boduo and His Brothers* employs mainly the round stroke interspersed with the square stroke. Due to it being carved without the guidance of a calligrapher's cinnabar tracing, the work has an added esthetic appeal resulting from rich variations in character size and posture.

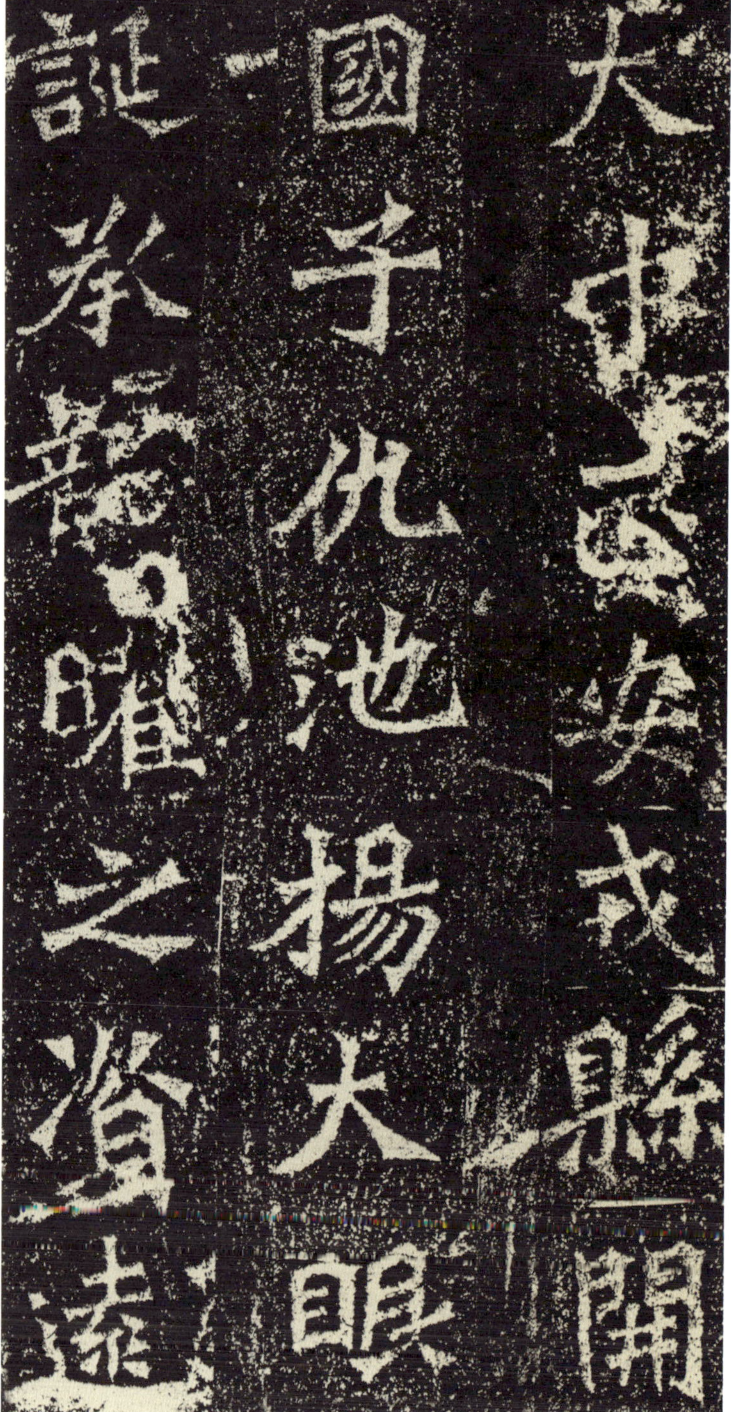

Rubbing from *Chronicle of the Building of the Buddha Image by Yang Dayan* (杨大眼造像记 *Yang Da Yan Zao Xiang Ji*)

Unknown calligrapher, **Northern Wei of the Northern dynasties**
500 AD–506 AD (carving)
Regular script (*kai shu*)

Among the "Longmen 20," *Chronicle of the Building of the Buddha Image by Shi Pinggong* and *Chronicle of the Building of the Buddha Image by Yang Dayan* are of particular note. In calligraphic style, *Chronicle of the Building of the Buddha Image by Yang Dayan* closely resembles *Chronicle of the Building of the Buddha Image by Shi Pinggong* in that both employ square, angular strokes and have a character structure that is contractive in the interior and expansive around the periphery, except that the degree of interior tautness is slightly less than in *Chronicle of the Building of the Buddha Image by Shi Pinggong*, a difference perhaps attributable to the fact that one is an intaglio carving and the other is a carving in relief. This piece was likened by one critic to a "young commandant, full of muscular strength and heroism."

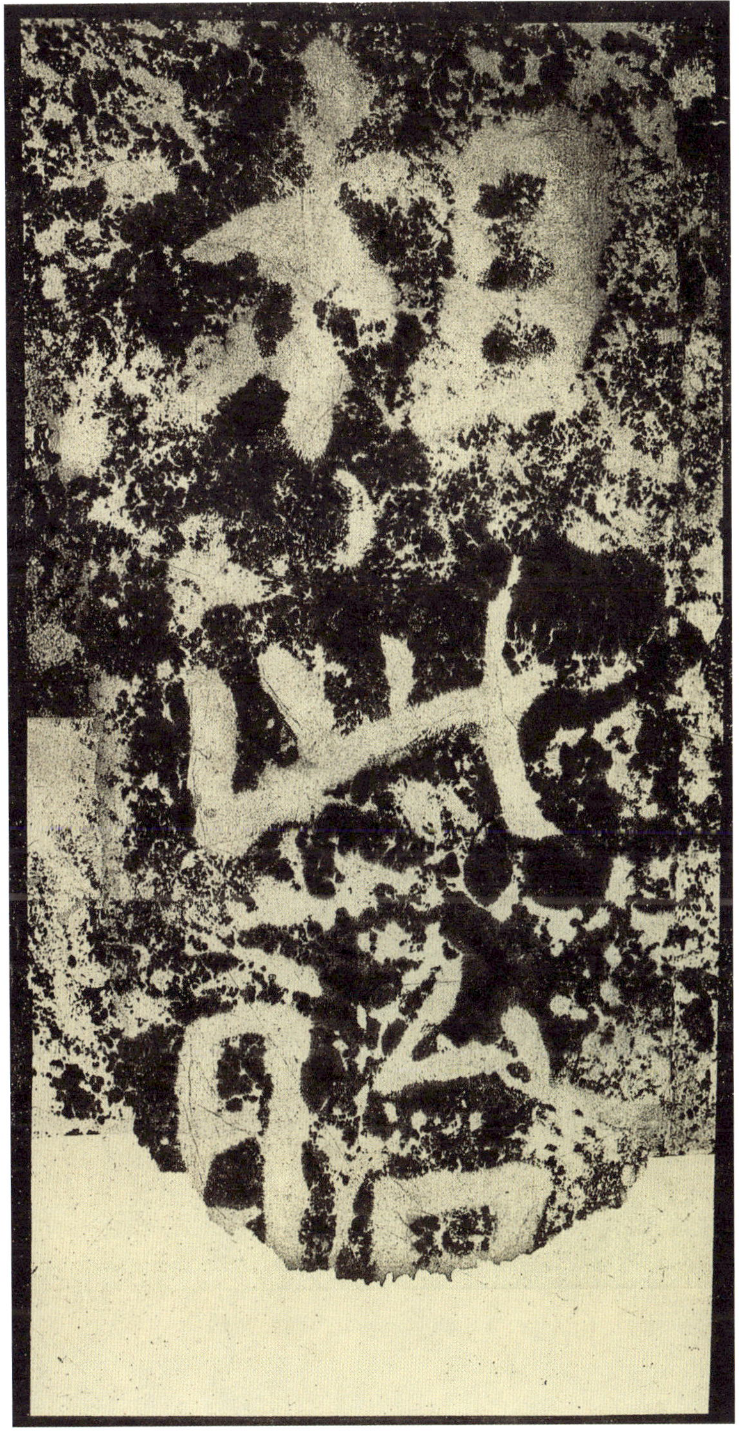

Rubbing from *Inscription on Stone Gate* (石门铭 *Shi Men Ming*)

Wang Yuanshu 王远书 (year of birth/ death unknown, Northern Wei of the Northern dynasties)
509 AD (carving)
Regular script (*kai shu*)
Cliff carving

The strokes in *Inscription on Stone Gate* are supple, unrestricted and open. The character structure is "lower at left and higher at right," airy but not disjointed. In the words of one critic, it "floats effortlessly in the air, with a simple grace, like an ascending fairy goddess." This is consistent with the natural environment surrounding the "Stone Gate cliff-side hanging plank trail" celebrated in the writing, which states "a winding, perilous trail with nine bends was cut into the cliff side," just as the jagged lines incised into the stone twist and turn, forming sharply leaning characters. *Stone Drum Inscriptions* (石鼓文 *shi gu wen*), *Ode to Stone Gate and Inscription on Stone Gate* would later be called the "Three Stones" (" 三石 " *san shi*), grouping together the three spiritually kindred pieces representing respectively the seal script, the clerical script and the regular script styles of calligraphy.

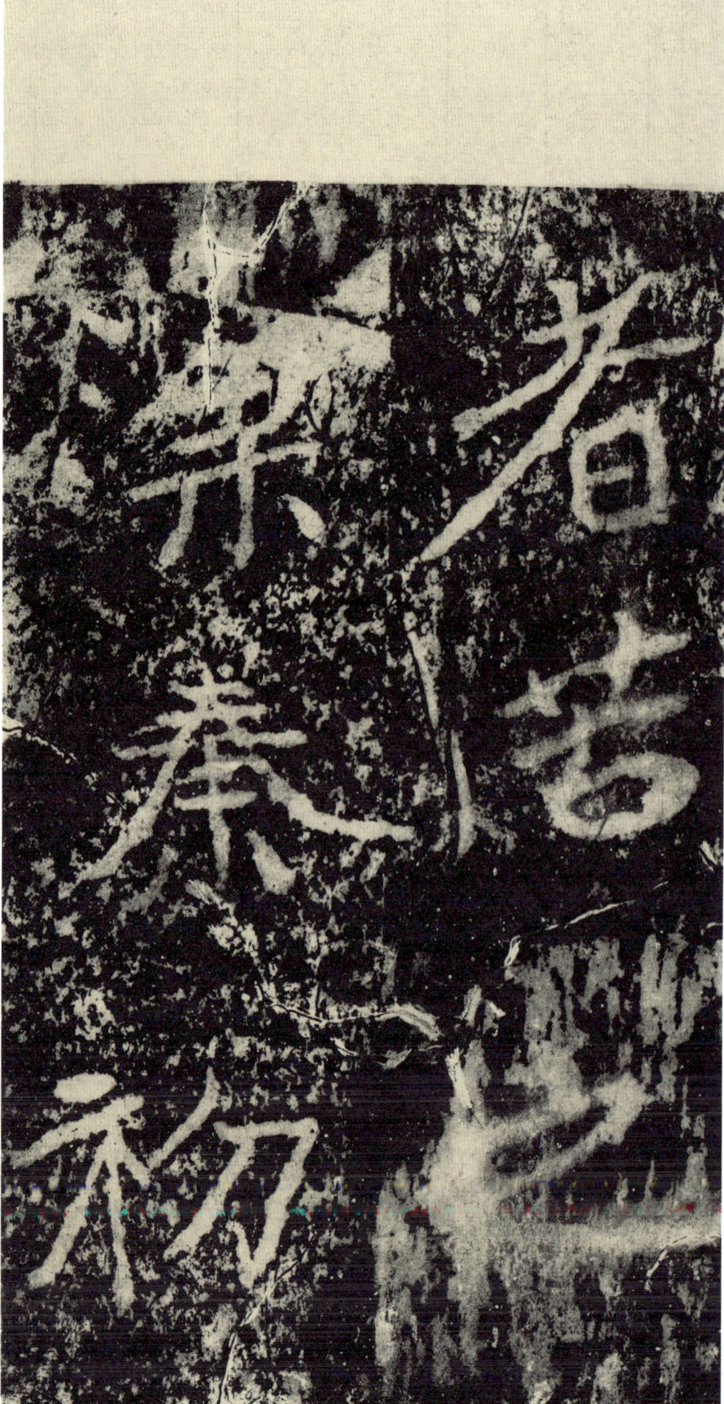

Rubbing from *In Memory of a Buried Crane* (瘗鹤铭 *Yi He Ming*)

Unknown calligrapher, Liang of the Southern dynasties
514 AD (carving)
Regular script (*kai shu*)
Cliff carving

During the Southern and Northern dynasties, the disruption of cultural exchanges in a China divided for prolonged periods into separatist feudal powers and the different natural environments and ways of life between the north and south contributed to the formation of distinct esthetic values and calligraphic styles. *In Memory of a Buried Crane* is a famous example of the Southern dynasties stone inscriptions. It displays a feminine softness (阴柔 *yin rou*) style, with simple, clean lines, and elegant, open character structures and shapes. As a result it conveys a relaxed, carefree spirituality that was a hallmark of the southern literati of the time, who were much influenced by Buddhist philosophy.

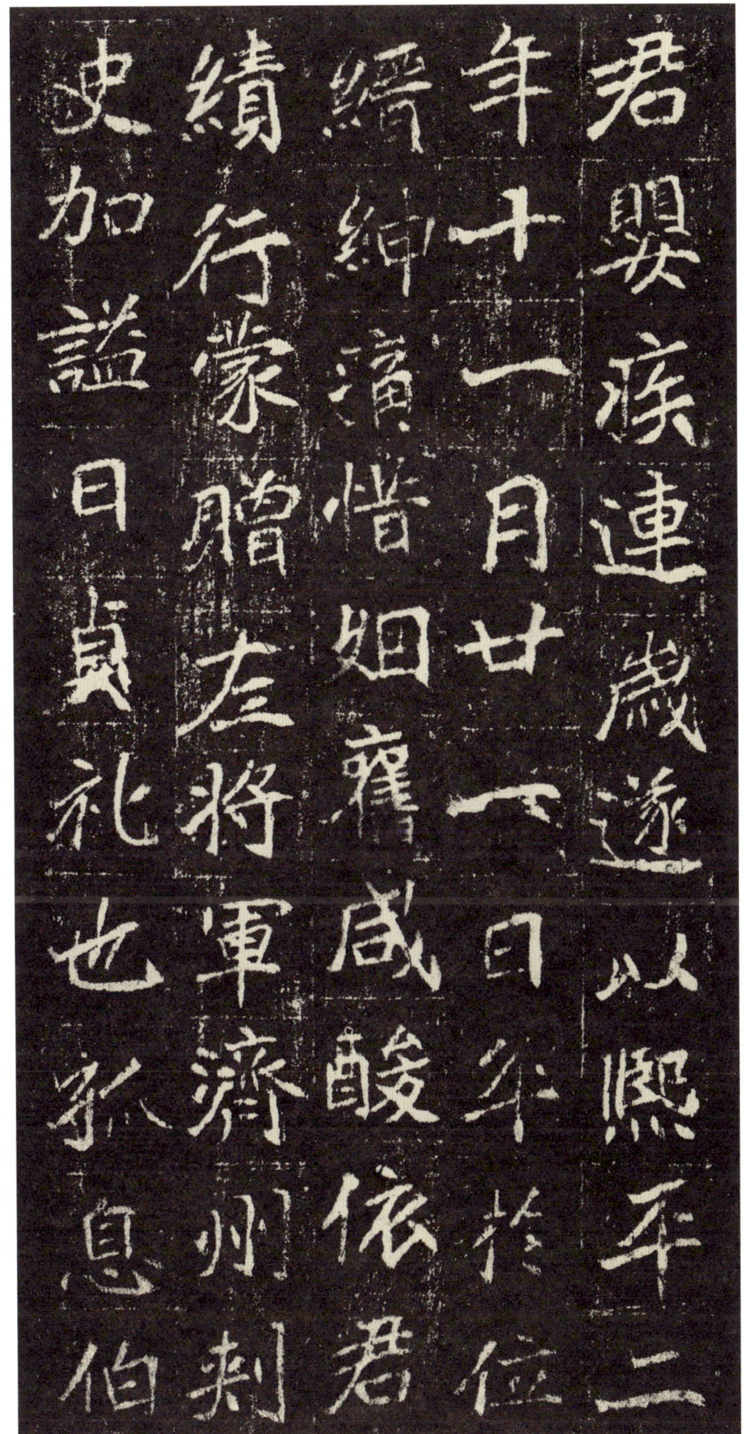

Rubbing from *Epitaph for Cui Jingyong* (崔敬邕墓志 *Cui Jing Yong Mu Zhi*)

Unknown calligrapher, Northern Wei of the Northern dynasties
517 AD (carving)
Regular script (*kai shu*)

The Cui clan was a prominent family in Boling during the Northern Wei dynasty. Cui Jingyong's paternal cousin Cui Ting was a well-known calligrapher of the time and was commissioned by the emperor to inscribe *Prince Xuan of Yan Tablet* (燕宣王碑 *yan xuan wang bei*) in memory of the father of Dowager Queen Wenming. It can be inferred that this epitaph must also have been from the hand of a contemporary calligrapher of note. Pre-Tang calligraphers did not normally put their name to the piece they wrote, so this work is also unsigned. The calligraphic style in this epitaph, compared to other epitaphs of the later years of the Northern Wei, leans more toward an energetic, imposing brushwork characterized by brushstrokes employing contrasting pressures and ways of pressing and lifting the brush, creating a strong sense of movement and rhythm. The amount of brush pressure used to make a stroke and determine its thickness (width) is closely related to the surrounding strokes. The entire inscription conveys a sober, solemn mood with its handsome, slender and forceful strokes.

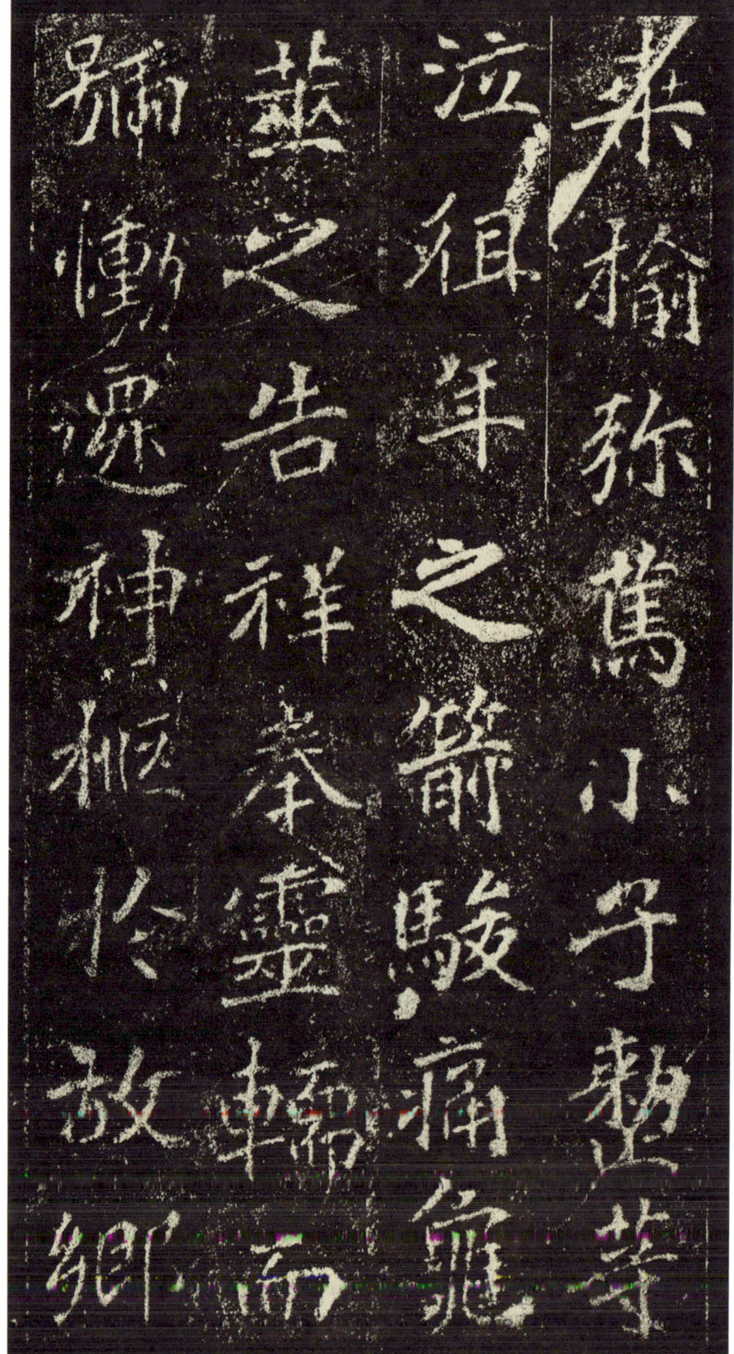

Rubbing from *Epitaph for Diao Zun*
(刁遵墓志 *Diao Zun Mu Zhi*)

Unknown calligrapher, Northern Wei of the Northern dynasties
517 AD (carving)
Regular script (*kai shu*)

Epitaph for Diao Zun exhibits a calligraphic style very much at odds with the virile, rough-hewn style prevalent on epitaphs of the Northern Wei dynasty. It draws on the calligraphic style of two Jin dynasties and the Southern dynasties and merges it with Northern calligraphy. Its stately, soft character structures and bright, open composition foreshadow the Sui and Tang calligraphy to follow. In the words of one critic, "This piece contains the embryo of the calligraphy of Xu Hao 徐浩 (703–782, Tang dynasty) and Yan Zhenqing of the Tang dynasty."

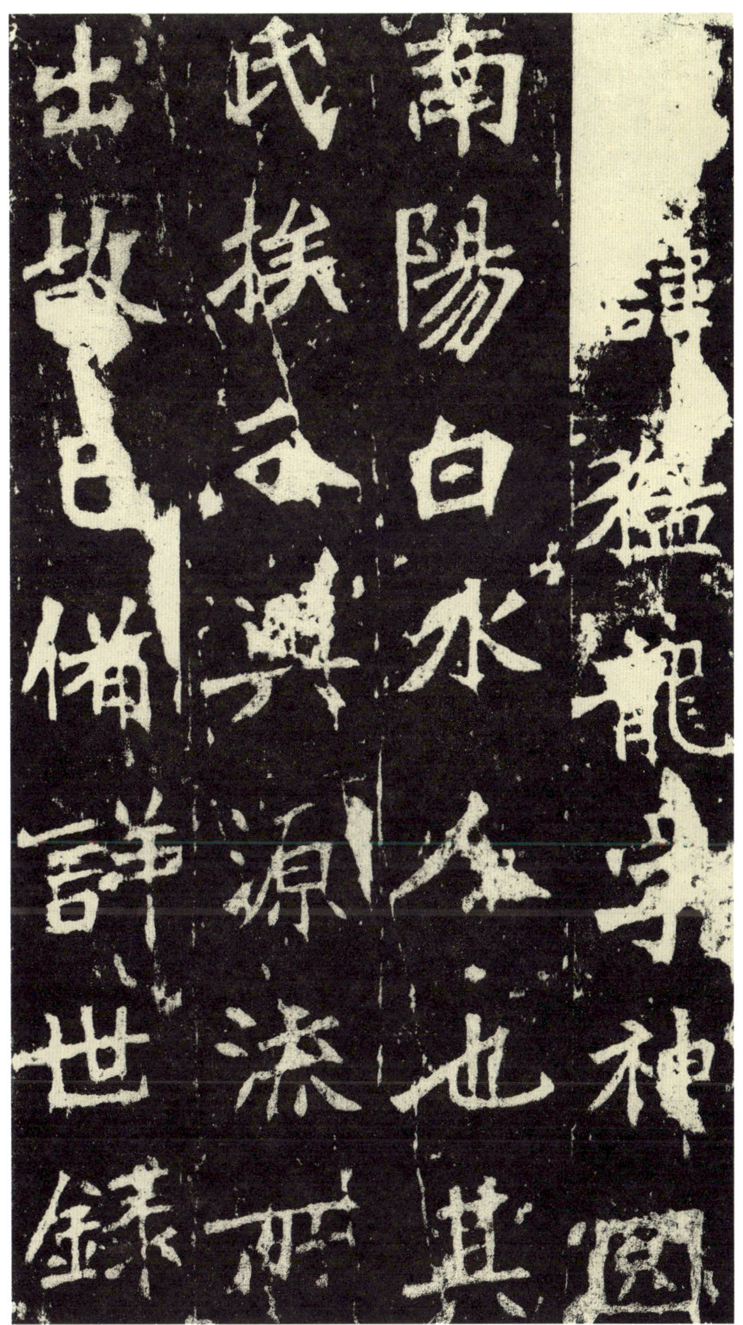

Rubbing made in the Ming dynasty from *Zhang Meng Long Tablet* (张猛龙碑 *Zhang Meng Long Bei*)

Unknown calligrapher, Northern Wei of the Northern dynasties
522 AD (carving)
Regular script (*kai shu*)

The brushwork in the inscription of *Zhang Meng Long Tablet* behaves "like a tool cutting metal and jade," resulting in crisp, clean strokes. In character structure, the strokes are concentrated in the middle, with a few strokes stretched very long. The contrast between compacting and stretching enlivens and invigorates the composition.

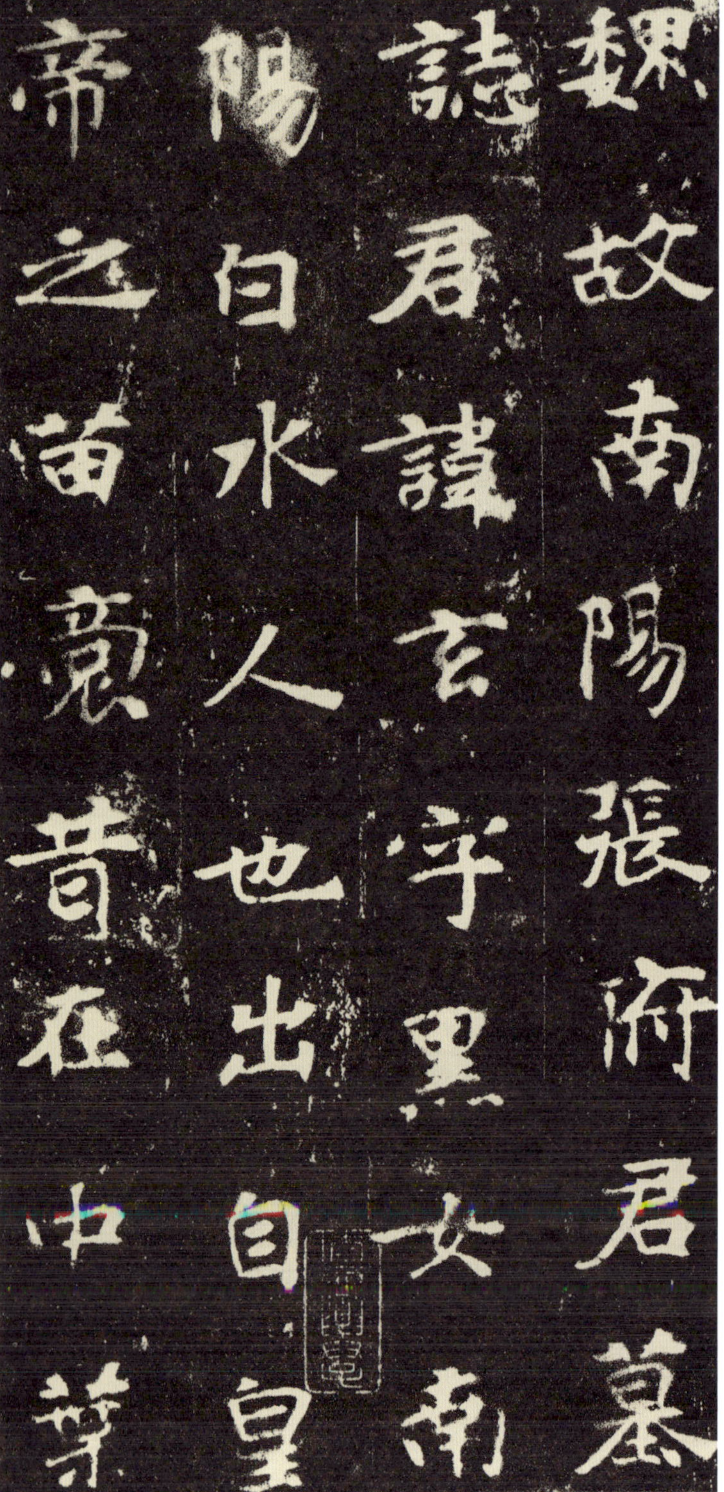

Rubbing from *Epitaph for Zhang Hei Nü* (张黑女墓志 *Zhang Hei Nü Mu Zhi*)

Unknown calligrapher, Northern Wei of the Northern dynasties
531 AD (carving)
Regular script (*kai shu*)
Shanghai Museum

Of the many Northern Wei epitaphs, the most famous is *Epitaph for Zhang Hei Nü*. Originally known as *Epitaph for Zhang Xuan* (张玄墓志 *zhang xuan mu zhi),* it was changed to the vernacular name *Epitaph for Zhang Hei Nü* in the reign of Kangxi emperor of the Qing dynasty because "xuan" happened to be a homophone for the "xuan" in "xuanye," part of the name of the emperor and therefore taboo. That both the calligrapher and the carver of this epitaph were accomplished artists can be clearly seen in the exquisite end product, whose every character is a gem and every column "fair as jade." The dominant square strokes are tempered by some rounded corners to give a refined look. The character structure is slightly squat and the posture upright. There is coexistence of the unorthodox and the orthodox, urgency and composure, openness and denseness, curvaceous beauty and smooth grace.

Rubbing from *Jing Shi Jun Tablet* (敬史君碑 *Jing Shi Jun Bei*)

Unknown calligrapher, Eastern Wei of the Northern dynasties
540 AD (carving)
Regular script (*kai shu*)

This late Wei-style stone inscription already shows signs of moving toward the future regular script style of the Tang dynasty. Both square and round techniques are used in starting and in ending a stroke. The brushwork leans toward restraint and not expansiveness to create a solid antique feel. These characteristics corroborate the claim that this inscription "pioneered the style of Yu Shinan 虞世南 (558–638, Tang dynasty) and Chu Suiliang 褚遂良 (596–658, Tang dynasty)." The strokes are rounded but not ornate, thick but not congested, and the entire piece is tinged with a literary coloring without losing its principal appeal of antique simplicity.

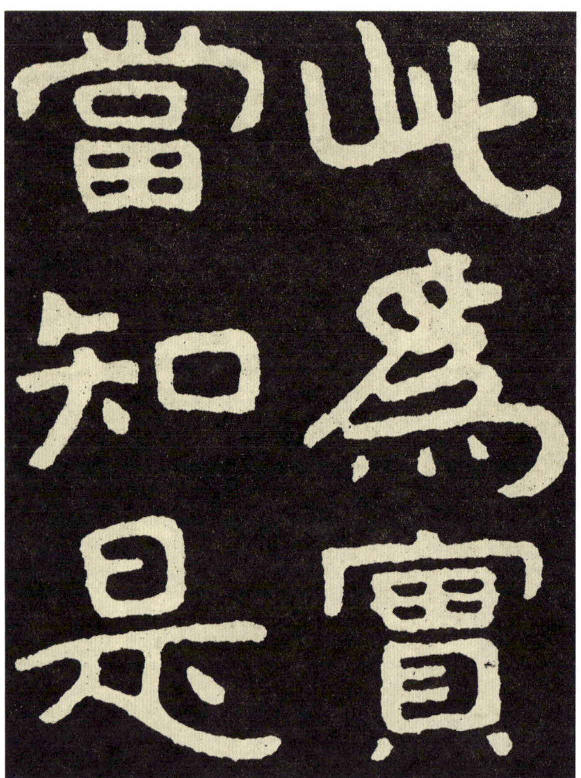

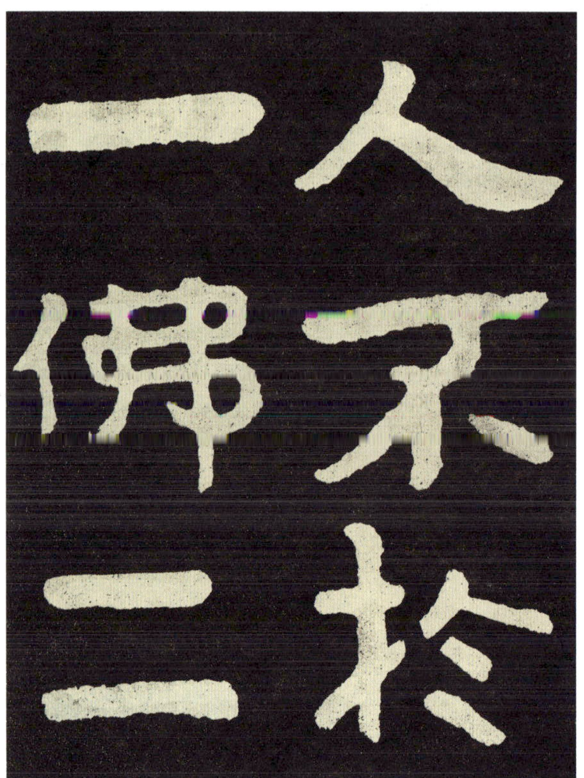

Rubbing from *Diamond Sutra of Jingshiyu on Mount Tai* (泰山经石峪金刚经 *Tai Shan Jing Shi Yu Jin Gang Jing*)

Unknown calligrapher, Southern and Northern dynasties
Regular script (*kai shu*)
Cliff carving

The giant characters of *Diamond Sutra* carved into a cliff on Mount Tai in Tai'an county, Shandong Province, were two feet wide each and the inscription takes up an area of 6,000 square meters, the largest calligraphic work in Chinese history. It effortlessly combines the seal script, the clerical script and the regular script styles. There is little width variation in the supple lines; the brushwork is leisurely and serene, solemn and reserved, with variations in brush pressure, pausing and transitional maneuvers deeply hidden in the heavily seal script-flavored strokes. The strokes are put together in the regular script style, with staggered long and short lines; the character postures appear to lean but remain upright. They appear to fly apart but are in fact cohesive. Anyone looking up at it cannot but be awed by the sheer monumentality of the work.

Sui, Tang and the Five Dynasties

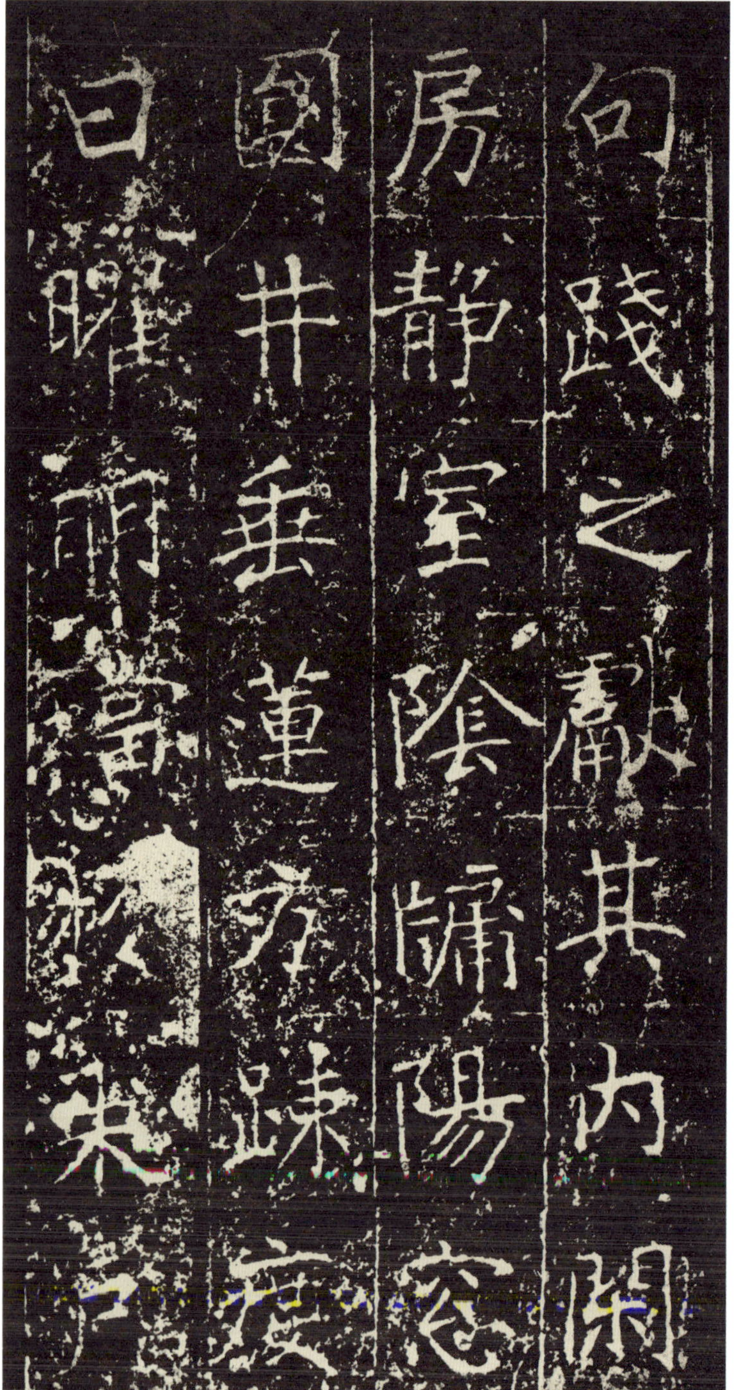

Rubbing from *Long Cang Temple Tablet* (龙藏寺碑 *Long Cang Si Bei*)

Unknown calligrapher, **Sui dynasty**
586 AD (carving)
Regular script (*kai shu*)
Long Cang Temple (also known as Long Xing Temple) in Zhengding, Hebei Province

Despite its brief timespan of only 29 years, the Sui dynasty was an important period of transition in the evolution of regular script. During this period, regular script matured, "melting the southern and the northern styles in one pot, and ushering in the Tang style of calligraphy." The brushwork in the inscription is crisp and forceful; the strokes, slender and hard but not without a mellow grace, are expertly executed; the plain-looking character structure is rich with pleasant surprises and the character postures are full of charm. The early Tang calligraphers, including Ouyang Xun 欧阳询 (557–641, Tang dynasty) and Yu Shinan, were influenced by this piece. In character structure and brushwork, Chu Suiliang's calligraphy bears a particularly close resemblance to *Long Cang Temple Tablet*.

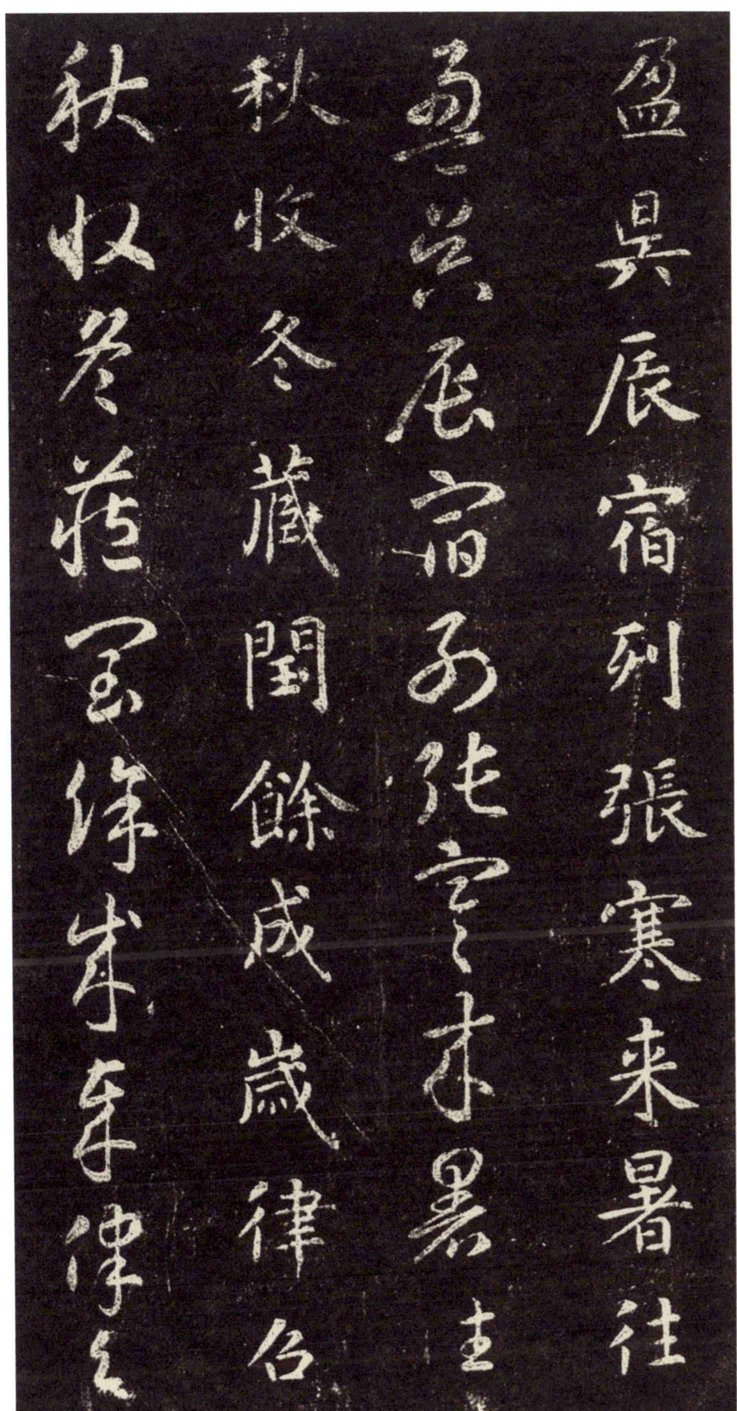

Rubbing from *Thousand Character Reader in Regular and Cursive Scripts* (真草千字文 *Zhen Cao Qian Zi Wen*)

Zhi Yong 智永 (years of birth/death unknown, Tang dynasty)
Regular script (*kai shu*) and cursive script (*cao shu*)
28 pages, each 22.5 cm × 12.2 cm
Palace Museum, Beijing

Zhi Yong was a seventh-generation grandson of Wang Xizhi. After becoming a monk, he went to live in Yong Xing Temple in Shanyin (present-day Shaoxing of Zhejiang Province) and was revered as Zen Master Yong (永禅师 *yong chan shi*). It is said that he handwrote 800 copies of *Thousand Character Reader in Regular and Cursive Scripts* and distributed them to temples in Eastern Zhejiang. In the process, he ruined enough brushes to fill five large bamboo baskets, which he buried in a "mass grave of ruined brushes." When the threshold of his dwelling was worn thin by devotees who trooped to his home seeking his works, he had it sheathed in metal sheeting and people started calling it the "iron threshold." Wang Xizhi's style of regular script flavored with the running script style is visible throughout this work by Zhi Yong, except that Wang's idiosyncratic character structure of "contractive left and expansive right" is lost in Zhi Yong's *Thousand Character Reader*. In this sense, Zhi Yong's calligraphic virtuosity may have been a handicap.

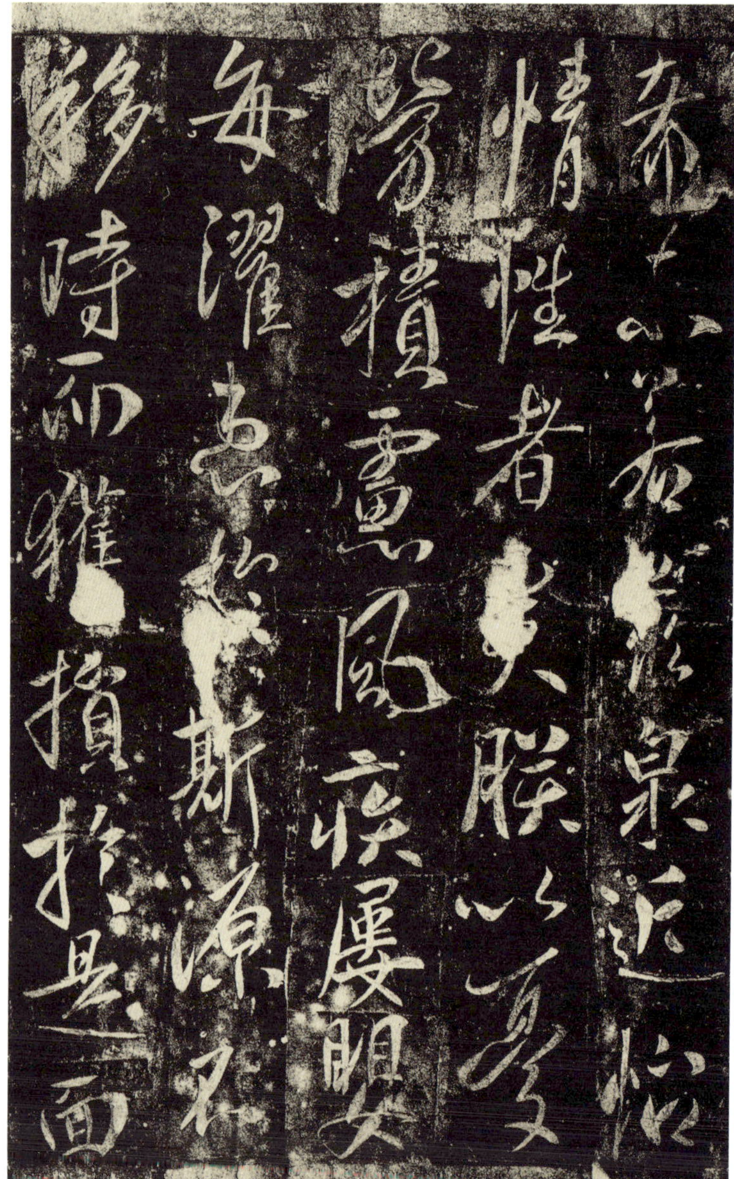

Spring (温泉铭 *Wen Quan Ming*)

Li Shimin 李世民 (599–649, Tang dynasty)
Running script (*xing shu*)
Bibliothèque Nationale de France, Paris

A serious connoisseur of calligraphy, Li Shimin, who was Emperor Taizong of the Tang dynasty, began acquiring original calligraphic works of Wang Xizhi immediately after his accession to the throne; he also wrote the monograph *On Wang Xizhi*. His initiative heralded the exaltation of the Wang style in Chinese calligraphy. He put great emphasis on bringing out shape and movement through brushwork characterized by "bone and strength," which is perfectly exemplified by his *Spring*. An aura of steely invincibility emanates from this graceful and elegant work. As far as brushwork and technique are concerned, however, the piece clearly has its flaws, mainly the gangling character structure and sloppy brushwork visible in some ideograms.

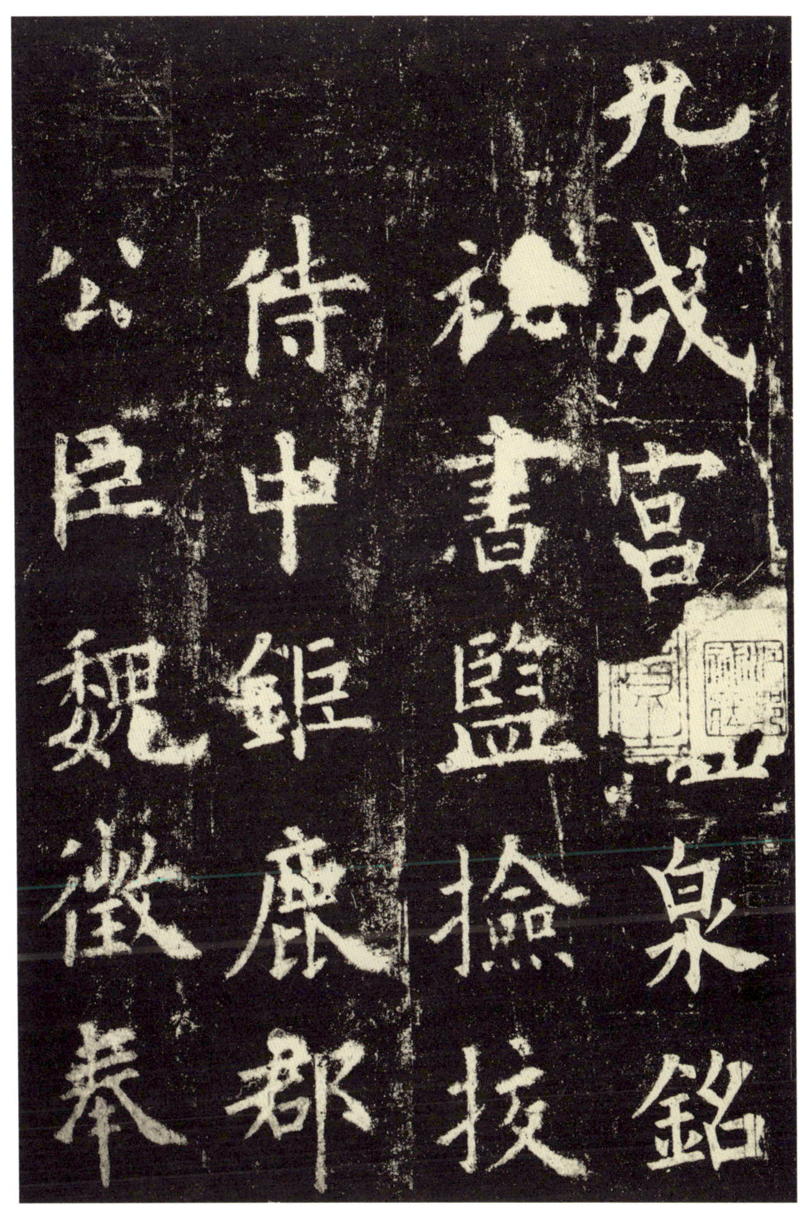

Rubbing made in the Tang dynasty from *Sweet Spring at Jiucheng Palace* (九成宫醴泉铭 *Jiu Cheng Gong Li Quan Ming*)

Ouyang Xun 欧阳询 (557-641, Tang dynasty)
Regular script (*kai shu*)
Palace Museum, Beijing

The calligraphy of Ouyang Xun, a follower of the calligraphic style of Wang Xizhi, has a "steeper" (险峻 *xian jun*) look than that of Wang Xizhi. *Sweet Spring at Jiucheng Palace* is his signature work in regular script and is, in the words of a critic, "like a mountain recluse who has achieved the ultimate wisdom, gaunt and lean in muscle but robust in spirit." Ouyang Xun's regular script style employs brushstrokes that are thicker at the two ends and thinner in the middle, falling in the contractive category. The indrawn strokes in turn produce an indrawn character structure, with outer lines drawn inward, forming arcs, and strokes concentrated as much as possible in the interior, creating a character structure that is compact in the center and less dense in the periphery. At the same time, some strokes are made longer than normal, transgressing the character grid, in order to avoid giving an overcautious look.

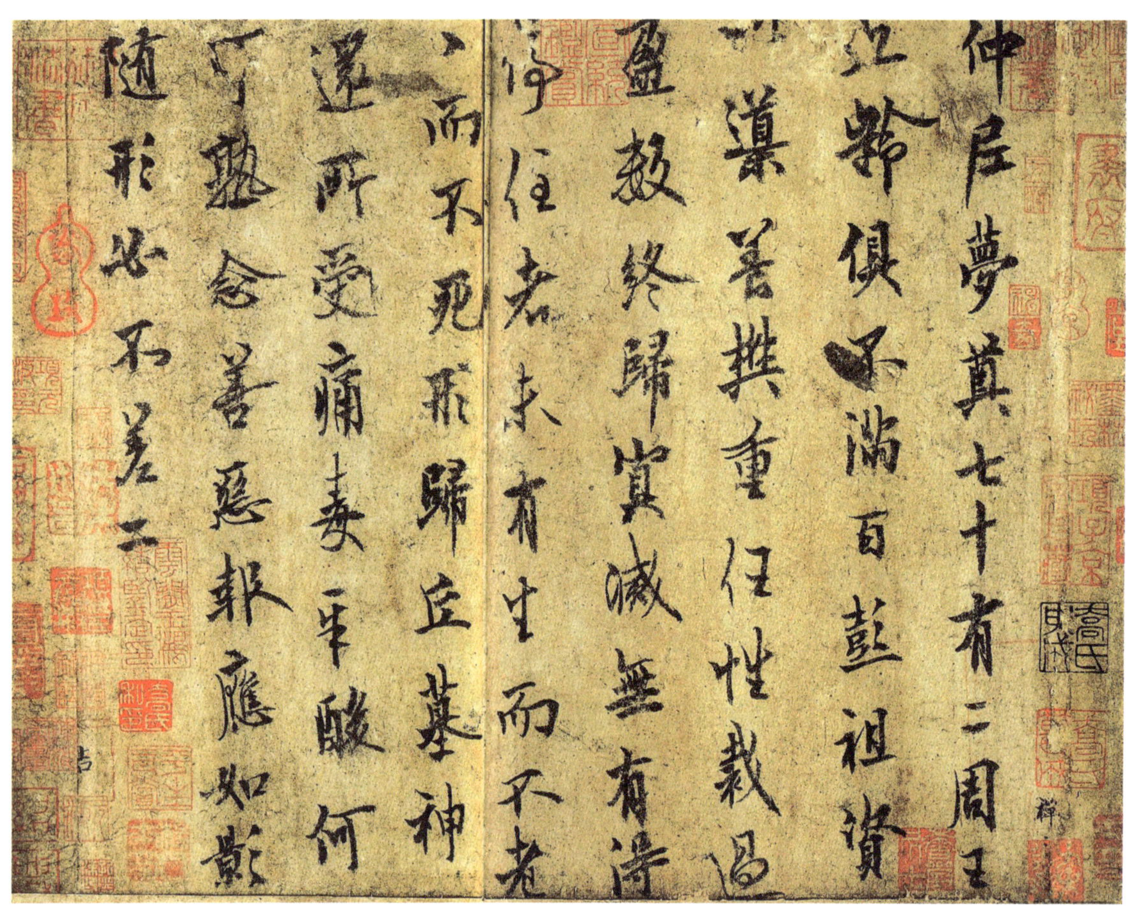

Confucius Dreams of His Death (仲尼梦奠帖 *Zhong Ni Meng Dian Tie*)

Ouyang Xun 欧阳询 (557-641, Tang dynasty)
Running script (*xing shu*)
25.5 cm × 33.6 cm
Provincial Museum of Liaoning

The calligraphy in *Confucius Dreams of His Death* gives the impression that it was written with a hard brush-tip and that there is a tension between the brush and the fingers holding it. This is particularly evident in the diagonal strokes. The central vertical in the character " 仲 " and the short diagonal to the left in " 尼 " are sharp and straight like a dagger. Structurally every character draws in toward the center or the midsection and the result is longer, slender-looking and therefore "steeper" characters with a hint of rebelliousness.

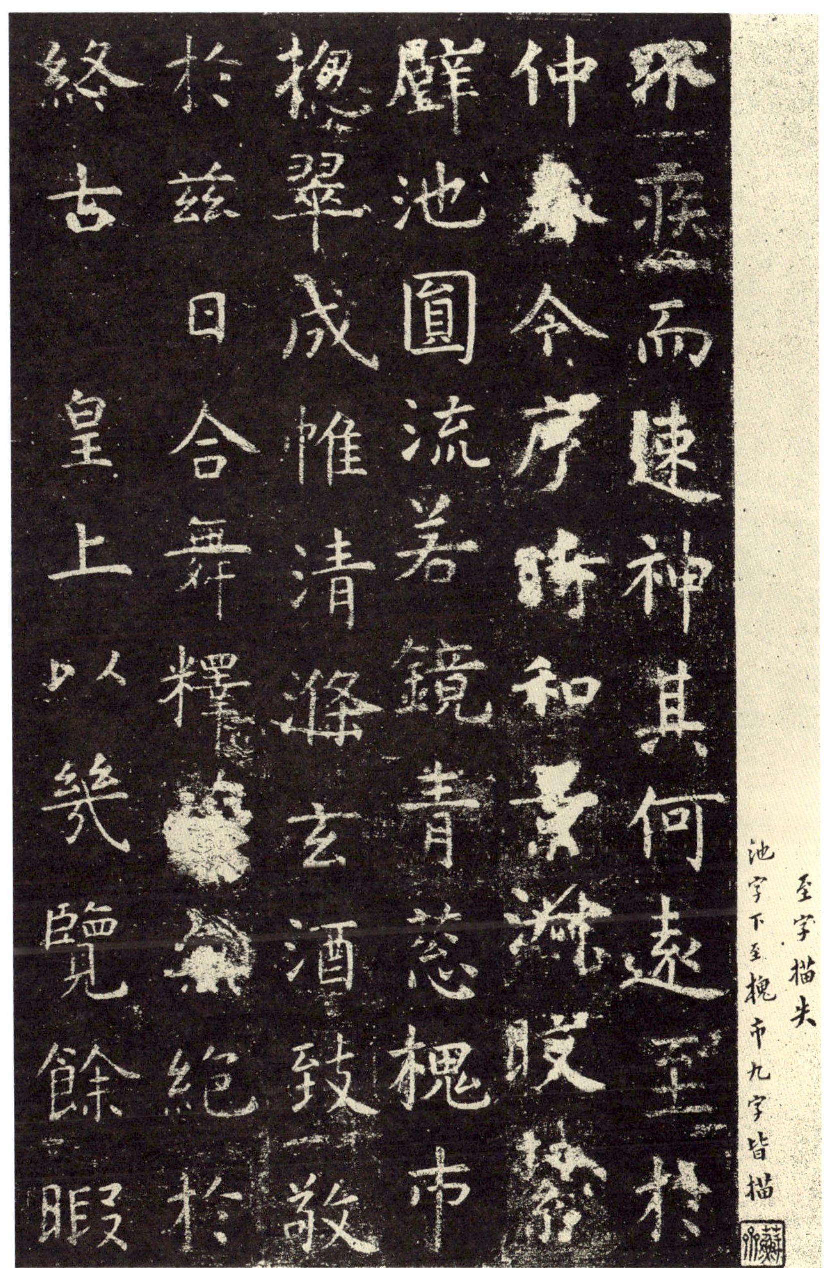

Rubbing made in the Tang dynasty from *Confucius Temple Tablet* (孔子庙堂碑 *Kong Zi Miao Tang Bei*)

Yu Shinan 虞世南 (558-638, Tang dynasty)
Regular script (*kai shu*)
28.3 cm in height
Mitsui Memorial Museum in Tokyo, Japan

The character structure in both *Confucius Temple Tablet*, a signature work by Yu Shinan, and Ouyang Xun's *Sweet Spring at Jiucheng Palace* tends toward the slender look. The spatial composition in both follows the rule of "compact upper part and looser lower part," creating a neat, forceful look. But the two pieces are radically different in the appearance of the strokes and the forms of the characters: Yu's strokes are slightly thicker in the middle than at the two ends, cleaving more to an expansive tradition. They present a more moderate, serene elegance than Ouyang's calligraphy, which often evokes a sense of "virile swords poised to strike" or "towering lone peaks."

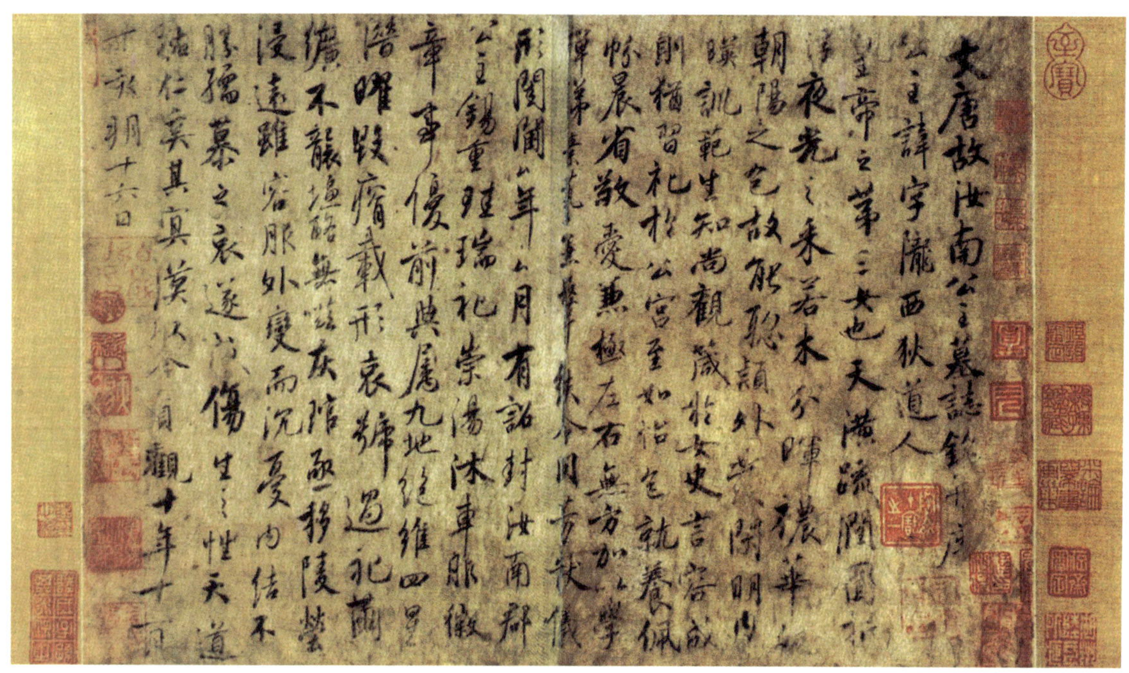

Epitaph for Princess Ru'nan (汝南公主墓志 *Ru Nan Gong Zhu Mu Zhi*)

Yu Shinan 虞世南 **(558–638, Tang dynasty)**
Running script (*xing shu*)
25.9 cm × 38.4 cm
Shanghai Museum

The "pace" of the brushwork in *Epitaph for Princess Ru'nan* is faster than in *Confucius Temple Tablet* but the short diagonals to the left and long diagonals to the right, the "slow" hooks and rounded corners, all marks of scholarly elegance, are still much in evidence in this piece. The brushwork seamlessly alternates between square and round strokes, with numerous variations. The brush begins the strokes cleanly and without hesitation, and moves with a resolute, brisk tempo. The skillful concatenation of strokes and the context-driven variation in the slant of the characters add life to ink and brush.

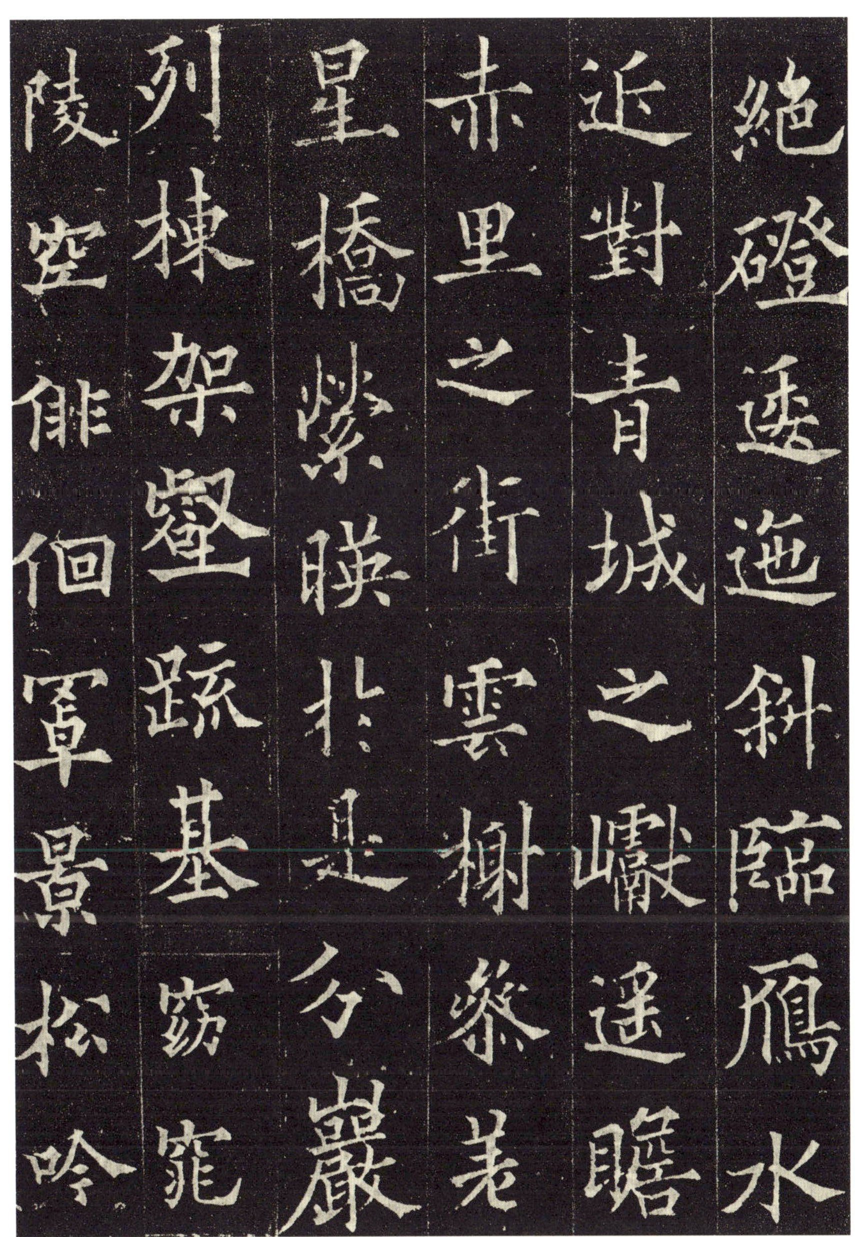

Rubbing made in the Song dynasty from *Monk Daoyin Tablet* (道因法师碑 *Dao Yin Fa Shi Bei*)

Ouyang Tong 欧阳通 (?-691, Tang dynasty)
Regular script (*kai shu*)
320 cm × 140 cm
Beilin Museum of Xi'an (stone tablet), Palace Museum, Beijing (Song rubbing)

Ouyang Tong, the fourth son of Ouyang Xun, shares calligraphic fame with his father. They are often referred to as "*Da Xiao* Ouyang" or "Ouyang Senior and Junior." A comparison with his father shows that what his style lacks in orthodox neatness he more than makes up for in "steepness" and energy. In other words, the "steepness" that is a hallmark of the Ouyang school of calligraphy reaches its zenith in Ouyang Tong. In the inscription on this tablet, he starts his strokes "like a falcon pecking at a rock with its beak" and does not seek to hide the tip of his brush. He unashamedly ends his strokes with deliberate pauses and heavy fold-backs. He wields his brush like a young artist without any baggage. The character structure of "a looser upper part and a compact lower part" creates a lower center of gravity that seemingly primes the character for an upward bounce.

Rubbing made in the Tang dynasty from *Monk Meng Tablet* (孟法师碑 *Meng Fa Shi Bei*)

Chu Suiliang 褚遂良 (596-658, Tang dynasty)
Regular script (*kai shu*)
25.1 cm in height
Mitsui Memorial Museum in Tokyo, Japan

This tablet is evocative of the clerical script and the supple charm of Yu Shinan's calligraphy. Great calligraphic works are always in possession of an inner balance, and this tablet attests to the soundness of this observation. Thus, in the 16-character matrix constituted by the characters " 法師碑銘 " and " 夫太陽始 ", " 若馳巨川 " and " 而不息是 " to the left, the characters are staggered in an intriguiging fashion without losing their cohesiveness and overall harmony. One gets the feeling that when the calligrapher is at work, he is mindful not only of the character he is actually working on, but also of those immediately surrounding it, and even of the entire inscription he sets out to complete.

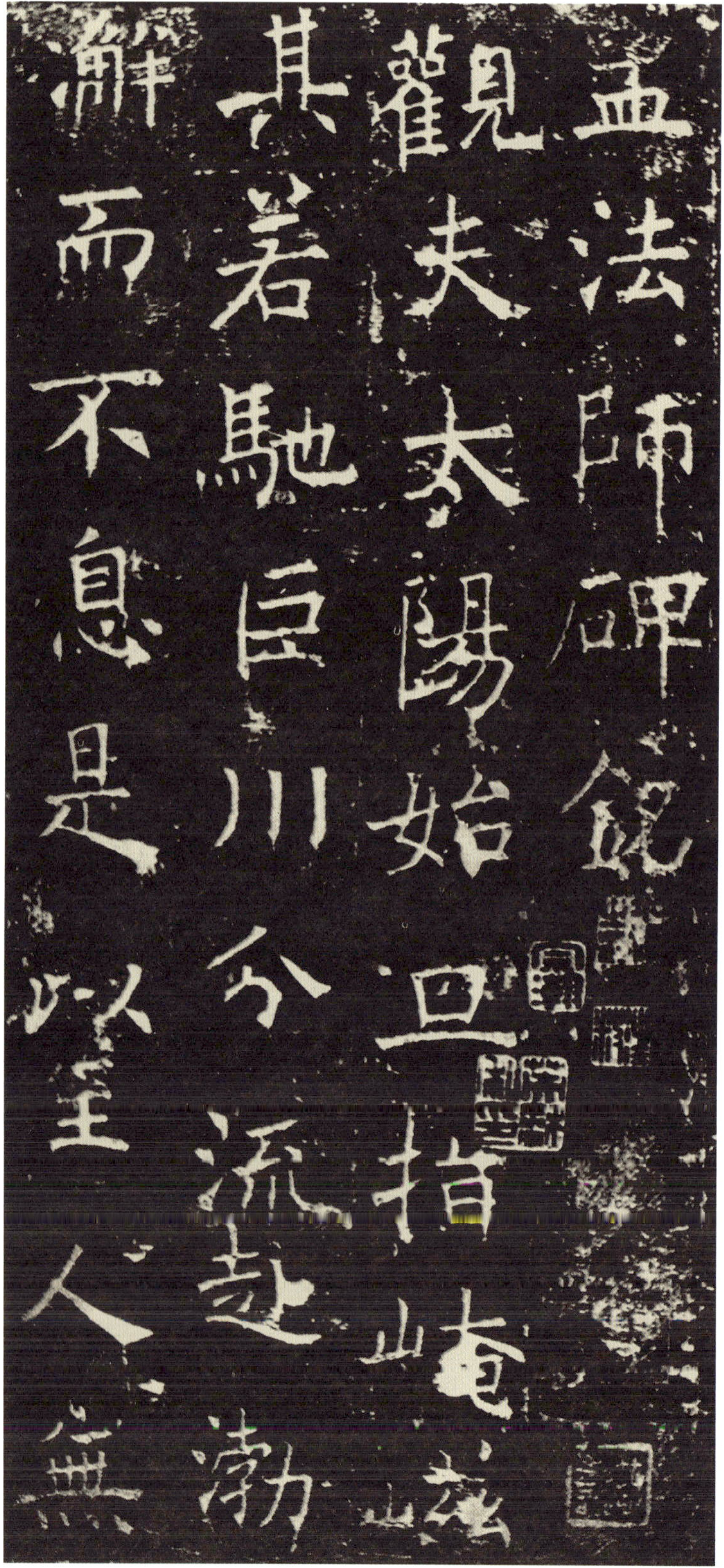

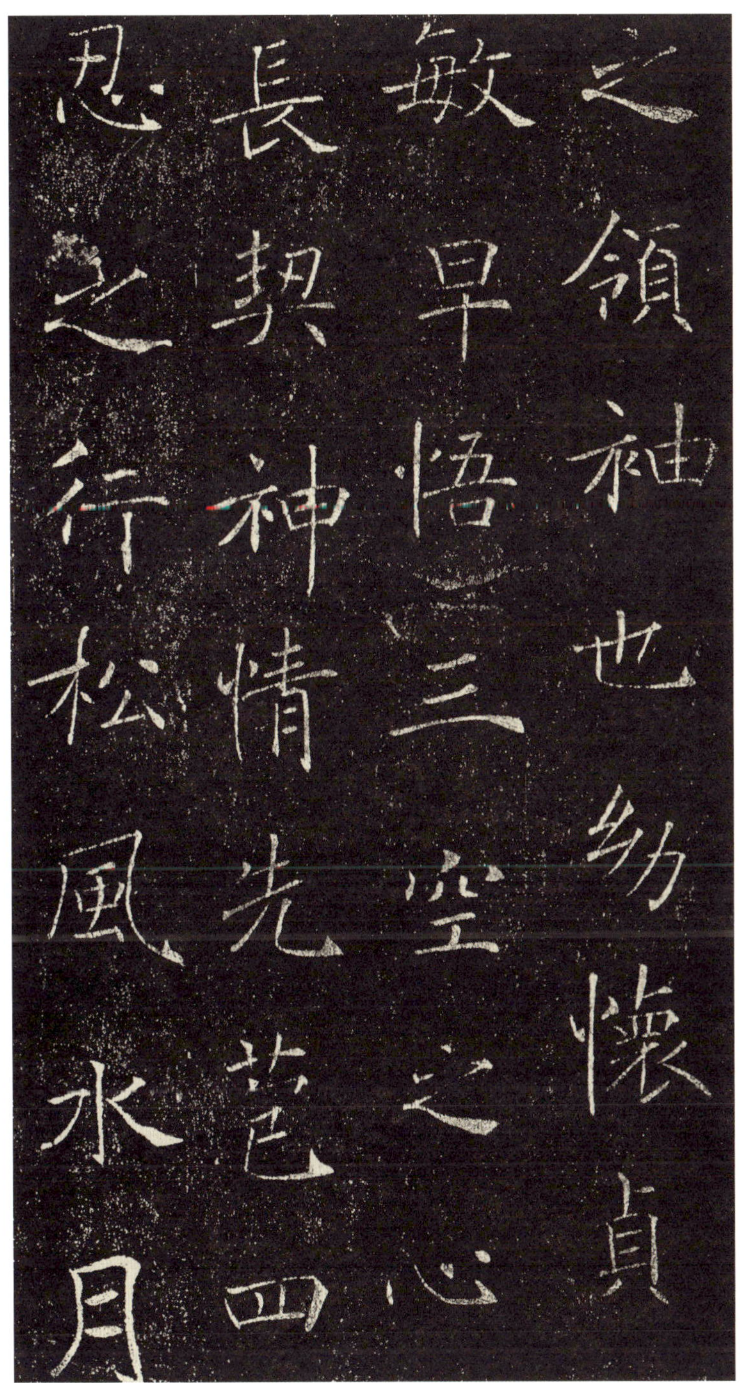

Rubbing made in the Ming dynasty from *Preface to Buddha's Teachings at Goose Pavilion* (雁塔圣教序 *Yan Ta Sheng Jiao Xu*)

Chu Suiliang 褚遂良 (596-658, Tang dynasty)
Regular script (*kai shu*)

The brushwork in *Preface to Buddha's Teachings at Goose Pavilion* is smooth and lively, its regular script style interspersed with running script, its lines graceful and full of vigor. It employs the "one wave, three reversals" technique to make horizontal strokes; when starting and ending a stroke, it meticulously observes the rules for lifting, pressing, pausing and reversing. The steady, forceful brushwork and the contrast between lines of varying thickness result in an ornate visual effect. In character structure, Chu Suiliang made a sharp departure from the elongated shape of characters of the early Tang and broadened the structure to make them square and squat, paving the way for the future evolution of calligraphic styles. It was on this basis that Yan Zhenqing further increased the width of the strokes and abandoned the contractive for the expansive structure, thereby achieving a radical change in calligraphic style.

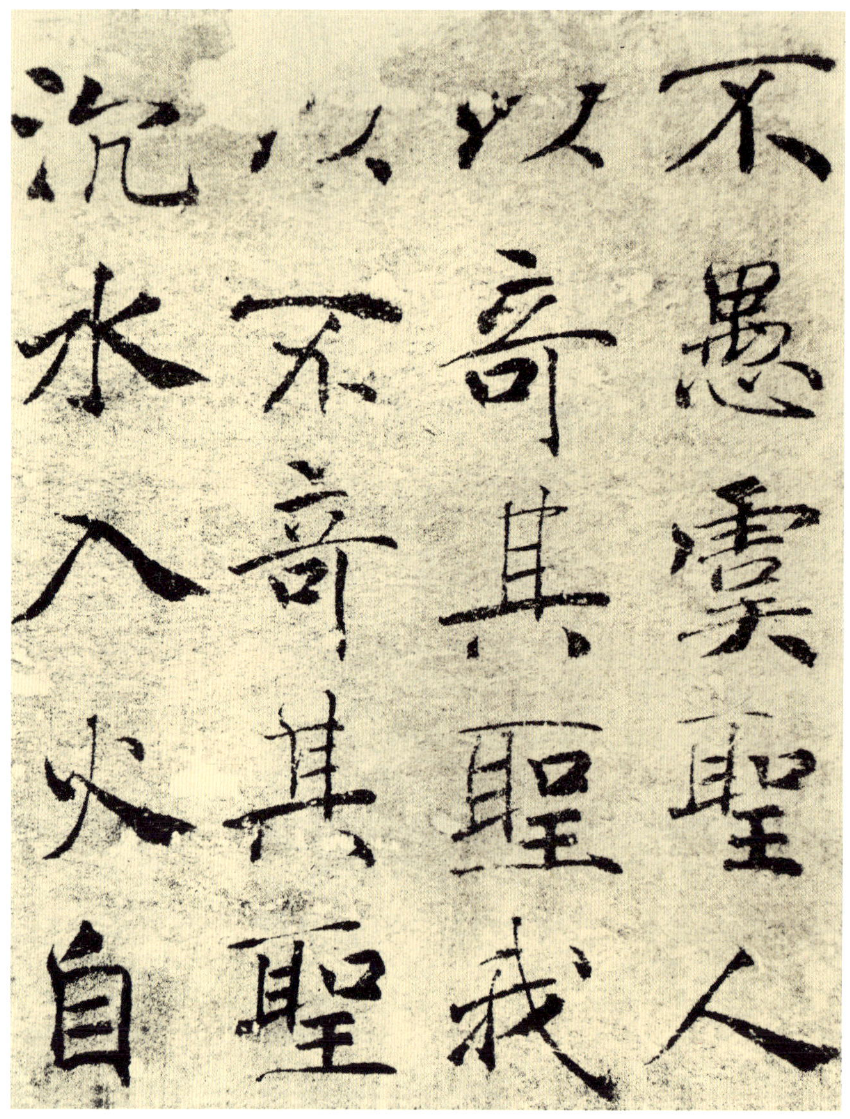

Classic of Secret Revelation (阴符经 *Yin Fu Jing*)

Chu Suiliang 褚遂良 (596-658, Tang dynasty)
Regular script (*kai shu*)
13 pages, each 24 cm × 19 cm
Taiwan

The regular script style of the Ouyangs and Yu Shinan of the early Tang is mainly characterized by a virile esthetic, with a square, energetic brushwork and solemn character shapes. Chu Suiliang was one of the few calligraphers in that period to defy the dominant "Northern Stone Inscriptions" (" 北碑 " *bei bei*) school of calligraphy and to use a relaxed, detached brushwork to express the beauty and rhythm of brushstrokes and lines. He perfected the contractive brush technique, seeking variation and contrast in the force used in making every vertical and every horizontal, and in character postures. Structurally his characters, generally compact in the center, appear relaxed without being disjointed, spacious but not sparse. From his early work *Monk Meng Tablet* to his later *Preface to Buddha's Teachings at Goose Pavilion* and *Classic of Secret Revelation* one can clearly see his progression from an inheritor of tradition to a creative innovator. Of the early Tang calligraphers, Chu Suiliang had arguably the deepest appreciation of the calligraphic art of the Jin masters and expertly combined the styles and techniques of the "Two Wangs" (Xizhi and Xianzhi).

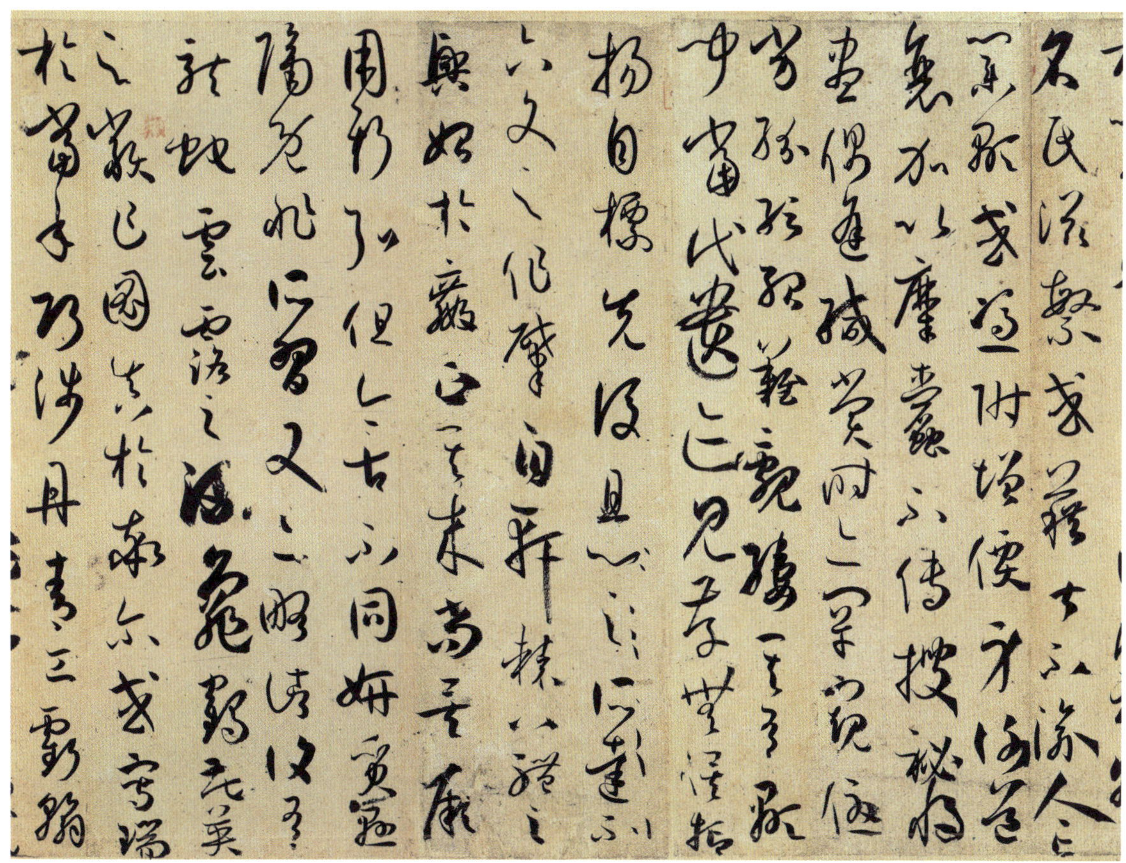

Discourse on Calligraphy (书谱 *Shu Pu*)

Sun Guoting 孙过庭 **(648-702?, Tang dynasty)**
Cursive script (*cao shu*)
Palace Museum, Taipei

In calligraphing the *Discourse on Calligraphy*, Sun Guoting draws on Wang Xizhi's style of merging square and round strokes in his cursive script works. Incongruence between character shapes does not stand in the way of maintaining contextual coherence. The brushwork is smooth and brisk without flouting rules. The use of ink is smooth and moist, making the strokes distinctly recognizable through the undulations. A sense of candid expressiveness prevails throughout the piece. The only flaw, if flaw it is, in this gem of a work is the uniform, repetitious appearance of some characters, in contrast to Wang Xizhi's *Orchid Pavilion Preface*, in which a total of 18 " 之 " are rendered in a colorful array of variations—a rare feat.

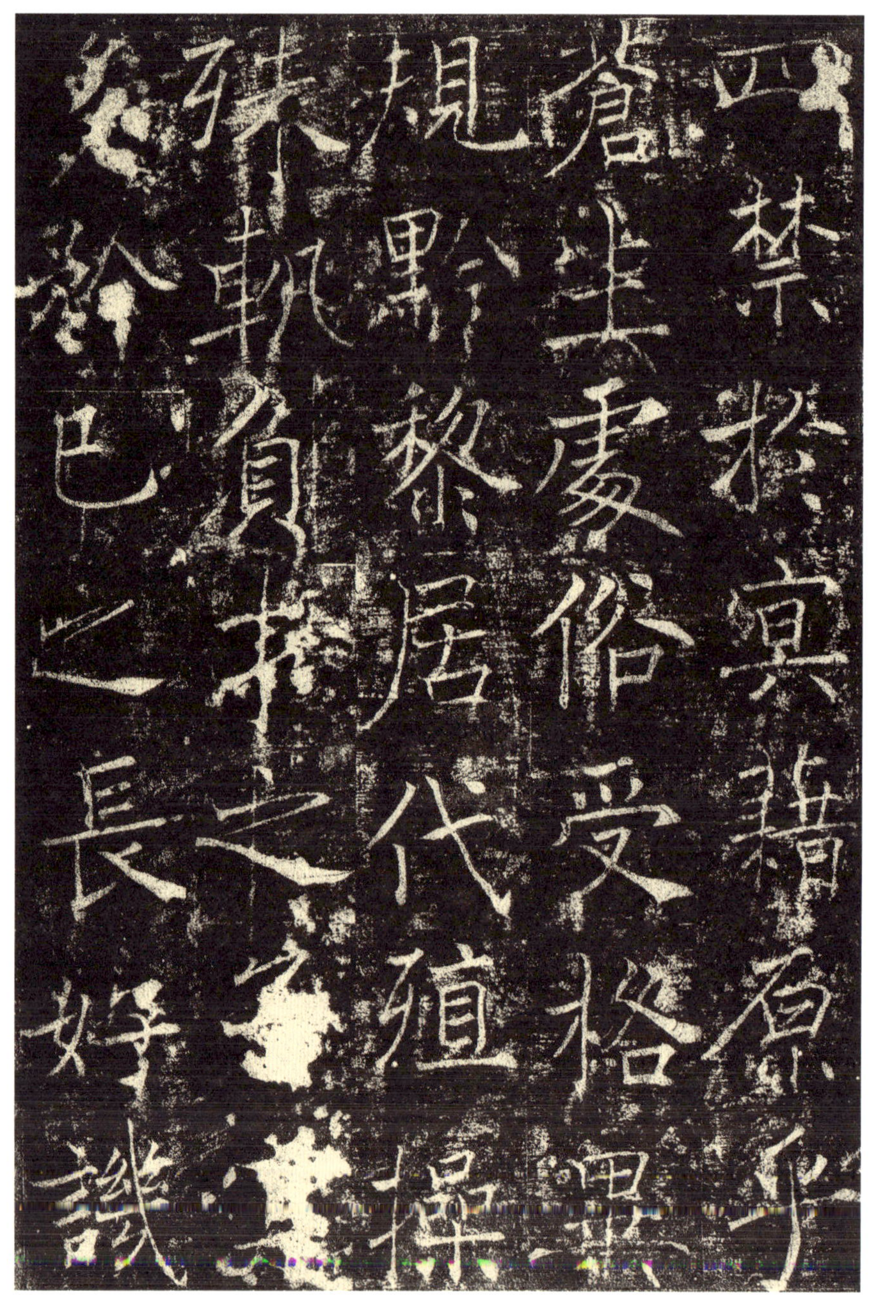

Rubbing made in the Song dynasty from *Zen Master Xinxing Tablet* (信行禅师碑 *Xin Xing Chan Shi Bei*)

Xue Ji 薛稷 **(649-713, Tang dynasty)**
Regular script (*kai shu*)
Otani University in Kyoto, Japan

"Four Masters of Early Tang" (初唐四家 *chu tang si jia*) refers to Xue Ji, Ouyang Xun, Yu Shinan and Chu Suiliang. Yu Shinan is famous for his robust, ornate, rounded and smooth brushwork, Ouyang Xun for his square, energetic and "steep" writing, whereas Chu Suiliang and Xue Ji are known for the spare beauty and boniness of their style. The slender brushwork and the "open and airy" character structure in this stone inscription had a direct influence on Liu Gongquan 柳公权 (778-865, Tang dynasty), master calligrapher of the late Tang, and foreshadowed the "slim gold" style (瘦金体 *shou jin ti*) initiated by Zhao Ji 赵佶 (1082-1135, Song dynasty), Emperor Huizong of the Song.

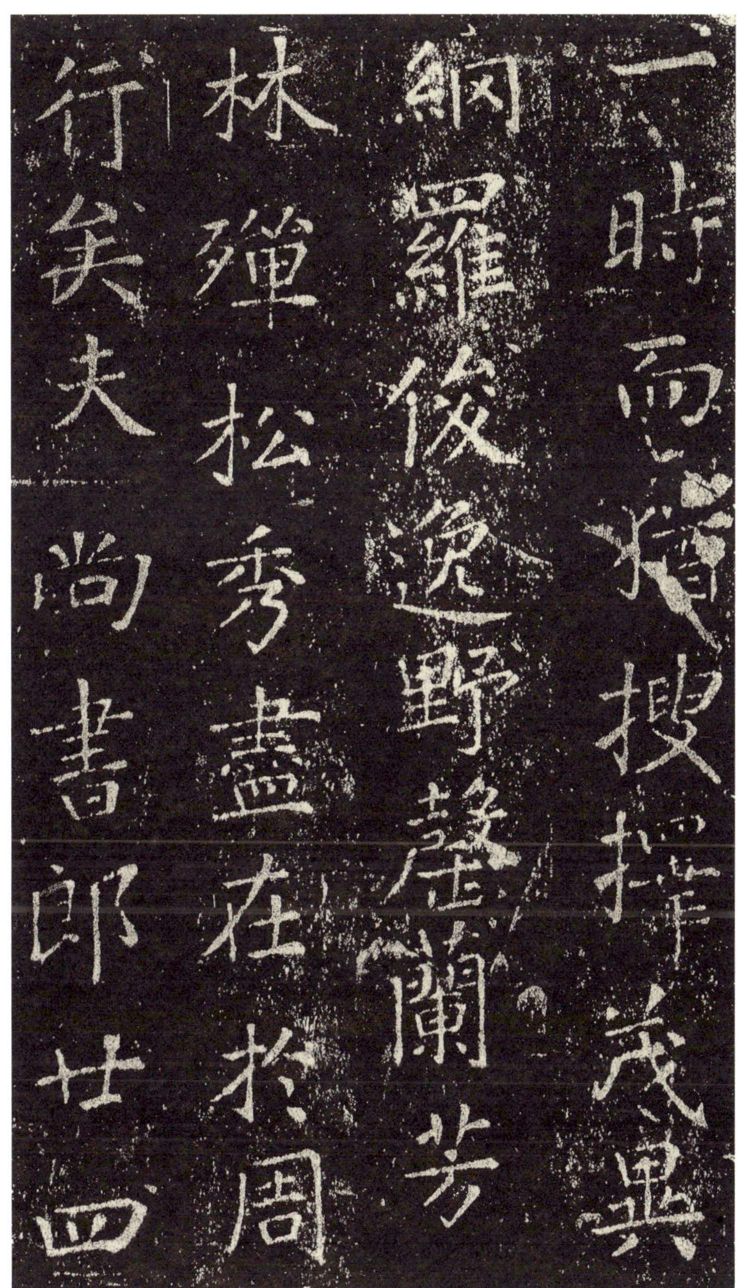

Preface to the Inscription of Officials' Name (郎官石柱记序 *Lang Guan Shi Zhu Ji Xu*)

Zhang Xu 张旭 (years of birth/death unknown; 675-750, Tang dynasty according to some sources)

Zhang Xu, a famous calligrapher in the Tang dynasty, was noted for his regular script and cursive script writing. He acquired the reputation of the "Sage of the Cursive Style" (草圣 *cao sheng*) and was one of the so-called "Three Last Authorities" (三绝 *san jue*) of the period, the other two being Li Bai 李白 (701-762, Tang dynasty) in verse and Pei Min 裴旻 in sword dance. *Preface to the Inscription of Officials' Name* is the only surviving regular script style work by Zhang Xu. The neatly and expertly executed piece is remarkable in three respects: 1. meticulous, orthodox brushwork that nonetheless exhibits an abundance of spirit, 2. serenity with a latent dynamic energy, and 3. an insouciant elegance that exudes composure.

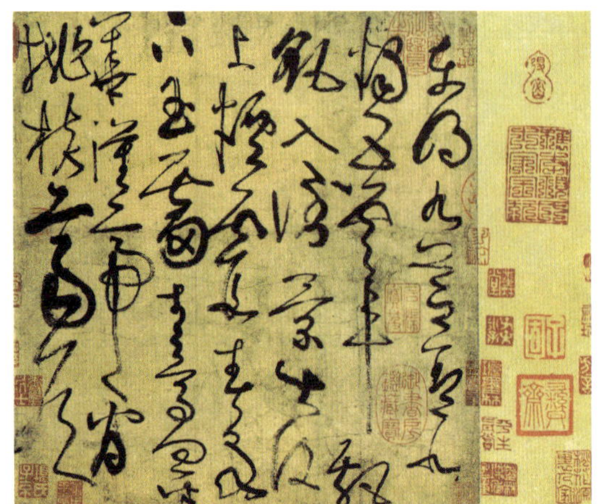

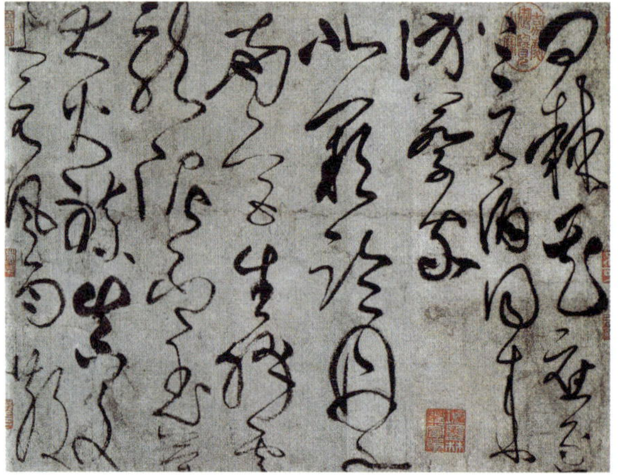

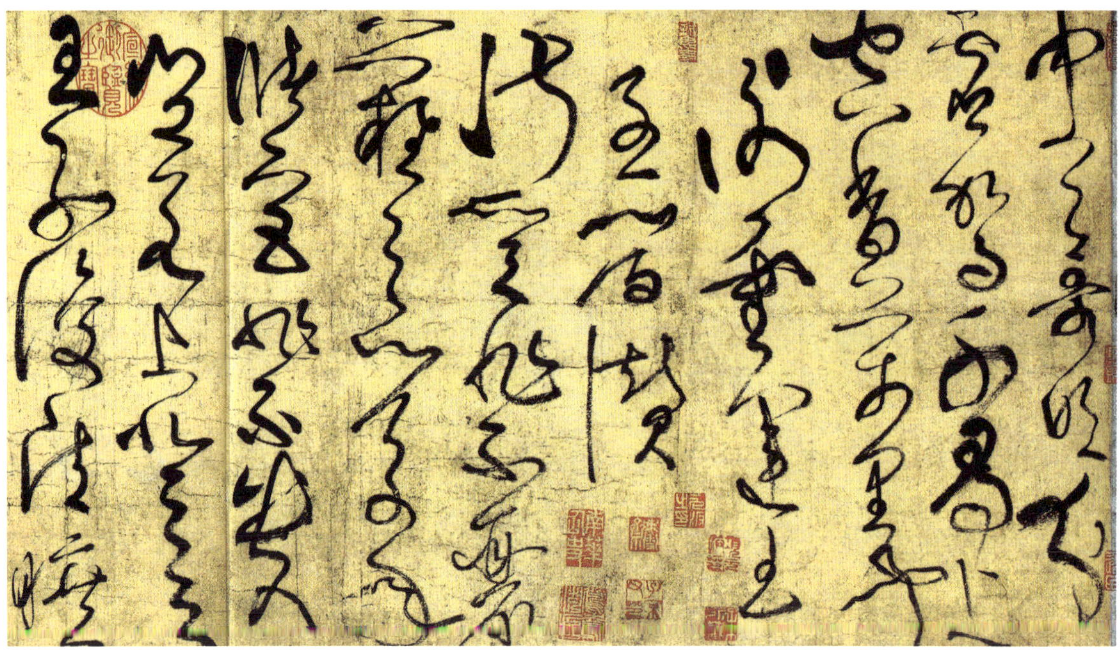

Four Ancient Poems (古诗四帖 *Gu Shi Si Tie*)

Zhang Xu 张旭 (years of birth/death unknown, Tang dynasty)
Cursive script (*cao shu*)
29.1 cm × 195.2 cm
Provincial Museum of Liaoning

Four Ancient Poems makes full use of the calligraphic techniques of emotional expression and imitation of external phenomena. According to Zhang Xu, he picked up cursive script from watching the sword dance performed by Gongsun Daniang 公孙大娘, a top dancer of the time, just as the famous Tang poet Du Fu 杜甫 (712–770, Tang dynasty) once got his inspiration for a poem when watching the same lady dance. In a departure from the tradition of writing discrete characters found in the cursive script style of Wang Xizhi and Sun Guoting, Zhang Xu adopted the mad cursive script (狂草 *kuang cao*) style of writing the characters in a continuum, broadening the horizon of calligraphic expression. His belief in imitating nature has greatly influenced generations of calligraphers. Su Dongpo's 苏东坡 (1037–1101, Song dynasty) observation "Watch carefully the things around you, you can usually make something interesting out of them" was inspired by this belief of Zhang Xu.

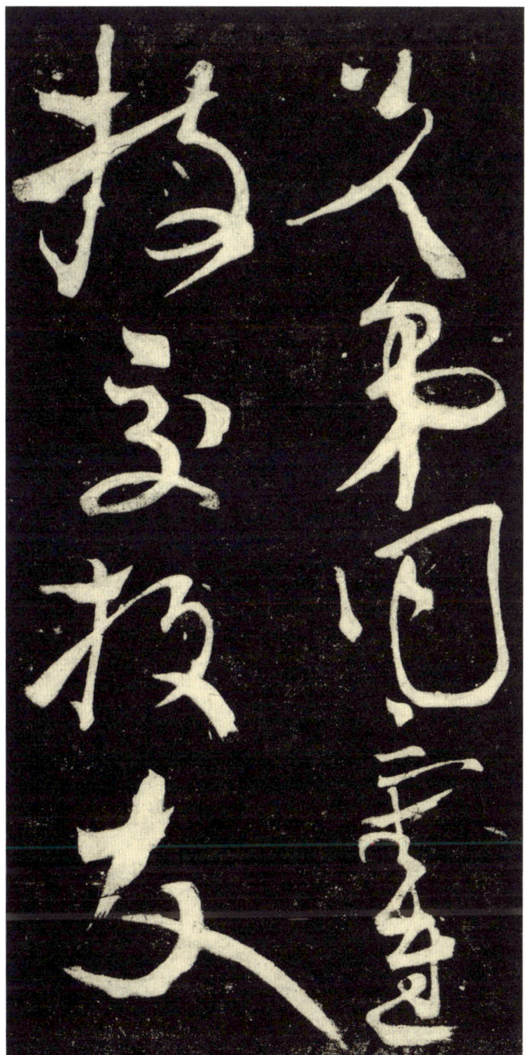

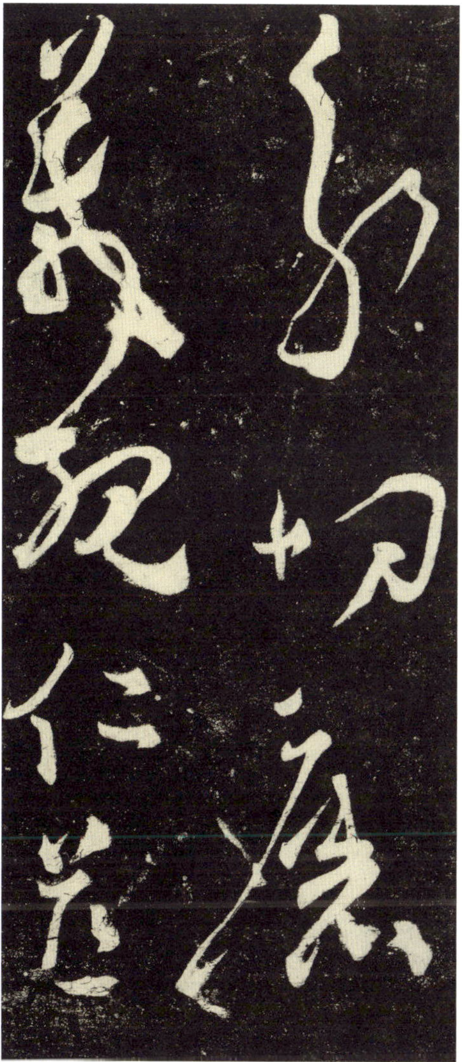

Rubbing from *Thousand Character Reader in Cursive Script* (草书断千文 *Cao Shu Duan Qian Wen*)

Zhang Xu 张旭 (years of birth/death unknown, Tang dynasty)
Cursive script (*cao shu*)
16 pages, each 25.9 cm × 14 cm
Shanghai Museum

Zhang Xu had the official title of Administrative Adjutant (长史 *zhang shi*) and was popularly known as "Administrative Adjutant Zhang" (张长史 *Zhang zhang shi*). In this piece written in cursive script style, the brushwork displays pronounced lifting and pressing, and distinct pausing and back-folding. Structurally the characters are open and imposing, undulating and majestic. The spatial composition shows a free spirit, with daring variations, but still succeeds in respecting established codes. Huang Tingjian 黄庭坚 (1045–1105, Song dynasty), after making a comparison between Zhang Xu and Huai Su, concluded "Huai Su's cursive style has its strength in 'slimness,' whereas Zhang's cursive script is strong in 'suppleness.' Bony slimness is much easier to achieve than energetic plumpness."

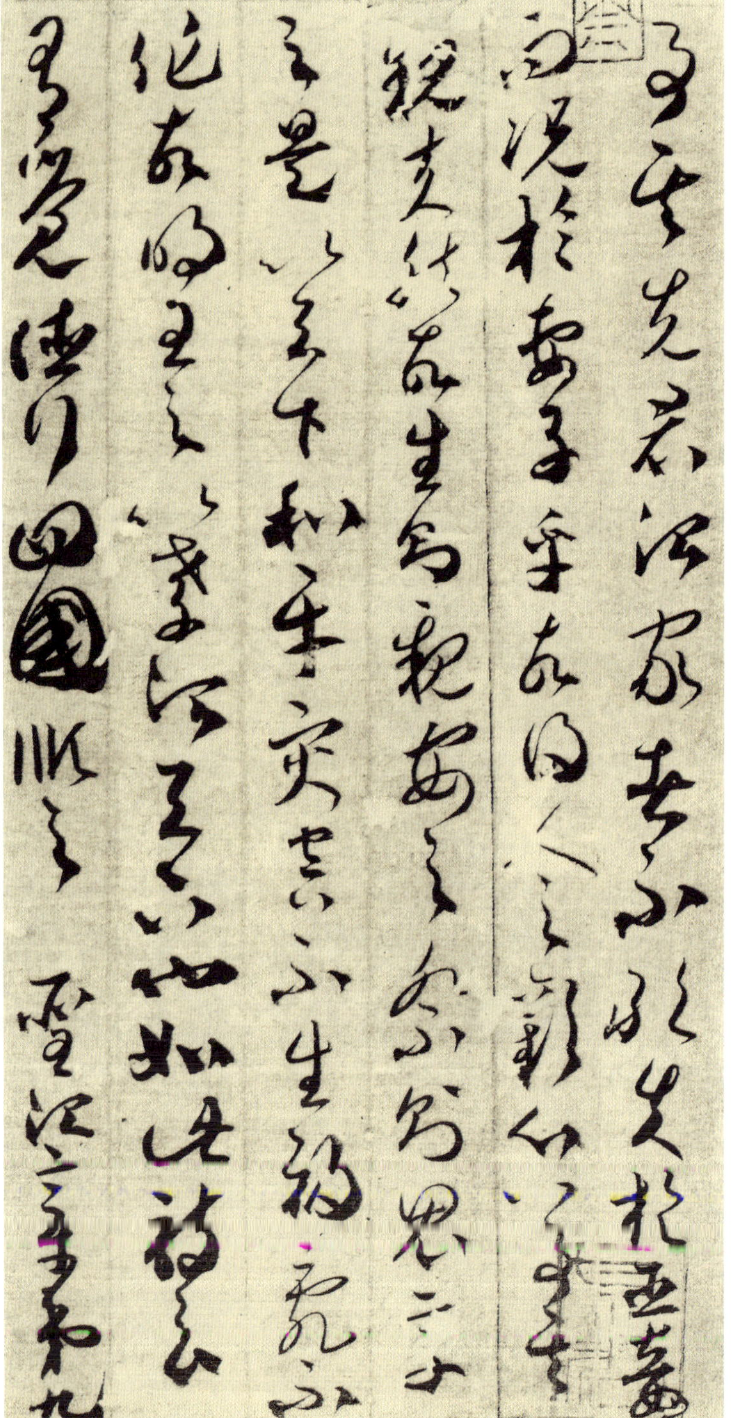

"Classic of Filial Piety" Scroll (孝经卷 *Xiao Jing Juan*)

He Zhizhang 贺知章 (659–c. 744, Tang dynasty)
Cursive script (*cao shu*)
26 cm × 265.1 cm
Sannomaru-Shozokan (Museum of the Imperial Collections) of the Imperial Household Agency of Japan

He Zhizhang was a major poet as well as a renowned calligrapher particularly accomplished in the cursive clerical script (草隶 *cao li*) style. This scroll in cursive script recalls the early cursive script style, which normally has a strong clerical script flavor with unlinked ideograms. In this piece, however, the fluent way in which characters are joined reflects more the contemporary cursive script style. Clearly the calligraphy in this work originates in early cursive script, but is also influenced by *Discourse on Calligraphy* of his contemporary Sun Guoting. The brush seems to fly through the columns, with expertly executed strokes, economically and crisply constructed ideograms, and an air of simplicity and conciseness that runs through the entire piece.

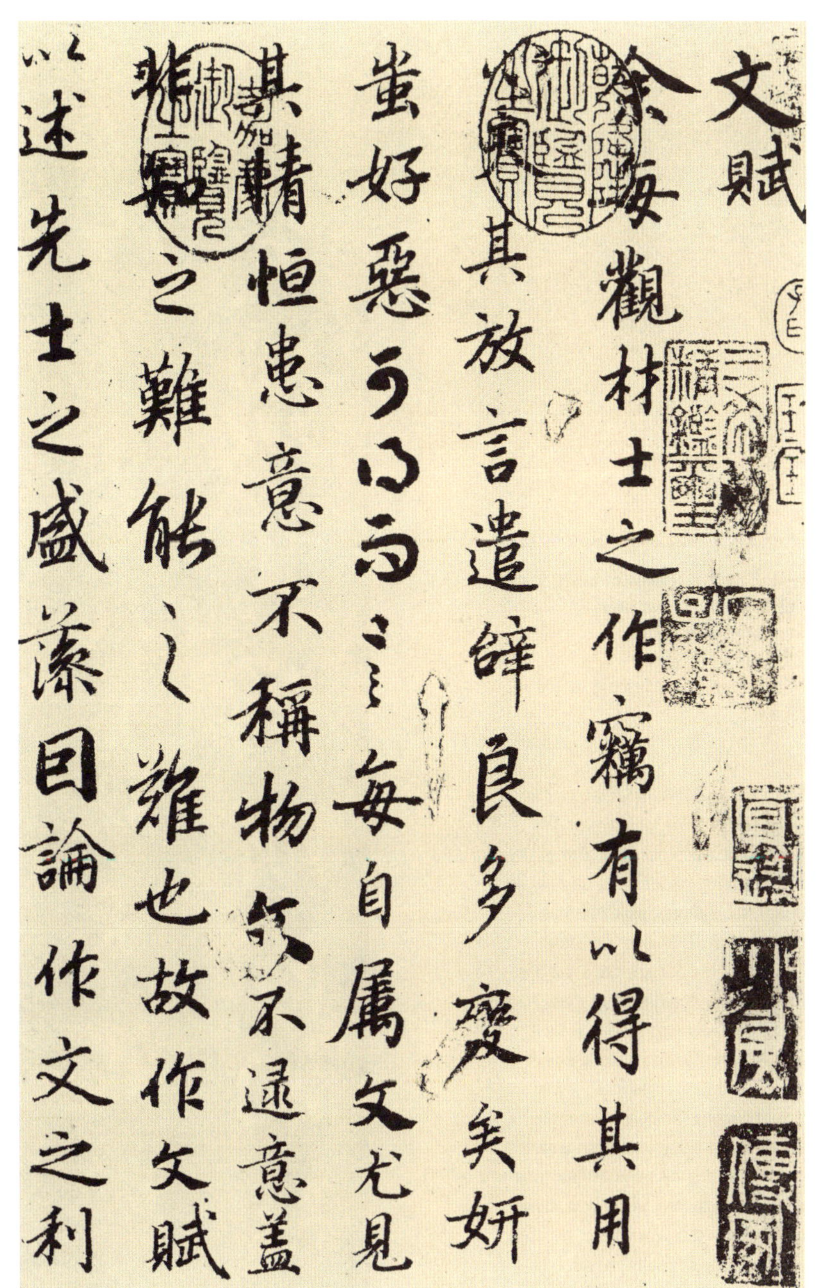

Rhyme Prose (文赋 *Wen Fu*)

Lu Jianzhi 陆柬之 (years of birth/death unknown, Tang dynasty)
Running regular script (*xing kai*)
Palace Museum, Taipei

Rhyme Prose was a work of parallel prose written by Lu Ji. *Rhyme Prose,* calligraphed by Lu Jianzhi, is therefore popularly referred to as "*Rhyme Prose* of the Two Lus" (二陆文赋 *er lu wen fu*). In this piece, Lu Jianzhi emulated the *Orchid Pavilion Preface* of Wang Xizhi, but with a brushwork that is more on the "rounded, vigorous" side. The dominant running regular script style is interspersed with the cursive script. The orthodox, level character postures are spiced with daring variations. The elegant strokes and fluid, free-spirited ideogram constructions are a testament to his mastery of Wang Xizhi's virtuoso brush techniques.

Preface to Buddha's Teachings Made by Pasting Together Ideograms from Wang Xizhi's Calligraphic Oeuvre (集王圣教序 *Ji Wang Sheng Jiao Xu*)

Huai Ren 怀仁 (years of birth/death unknown, Tang dynasty)
Running script (*xing shu*)
28.4 cm in height
Mitsui Memorial Museum in Tokyo, Japan

The Tang Buddhist monk Xuan Zang 玄奘 (602–664, Tang dynasty) undertook a perilous long journey to India to bring back a large number of Buddhist scriptures, which he translated into Chinese. Li Shimin, Emperor Taizong of the Tang, wrote a preface for these translated works—*Preface to Buddha's Teachings* (圣教序 *sheng jiao xu*). The crown prince Li Zhi 李治 (628–683, Tang dynasty), who would become Emperor Gaozong, also wrote a preface to these Buddhist classics. During his reign as Gaozong emperor, Huai Ren, who was a monk, undertook a ten-year project he knew would please the supreme ruler: he collected Wang Xizhi's calligraphic works and pasted together ideograms from these to create *Preface to Buddha's Teachings Made by Pasting Together Ideograms from Wang Xizhi's Calligraphic Oeuvre*, a collage that has proved an excellent model and guide for those interested in learning the Wang style. As a result of the publication of this work, the running script became all the rage during the period.

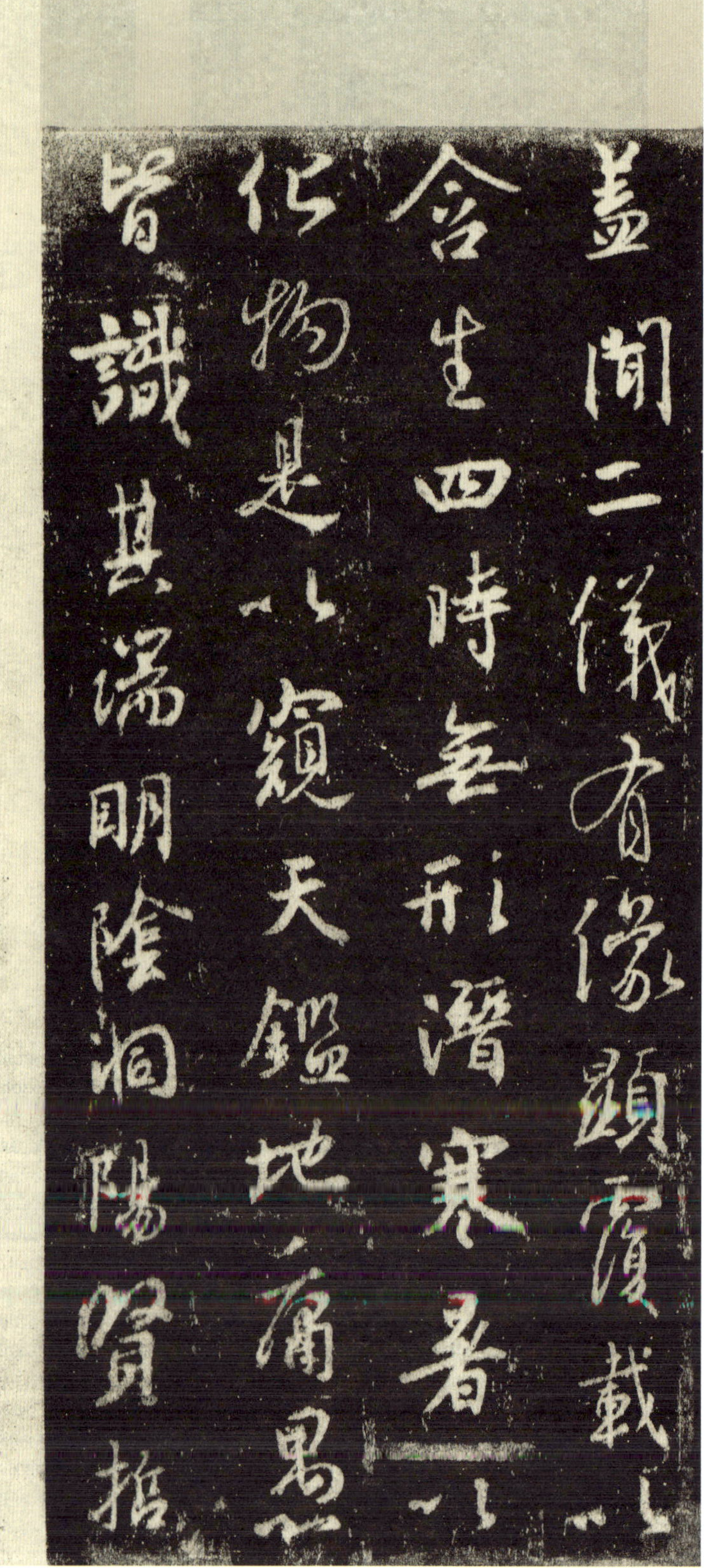

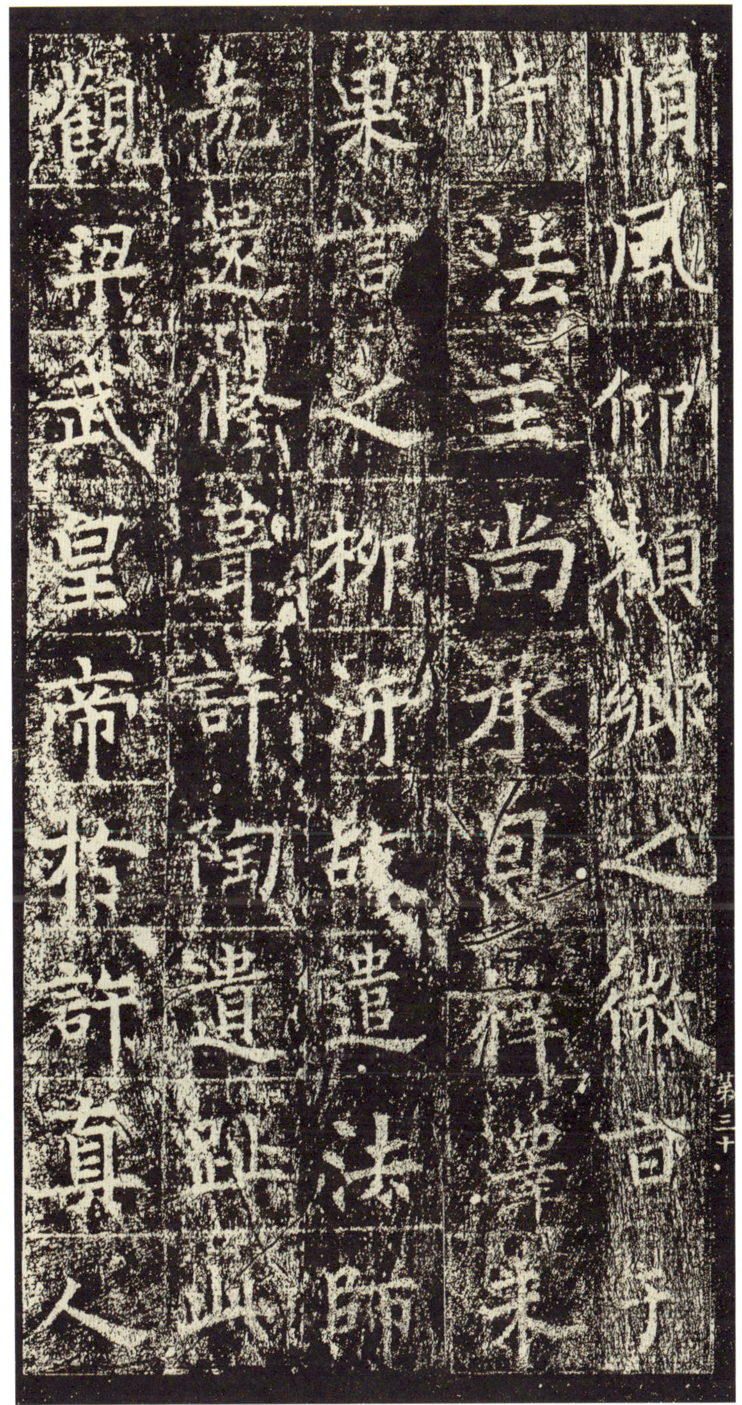

Rubbing from *Wang Hong Fan Tablet*
(王洪范碑 *Wang Hong Fan Bei*)

Wang Xuanzong 王玄宗 (years of birth/death unknown, Tang dynasty)
AD 667 (carving)
Regular script (*kai shu*)

Although the "Four Masters" won the highest acclaim in regular script calligraphy in the early Tang, the period produced many other accomplished regular script style calligraphers. Numerous calligraphic works by Tang calligraphers, discovered in later periods in the form of Buddhist sutras, epitaphs and stone tablets, may not have been authored by the renowned masters but possessed great artistic merit all the same. The stone inscription *Wang Hong Fan Tablet* was an important example of such works. It exhibits several characteristics of the style of Ouyang Xun and Chu Suiliang: the dots and strokes are square, vigorous and crisp; the character structure, though level and orthodox, is not without daring innovations; and the undulating character postures are intriguing.

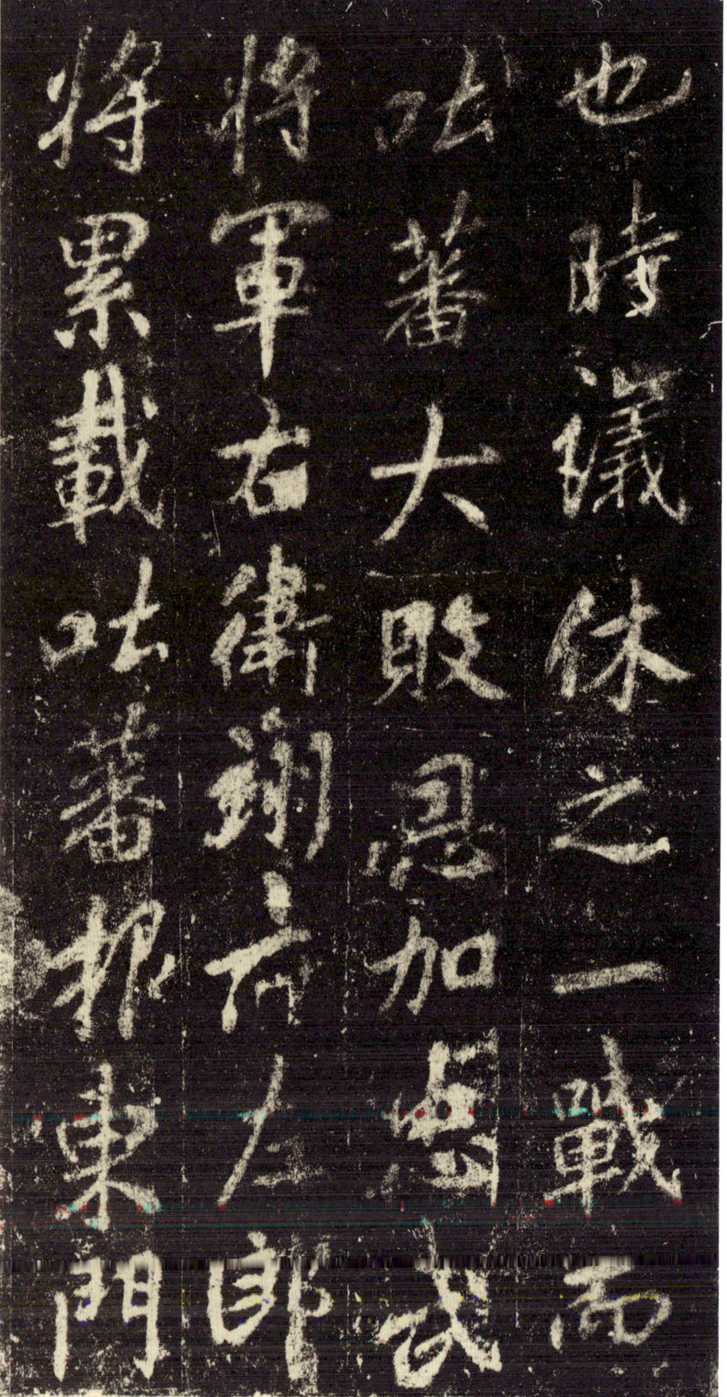

Rubbing from *Yunhui General Li Xiu Tablet* (云麾将军李秀碑 *Yun Hui Jiang Jun Li Xiu Bei*)

Li Yong 李邕 (678–747, Tang dynasty)
Running script (*xing shu*)
Shrine to Wen Tianxiang, Beijing
(fragmented tablet)

Li Yong was also popularly known as "Li Beihai" because he once held the position of Prefect (太守 *tai shou*) of Beihai. He started out learning the style of Wang Xizhi but later, abandoning the form of Wang's writing, struck out on his own to create a unique style by employing the running script hand when writing stone inscriptions. He was credited with a magic hand in calligraphy. By infusing Wang Xizhi's style with the flavor of stone inscriptions, he succeeded in adding a sense of simple solidity to Wang's writing and created his own unique style. According to some later writings, "Wang Xizhi's calligraphy recalls a dragon, whereas Li Beihai's style calls to mind an elephant." This *Yunhui General Li Xiu Tablet* was an excellent example of Li Yong's calligraphic style. The plumpness of the strokes in no way overwhelms the underlying bony energy; and the supple shapes and postures of the ideograms do not stand in the way of the virile esthetic running through the entire piece.

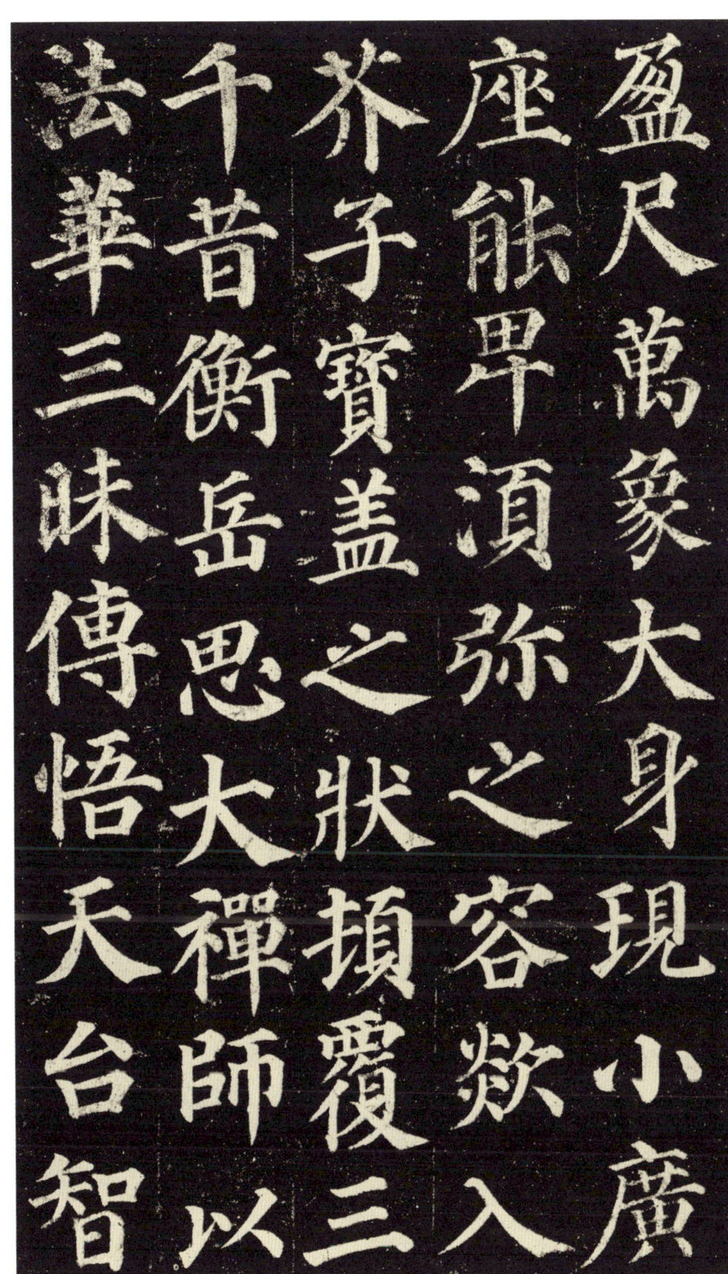

Rubbing made in the Song dynasty from *Prabhutaratna Buddha Pagoda Tablet* (多宝塔碑 *Duo Bao Ta Bei*)

Yan Zhenqing 颜真卿 **(708–784, Tang dynasty)**
Regular script (*kai shu*)

If early Tang calligraphy was dominated by the influence of the "Two Wangs," the middle Tang was a period of daring innovations. Li Yong, Xu Hao and Liu Gongquan, to name a few, were calligraphers of the period who pioneered their own unique styles. The greatest impact was made by Yan Zhenqing, who opened up a brave new world in calligraphy. He was also popularly known as the "Duke of Lu" (颜鲁公 *yan lu gong*) by reason of a title he held. In his regular script style calligraphy, which combines the forms and postures of the clerical script style of the Han dynasty and the "brush spirit" of seal script, reigns an aura of incorruptibility and uprightness, just as a minister presides over affairs of state with a forbidding solemnity. *Prabhutaratna Buddha Pagoda Tablet*, the earliest of his surviving works, is characterized by supple strokes, an energy-filled brushwork, a dense, compact character structure and neat, elegant postures. It remains a popular copybook for beginning learners of Chinese calligraphy.

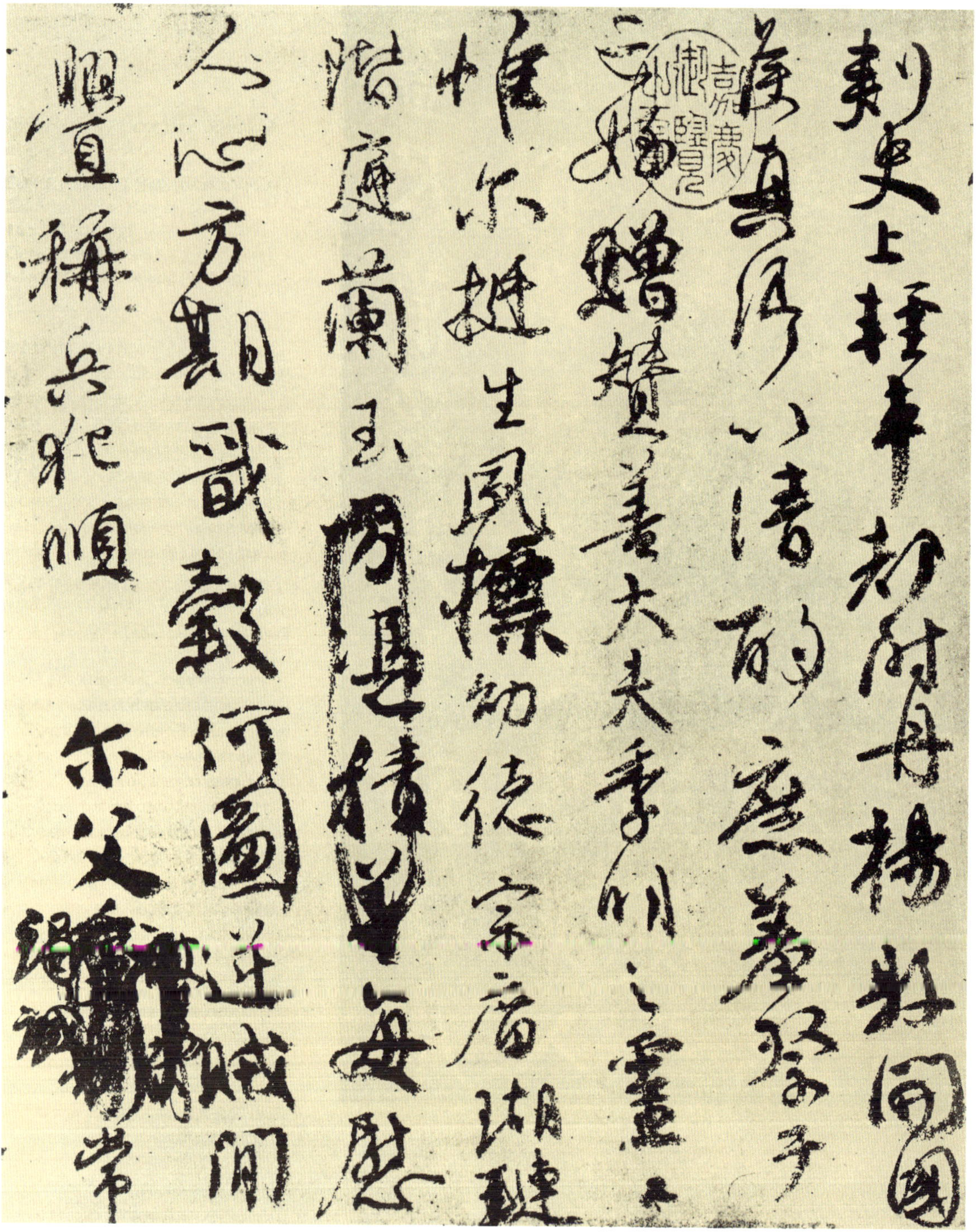

刺史上輕車都尉丹楊縣開國
侯真卿以清酌庶羞祭于
亡姪贈贊善大夫季明之靈曰
惟爾挺生夙標幼德宗廟瑚璉
階庭蘭玉方憑積善每慰
人心方期戩穀何圖逆賊間
釁稱兵犯順爾父竭誠常

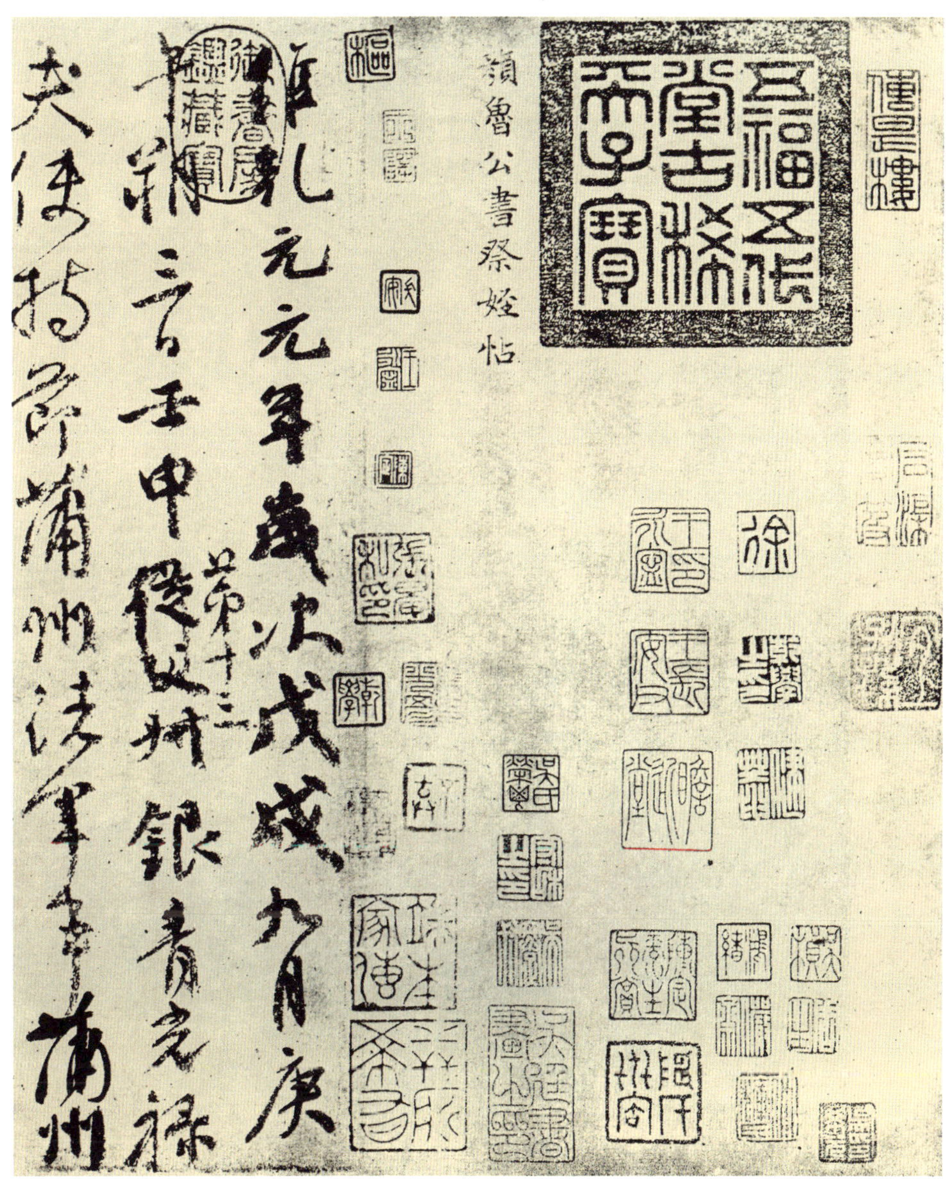

Draft Eulogy for a Nephew (祭侄文稿 *Ji Zhi Wen Gao*)

Yan Zhenqing 颜真卿 (708–784, Tang dynasty)
Running cursive script (*xing cao*)
28.2 cm × 75.5 cm
Palace Museum, Taipei

Upon learning of the death of his cousin Yan Gaoqing 颜杲卿 (692–756, Tang dynasty) and the latter's son in An Lushan's Rebellion, the deeply distraught Yan Zhenqing composed in one breath this eulogy for his nephew. In the emotional outpouring, he was driven on by sorrow and anger, paying no heed to the neatness of his calligraphy; but "the beauty of the handwriting shows despite his inattention to the calligraphy." He starts in with the seal script style, continues in center-brush, and exits with deliberate speed. The virtuoso brushwork is imposing, full of variety and leaps with energy and flair. The heaving emotions come through in the calligraphy, which seems to come to a sobbing pause at some points, and to launch into lamentation at others, the sorrow and indignation racing like a torrent. The numerous erasures and corrections in the draft do not detract from its soul-wrenching artistic impact. Xianyu Shu 鲜于枢 (1256–1301, Yuan dynasty), a Yuan calligrapher, called it the "second masterpiece in running script."

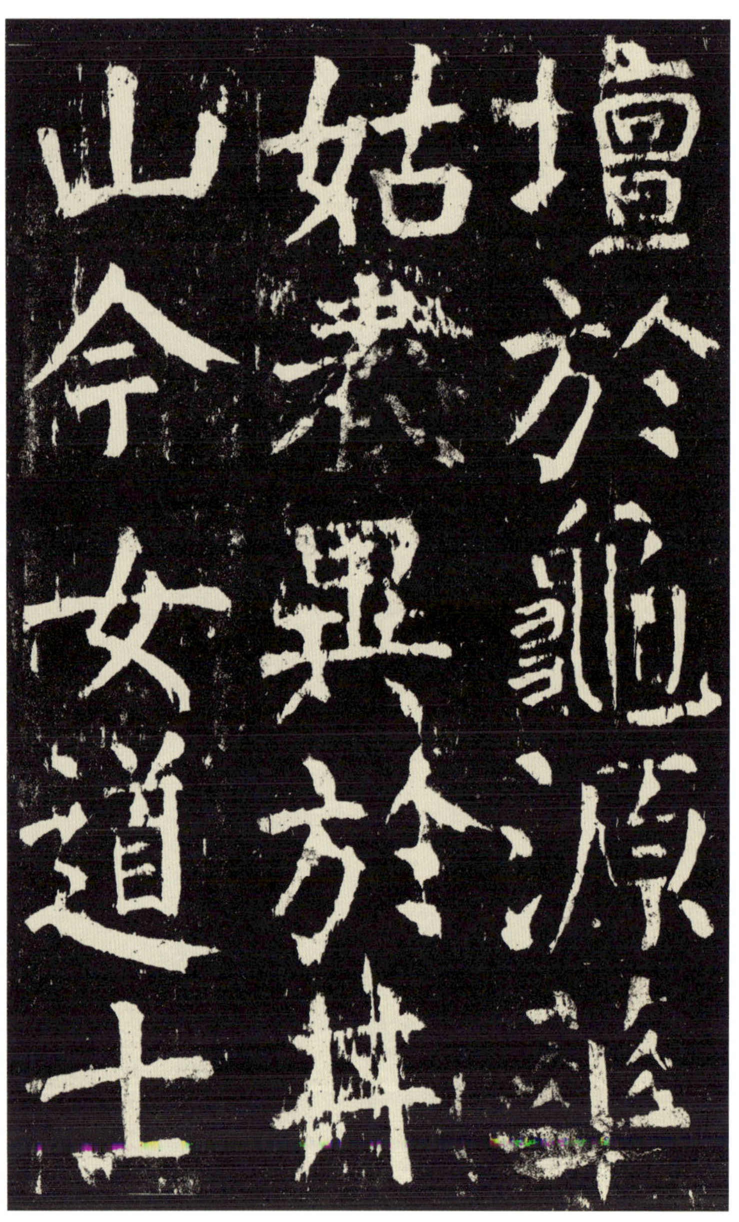

Rubbing made in the Ming dynasty from *Altar to an Immortal on Mount Magu* (麻姑仙坛记 *Ma Gu Xian Tan Ji*)

Yan Zhenqing 颜真卿 (708–784, Tang dynasty)
Regular script (*kai shu*)
Palace Museum, Taipei

Yan Zhenqing's regular script style is characterized by energetically executed strokes, elegant character structures, and well-arranged spatial composition and column spacing. Its fat strokes belie the energy with which they are executed; the seeming murkiness hides a genuine clarity; an exquisite hand lies just beneath the clumsy appearance; and despite the antique look there is no lack of innovativeness. All but the most astute connoisseurs would likely miss the subtle nuances. Yan's regular script style had not initially been valued widely. Thus, Li Yu 李煜 (937–978, Southern Tang dynasty), last emperor of the Southern Tang, disparagingly likened Yan's calligraphy to "a coarse, bumbling country farmer." But Yan's calligraphic works endeared themselves to succeeding generations. In Ouyang Xiu's words, "the more one looks at this stone inscription, the more its merit becomes evident, and one realizes that Yan Lugong alone is capable of writing such a good hand."

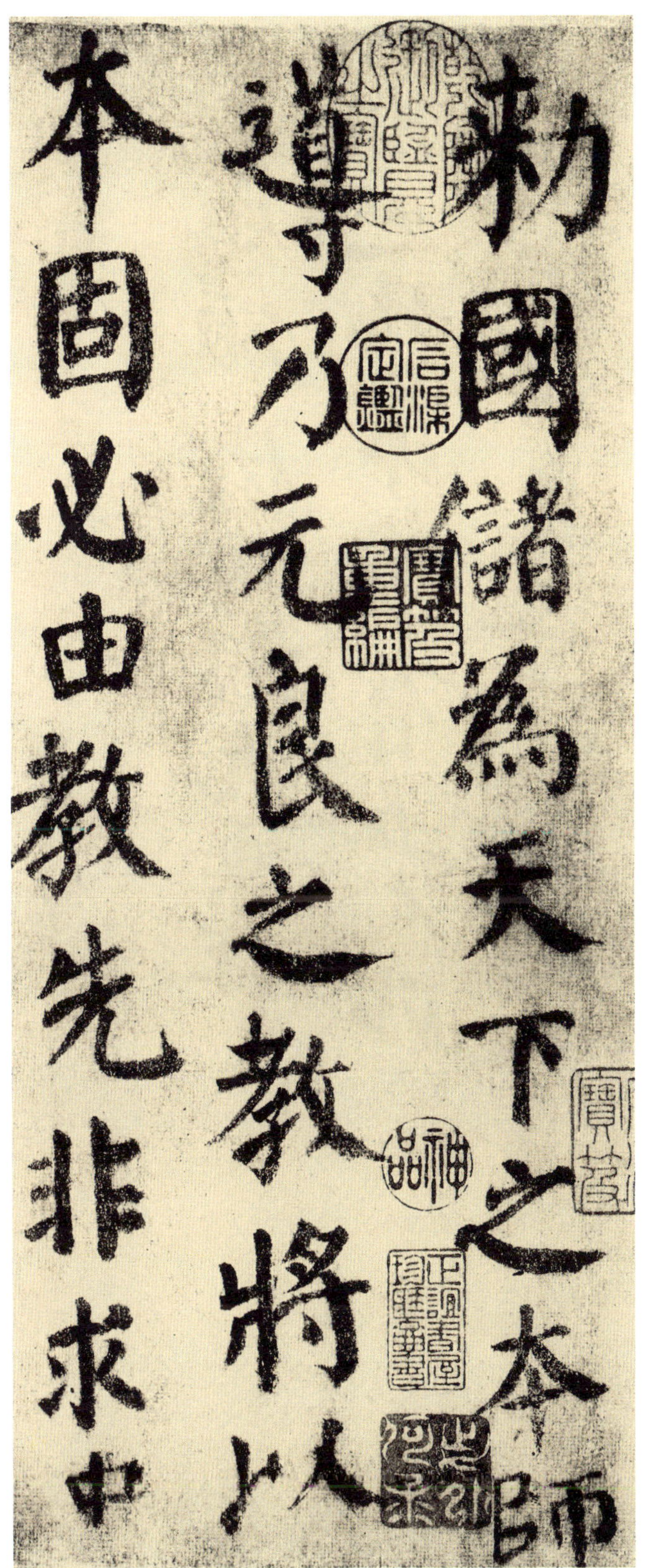

Letter of Attorney (自书告身 *Zi Shu Gao Shen*)

Yan Zhenqing 颜真卿 **(708–784, Tang dynasty)**
Regular script (*kai shu*)
29.7 cm × 220.8 cm
Private collection of Nakamura Fusetsu

This is the only surviving original work in regular script style by Yan Zhenqing. The characters in this scroll vary in size, angle of inclination, length and levelness of the strokes, its awkward appearance belying ingenious touches; the spaces between characters also vary, with vertical, but no discernable horizontal, alignment. The piece exhibits a brisk tempo and a genial antique feel. Although it employs the calligraphic style for stone inscriptions, a literary flavor suffuses the piece. This led the Qing dynasty calligrapher Yang Shoujing 杨守敬 (1839–1915, Qing dynasty) to state, "Yan Lugong's regular script style in this piece is radically different from the style displayed in his stone inscriptions."

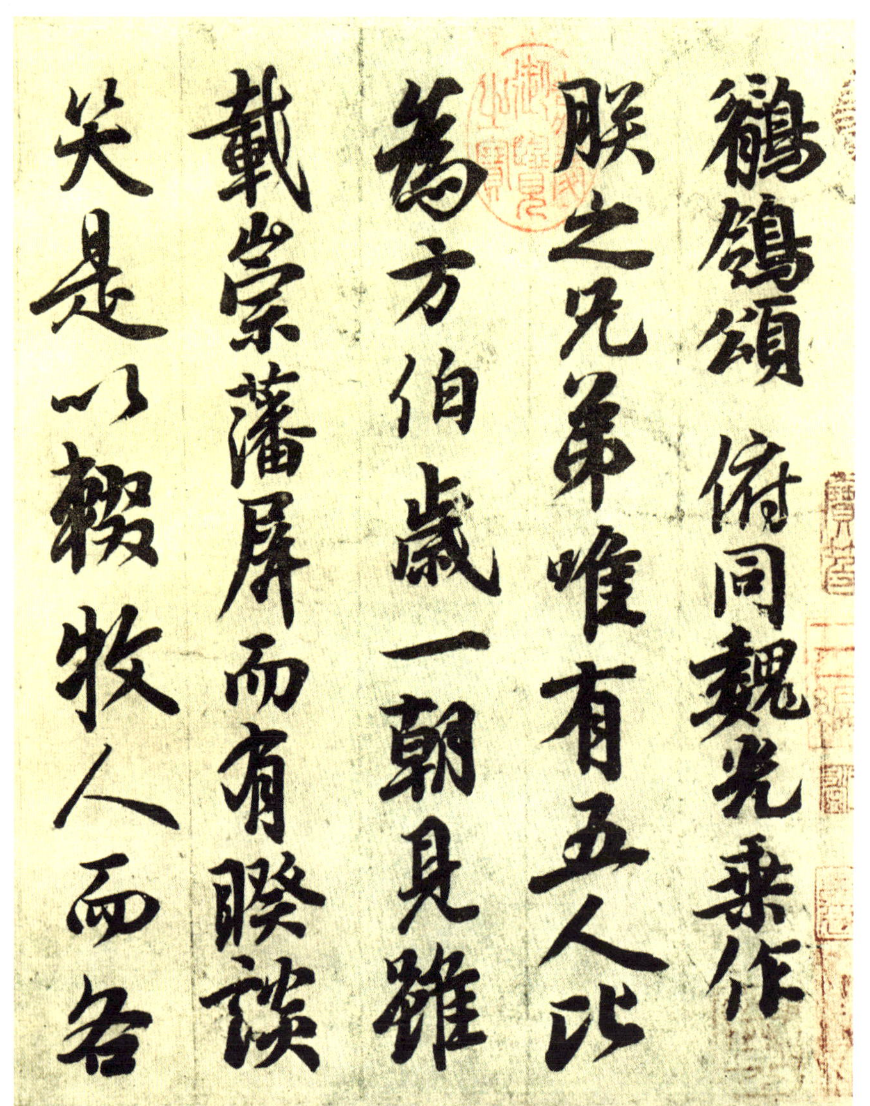

Ode to a Wagtail (鹡鸰颂 *Ji Ling Song*)

Li Longji 李隆基 (685-762, Tang dynasty)
Running script (*xing shu*)

Li Longji is Emperor Xuanzong of the Tang dynasty, also known as Tang Ming Huang. The characters in his elegant *Ode to a Wagtail* in running script are plump, with no visible "flesh." The "plump" esthetic received a mighty boost with the emperor's endorsement. In the history of Chinese calligraphy, the most accomplished emperor-calligrapher is indisputably Zhao Ji of the Song dynasty, known for his "slim gold" style. The next to come to mind is probably Li Longji for his "plump" style.

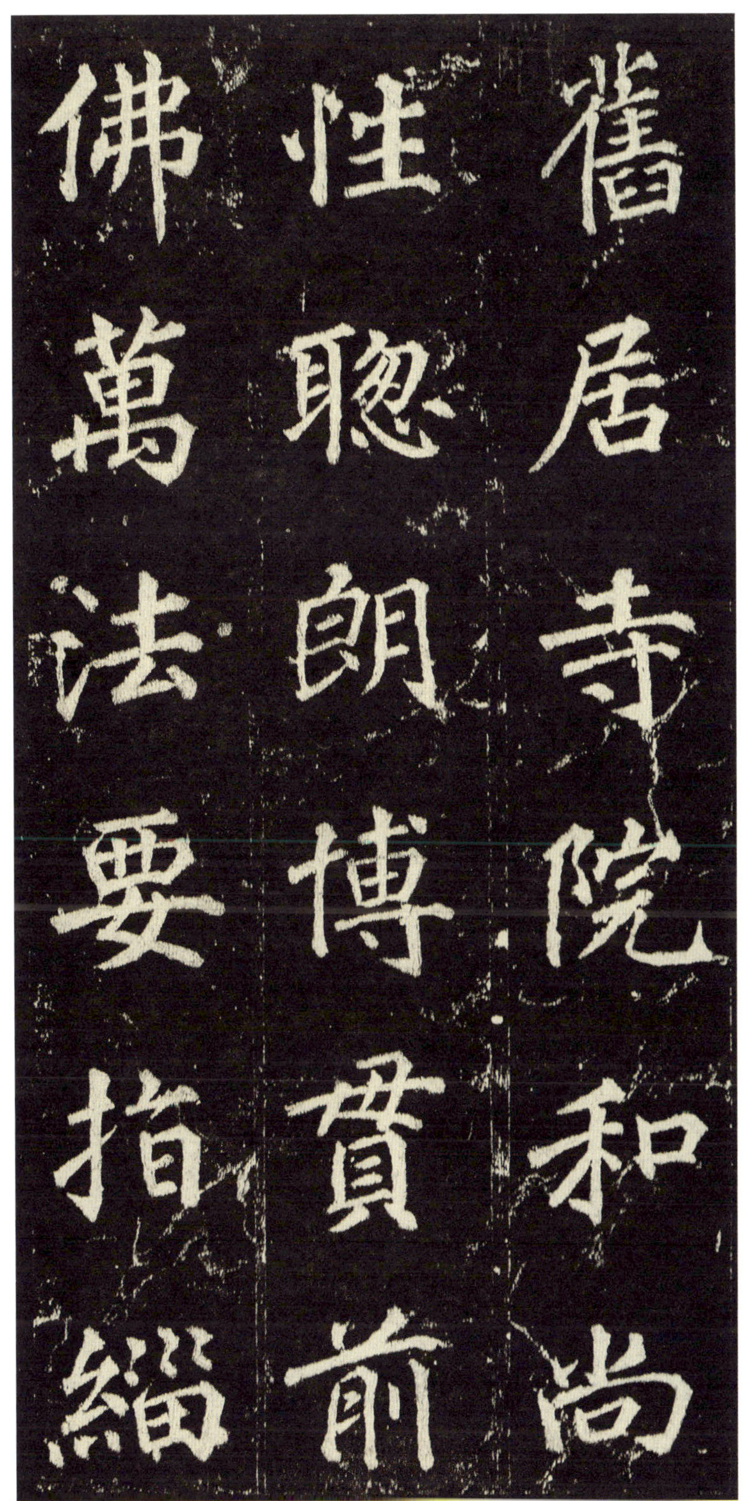

Rubbing from *Amogha Tablet* (不空和尚碑 *Bu Kong He Shang Bei*)

Xu Hao 徐浩 (703-782, Tang dynasty)
Regular script (*kai shu*)
Provincial Museum of Shaanxi

Xu Hao and Yan Zhenqing are the two calligraphers that most epitomize the calligraphy of the Tang dynasty at its zenith. Xu's regular script style is characterized by the center-brush technique and a deliberate brush movement, as if sailing against the current. The robust, rounded brushwork produces strong-boned, full-fleshed characters. Mi Fu 米芾 (1051-1107, Song dynasty), a renowned Song calligrapher, likened Xu's writing to "a mellow, urbane gentleman imbued with virtue," aptly describing Xu Hao's emphasis on content above form.

Taoist Scripture "Ling Fei" (灵飞经 *Ling Fei Jing*)

Unknown calligrapher, Tang dynasty
713-741, Kaiyuan period of the Tang dynasty
Regular script (*kai shu*)

During the middle Qing dynasty a small number of religious texts copied by Tang calligraphers emerged into public view. *Taoist Scripture "Ling Fei"* was one of the most prominent of these discoveries. Also known as *Taoist Scripture "Ling Fei Liu Jia"* (灵飞六甲经 *ling fei liu jia jing*), it is a Taoist classic purportedly created by Zhong Shaojing 钟绍京 . Qi Gong 启功 , a contemporary calligrapher, dismissed the attribution as pure speculation. Taoist Scripture *"Ling Fei,"* with its graceful style tinged with an antique charm, an open but cohesive character structure and a leisurely but varied brushwork, is the epitome of Tang calligraphy.

七日跪有經之師上金六兩白素六十尺金
鐶六雙青絲六兩五色繒各廿二尺以代翦
髮歃血登壇之誓以盟奉行靈符玉名不洩
之信矣違盟負信三祖父母獲風刀之考詣
積夜之河運蒙山巨石塡之水津有經之師

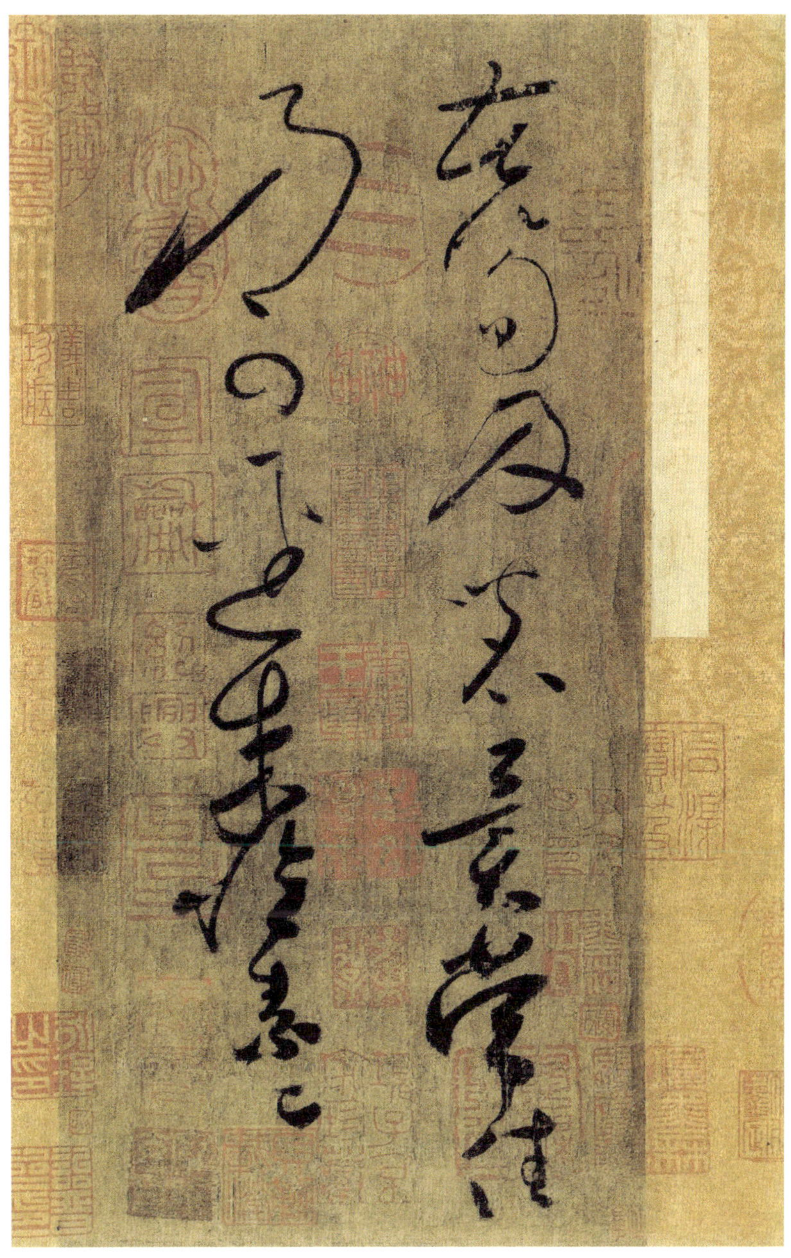

Bitter Bamboo Shoot (苦笋帖 *Ku Sun Tie*)

Huai Su 怀素 **(725–785, Tang dynasty)**
Cursive script (*cao shu*)
Silk tabby calligraphy
25.1 cm × 12 cm
Shanghai Museum

This piece, characterized by center-brush strokes and rounded characters, throbs with life: the diagonal stroke in the character " 乃 " appears ready to spring, and the curved, easy-flowing brush turnings in the character " 迳 " convey a wonderful sense of "a bird fluttering out of a wood and a frightened snake slithering into the grass for cover." The seven characters " 乃可迳来懷素上 " were completed in one flourish of the brush in one breath; they flow like a river cascading down a cataract.

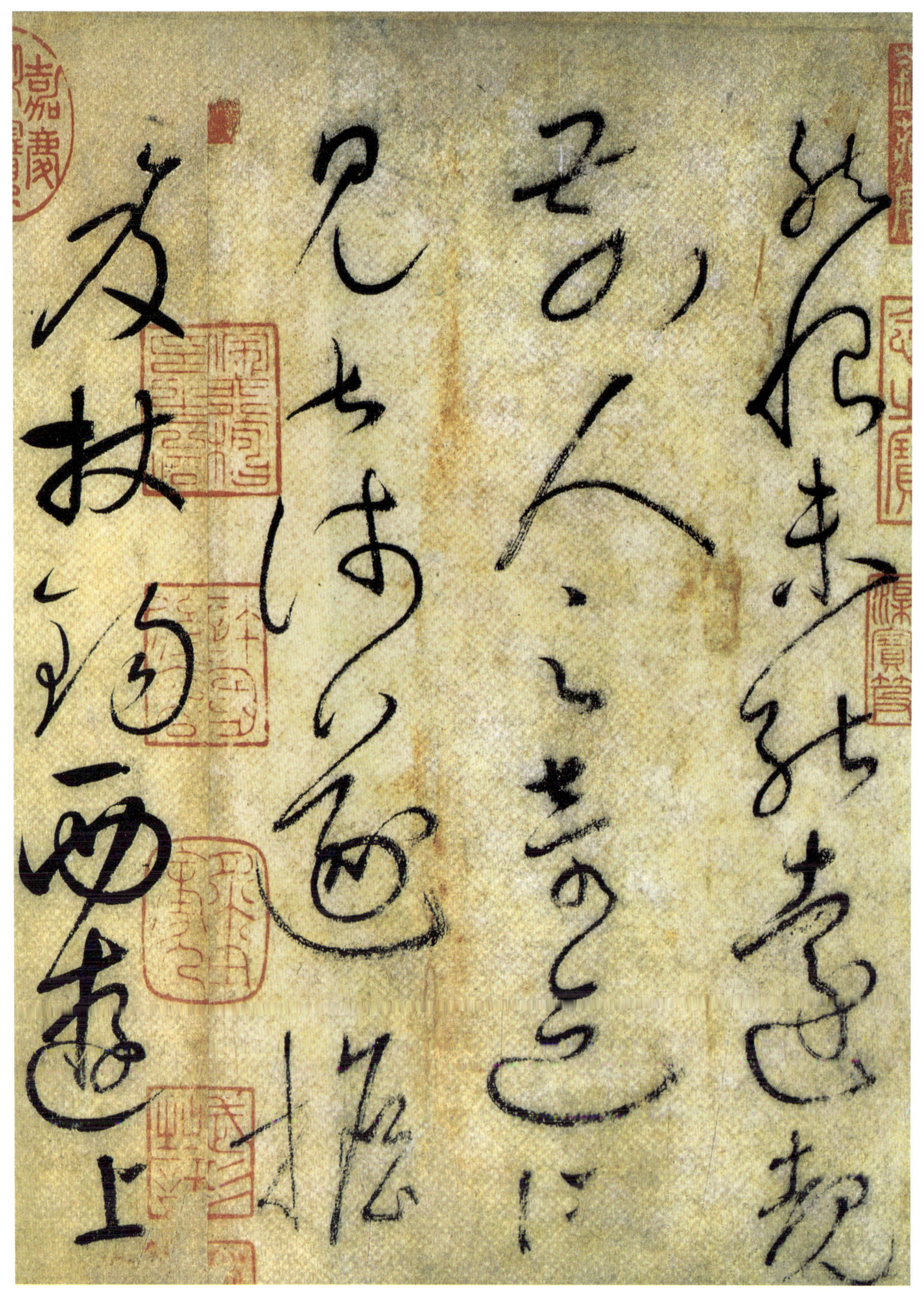

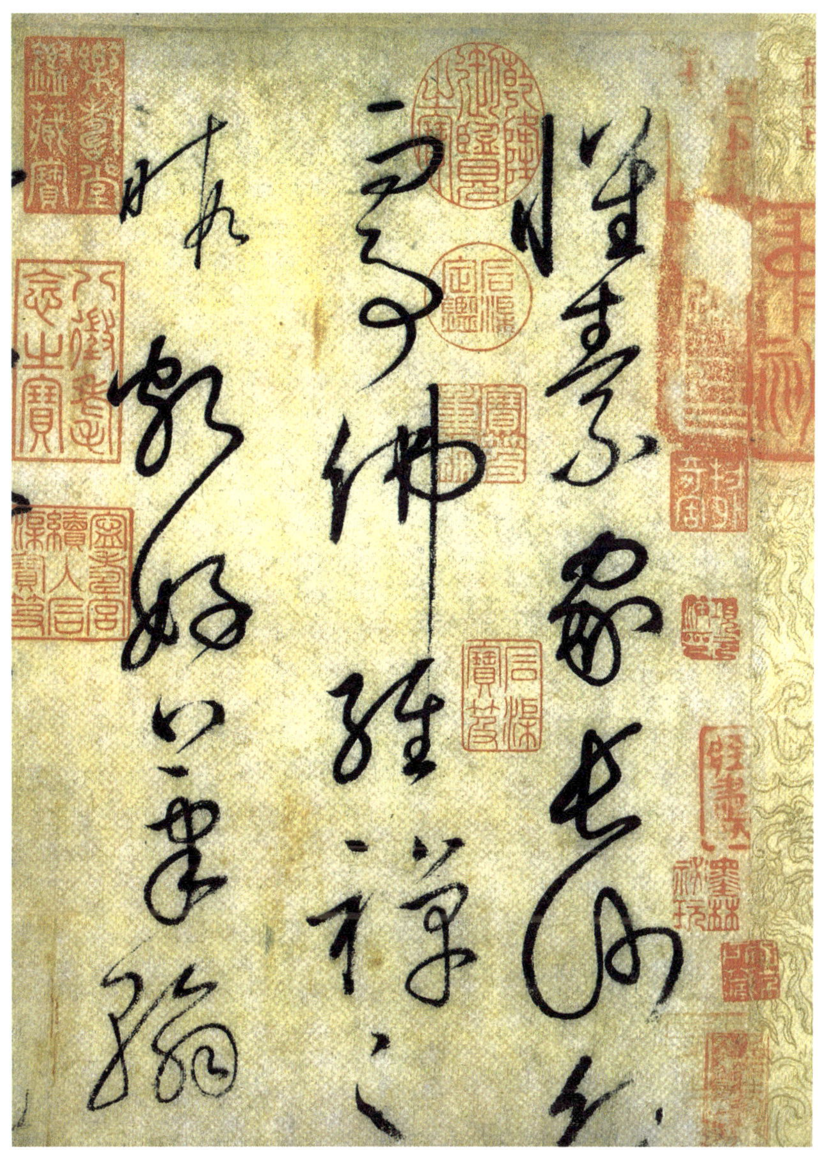

Autobiographical Notes (自叙帖 *Zi Xu Tie*)

Huai Su 怀素 **(725-785, Tang dynasty)**
Cursive script (*cao shu*)
28.3 cm × 755 cm
Palace Museum, Taipei

The family name of Huai Su, who became a monk at 7, was Qian. Penniless and unable to afford paper for calligraphic practice, he grew a grove of banana trees outside his temple, which he named "Green Sky Temple" (绿天庵 *lü tian an*), harvesting the broad leaves as writing support. He adopted Zhang Xu's mad cursive script style and further developed it. The two are popularly referred to as "Crazy Zhang and Drunken Su" (颠张醉素 *dian zhang zui su*). Huai Su's cursive script style *Autobiographical Notes* is truly a vivid demonstration of the observation "calligraphy is a painting of one's interior landscape." His personality, spirit and unstoppable passion pour through the tip of his brush as he enters, so to speak, a state of trance, of "self-oblivion," and at the same time releases his "self" through the brush to create, as if aided by a divine hand, a masterpiece.

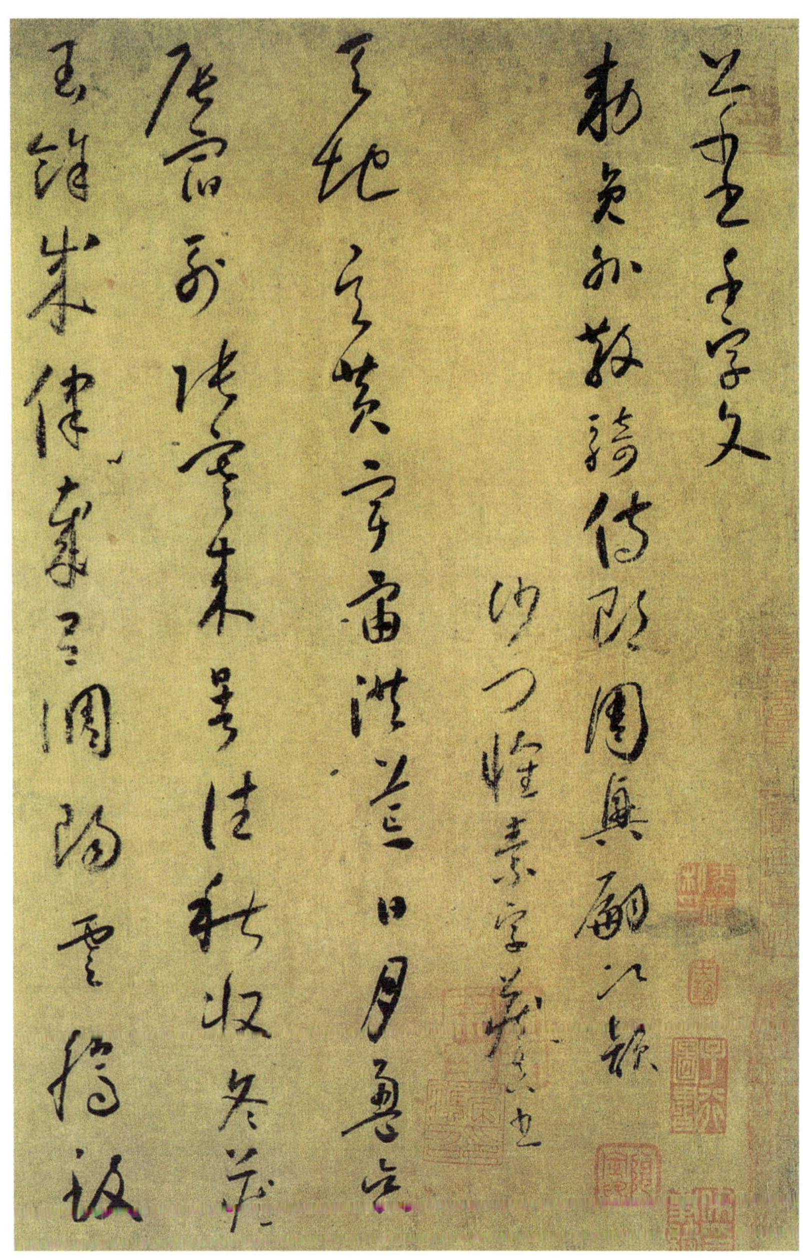

Thousand Character Reader in Small Cursive Hand (小草千字文 *Xiao Cao Qian Zi Wen*)

Huai Su 怀素 (725–785, Tang dynasty)
Cursive script (*cao shu*)
26.8 cm × 278.9 cm
Taiwan

This piece is also known as "Calligraphic Model Worth a Thousand Taels of Gold" (千金帖 *qian jin tie*) after Yao Gongshou 姚公绶 of the Ming dynasty gushed, "Each word in this calligraphic model is worth a tael of gold!" It is a signature work of Huai Su in his later years. Its simple style, evocative of an antique elegance, has nothing of the untrammeled freedom found in his *Autobiographical Notes*. In the use of the brush, there are fewer linked characters, but spirit and energy run through the entire work. The wide open spaces between characters and columns create an impression of a return to the simplicity of rarified antiquity.

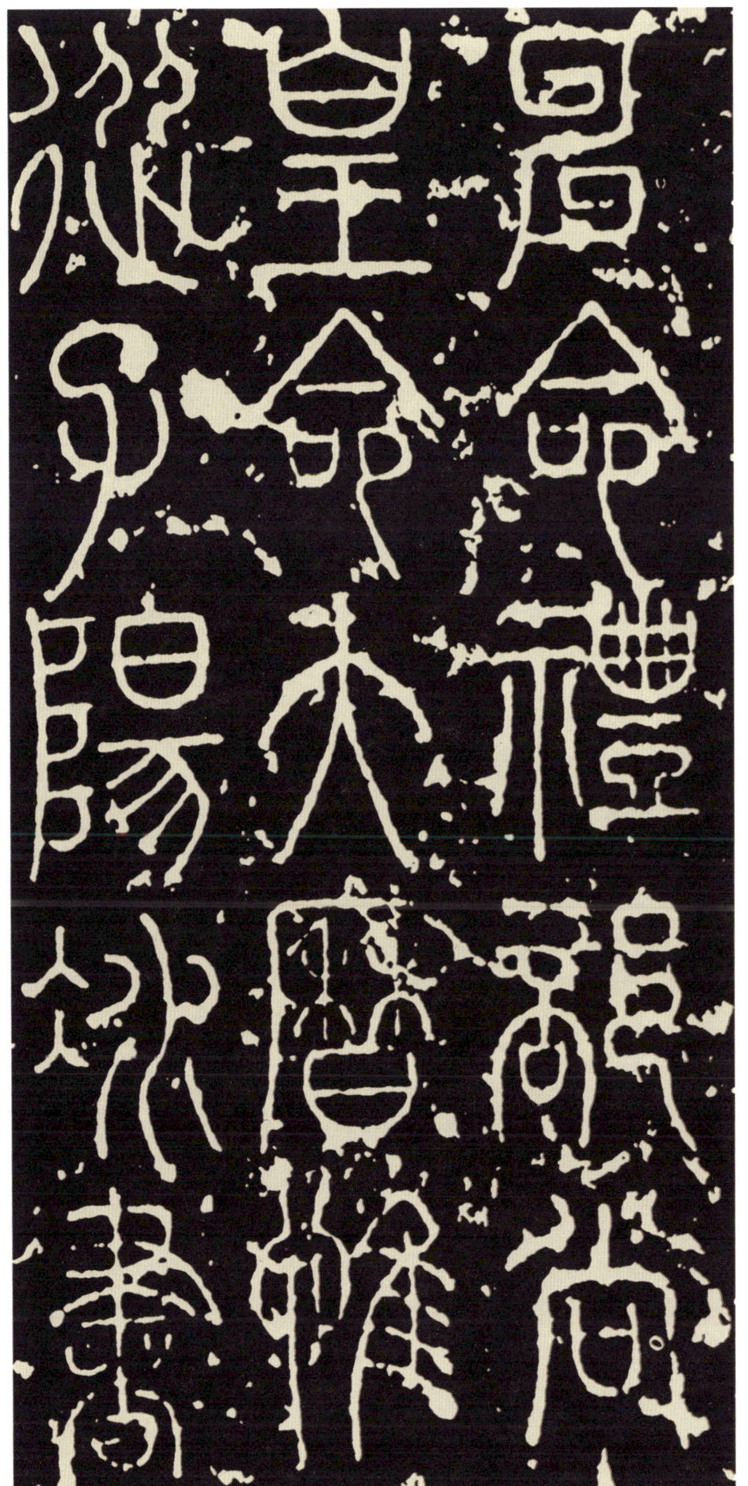

Rubbing from *Tombs of Ancestors* (栖先茔记 *Qi Xian Ying Ji*)

Li Yangbing 李阳冰 (years of birth/death unknown, Tang dynasty)
767 AD (carving)
Seal script (*zhuan shu*)
Beilin Museum of Xi'an, Shaanxi (stone tablet re-carved in the Song dynasty)

The seal script of the Qin dynasty was no longer recognizable as such in the wake of its many transformations through the Han, the Wei and the Two Jins. With the high premium placed by calligraphers in the Tang dynasty on rules and conventions in calligraphy, the neat Qin seal script style came back into vogue, because it was attuned to the esthetic of the time. Li Yangbing's seal script style boasts an orthodox brushwork and bright, easy-flowing character structures. He once made the claim, "None but your humble servant after Master Li Si," meaning in the millennium after Qin's Li Si, there had been no other master of the seal script style, except himself; he alone could claim to be the interpreter of the spirit of Li Si's seal script style and a keeper of his legacy. His claim is to a considerable extent borne out by the merit of his works.

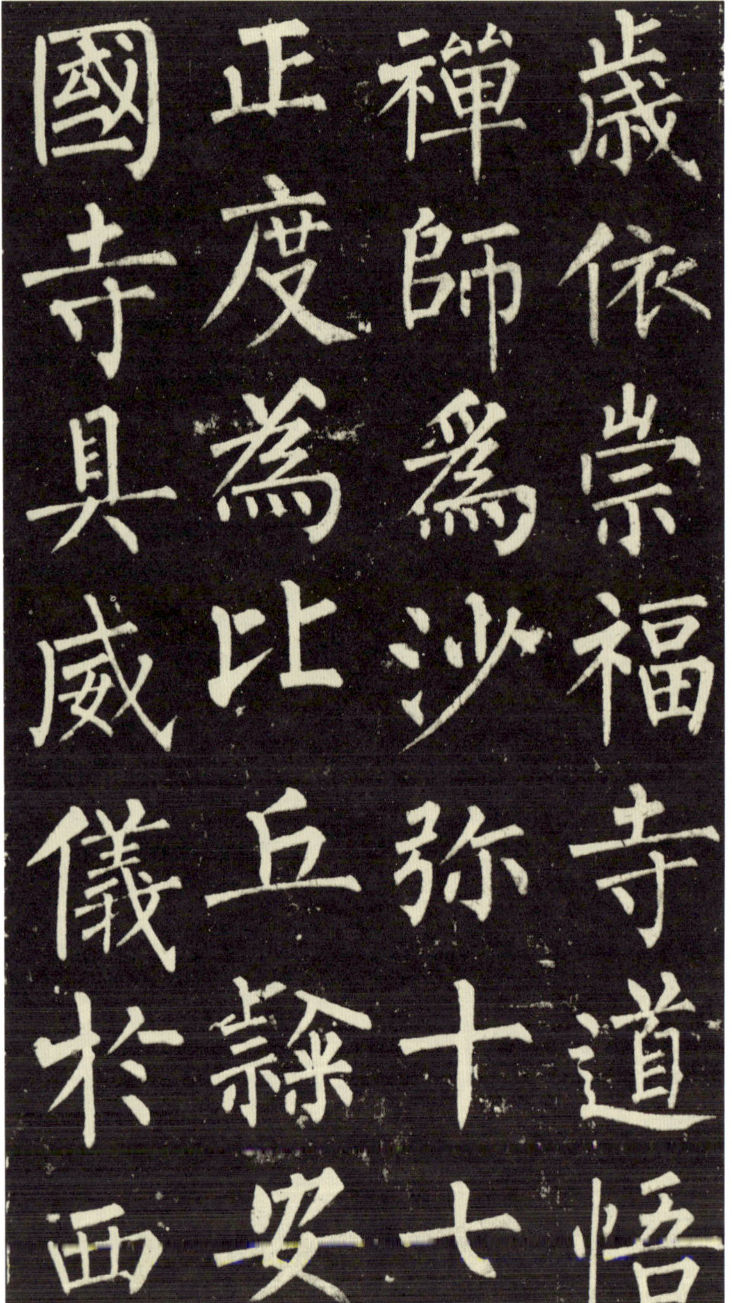

Rubbing made in the Song dynasty from *Tablet of the Xuanmi Pagoda* (玄秘塔碑 *Xuan Mi Ta Bei*)

Liu Gongquan 柳公权 **(778–865, Tang dynasty)**
Regular script (*kai shu*)
Beilin Museum of Xi'an, Shaanxi

In addition to Ouyang Xun, Chu Suiliang and Yan Zhenqing, the other Tang calligrapher to have left a major legacy in the regular script style is Liu Gongquan. Liu's calligraphy, often characterized as abounding in "strong sinews and hard bone," metamorphosed from the Yan Zhenqing tradition into a distinct style whose "elegance, sharpness, boniness and sinewy feel" contrasts with Yan's "grand, epic, solemn and exuberant" writing. This difference in style is summed up in the popular saying "Yan's sinews and Liu's bone" (颜筋柳骨 *yan jin liu gu*). Legend has it that when asked by Emperor Muzong of the Tang for calligraphic advice, Liu Gongquan replied, "The key to the brush is the heart, when the heart is in the right place, the brush will move itself." *Tablet of the Xuanmi Pagoda* is a perfect realization of this candid advice to an emperor.

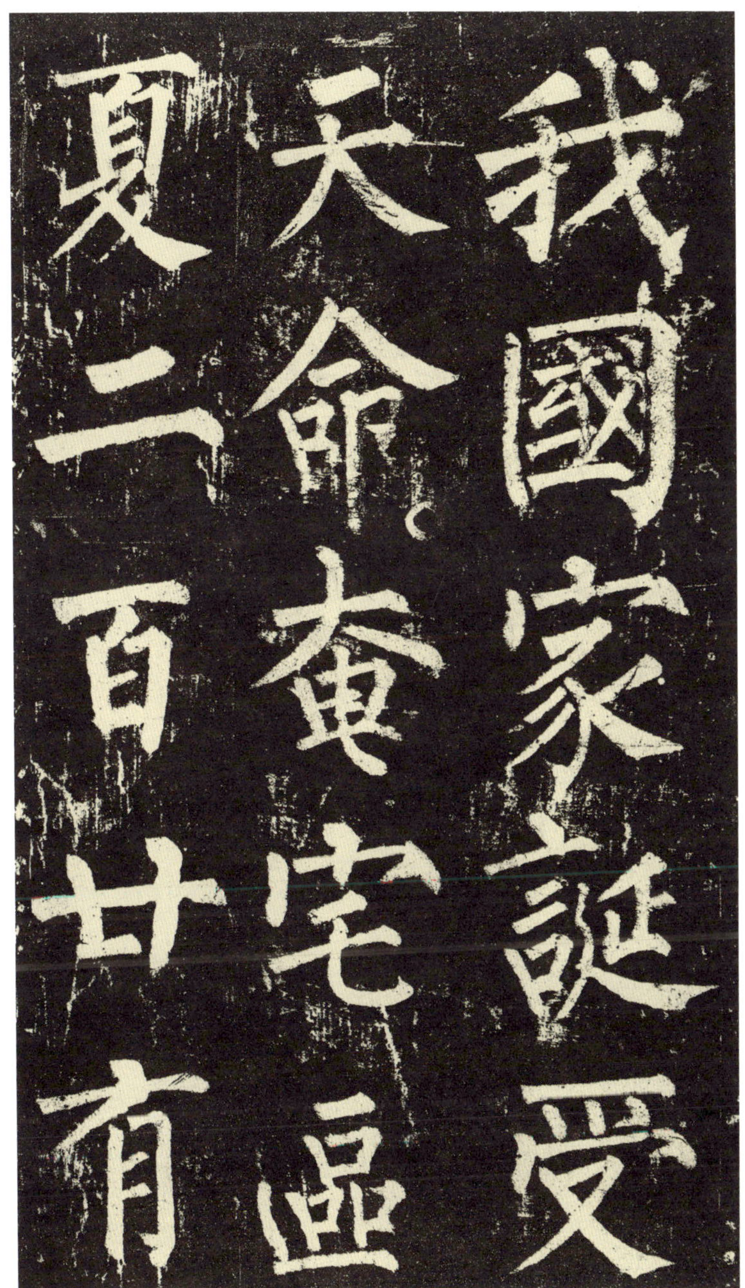

Rubbing made in the Song dynasty from *Imperial Guard Tablet* (神策军碑 *Shen Ce Jun Bei*)

Liu Gongquan 柳公权 **(778-865, Tang dynasty)**
Regular script (*kai shu*)
National Library of China, Beijing

The Liu style is characterized by strong bone and fine structure. His brushwork is crisp and decisive as if he were "cutting through metal," using almost exclusively straight lines and square corners, rarely resorting to curves except in diagonal strokes. He felt strongly about structure, but unlike calligraphers before his time he broke away from the conventional linkages and relationships between strokes, arranging them instead in any way that would enhance the esthetics, the elegance and grace of the work. *Imperial Guard Tablet*, written in his later years, exhibits greater energy and majesty than his *Tablet of the Xuanmi Pagoda*.

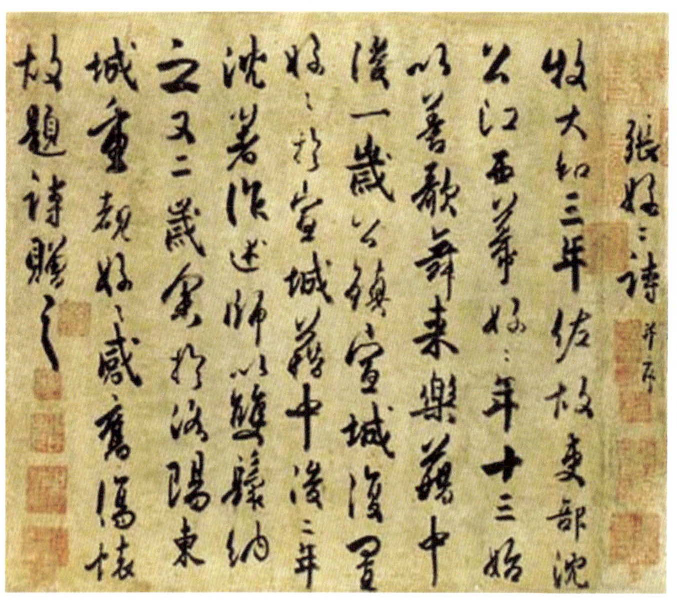

Poem about Zhang Haohao (张好好诗 *Zhang Hao Hao Shi*)

Du Mu 杜牧 (803-853, Tang dynasty)
Running script (*xing shu*)
28.2 cm × 162 cm
Palace Museum, Beijing

Many of the famous Tang poets were also accomplished calligraphers. It is a pity that few of their calligraphic works have survived. For this reason Du Mu's *Poem about Zhang Haohao* and He Zhizhang's *"Classic of Filial Piety" Scroll* are all the more to be treasured. Du Mu wrote this five-character ancient verse for the singer-courtesan Zhang Haohao, using her sad life story as a vehicle to express his "nostalgia and sad thoughts." His masculine, free flowing and charismatic calligraphy shows a sure grasp of the legacy of the Six dynasties, and is in perfect harmony with the poetic content.

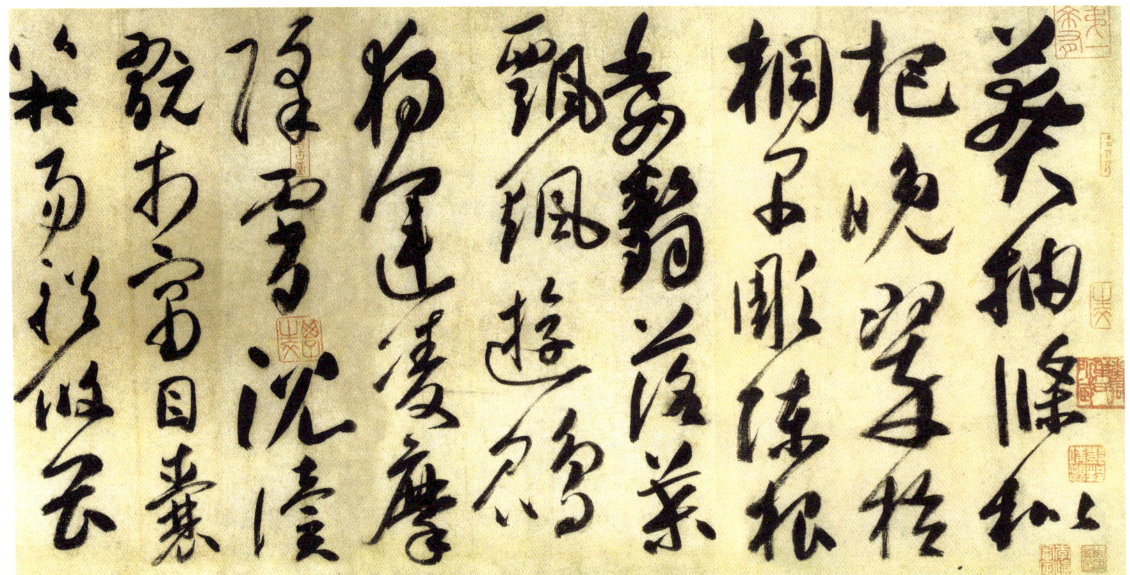

Thousand Character Reader (千字文 *Qian Zi Wen*)

Gao Xian 高闲 (years of birth/death unknown, Tang dynasty)
Cursive script (*cao shu*)
30.8 cm × 331.3 cm
Shanghai Museum

Like Huai Su, Gao Xian was a monk. In contemporary cursive script calligraphy, Wang Xizhi pioneered a style where the characters were unlinked; Zhang Xu and Huai Su abandoned that principle and formed the mad cursive script style where the characters were strung together in a mad gallop. In Gao Xian's *Thousand Character Reader* in cursive script, he combines the styles in a seamless manner; his forceful strokes throb with life and energy, producing a cathartic esthetic effect.

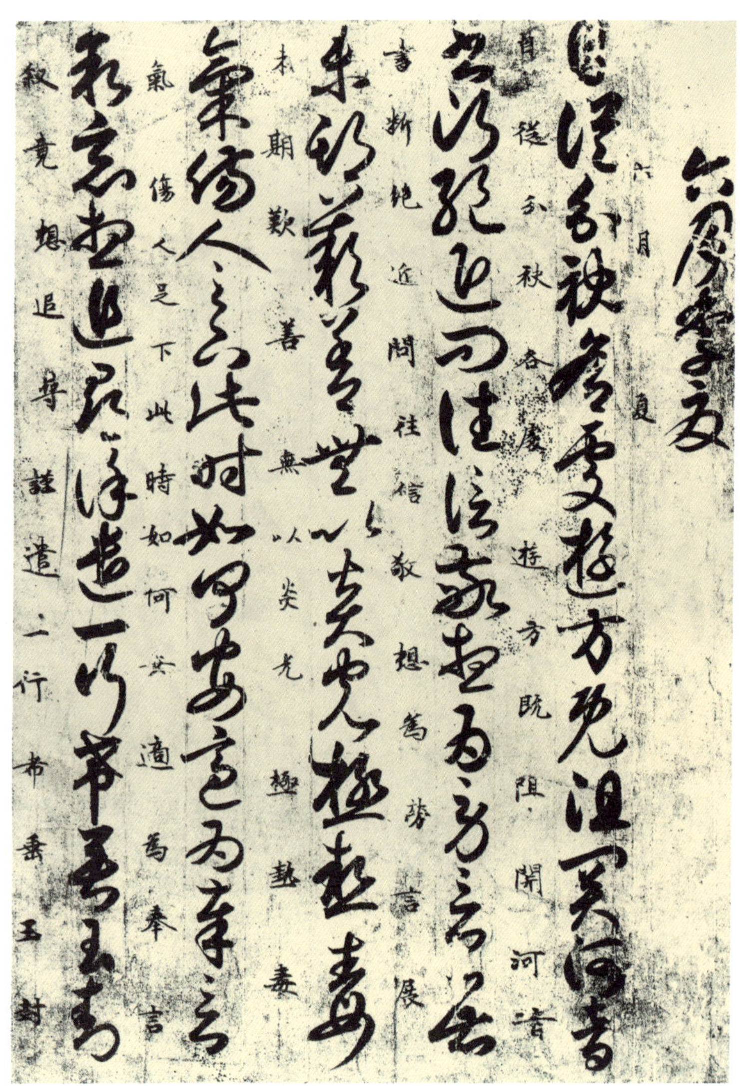

Greetings among Friends (唐人月仪帖 *Tang Ren Yue Yi Tie*)

Unknown calligrapher, Tang dynasty
Cursive script (*cao shu*) for the larger characters; regular script (*kai shu*) for the smaller ones
Palace Museum, Taipei

The brushwork, character structure and spatial composition in *Greetings among Friends* do full justice to the spirit of the "Two Wangs." The main text, although written in cursive script, appears self-assured, graceful and elegant, presenting a pleasing, coherent whole. The small-character explanatory text between the main columns is also exquisitely rendered. Later calligraphers made an enlarged version of the explanatory text as a model to emulate.

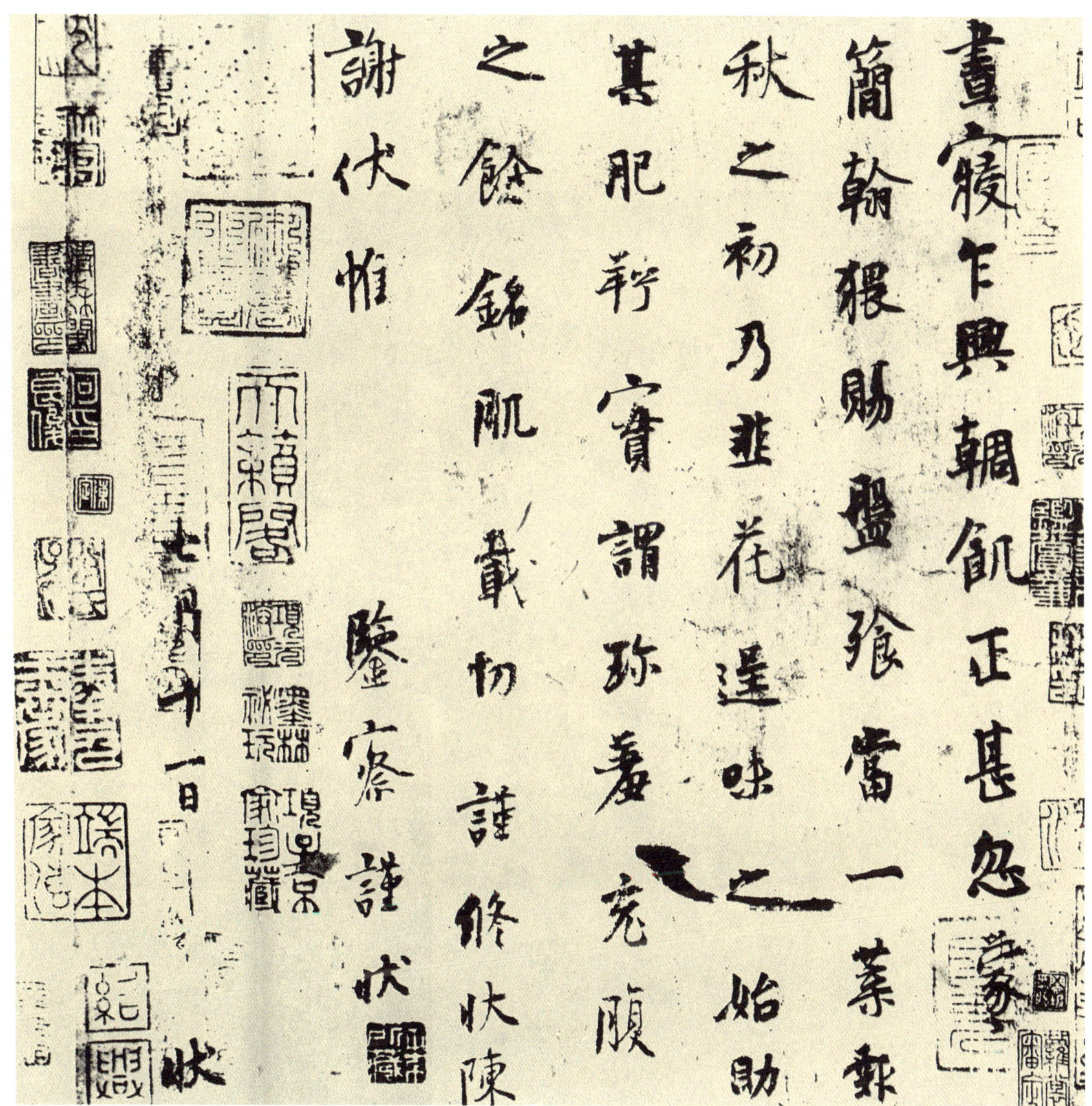

A Gift of Chives (韭花帖 *Jiu Hua Tie*)

Yang Ningshi 杨凝式 (873-954, Five dynasties)
Running regular script (*xing kai*)
26 cm × 28 cm
Lan Qian Shan Museum of Taiwan; Office of Culture of the Municipality of Wuxi

The brushwork in this piece is characterized by energy and reserve, conciseness and neatness. Some critics even go so far as to argue that in its use of the brush and verve, this work is superior to *Orchid Pavilion Preface*. Structurally, *A Gift of Chives* expertly manages the writing space, creating an intriguing horizontal and vertical zigzag and, especially, lively, charming, intra-character spaces, for example, in characters like "寢", "翰", "實", "謂", "差" and " 察 ", spaces "so open that a horse can trot through them or so dense light cannot pass through." The spatial composition in this work is also very distinctive, with widened distances between characters and columns. In some places the blank space between two consecutive characters can be as wide as a character, a rare occurrence in calligraphic works before his time. This innovation was praised by later critics.

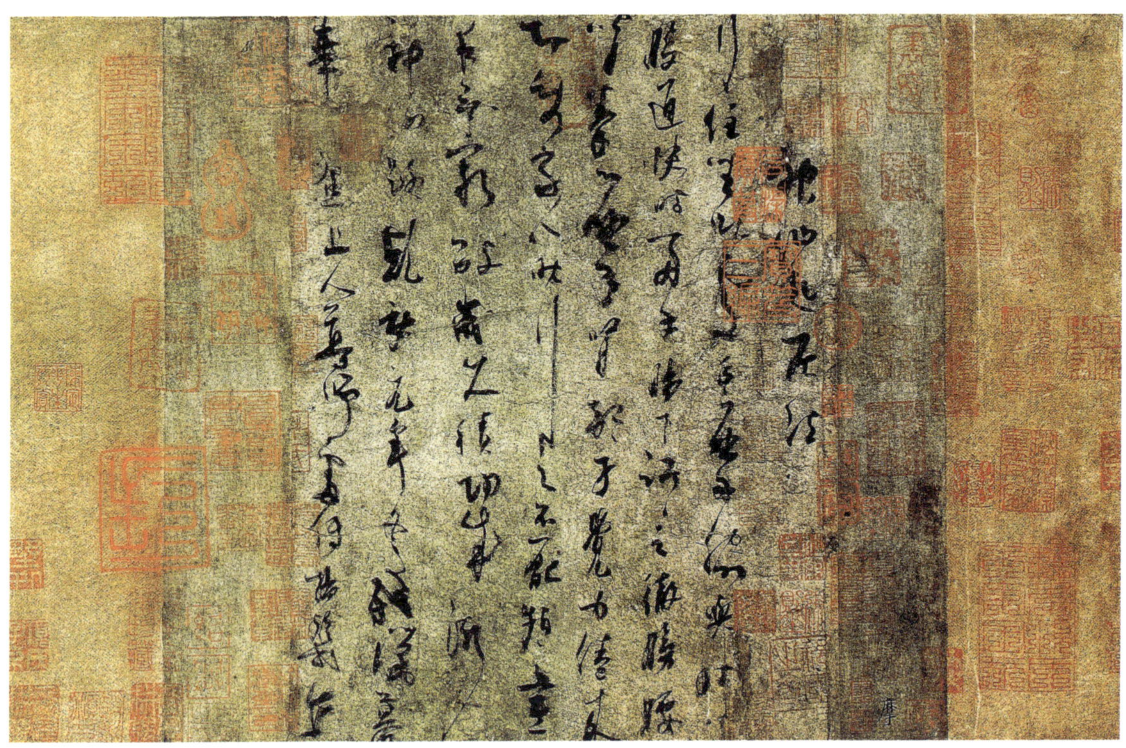

The Practical Way to Immortality (神仙起居法 *Shen Xian Qi Ju Fa*)

Yang Ningshi 杨凝式 (873-954, Five dynasties)
Cursive script (*cao shu*)
27 cm × 21.2 cm
Palace Museum, Beijing

Musicality is a distinctive mark of Chinese calligraphy, particularly in the cursive script. This musicality is clearly demonstrated in Zhang Xu's cursive script style, with its clearly defined pauses and brush reversals and undulations, and in Huai Su's style, with its passionately flying, winding, cascading strokes. Yang Ningshi developed this musicality to its utmost in *The Practical Way to Immortality*, creating a distinctly personal, albeit somewhat nervous, musical rhythm by varying the thickness and length of lines, brush pressure and turning, shifting of the central axis of the columns left and right as a result of varied horizontal and vertical inclinations and the back-and-forth links between strokes.

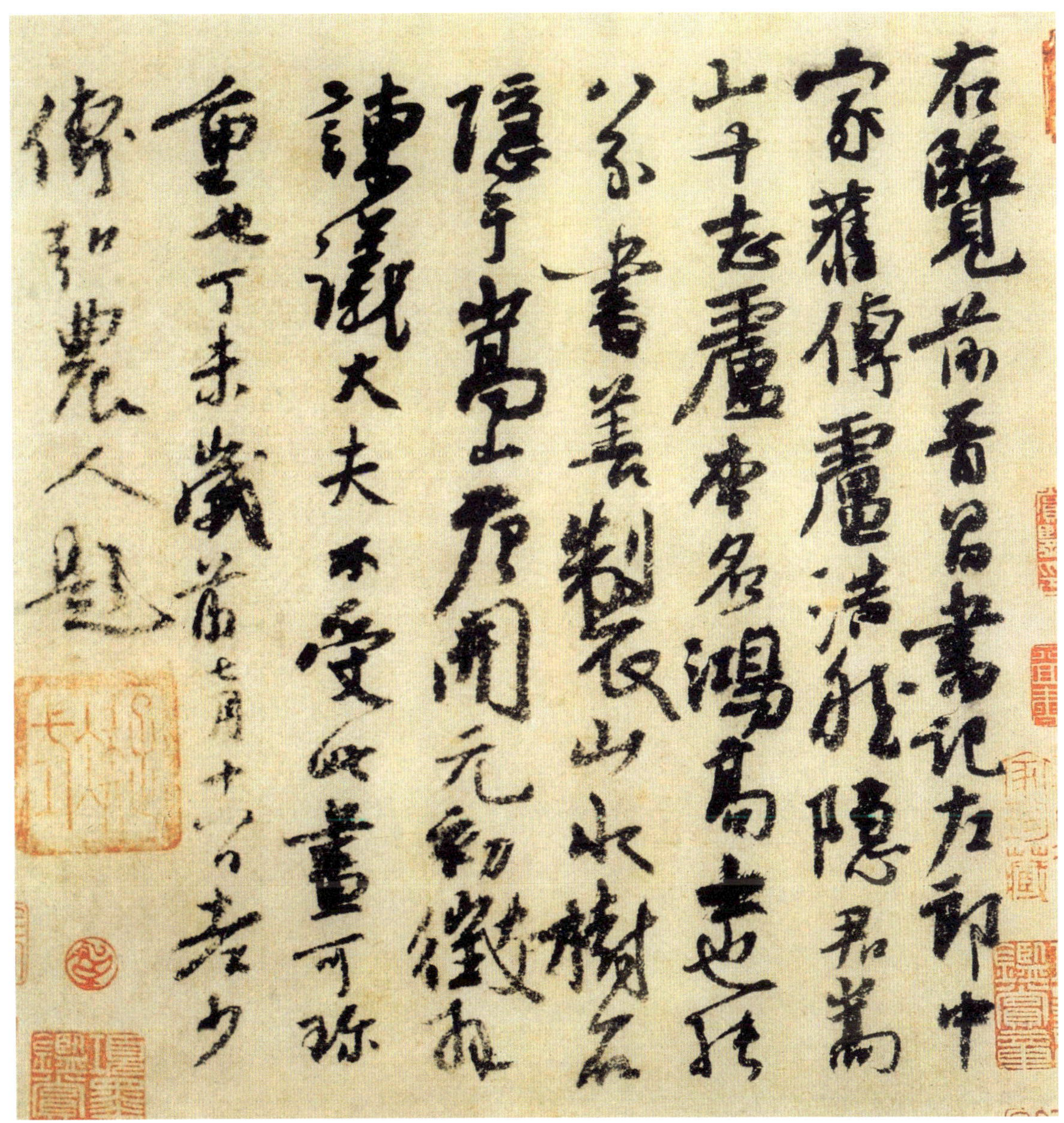

Colophon to Lu Hong's Painting of Ten Scenic Attractions around His Thatched Hut (卢鸿草堂十志图跋 *Lu Hong Cao Tang Shi Zhi Tu Ba*)

Yang Ningshi 杨凝式 (873-954, Five dynasties)
Running script (*xing shu*)
Palace Museum, Taipei

A septuagenarian Yang Ningshi wrote this colophon for the famed Tang painter Lu Hong's painting of *Ten Scenic Attractions around His Thatched Hut*. The exceptionally fine calligraphy looks as ancient as Yang, who was in his seventies when he wrote it. The entire piece is densely populated by lively characters without losing composure and clarity. The variations in character inclinations do not detract from the solid, stately elegance of the characters. Behind the serene, rounded and supple brushwork lies a majestic, vigorous spirit. Later critics have rightly considered the calligraphy in this piece comparable in artistic merit to Yan Zhenqing's running script.

Song Dynasty

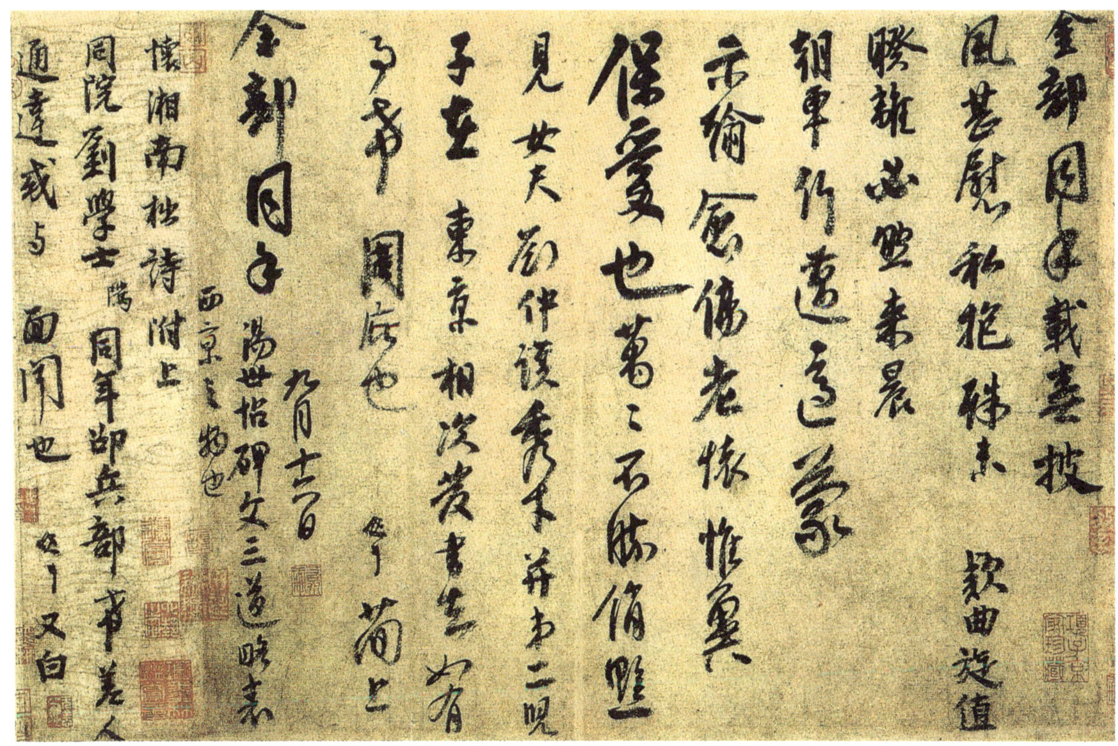

Letter to Colleague in the Department of Treasury (同年帖 *Tong Nian Tie*)

Li Jianzhong 李建中 (945-1013, Song dynasty)
Running script (*xing shu*)
33 cm × 51 cm
Palace Museum, Beijing

The calligraphy in this piece, unsophisticated but graceful despite a clumsy appearance, dense but fluid, with a mellow charm fortified by an inner strength, was described by Huang Tingjian as "plump yet free of excess fleshiness, like a chubby lady that radiates a delicate beauty." This work already suggests the beginnings of a transition from the thick, round calligraphic style of the Tang dynasty to the clean, vigorous style of the Song dynasty.

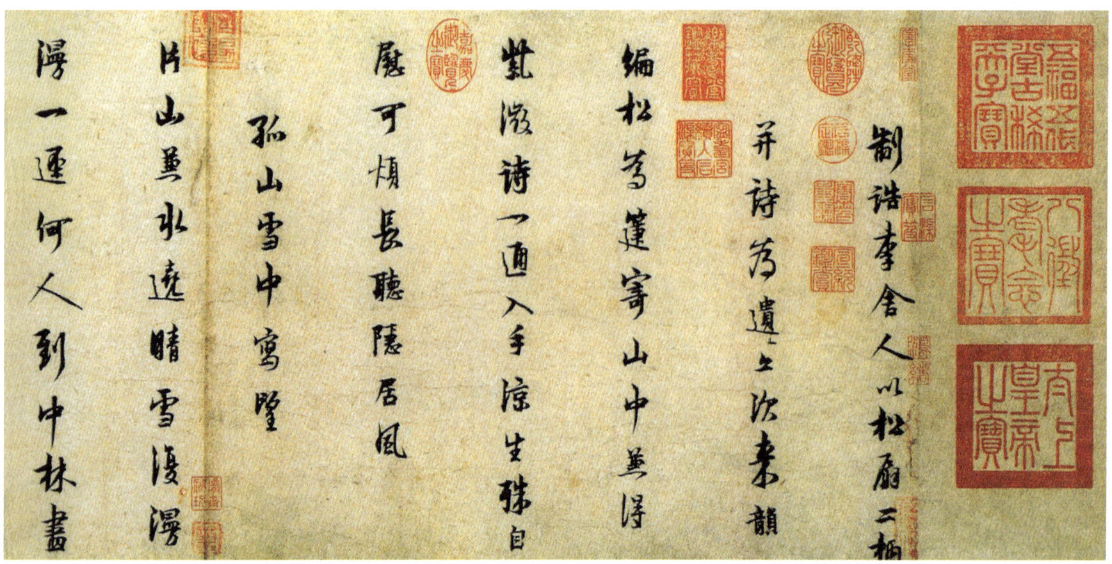

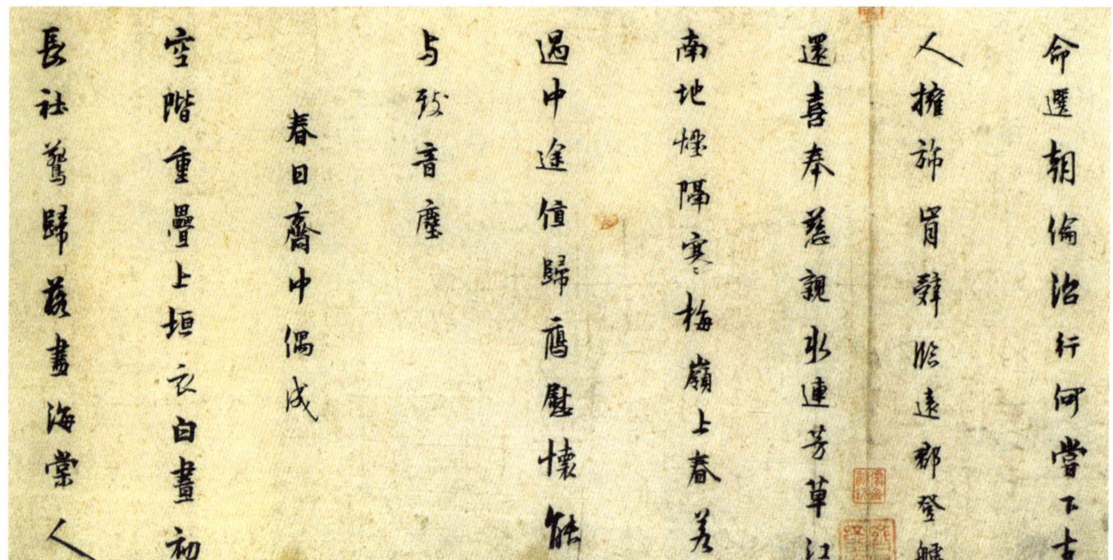

Note of Poems Composed and Calligraphed by the Author (自书诗帖 *Zi Shu Shi Tie*)

Lin Bu 林逋 (967–1029, Song dynasty)
Running script (*xing shu*)
32 cm × 302.6 cm
Palace Museum, Beijing

Lin Bu was uninterested in fame or fortune and maintained his celibacy to the end. He grew plum trees and raised cranes instead of children, and liked to say he had plum trees for a wife and cranes for children. *Note of Poems Composed and Calligraphed by the Author* has a spacious look; the wide spaces between characters and between columns create an aura of spiritual freedom and detachment that recalls his famous verse line "dappled shadows cast across a clear shallow creek, an unknown fragrance wafting through the moonlit twilight."

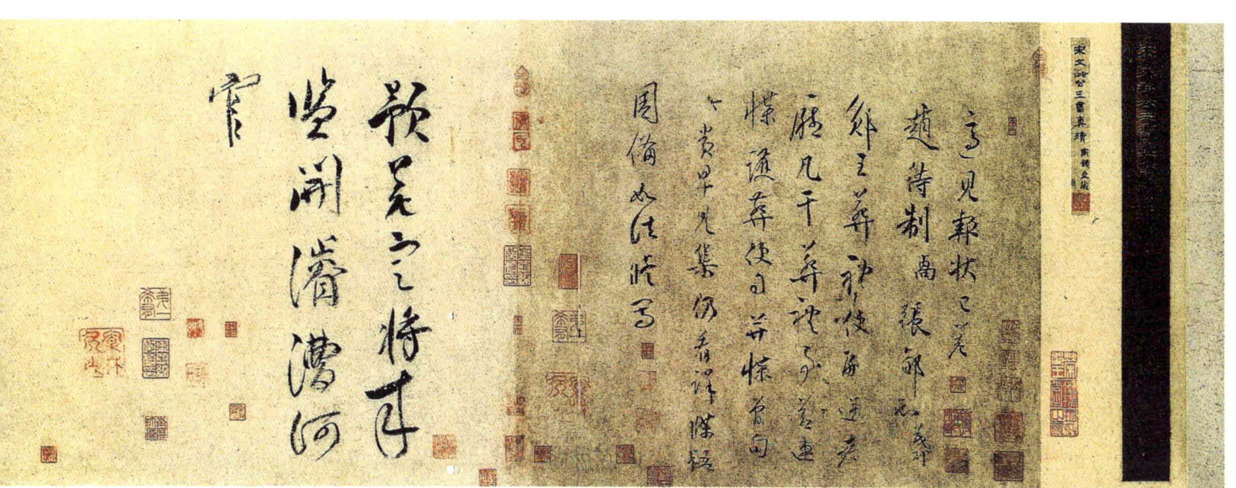

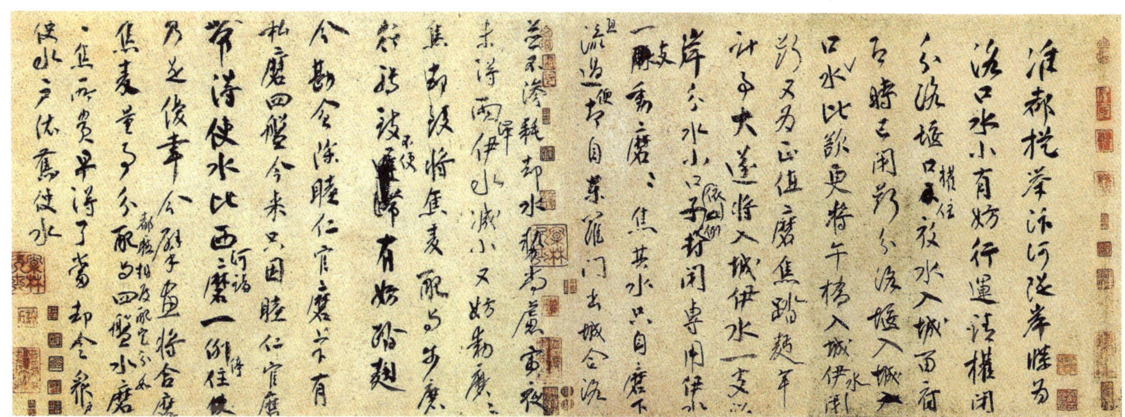

Note of Running Cursive Script (行草札 *Xing Cao Zha*)

Wen Yanbo 文彦博 (1006-1097, Song dynasty)
Running cursive script (*xing cao*)
43.6 cm × 223 cm
Palace Museum, Beijing

Wen Yanbo used a drier-than-usual brush in this piece. The calligraphy is sharp and refined in the first part, untrammeled in the second part, with open, dynamic character postures and square, sharp corners, displaying a natural charm. In the third part, the writing appears to become more casual, with larger variations in brush pressure, leading the viewer to wonder if the calligrapher's attention has strayed from the writing at hand. Since this was a draft, numerous corrections were made.

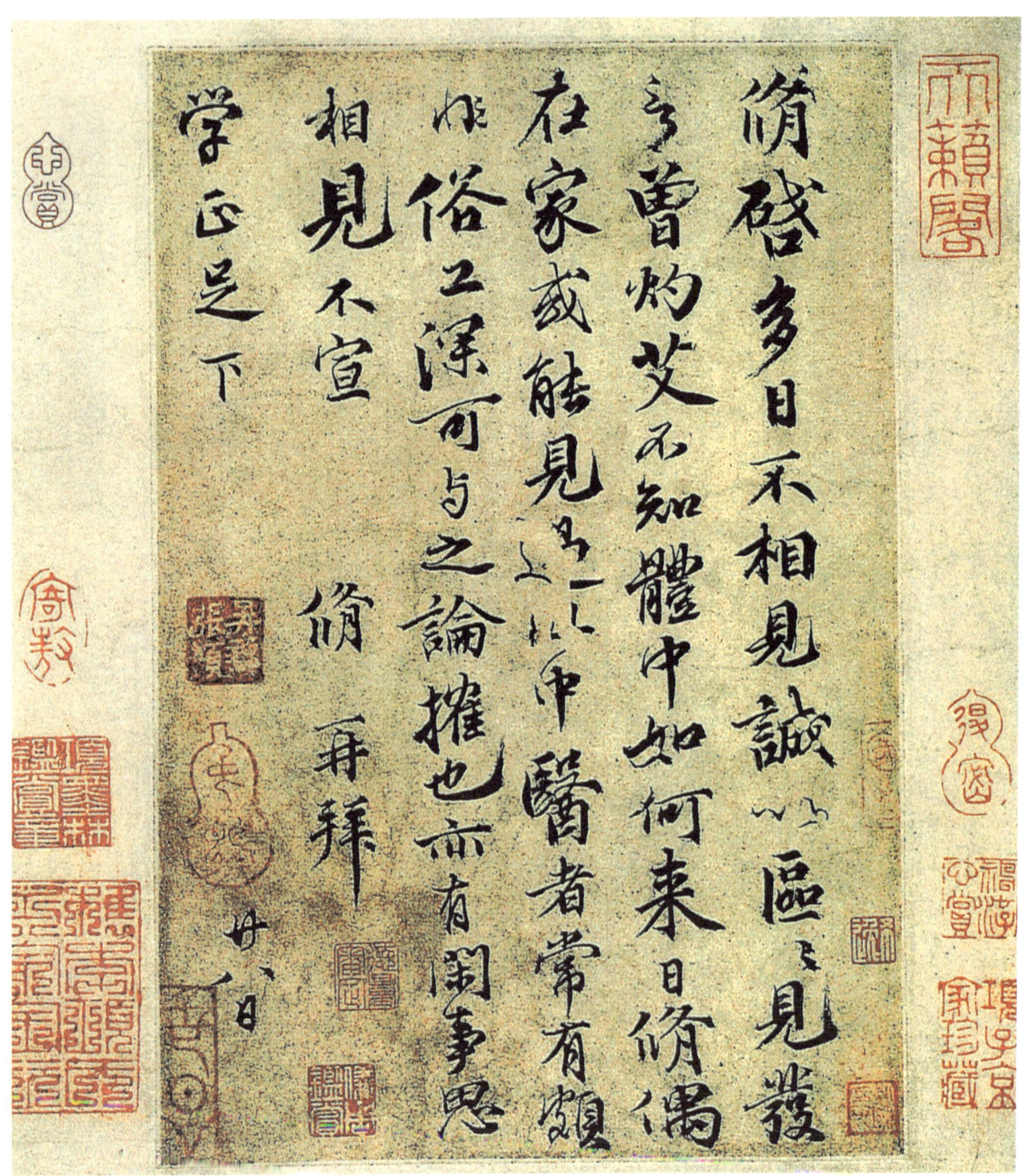

Letter on a Matter of Moxibustion (灼艾帖 *Zhuo Ai Tie*)

Ouyang Xiu 欧阳修 (1007-1072, Song dynasty)
Running script (*xing shu*)
25 cm × 18 cm
Palace Museum, Beijing

Ouyang Xiu was a great essayist of his time. As a calligrapher, he wrote with an energetic hand and created an individualistic style with his refreshingly pleasing character forms. This piece is clearly influenced by the calligraphic greats Ouyang Xun and Yan Zhenqing of the Tang dynasty: the structure of the characters exhibits the broadness of the Yan style and the brushwork has the steepness and vigor of the style of Ouyang Xun. In the opinion of Su Shi 苏轼 (1037-1101, Song dynasty), this work "employs a sharpened brush-tip and dry ink to produce square, smooth characters that radiate a grace of great suavity."

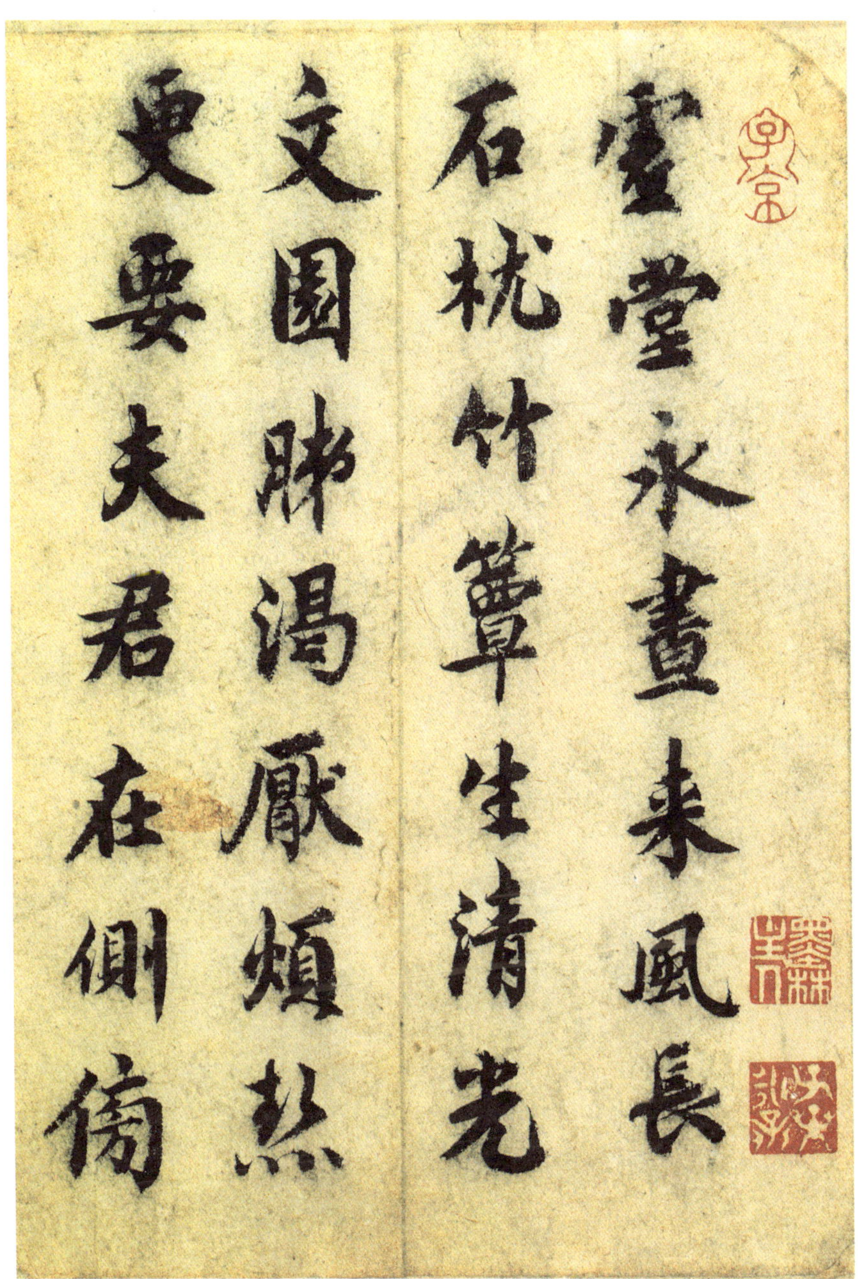

Note of a Poem (虚堂诗帖 *Xu Tang Shi Tie*)

Cai Xiang 蔡襄 (1012-1067, Song dynasty)
Regular script (*kai shu*)
22.6 cm × 16 cm

Cai Xiang was a renowned calligrapher in the Northern Song and was one of the "Four Great Masters of the Song dynasty," the other three being Su Shi, Huang Tingjian and Mi Fu. He wrote this piece when he was about 35 years of age and had not yet forged a distinct calligraphic style of his own. The structure of his characters is solid and heavy; the ideograms are executed with care and the strokes appear plump, clumsy and plodding as well as elastic, closely resembling the style of Yan Zhenqing.

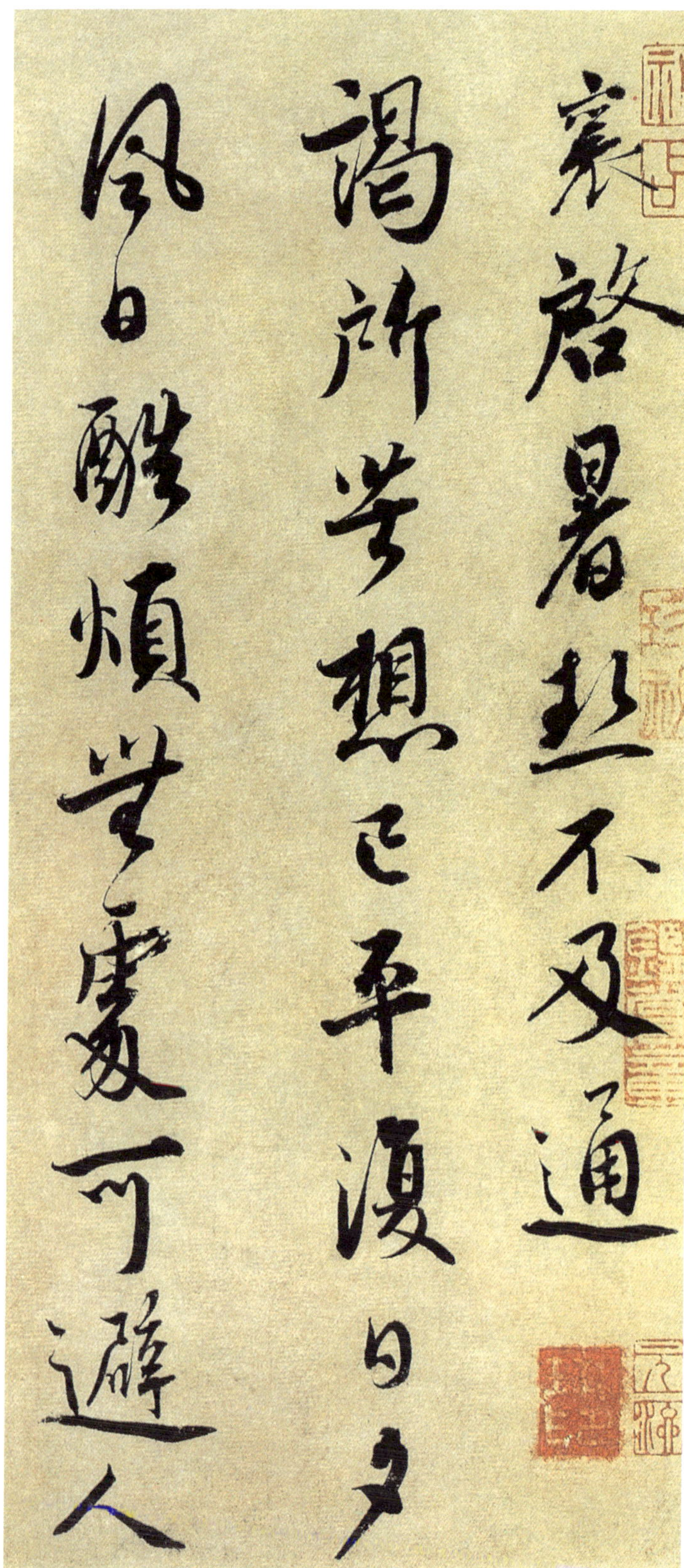

Letter about Tea (暑热帖 *Shu Re Tie*)

Cai Xiang 蔡襄 (1012–1067, Song dynasty)
Running script (*xing shu*)
23 cm × 29.2 cm

This piece is a good example of Cai Xiang's simple, vigorous and virile style. His running script calligraphy is characterized by a reserved elegance and a softness underpinned by a hard edge. Mi Fu aptly compared his calligraphy to "a young woman with a lithe and graceful carriage, all decked up in fine jewelry and flowers, taking a leisurely stroll."

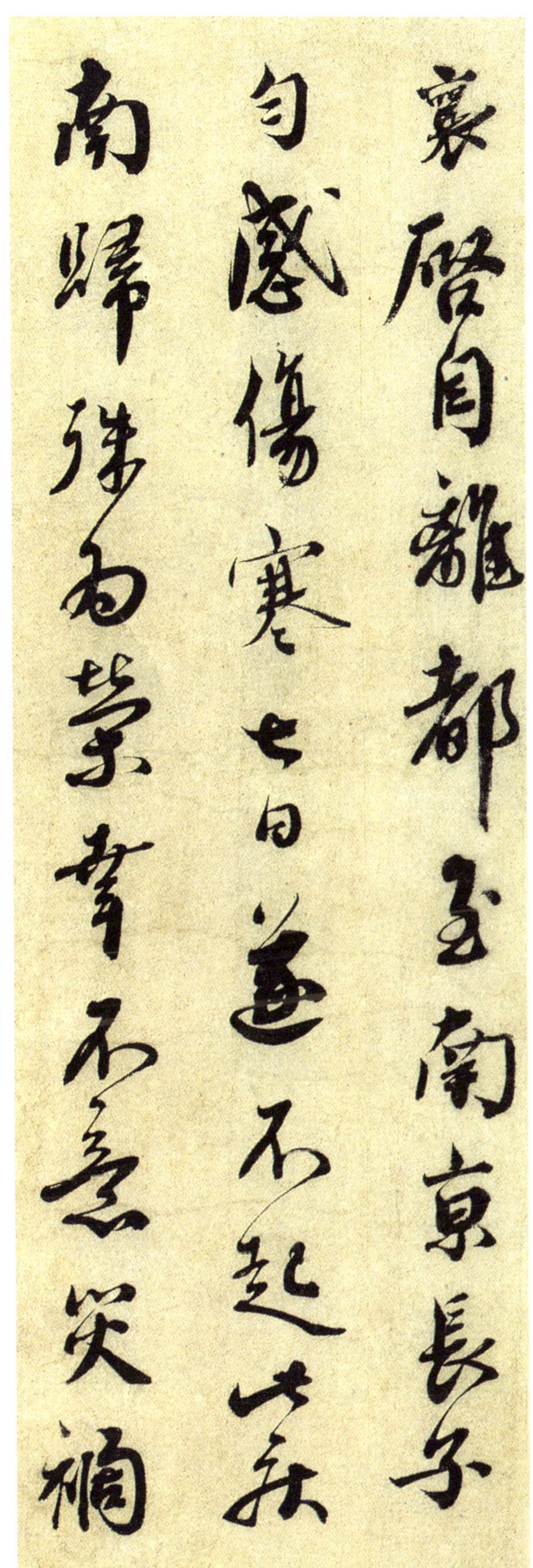

Letter to Appreciate Friend's Solicitude (离都帖 *Li Du Tie*)

Cai Xiang 蔡襄 **(1012-1067, Song dynasty)**
Running script (*xing shu*)
29.2 cm × 46.8 cm

The style of Cai Xiang mellowed in his old age and showed a muted elegance. Viewing the calligraphy of his later years is like drinking well aged wine with a long lingering aftertaste; he gives a lot of thought to fine details, especially when starting a stroke. Su Shi offered this unqualified praise for Cai Xiang, "He is not only gifted but also erudite. The perfect coordination between his hand and his mind helps produce a richly varied calligraphy. He is therefore arguably the best of our time."

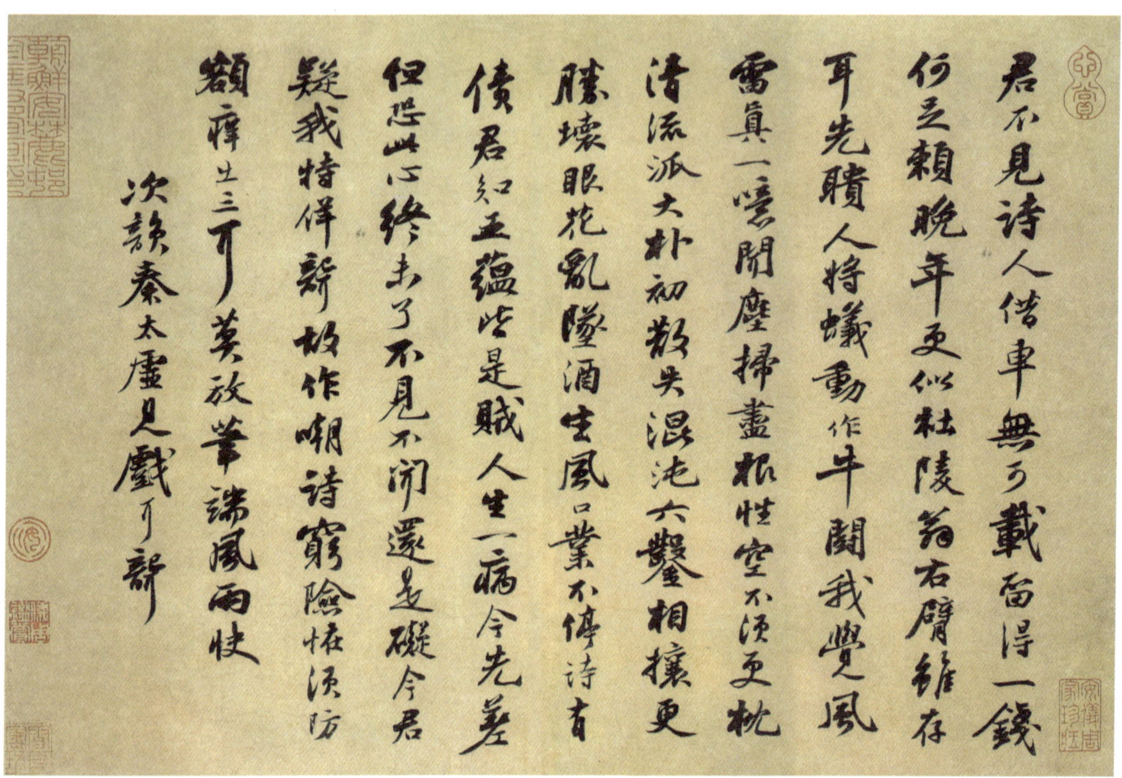

Poem about Deafness (次韵秦太虚诗帖 *Ci Yun Qin Tai Xu Shi Tie*)

Su Shi 苏轼 (1037-1101, Song dynasty)
Running script (*xing shu*)
30.7 cm × 45.3 cm

Su Shi's versatile talents earned him deserved acclaim in the fields of verse, literature, calligraphy and painting. In calligraphy, he did not take the beaten path but struck out on his own to create a new style attuned to the ethos of the Song dynasty, in which the expressive quality of calligraphy was highly valued. He may have described calligraphy as a "play with ink," but, as Huang Tingjian aptly put it, "his erudition and literary verve that shine through ink and brush are what leave many others in the dust." True to his style, the horizontal strokes in this piece by Su Shi are light and executed with the center-brush method, and the verticals are heavy and written with the side-brush method.

In Memory of Huang Jidao (祭黄几道文 *Ji Huang Ji Dao Wen*)

Su Shi 苏轼 (1037–1101, Song dynasty)
Regular script (*kai shu*)
31.6 cm × 121.7 cm
Shanghai Museum

In this piece, Su Shi is not enslaved to the center-brush technique. There is a great deal of wrist flipping in his brushwork, which is peppered with side-brush touches. The regular script writing interspersed with running script characters appears all the more supple, dignified, simple and without artifice. The left and right diagonal strokes are ended with conspicuous "swallow tails," which seem to add graceful wings to the characters. The structure of the characters is squarish and squat, lower on the left and higher on the right, thus giving the characters an air of flying at a banking angle.

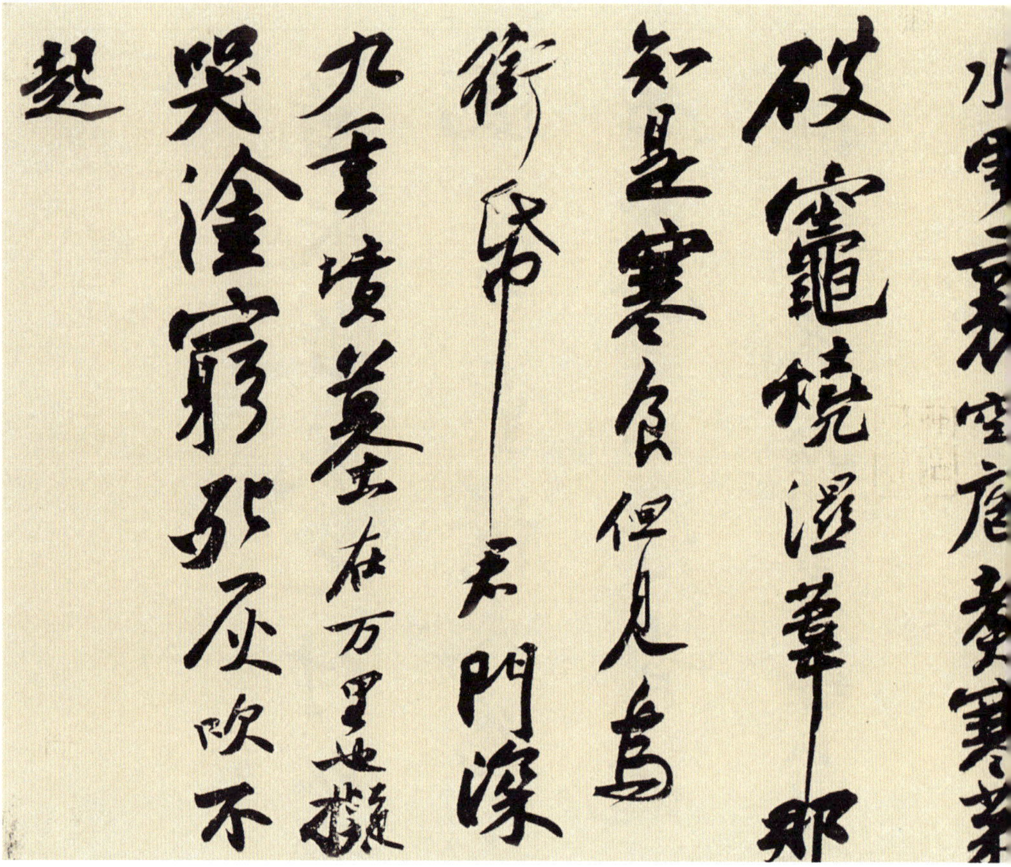

水雲裏空庖煮寒菜
破竈燒濕葦那
知是寒食但見烏
銜紙君門深
九重墳墓在万里也擬
哭塗窮死灰吹不
起

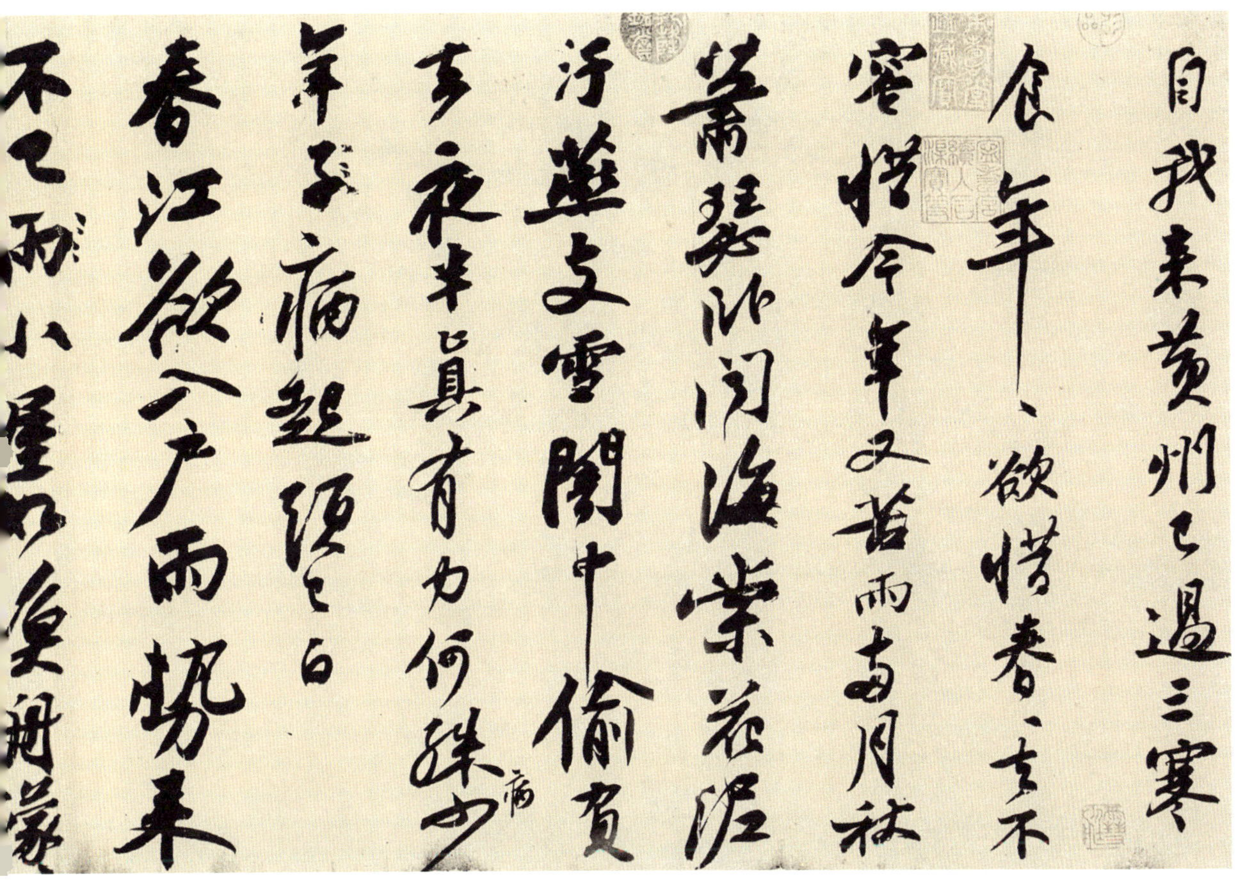

Poem to Express Melancholy after Demotion (黃州寒食诗卷 *Huang Zhou Han Shi Shi Juan*)

Su Shi 苏轼 (1037-1101, Song dynasty)
Running script (*xing shu*)
33.5 cm × 118 cm
Palace Museum, Taipei

Poem to Express Melancholy after Demotion is a draft of a poem in five-character meter written by Su Shi after being demoted and posted to remote Huangzhou prefecture. The characters in the first three to five columns are supple and dignified, as if in a leisurely, intimate chat; as passion seizes the author, the ideograms increase in size, the strokes become thicker, and the spatial composition shifts and fluctuates. In the last few lines, the author seems to be carried away, writing furiously: the characters " 破灶 " and " 涂穷 " are shockingly large and the ideograms " 湿苇 " and " 衔纸 " end with a long trailing tail, mirroring his anger and unhappiness. This impromptu piece of verse composed and calligraphed on the spur of the moment perfectly encapsulates Su Shi's esthetic observation that "a work that does not set out to be a great piece often has a better chance of becoming one." Xianyu Shu, a critic of the Yuan dynasty, characterized this work as the "Third Masterpiece of Running Script Calligraphy" after Wang Xizhi's *Orchid Pavilion Preface* and Yan Zhenqing's *Draft Eulogy for a Nephew*.

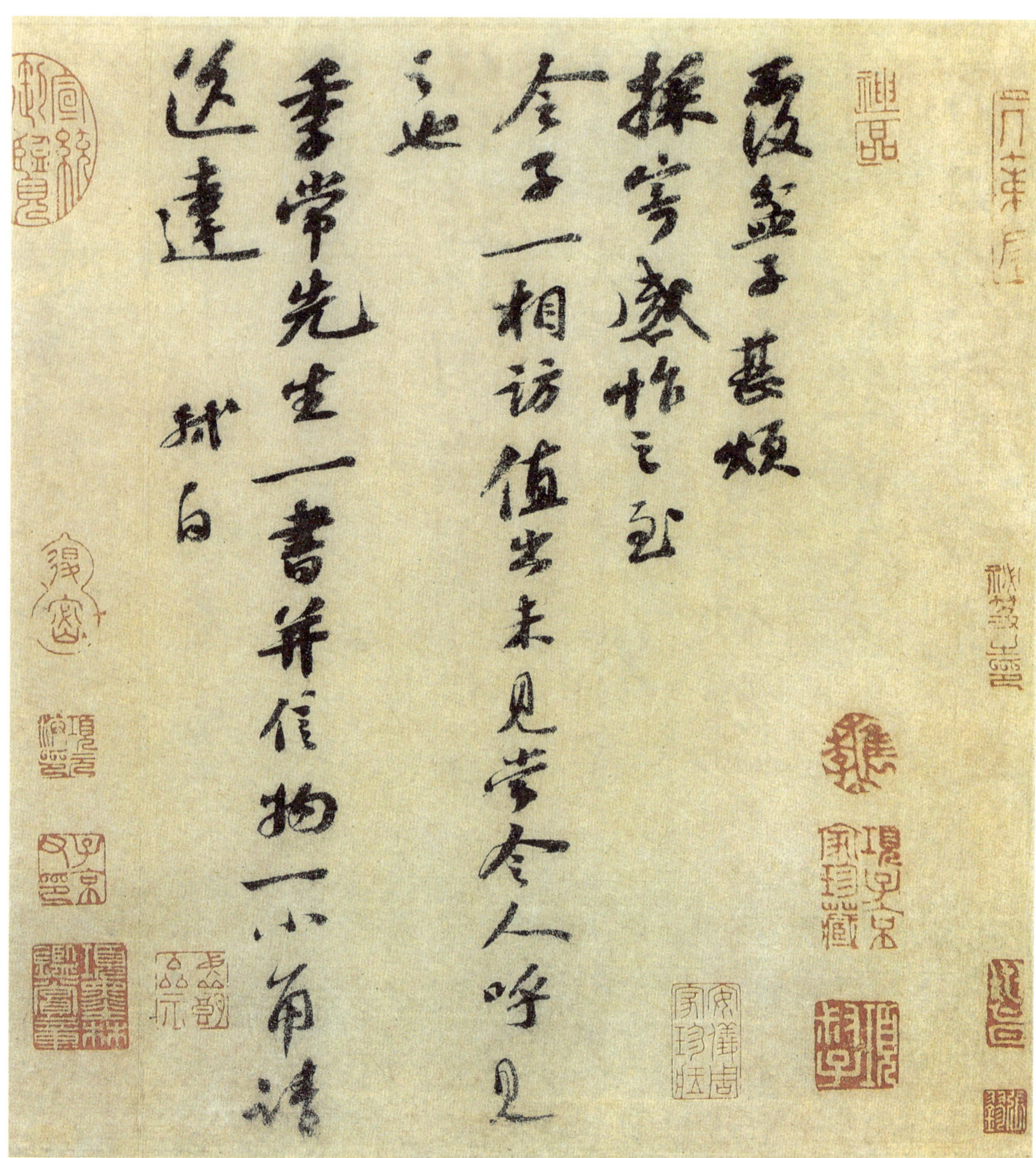

Picking Raspberry (覆盆子帖 *Fu Pen Zi Tie*)

Su Shi 苏轼 (1037-1101, Song dynasty)
Running script (*xing shu*)
27.7 cm × 44.8 cm

Though only a casual note, *Picking Raspberry* is a joy to look at. Su Shi liked to say, "My calligraphic ideas do not obey any rules; I let my brush form the strokes freely and spontaneously without any forethought." The fact is that he had assiduously copied and emulated the calligraphies of great masters like Zhong You, Wang Xizhi, Wang Sengqian, Yan Zhenqing, Liu Gongquan, Xu Hao, Li Yong and Yang Ningshi. This enthusiasm lasted well into his old age. Therefore, even if he claimed to obey no rules, he was solidly grounded in all the rules and codes of calligraphy.

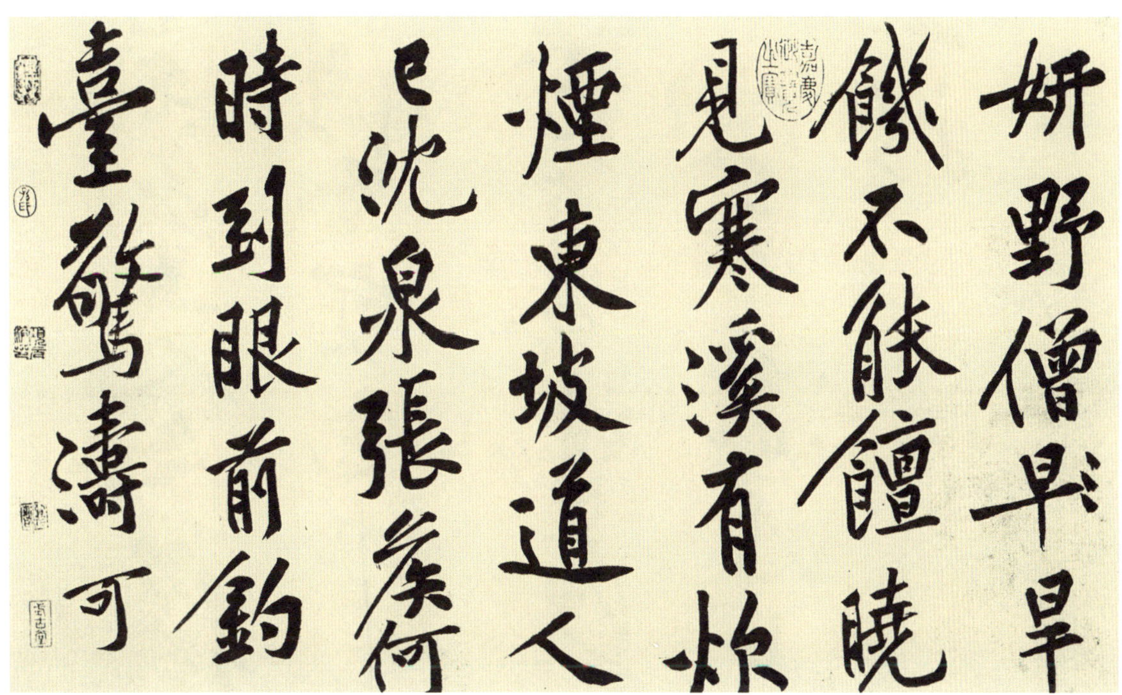

Pine Pavilion (松风阁诗 *Song Feng Ge Shi*)

Huang Tingjian 黄庭坚 (1045-1105, Song dynasty)
Running script (*xing shu*)
Palace Museum, Taipei

In the Song ethos, the expressive quality of calligraphy was highly regarded and the free expression of artistic personality was given greater weight than in previous eras. Huang Tingjian was among the most creative of the calligraphers of the time. One of the major characteristics of his works is the freedom of his strokes and the liberation of his calligraphy from the traditional verticality. Another is the undulating quality of the midstream movement in the strokes resulting from continuous alternation between lifting and pressing of the brush, which imparts a distinctive rhythm to his writing. In Huang Tingjian's own words, his calligraphy has "the eye in the verse" of Zen philosophy.

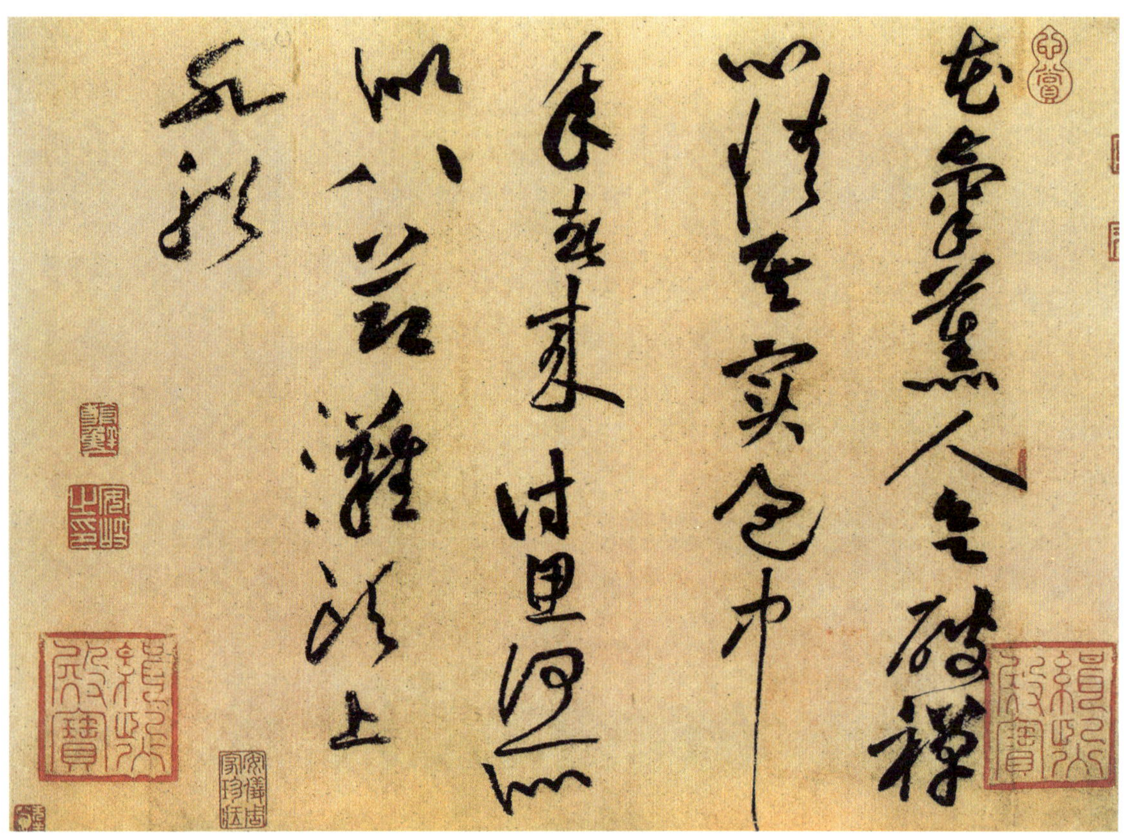

Flower Fragrance (花气诗帖 *Hua Qi Shi Tie*)

Huang Tingjian 黄庭坚 (1045-1105, Song dynasty)
Cursive script (*cao shu*)
30.7 cm × 43.2 cm

Huang Tingjian was proud of his cursive hand and believed that, over the centuries, only Zhang Xu, Huai Su and himself had really mastered the art of cursive writing. His great achievement in cursive script has indeed been recognized by later generations. This piece is a quatrain in seven-character meter (七绝 *qi jue*) written in five columns, totaling 28 ideograms. The first two columns are a mix between the running and the cursive scripts. Starting from the third column, the writing turns to free style and becomes heedless of the codes. The result is a work with an unaffected charm.

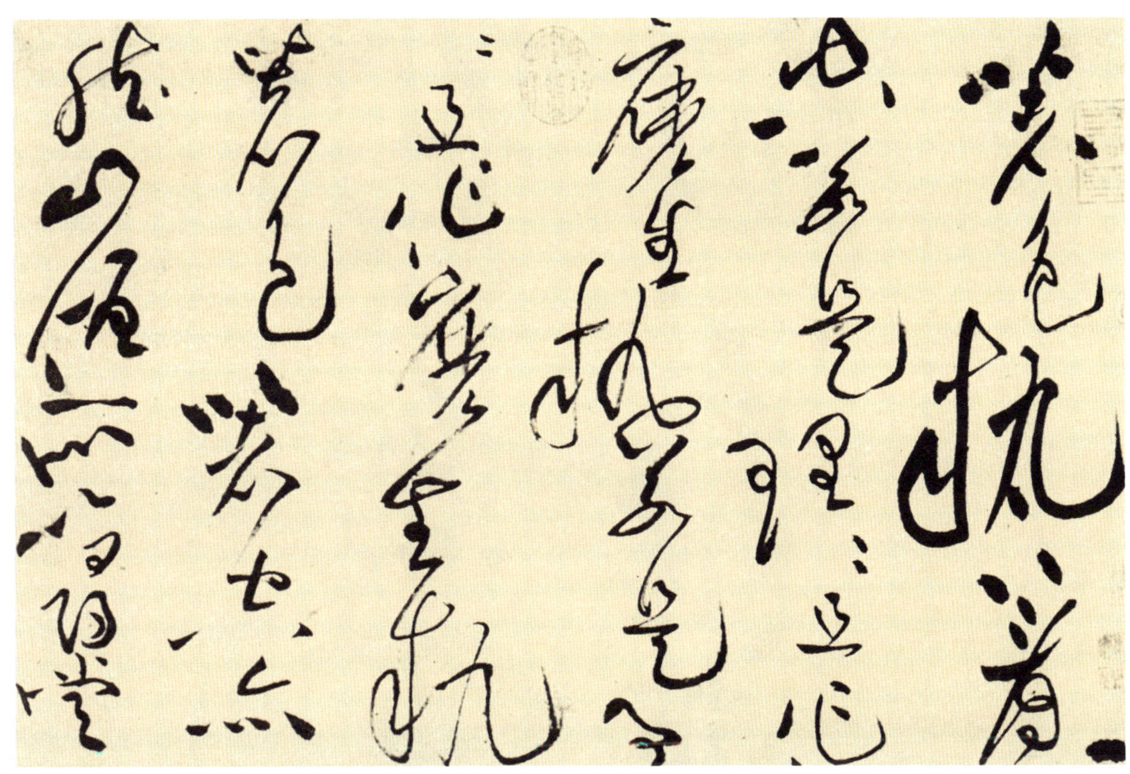

Speech of Monks with High Moral Integrity (诸上座帖 *Zhu Shang Zuo Tie*)

Huang Tingjian 黄庭坚 (1045-1105, Song dynasty)
Cursive script (*cao shu*)

Speech of Monks with High Moral Integrity is an excellent example of Huang Tingjian's cursive script style. It was seemingly completed in one breathless motion, with the brush galloping like a dragon at one moment and slithering like a snake the next, tensing and relaxing at will, giving the characters a restrained energy. The variation in the size of the characters creates a strong rhythm, reminding one of the imagery of "pearls of varying sizes cascading into a jade bowl." Although this work is in large cursive script (大草 *da cao*), there is nothing coarse or uncouth about it, because the brushwork is serene and leisurely, undoubtedly reflecting the inner peace of the author.

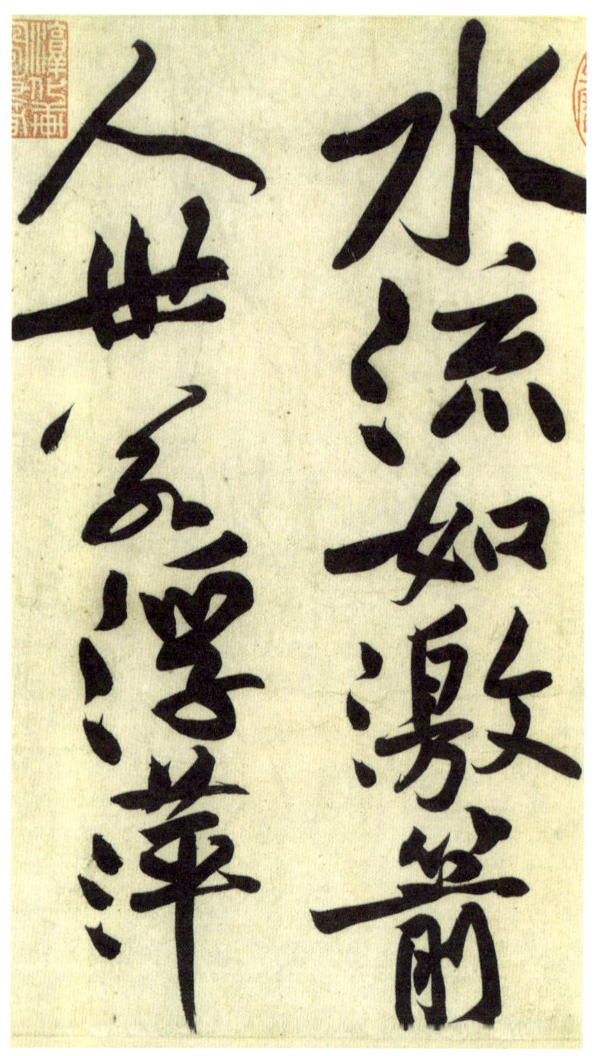

Poems of Han Shan and Pang Yun (寒山子庞居士诗 *Han Shan Zi Pang Ju Shi Shi*)

Huang Tingjian 黄庭坚 (1045-1105, Song dynasty)
Running script (*xing shu*)
29.1 cm × 213.8 cm
Palace Museum, Taipei

This panoramic running script piece is a work by Huang Tingjian in his old age. Its robust diagonals and the solid, bold strokes seeming to land spiraling down on the paper convey a sense of flight. The structure of the characters exhibiting daring variations in inclination and shape, the airy elegance and the use of the reversed brush-tip method (brush slanted and moved in the direction of the tip of the brush) are typical of Huang Tingjian's calligraphy.

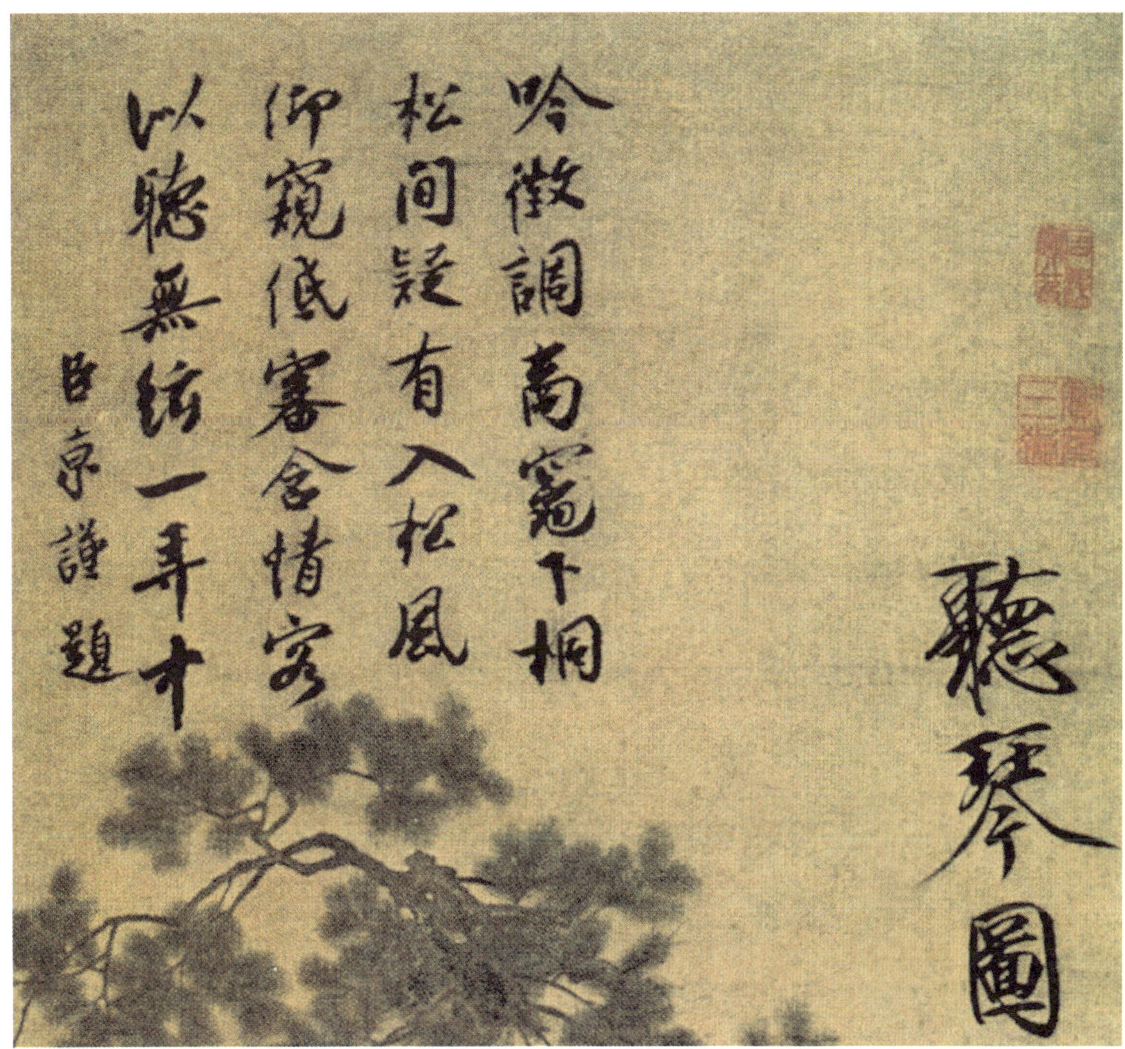

Poem on the Painting "Listening to the Zither" (听琴图题诗 *Ting Qin Tu Ti Shi*)

Cai Jing 蔡京 (1047-1126, Song dynasty)

There were two theories about the true identity of the "Cai" in the "Four Great Masters of the Song"—"Su, Huang, Mi, Cai." Some theorize it is Cai Xiang, others, Cai Jing. However, Cai Jing was a notoriously dishonest and scheming chief minister to Emperor Huizong of Song. Calligraphy historians, following the tradition of "denigrating the calligraphy of a disgraced person, regardless of its artistic merit", blackballed him in favor of Cai Xiang. This piece is a quatrain in seven-character meter written by Cai Jing as an inscription to Emperor Huizong's painting *Listening to the Zither*. The writing shows an elegant hand and a thorough grounding in the techniques of calligraphy.

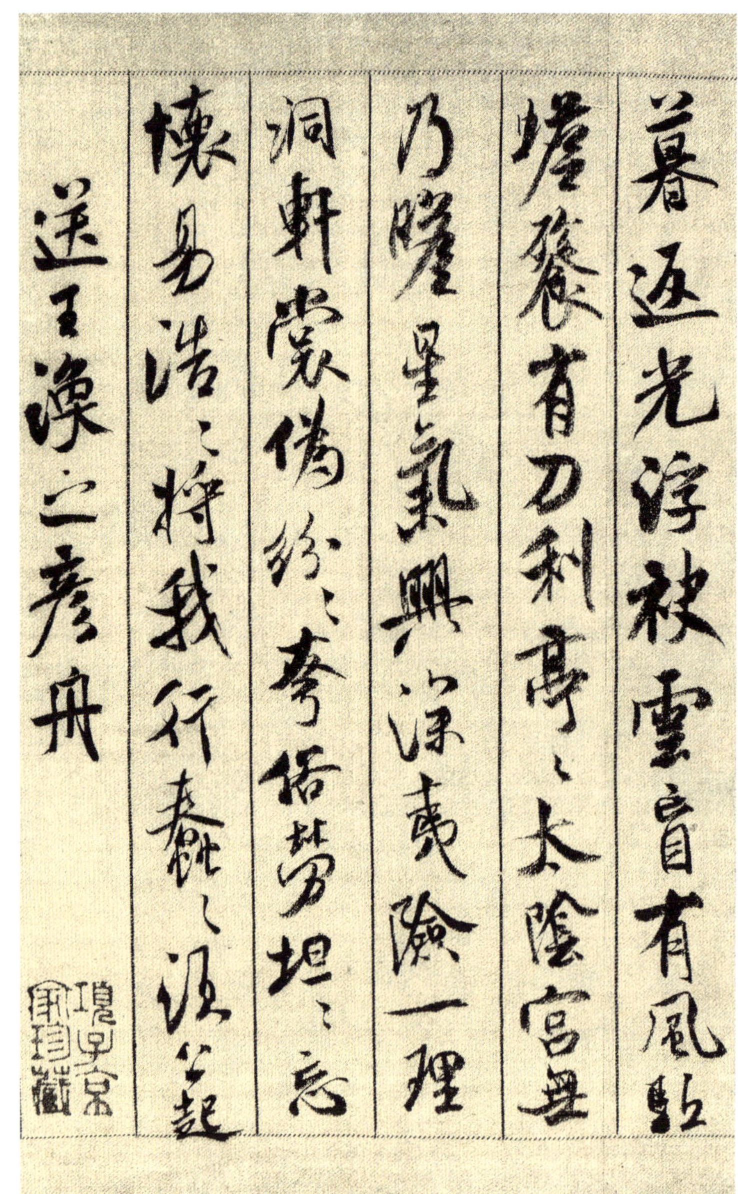

Poems Written on Sichuan Silk (蜀素帖 *Shu Su Tie*)

Mi Fu 米芾 (1051-1107, Song dynasty)

Mi Fu had an irreverent and wildly eccentric personality. Though serving in the Song government, he dressed in the Tang style. When he saw an uncommon rock that took his fancy, he would give obeisance to it and call it in all seriousness his "brother rock." His lunatic behavior earned him the nickname of "*Mi Dian*" or "the lunatic Mi." He forged his personal calligraphic style by emulating Wang Xizhi and Wang Xianzhi and assimilating the strengths of all masters before his time without discrimination. Su Shi praised his running cursive script style in these words, "It is like boats with wind in their sails and steeds riding into battle, robust and fleet. It has nothing to envy from the works of Zhong You or Wang Xizhi." Dong Qichang, a calligrapher of the Ming dynasty, aptly described this representative work of Mi Fu as "one of his best, to which he gave his all, like a lion going after an elephant."

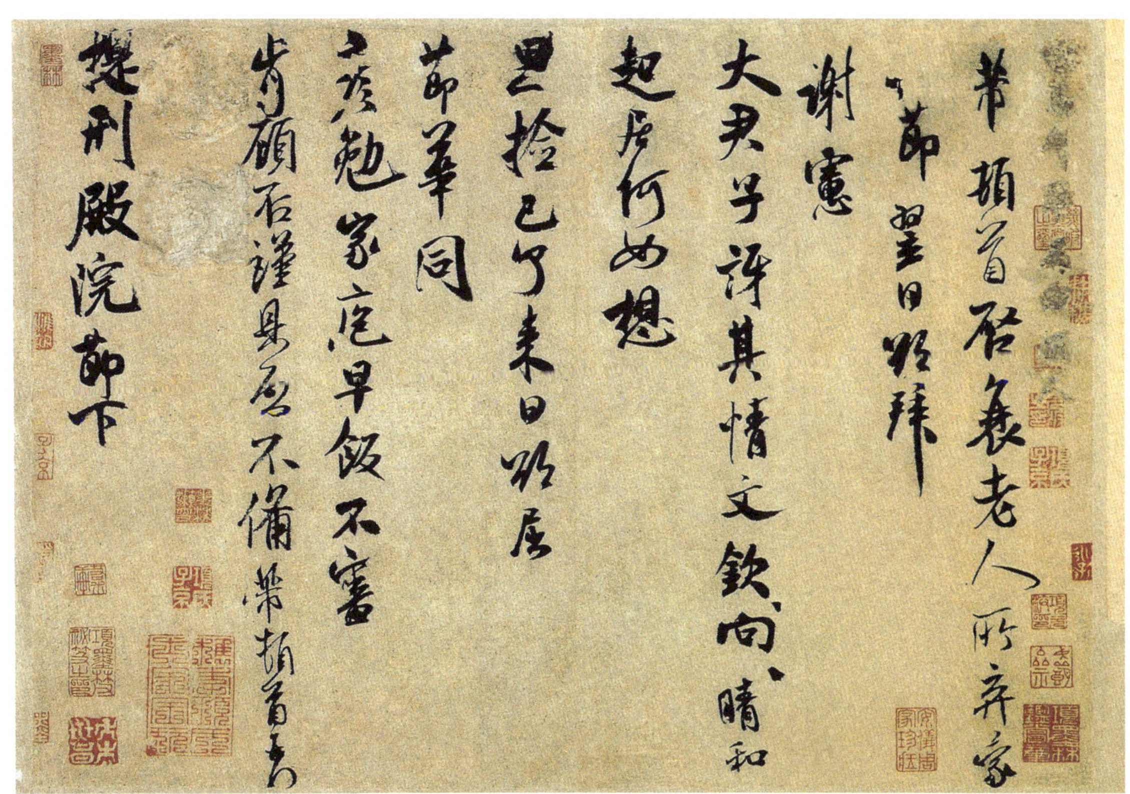

Frail Old Man (衰老帖 *Shuai Lao Tie*)

Mi Fu 米芾 (1051-1107, Song dynasty)
Running script (*xing shu*)
34.5 cm × 49.2 cm
Palace Museum, Beijing

Here the calligrapher was writing a letter without consciously setting out to create a work of art but the result was a wonderful piece vibrating with calligraphic interest. In *Frail Old Man*, Mi Fu wielded a powerful brush, with enough energy to "pierce the paper." The fine strokes brim with the energy of a swift moving dragon, thin but showing no traces of boniness; the plump strokes make graceful turns and do not give an impression of fatness.

菱謳纔會圭鱸堆峯
圖金橋瀾洲水宮無限
景載與謝公遊
半歲依脩竹，時看好
花懶傾惠泉酒點盡

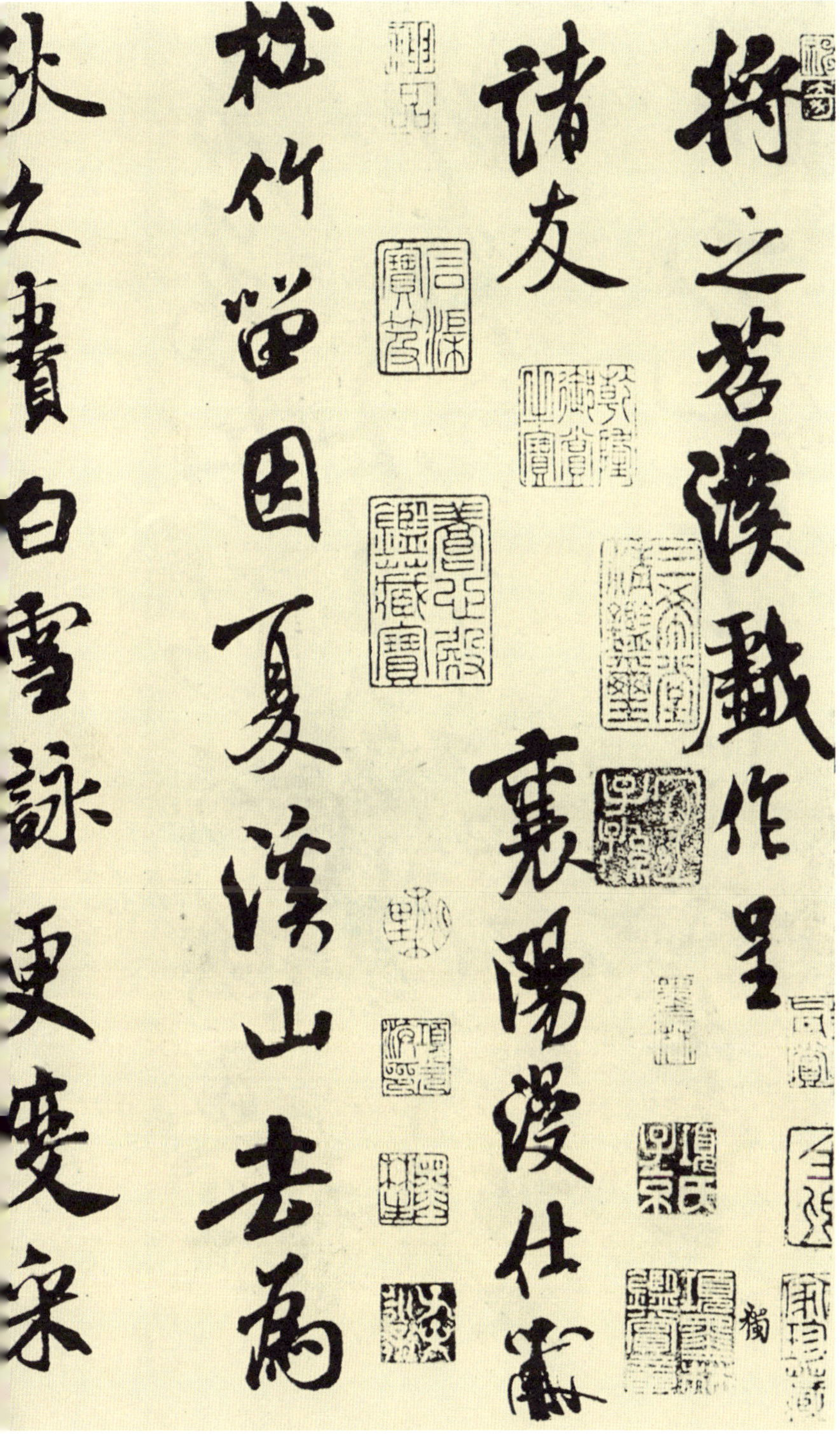

Poems to Share with Friends before Leaving for Tiaoxi (苕溪帖 *Tiao Xi Tie*)

Mi Fu 米芾 (1051-1107, Song dynasty)
Palace Museum, Beijing

Mi Fu's swift brushwork demonstrates an ability to use "all eight facets" of the brush, landing the brush-tip on the paper in a variety of ways. He described his style as "brushing," not merely "writing," the characters. His works generally exhibit a robust energy, alternation between wet and dry ink tones, and a powerful momentum that evokes the image of "a celestial steed streaking across the sky." The inclination of the character structure and varied character size impart a charming naiveté and whimsy to the piece. *Poems to Share with Friends before Leaving for Tiaoxi* is a proud work of Mi Fu in his middle years.

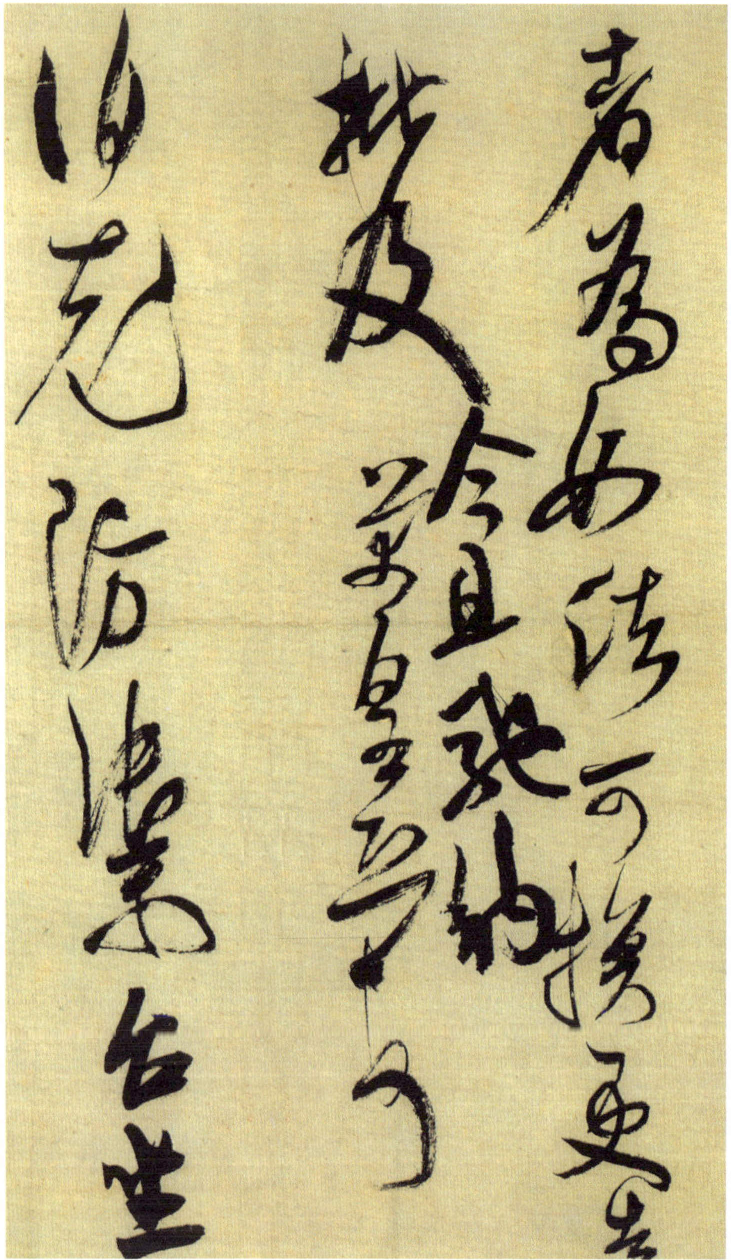

Letter to Bo Chong Inquiring about a Decision Made by the Court (值雨帖 *Zhi Yu Tie*)

Mi Fu 米芾 (1051-1107, Song dynasty)
Running script (*xing shu*)
25.6 cm × 38.6 cm

Running script is a forte of Mi Fu, but his brush strokes are grounded in his regular script. This has enabled him to let his spirit move the brush as it pleases. In character structure, he abandons the conventional requirements of stability, levelness and equilibrium in favor of "stability without losing originality, daring without being outlandish, age without drying up and plumpness without being fat."

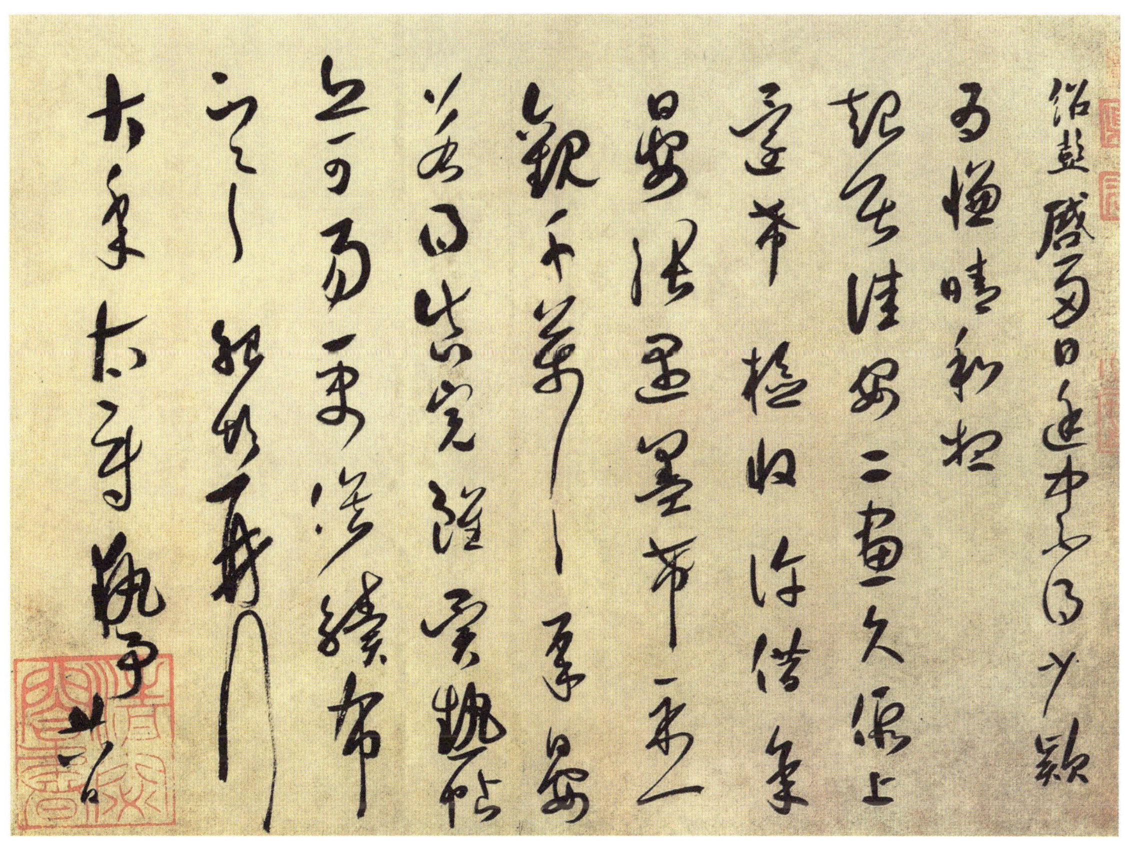

Letter to Friend about the Exchange of Precious Objects (*大年帖 Da Nian Tie*)

Xue Shaopeng 薛绍彭 (years of birth/death unknown, Song dynasty)
Cursive script (*cao shu*)
25.1 cm × 34.8 cm
Palace Museum, Beijing

Mi Fu's contemporary, Xue Shaopeng, shared calligraphic fame with him. They were often mentioned in the same breath as "Xue Mi." In his discourse on masters of calligraphy, Zhao Gou (1107–1187, Song dynasty), Emperor Gaozong of the Song, ranked Xue Shaopeng among the likes of Su Shi, Huang Tingjian and Mi Fu, an measure of the significant influence of Xue in that period. His style is considered to have a contractive character structure, a preference for "hiding the brush-tip," a quaint charm and an aversion to adventuristic experimentation with character postures.

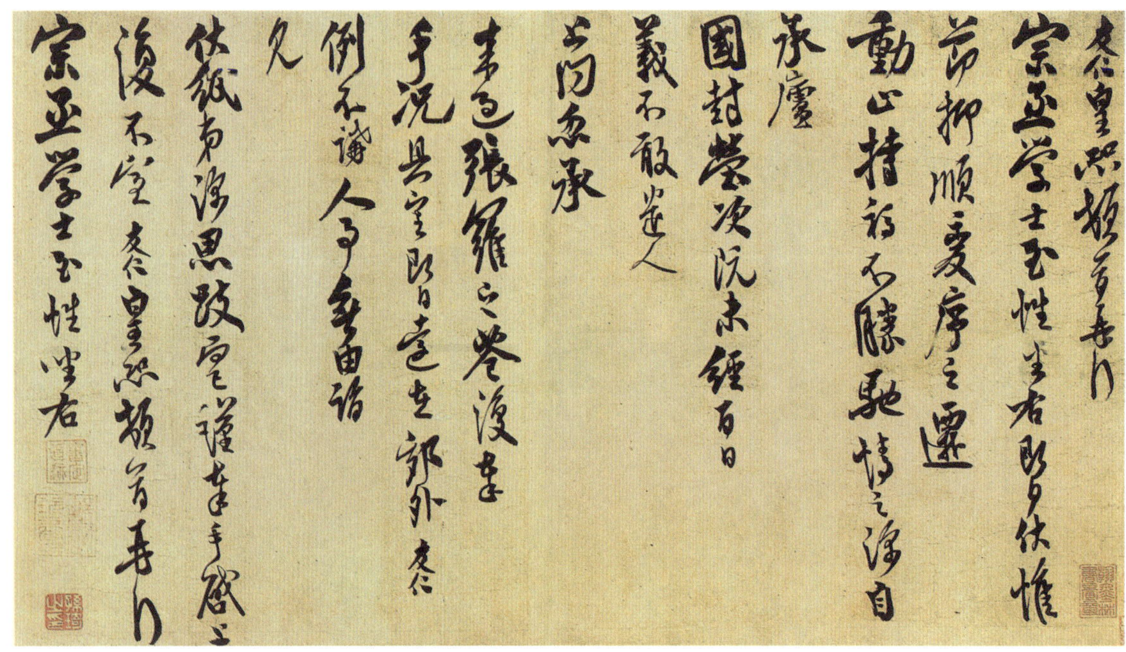

Letter to Colleague in Court (动止持福帖 *Dong Zhi Chi Fu Tie*)

Mi Youren 米友仁 (1074-1153, Song dynasty)
Running script (*xing shu*)
33.1 cm × 59.6 cm
Palace Museum, Beijing

Mi Youren, Mi Fu's eldest son, was also renowned for his painting and calligraphy. His calligraphic style is similar to his father's, and places great emphasis on the generation of calligraphic interest by manipulating character structure and postures, seeking equilibrium in precariousness, and varying the inclinations of the ideograms. In contrast to his father's trenchant and bold brushwork, Mi Jr.'s style leans toward softer lines and a more contracted character structure, making for a full-bodied flavor.

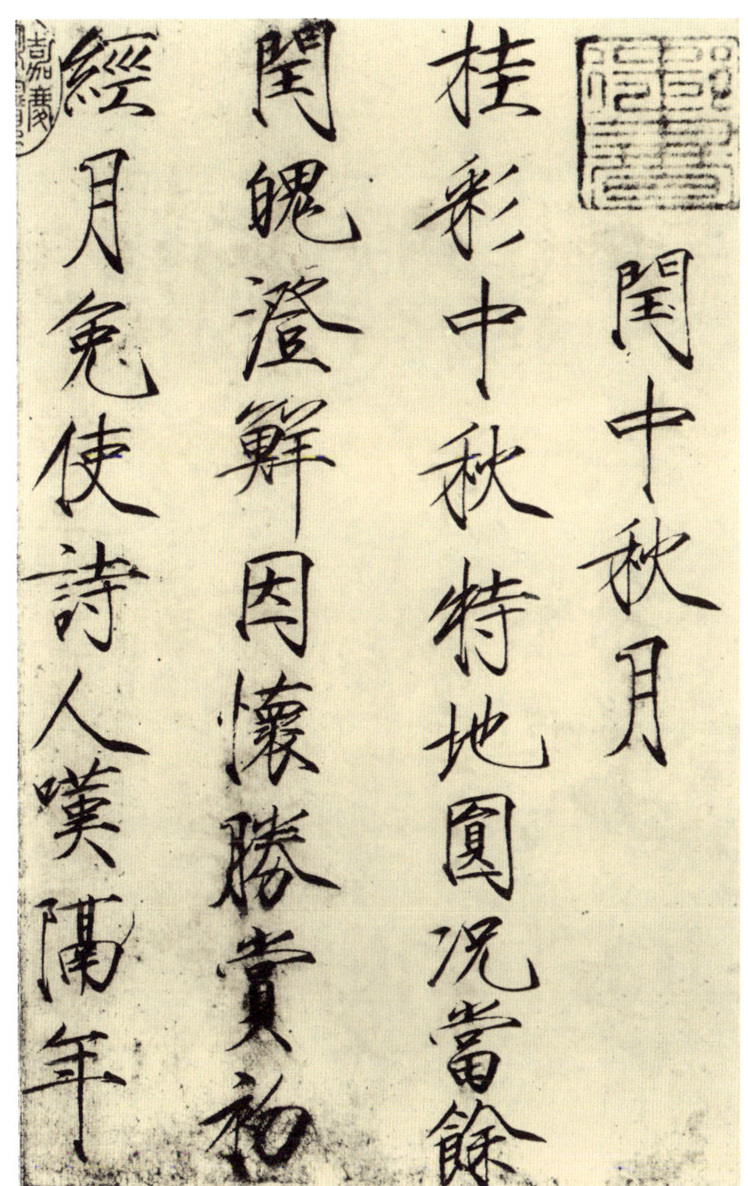

Moon in the Mid-Autumn Festival (闰中秋月诗 *Run Zhong Qiu Yue Shi*)

Zhao Ji 赵佶 (1082–1135, Song dynasty)
Regular script (*kai shu*)
35 cm × 44.5 cm
Palace Museum, Beijing

Zhao Ji, also known as Emperor Huizong of the Song, was a notoriously cowardly and fatuous emperor but a talented artist. His calligraphy is a variation on the style of Xue Ji of the Tang dynasty, known for his slim strokes. Zhao Ji further slimmed down the Xue style and gave it more sinew to create the so-called "slim gold" or "slim sinewy" style. If one looks beneath the surface of his energetic strokes, however, one will find an inner grace and tenderness.

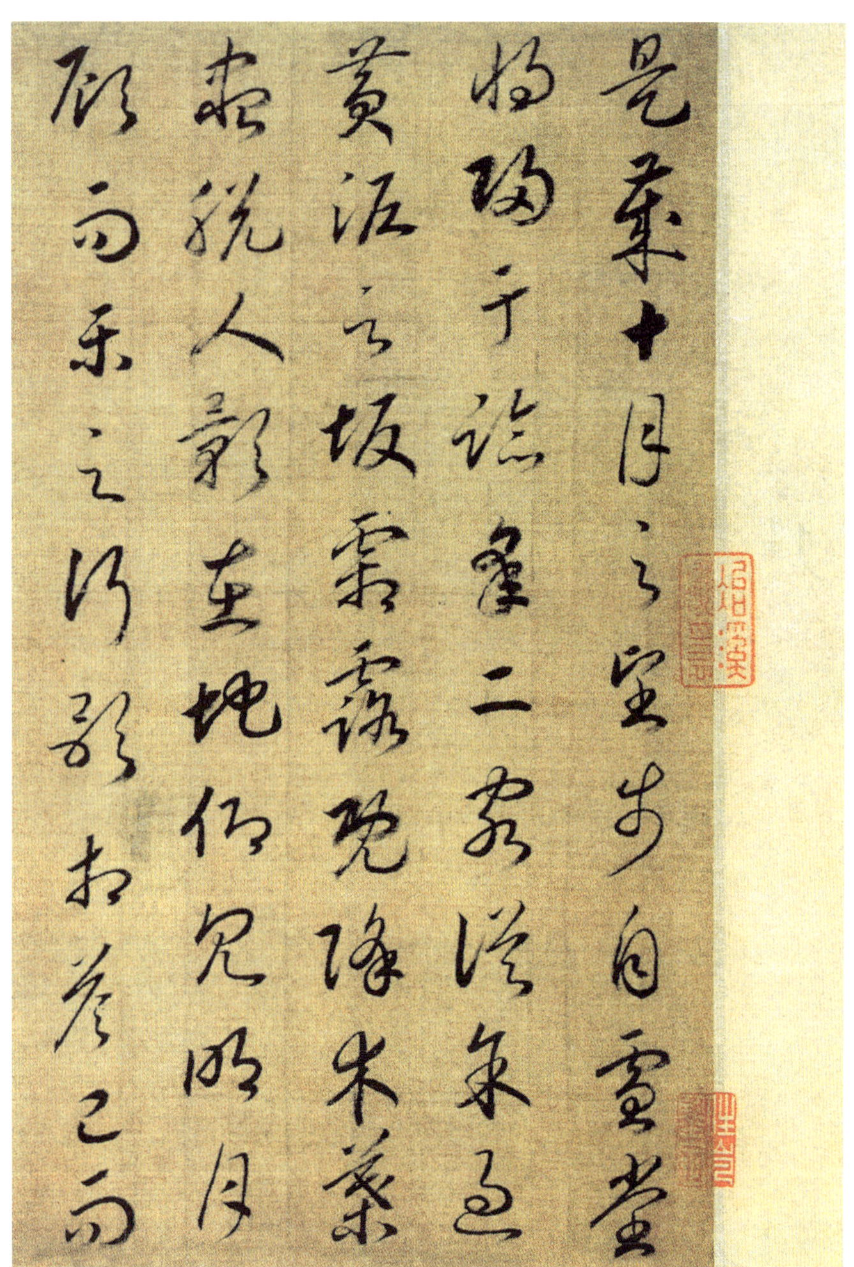

Latter Red Cliff Rhapsody (后赤壁赋 *Hou Chi Bi Fu*)

Zhao Gou 赵构 (1107-1187, Song dynasty)
Cursive script (*cao shu*)
29.5 cm × 143 cm
Palace Museum, Beijing

Zhao Gou, the ninth son of the Huizong emperor, ascended the throne as Emperor Gaozong of the Song, and was later forced to move his court to the south in a divided China. A passionate lover of the calligraphic art, he actively promoted it, so much so that "when the Gaozong emperor started to study and emulate the calligraphy of Huang Tingjian, everybody in his realm jumped on the bandwagon; and when later he studied the art of Mi Fu, the Mi style became the rage; and when finally he turned his attention to the style of Sun Guoting, the Sun style came into vogue." Zhao Gou boasted an untrammeled, graceful brushwork, whose spontaneity and fluidity captured the spirit of calligraphy of the previous Jin dynasty.

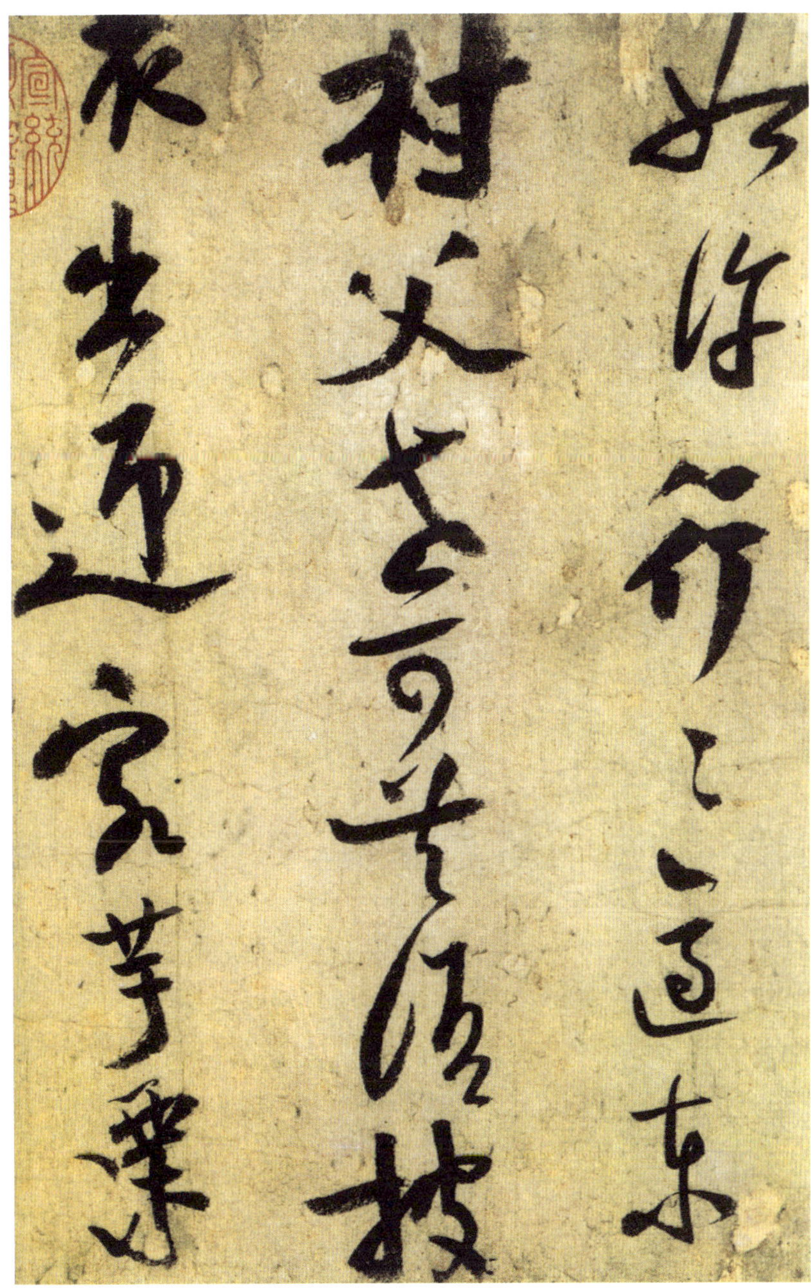

Scroll of Poems Composed and Calligraphed by the Author (自书诗卷 *Zi Shu Shi Juan*)

Lu You 陆游 (1125-1210, Song dynasty)
Running cursive script (*xing cao*)
30 cm × 701.5 cm
Provincial Museum of Liaoning

Lu You was a renowned poet of the Song dynasty. This scroll collects a number of poems calligraphed by him. The writing is casual but the characters exude an ethereal charm, and the strokes are full of energy. Upon close scrutiny, one will find that while this work by Lu You has retained some brush techniques and stroke idiosyncrasies picked up from Yan Zhenqing and Su Shi in his early study of these masters, it has also incorporated some strengths of the running script of Yang Ningshi and Mi Fu, and the cursive script of Zhang Xu. He writes "as the whim takes him," his heart and mind going directly through his hand and brush to paper without kowtowing to tradition or contemporary fashion.

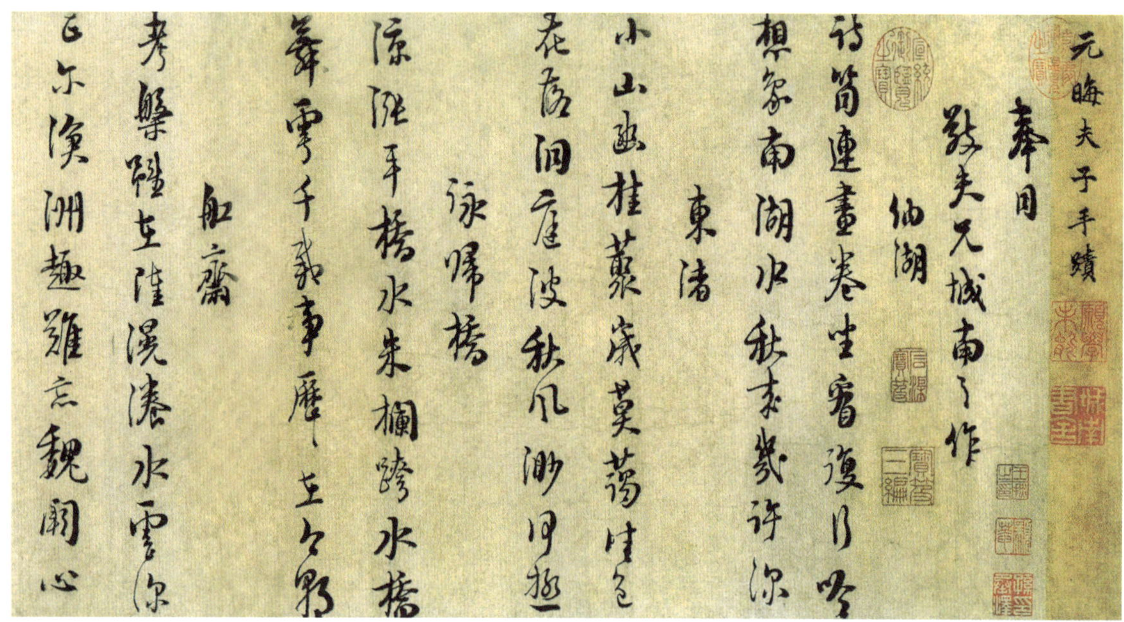

A Visit to Chengnan (城南唱和诗 *Cheng Nan Chang He Shi*)

Zhu Xi 朱熹 (1130-1200, Song dynasty)

Zhu Xi emulated the calligraphies of the Han and Wei dynasties in the early stages of his calligraphic studies. He later came to value the Tang and Jin calligraphic styles and advocated an undogmatic return to antiquity, while maintaining his personal style. In the words of later critics, he "excelled in the running cursive script, especially in elegant small-size writing." One of Zhu Xi's early works, this piece is characterized by brush speed and inattention to finer details that belies an adherence to all calligraphic codes in the forming of the strokes. This exquisite and charming piece is one of Zhu Xi's representative works.

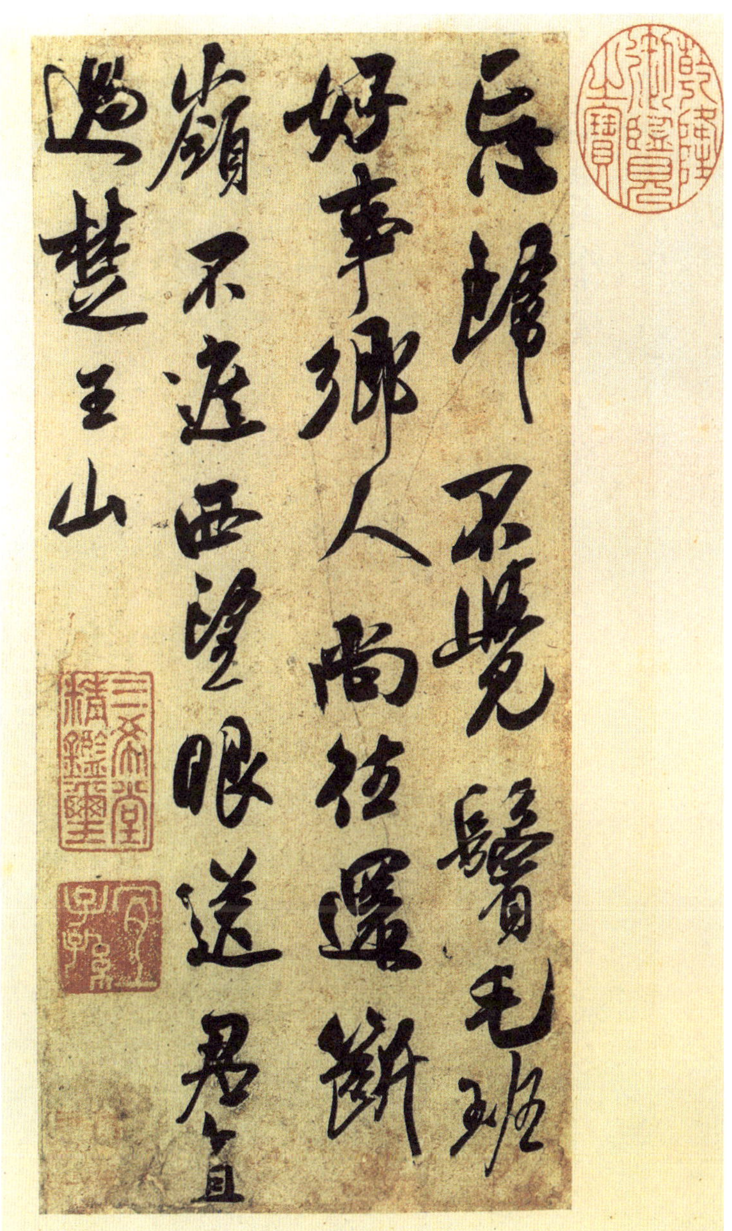

Note of Poems (望君诗帖 *Wang Jun Shi Tie*)

Wu Ju 吴琚 (years of birth/death unknown, Song dynasty)

Wu Ju was a nephew of Emperor Gaozong of the Song. He was nicknamed "Prince Wu of Seven" (吴七郡王 *wu qi jun wang*) because of his seven successive appointments to high office. Of all calligraphic masters, he admired Mi Fu the most and was dedicated to the study of Mi's calligraphy all his life. He was eventually able to closely simulate Mi Fu's calligraphy in both style and spirit. If Wu Ju succeeded in "adding his own ideas" to the Mi style, it is reflected in his ability to apply the square stroke technique more smoothly and in a mellower fashion. The flip side of this refinement is that his calligraphy lost some of the vigor of the Mi style.

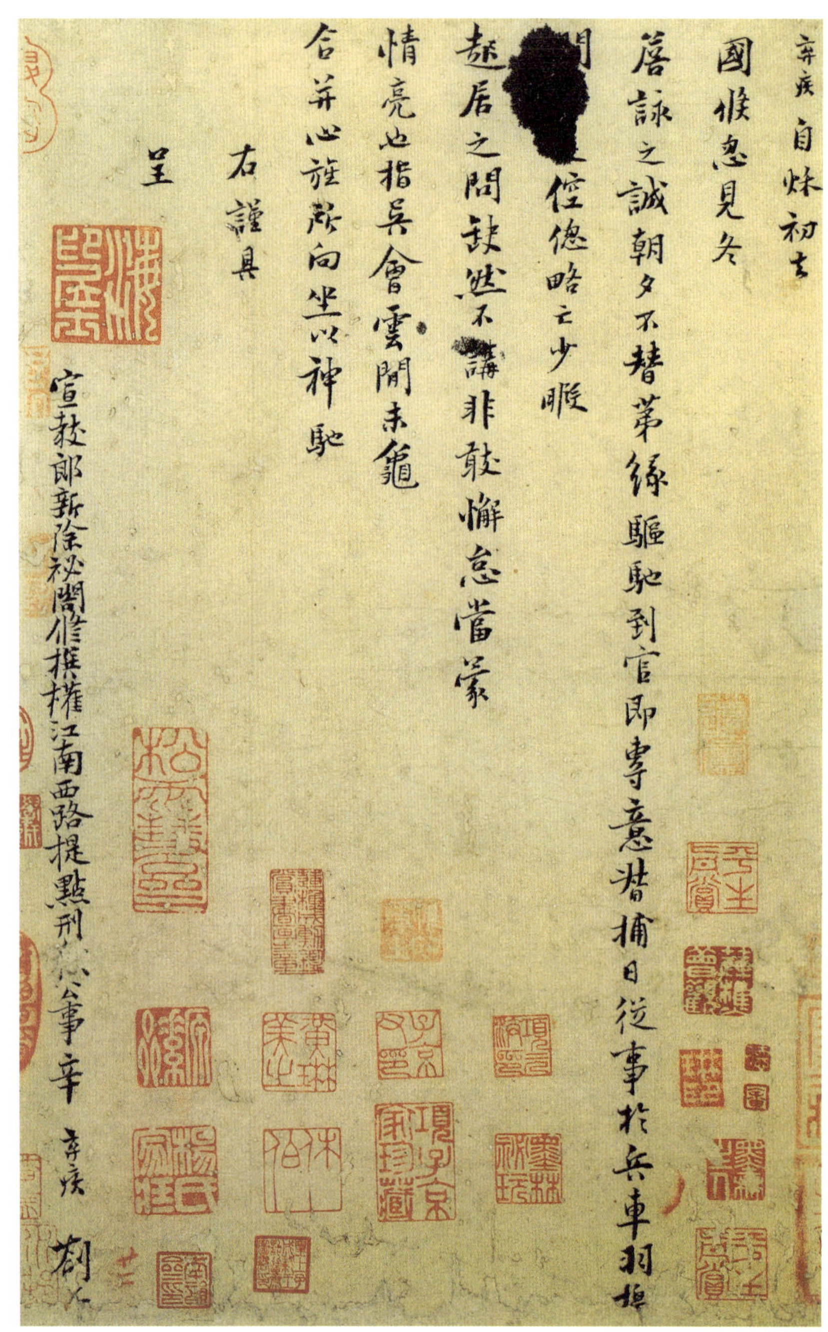

Letter about Government Affairs (去国帖 *Qu Guo Tie*)

Xin Qiji 辛弃疾 (1140–1207, Song dynasty)
Running regular script (*xing kai*)
33.5 cm × 21.5 cm
Palace Museum, Beijing

This is the only extant calligraphic work of the famous Song poet Xin Qiji. Written when he was 36 years of age, this piece shows a simple grace and energetic neatness, and reveals the influence of the ink and brush styles of Su Shi and Huang Tingjian.

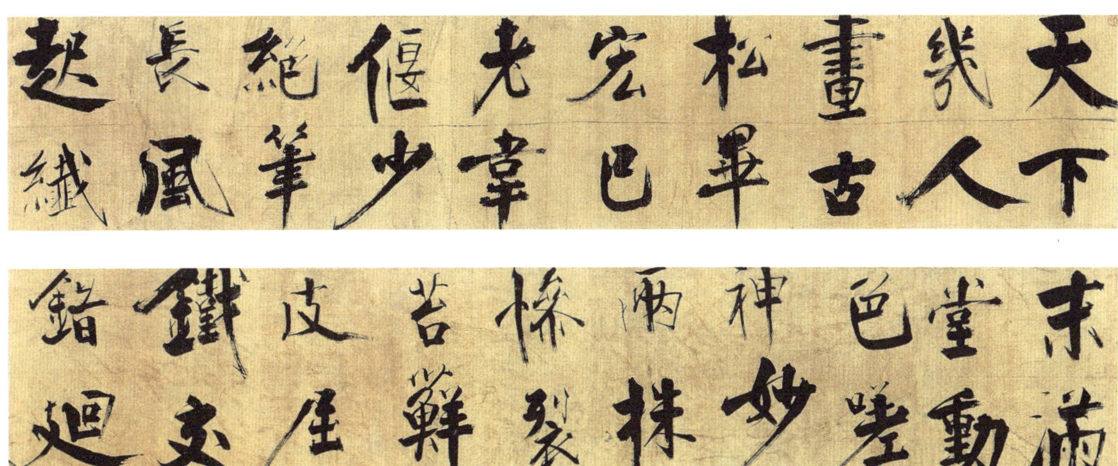

Poem on the Painting "Two Pines" (*双松图歌卷 Shuang Song Tu Ge Juan*)

Zhang Jizhi 张即之 (1186–1263, Song dynasty)
Regular script (*kai shu*)
33.8 cm × 1196 cm
Palace Museum, Beijing

Zhang Jizhi followed the Tang calligraphic tradition in strictly adhering to the codes for the structure of the characters. His style had a large following among the calligraphers of his time and his calligraphic fame spread far and wide. His regular script is characterized by an uncommon vigor, a brushwork that attends to fine details and a preference for starting strokes with the forward brush tip technique (搭锋 *da feng*) instead of the reversed brush-tip. The way his strokes interrelate gives his writing a flavor of the running cursive script. His skilled use of the square stroke and the center-brush techniques results in an exquisite, vibrant calligraphy.

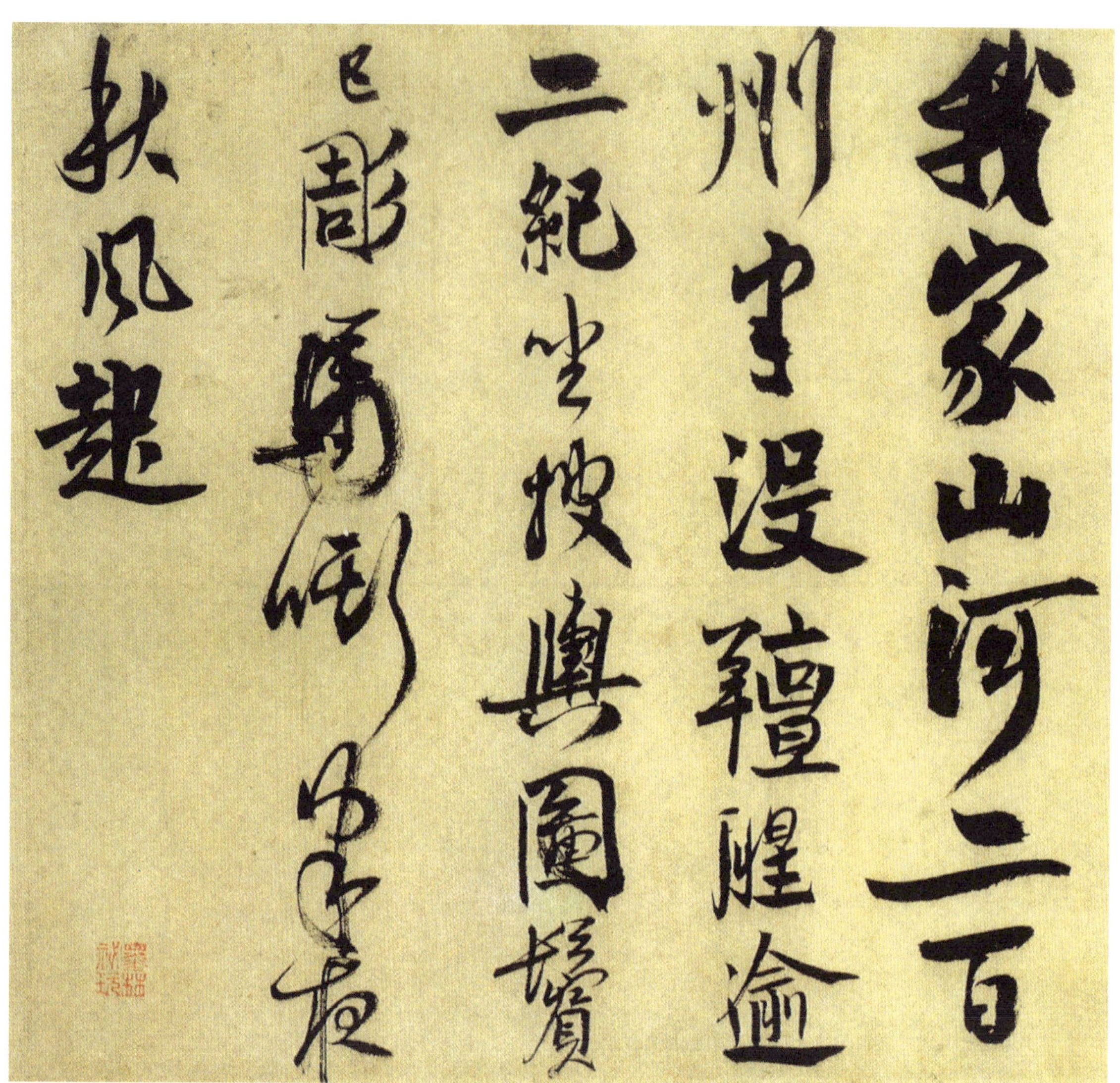

Poems Composed and Calligraphed by the Author (自书诗 *Zi Shu Shi*)

Zhao Mengjian 赵孟坚 **(1199–before 1267, Song dynasty)**
Running script (*xing shu*)
35.8 cm × 675.6 cm
Palace Museum, Beijing

Zhao Mengjian was an accomplished painter-calligrapher, among whose legacy is *A Guide to Plum Flower Painting* (梅谱 *mei pu*). *Poems Composed and Calligraphed by the Author*, a work in his old age, is strongly suggestive of the style of Huang Tingjian in its vigorous, untrammeled brushwork and recalls Mi Fu in its slim, contractive character structure and the inclinations of character postures. Importantly, he had the uncommon ability to create a distinctly individualistic style despite his inheritance of the legacy of past masters.

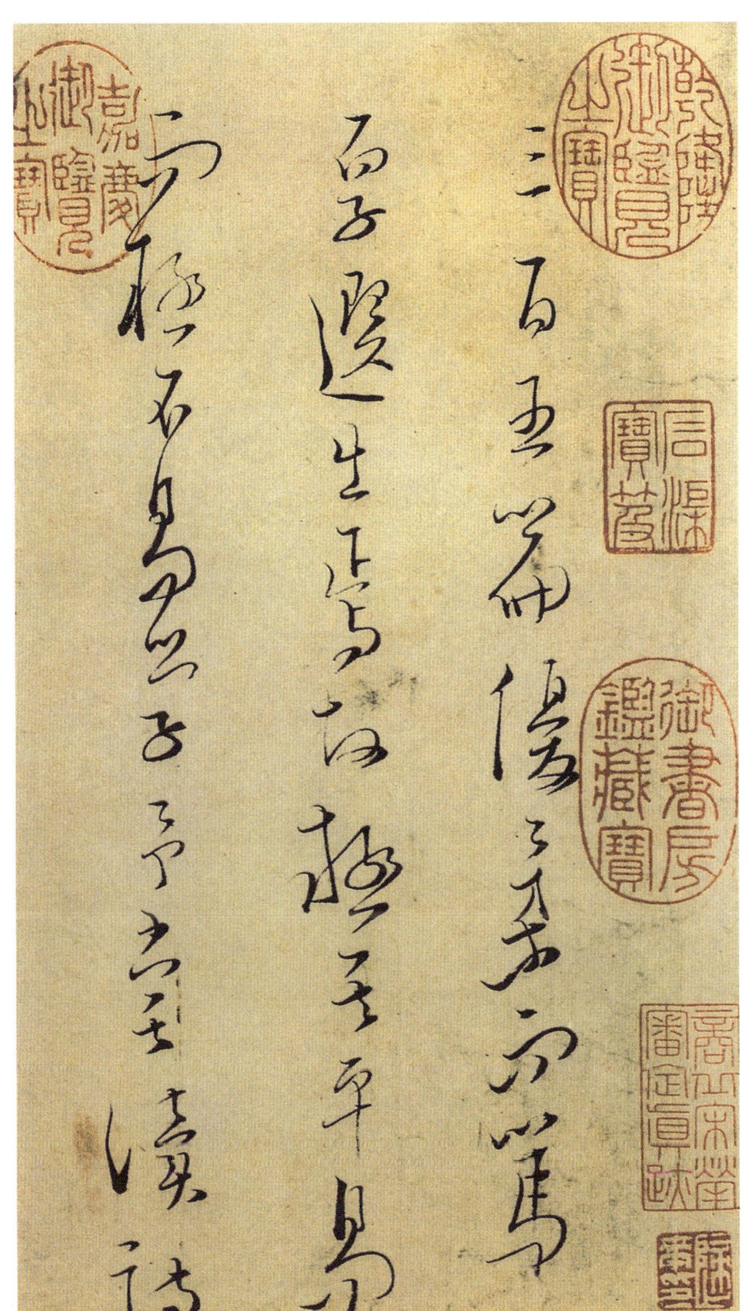

Preface to the Collected Writings of Zhang Zongfu (木鸡集序 *Mu Ji Ji Xu*)

Wen Tianxiang 文天祥 **(1236-1283, Song dynasty)**

Wen Tianxiang's calligraphy is modeled on the style of the "Two Wangs" (Wang Xizhi and Wang Xianzhi). There is little variation in the thickness of the strokes in his works, but great attention is paid to the spatial composition. A breath of fresh air seems to course through his calligraphy. In this piece, the slender, lithe strokes alight and lift off gently in an open, airy field. Wide blank spaces are deliberately left in to create an airy character structure. The continuity from character to character is ensured not so much by physical links between succeeding strokes but by the flow and momentum of the writing.

Yuan Dynasty

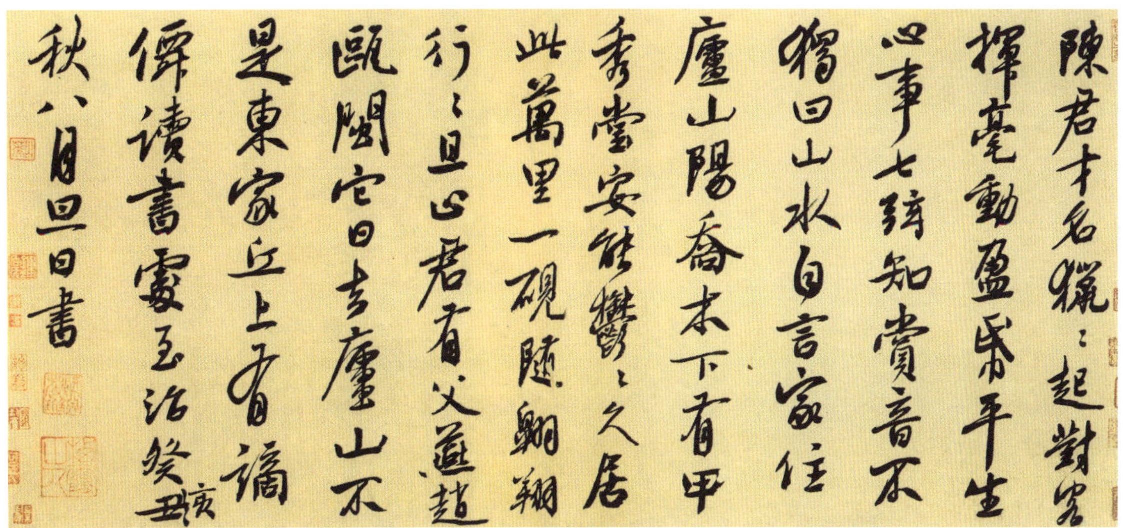

A Poem to Chen Zheng (陈君诗帖 *Chen Jun Shi Tie*)

Bai Ting 白珽 (1248-1328, Yuan dynasty)
Running script (*xing shu*)
31.2 cm × 68.2 cm
Palace Museum, Beijing

This work is characterized by a smooth and spontaneous brushwork, freedom in stroke formation and a lean and simple style. While Mi Fu's influence peeks out at numerous points in the piece, there is no lack of originality. Thus, the characters such as "纸", "不" and "水" strongly suggest an idiosyncratic, personal style.

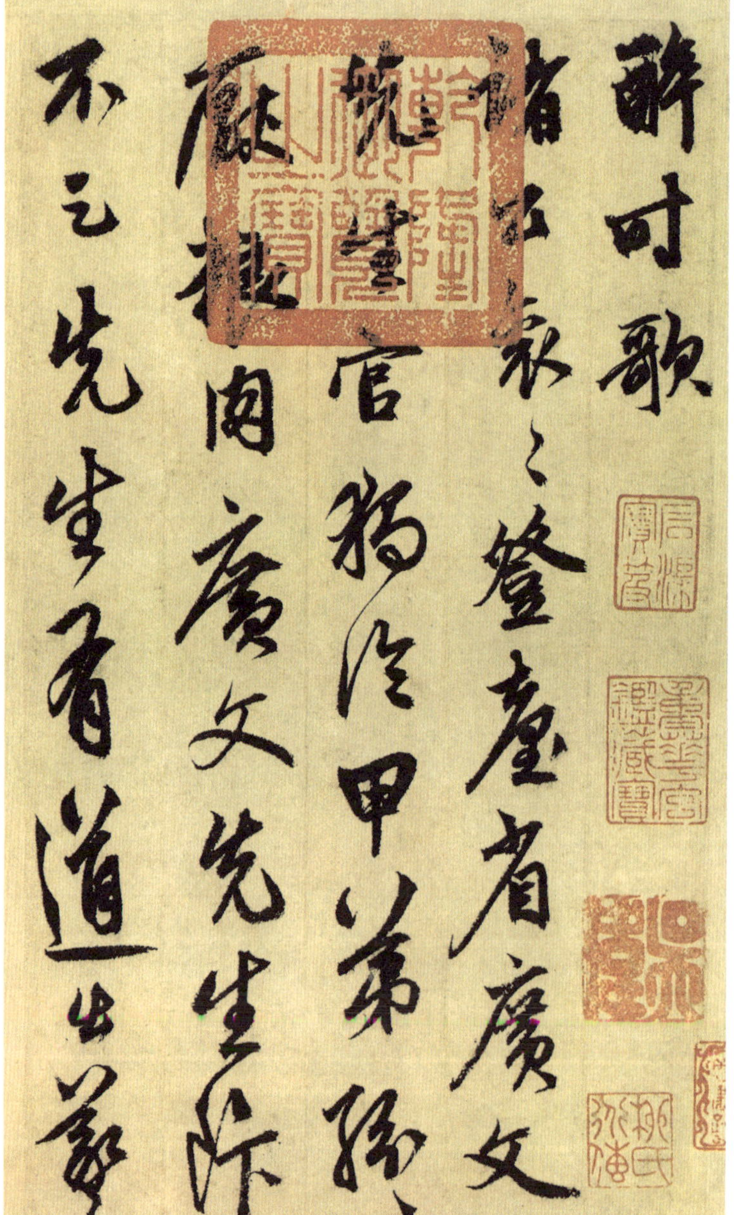

Twelve Tang Poems (唐人诗十二首 *Tang Ren Shi Shi Er Shou*)

Xianyu Shu 鲜于枢 (1256-1301, Yuan dynasty)
Running cursive script (*xing cao*)
Palace Museum, Taipei

An important calligrapher of the Yuan dynasty, Xianyu Shu was best known for his cursive script. His cursive script is modeled on three Tang masters of this style: from Sun Guoting he acquired the forceful lines with square corners; from Zhang Xu the plump, smooth grace; and from Huai Su the lean energy. In character structure, he abandoned the elongated form of Sun and Huai in favor of the broad form of Zhang Xu. In spatial composition, his calligraphy resembles that of Sun Guoting in that the space between characters is less than the space between columns. *Twelve Tang Poems* exhibits a solid, serene, forceful and fluid brushwork.

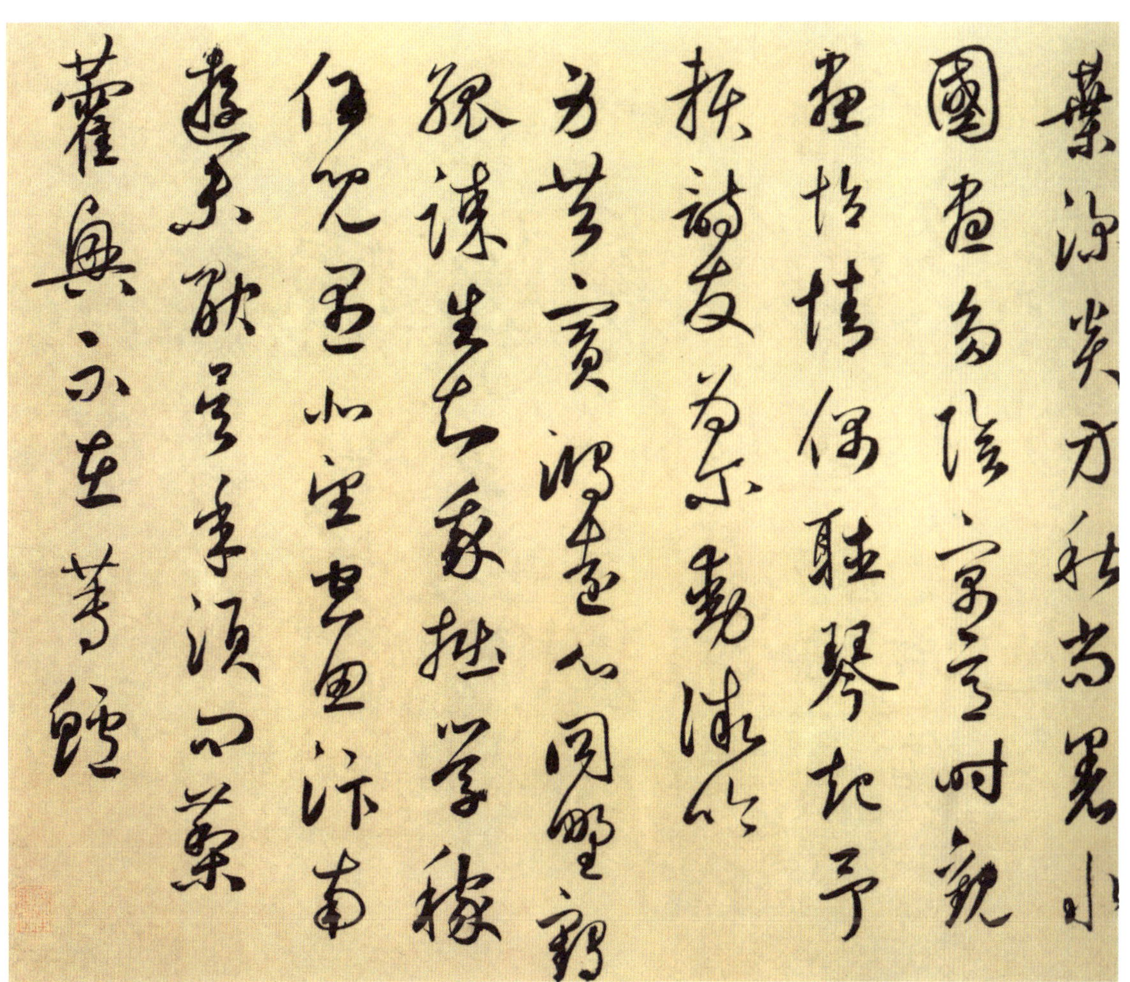

Autumn Thoughts, a Poem (秋兴诗 *Qiu Xing Shi*)

Xianyu Shu 鲜于枢 (1256-1301, Yuan dynasty)
Running script (*xing shu*)
33.6 cm × 40.6 cm
Palace Museum, Beijing

Xianyu Shu was a stickler for "looseness of the wrist" in calligraphy. This work in running script encapsulates this idea of his. The piece is characterized by a steady, palpable rhythm, a free and fluid movement of the brush and a solid, hefty touch of the brush; it does a good job of evoking "a cloud of autumn insects flitting about and leaves fluttering down to the ground."

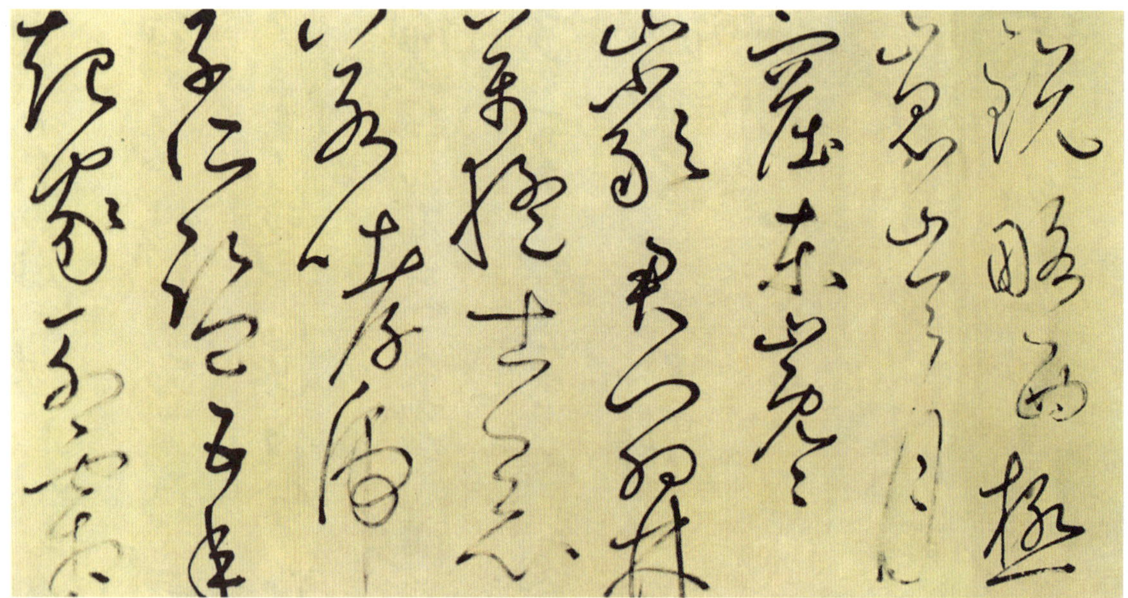

In Praise of General Wei (杜诗魏将军歌 *Du Shi Wei Jiang Jun Ge*)

Xianyu Shu 鲜于枢 (1256-1301, Yuan dynasty)
Running cursive script (*xing cao*)
48 cm × 462 cm
Palace Museum, Beijing

When asked about the secret to a good cursive hand, Xianyu Shu replied, "Dare! Dare! Dare!" or "let the spirit prevail." This *In Praise of General Wei* by the Tang poet Du Fu, calligraphed in cursive script style, exhibits a great freedom, a smooth, fluid continuum of ink and brush that imparts a sense of having been completed in one heroic breath.

Autumn Thoughts, a Prose Poem (秋兴赋 Qiu Xing Fu)

Zhao Mengfu 赵孟頫 (1254-1322, Yuan dynasty)
Running script (*xing shu*)

Zhao Mengfu is the most important calligrapher of the Yuan dynasty. He blended the styles of the calligraphic masters of the Jin and Tang dynasties to create a form of calligraphy that proved very popular with the educated elite of his time. Whereas this "Zhao style" characterized by supple, smooth strokes, graceful character structures, a neat and balanced spatial composition and a stately elegance lacks the free spirit of the mountains and woods that is the mark of the "Two Wangs," it compensates with an opulence worthy of the imperial court.

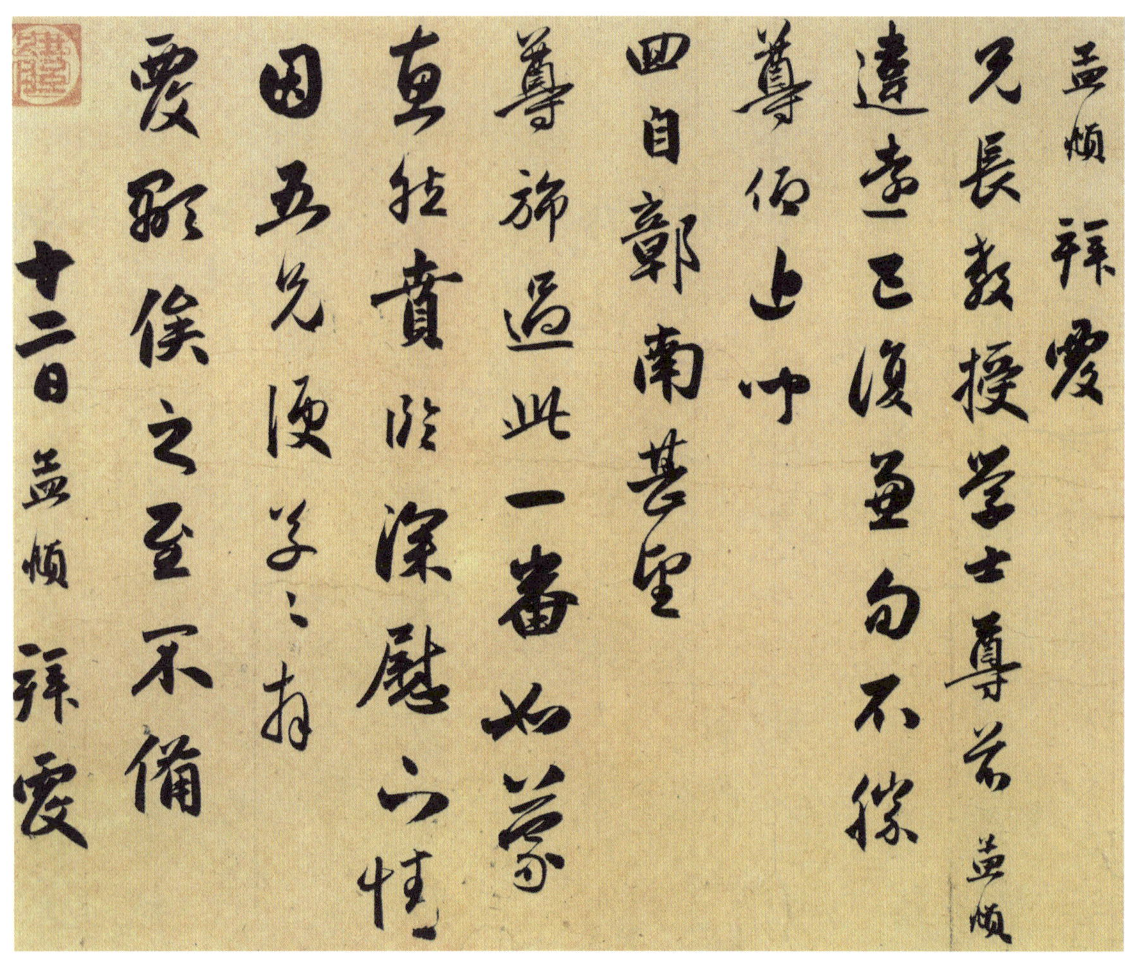

Long Absence (违远帖 *Wei Yuan Tie*)

Zhao Mengfu 赵孟頫 (1254-1322, Yuan dynasty)
Running script (*xing shu*)
27.5 cm × 28.7 cm
Palace Museum, Beijing

According to historical chronicles, Zhao Mengfu calligraphed at an amazing speed, often writing ten thousand characters a day without feeling any fatigue. When asked how he managed to do it, he replied, "Because I am well practiced." Being well practiced is a major factor in Zhao Mengfu's calligraphy. The proficiency that comes from practice allows him to reject the mentality of subjective treatment, contrary to the "conscious creativity" valued by the Song calligraphers. Proficiency also helps him to forge a calligraphic style characterized by delicate grace, neatness, elegance and ease of mastery.

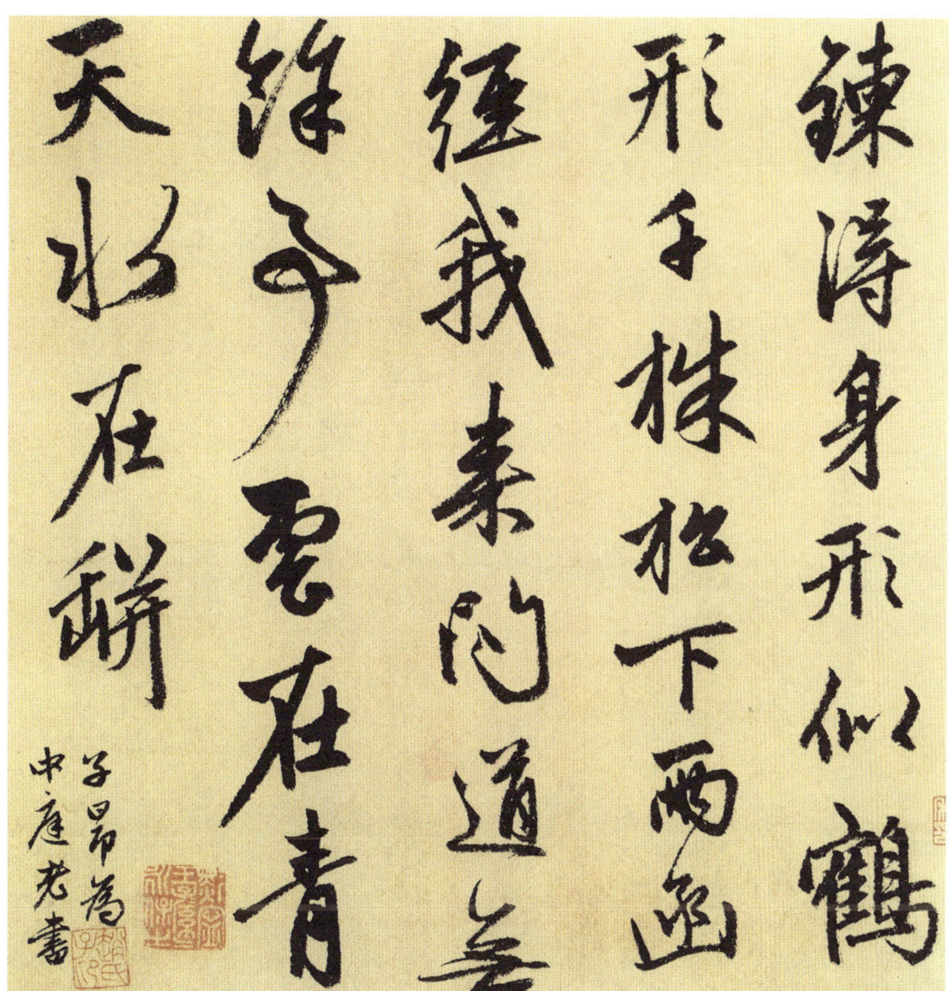

Quatrain in Seven-character Meter in Running Script (行书七绝 *Xing Shu Qi Jue*)

Zhao Mengfu 赵孟頫 (1254–1322, Yuan dynasty)
Running script (*xing shu*)
34.7 cm × 35.3 cm
Palace Museum, Beijing

Written by Zhao Mengfu in his old age, this piece is characterized by a steady hand, an irresistible momentum and a punctiliously regular character structure. Although consisting of only five columns of large characters, the piece is rich in variations. An uncontrived elegance comes through despite a calligraphic style that was beginning to show its age.

Rhapsody on the Luo River Goddess in Small Regular Script (小楷洛神赋 *Xiao Kai Luo Shen Fu*)

Zhao Mengfu 赵孟頫 (1254–1322, Yuan dynasty)
Regular script (*kai shu*)
25.7 cm in height
Palace Museum, Beijing

This was calligraphed by a 66-year-old Zhao Mengfu. In small regular script, Zhao Mengfu took the "Two Wangs" as his model and benefited hugely from a Taoist classic *Huang Ting Scripture* (黄庭经 *huang ting jing*) by Wang Xizhi and *Rhapsody on the Luo River Goddess* by Wang Xianzhi. Drawing inspiration from the religious texts copied by Jin and Tang calligraphers, he was able to add charm to his meticulously executed calligraphy, a charm that embodies this verse line in the piece "the grace of a frightened swan goose in flight and a lithe dragon riding the waves."

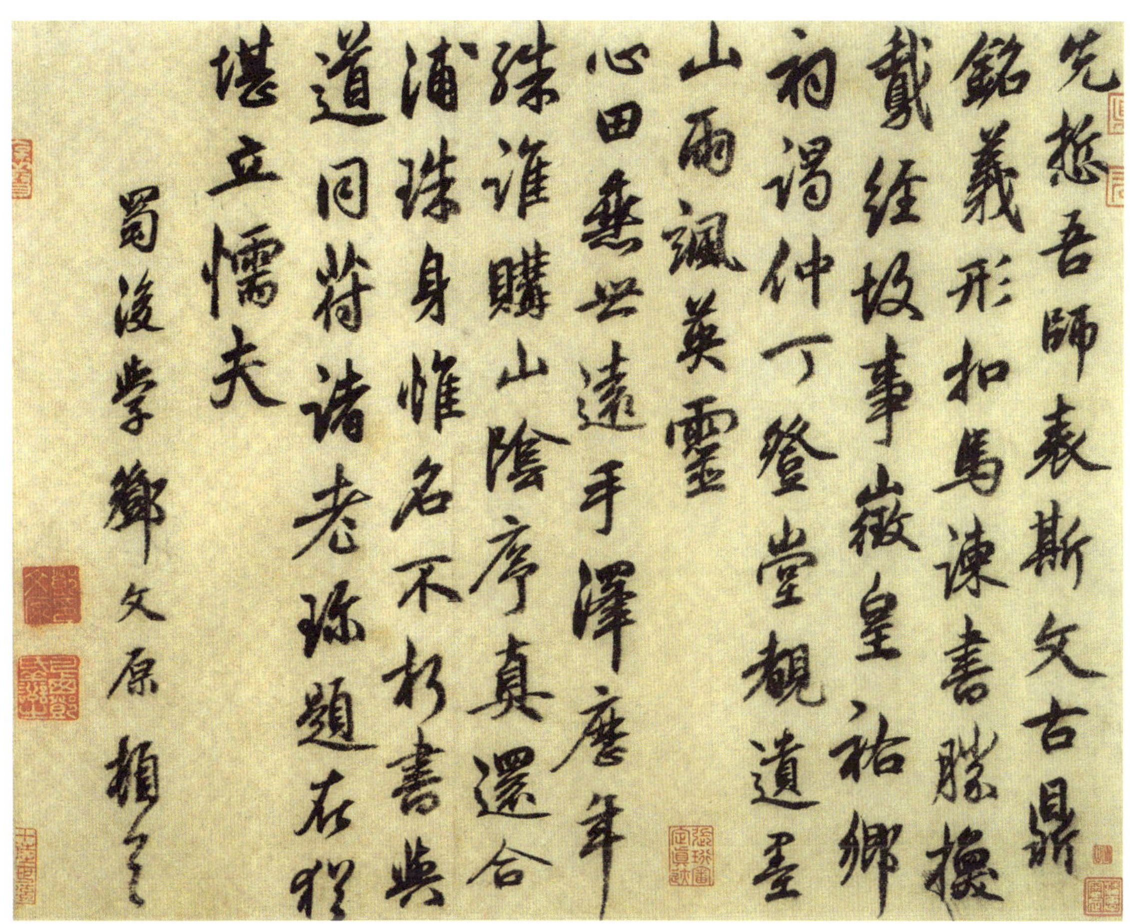

Eight-line Regular Poem in Five-character Meter (五言律诗帖 *Wu Yan Lü Shi Tie*)

Deng Wenyuan 邓文原 (1258-1328, Yuan dynasty)
Running script (*xing shu*)
32.7 cm × 40.9 cm
Palace Museum, Beijing

The Ming calligrapher Wu Kuan 吴宽 rated Deng Wenyuan, Zhao Mengfu and Xianyu Shu as the three pillars of Yuan calligraphy, each supreme in his own area of specialty. Relatively speaking, Zhao is stronger in technical virtuosity, Xian in his energy-packed strokes and Deng in the scholarly urbanity of his calligraphy. Deng Wenyuan's calligraphy has a spare beauty that is not without a tender charm; his brushwork may not be free-spirited but its smoothness and fluidity is absent in Zhao Mengfu.

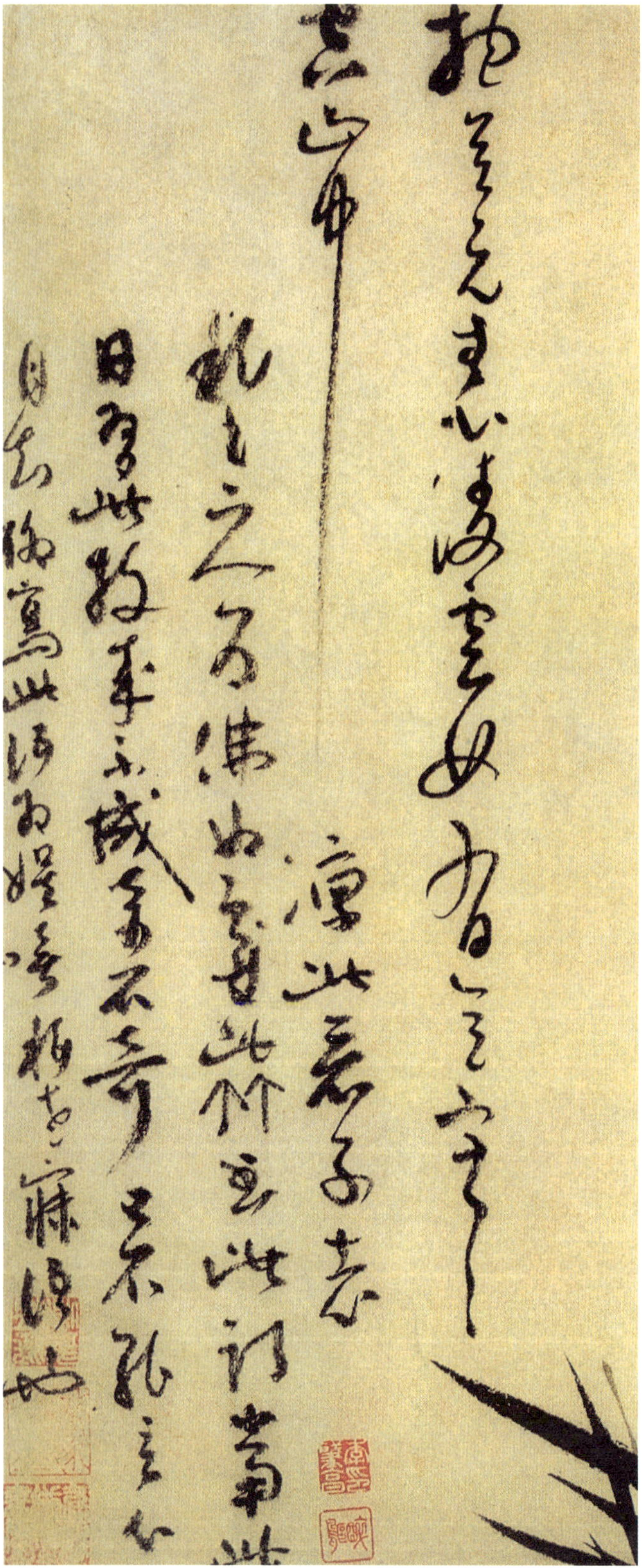

Colophon to Bamboo Painting Guide
(题墨竹谱之十三 *Ti Mo Zhu Pu Zhi Shi San*)

Wu Zhen 吴镇 **(1280–1354, Yuan dynasty)**
Cursive script (*cao shu*)

Wu Zhen, Huang Gongwang 黄公望 (1269–1354, Yuan dynasty), Ni Zan 倪瓒 (1306 or 1301–1374, Yuan dynasty) and Wang Meng 王蒙 (1308 or 1301–1385, Yuan dynasty) are commonly referred to as the "Four Masters of Yuan Painting." Wu Zhen is well known for his cursive script calligraphy and this *Colophon to Bamboo Painting Guide* is a representative calligraphic work of his in his old age. It was written on the spur of the moment, with little regard for codes and no hesitation or inhibition whatsoever but nonetheless exudes a natural charm.

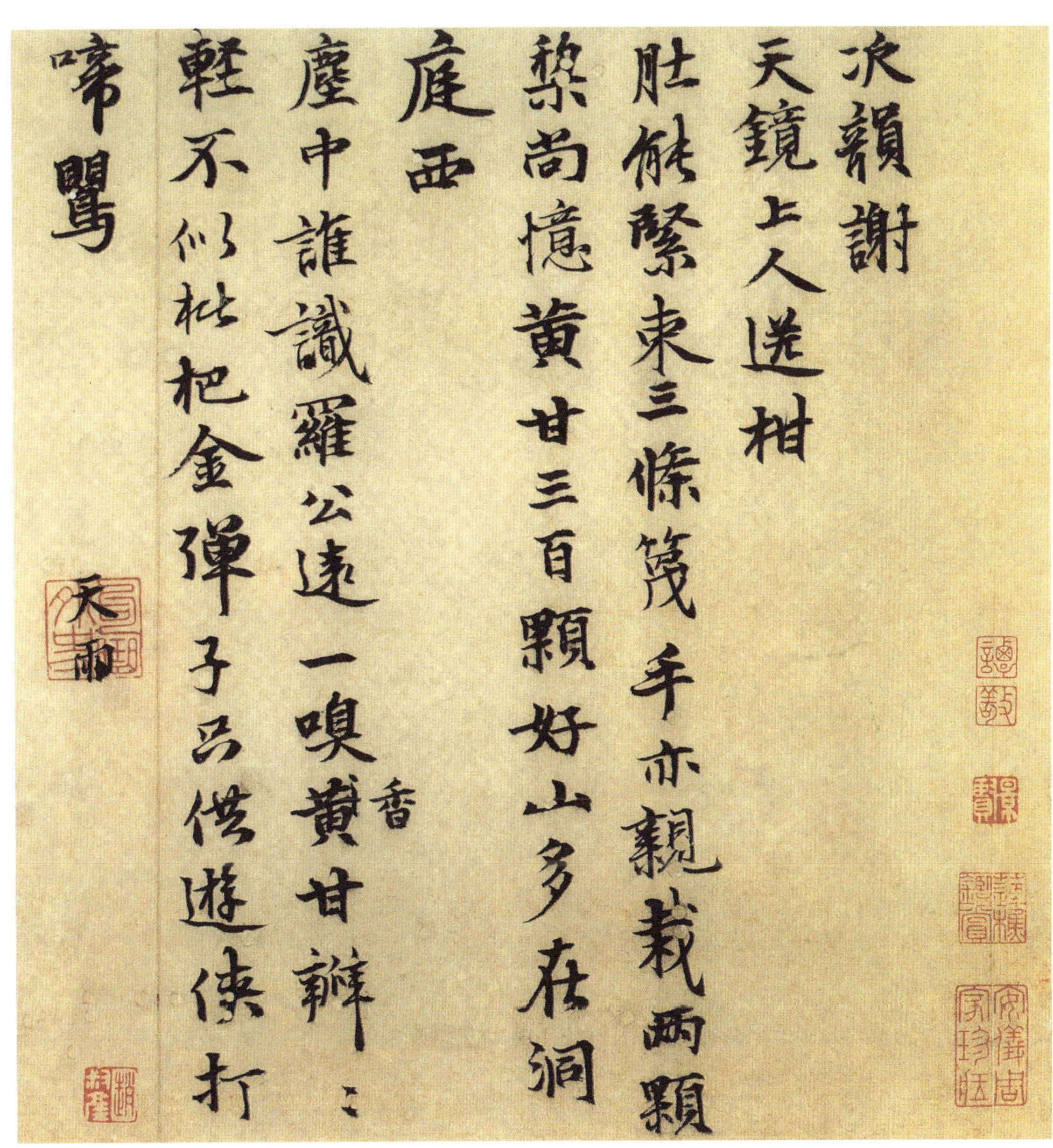

Giving Tangerine (送柑诗帖 *Song Gan Shi Tie*)

Zhang Yu 张雨 (1283-1350, Yuan dynasty)
Running script (*xing shu*)
26.5 cm × 29.4 cm
Palace Museum, Beijing

Zhang Yu left his home in his twenties to become a Taoist priest and traveled through the mountains in the eastern part of Zhejiang. His poetry, paintings and calligraphy have a serene and leisurely air that prompts the comment that they have "the ethereal aura of an immortal." The relaxed elegance of this piece has a lot in common with the Zhao Mengfu style, but its inner strength is reminiscent of Li Yong' s brushwork.

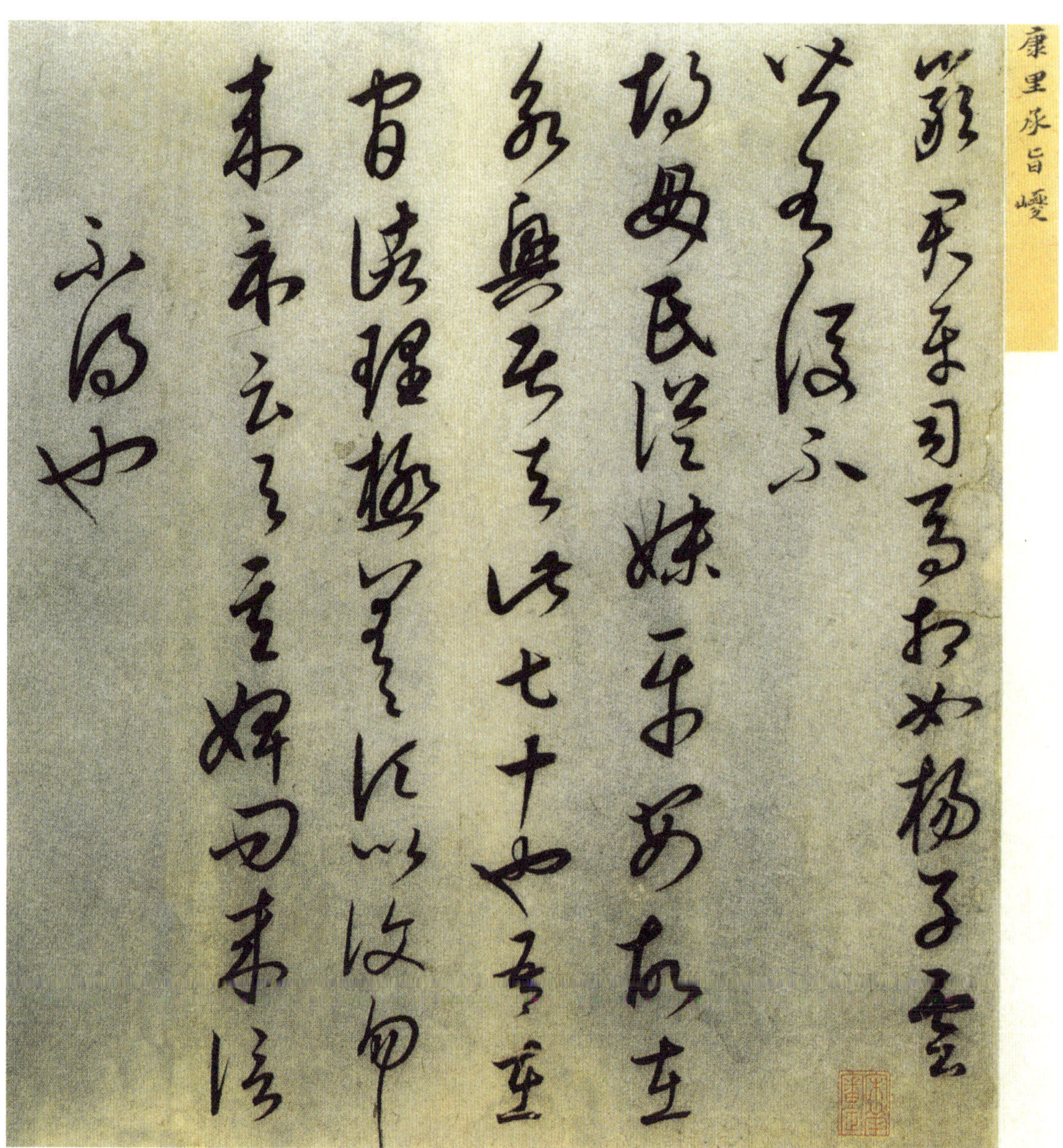

Copy of "on the Seventeenth Day" (临十七帖 *Lin Shi Qi Tie*)

Kang Li'nao 康里巎 (1295-1345, Yuan dynasty)
Cursive script (*cao shu*)
28.5 cm × 42.6 cm
Palace Museum, Beijing

Kang Li'nao, also known as Kangli Naonao, was a member of the Kangli tribe in present-day Xinjiang. He was a calligraphy enthusiast throughout his life, excelling in regular script, running script and cursive script, and was especially famous for the latter. His calligraphy has been likened to "a towering sword thrusting into the sky, a majestic rainbow spanning the sea," because of the fluent and speedy brushwork and the charisma glowing just beneath the veneer of his free and easy strokes. Coming from a non-Han background, he was able to achieve great depth in his knowledge of Chinese Han culture through assiduous study. When told that Zhao Mengfu wrote ten thousand characters a day, he was unimpressed, saying, "I write thirty thousand characters a day without ever laying down the brush because of fatigue."

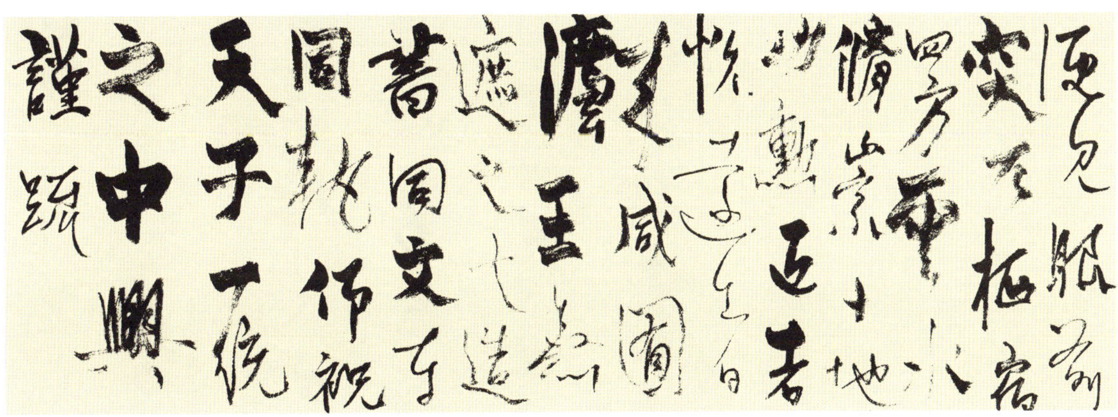

Appeal for Funds for True Mirror Temple (真镜庵募缘疏卷 *Zhen Jing An Mu Yuan Shu Juan*)

Yang Weizhen 杨维桢 **(1296-1370, Yuan dynasty)**
Running script (*xing shu*)
33.3 cm × 278.4 cm
Shanghai Museum

Yang Weizhen's calligraphy is marked by a "disheveled and uncouth" look and a rebellious, arrogant vein that is often associated with troubled times. In this piece, the calligrapher wields a willful, untrammeled, cathartic brush, with a boldness and energy that could cut through metal, combining square and round strokes, speed and deliberation. With its unambiguous, sharp turns and right diagonals' "swallow tails," the piece has the feel of early cursive script. The sense of movement in the piece gives the impression of a busy battlefield, bristling with arms and with war horses charging about.

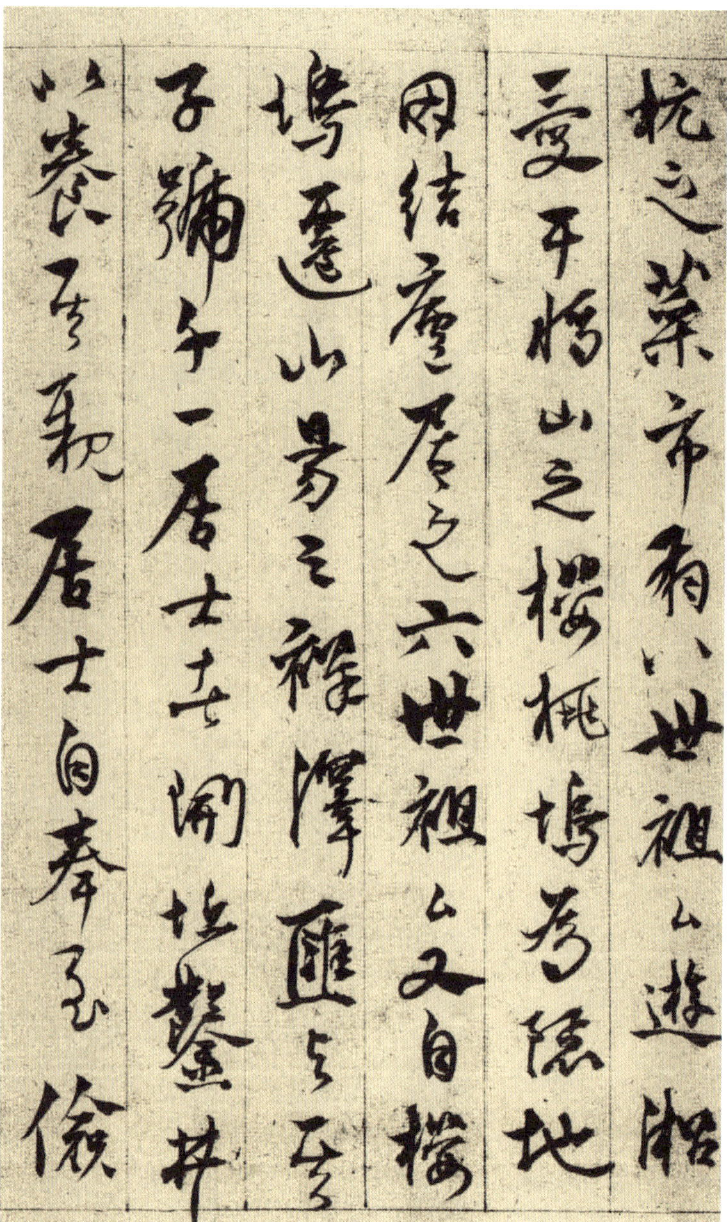

Epitaph of the Zhang's Ancestors (张氏通波阡表 *Zhang Shi Tong Bo Qian Biao*)

Yang Weizhen 杨维桢 (1296-1370, Yuan dynasty)
Running script (*xing shu*)
28.9 cm × 146.1 cm
Tokyo National Museum, Japan

The spatial composition of this work is dense and the strokes are dynamic and leap about. The clumsy appearance of the early cursive script style and the bold revelation of the brush-tip at stroke endings bring to mind the cold, steely flash of a sword. In contrast to the mellow, graceful style of Zhao Mengfu that monopolized the field of calligraphy of the time, Yang Weizhen's calligraphic style stood out like a "lone peak."

A Poem for Zong Dao (淡室诗 *Dan Shi Shi*)

Ni Zan 倪瓒 (1306 or 1301-1374, Yuan dynasty)
Running regular script (*xing kai*)
64 cm × 27 cm
Palace Museum, Beijing

This calligraphy has a painterly quality to it. It emphasizes spatial composition and places the inter-character relationship above the structure of individual characters. The author pays great attention to the execution of the strokes, and does his best to convey a clerical script flavor.

Ming Dynasty

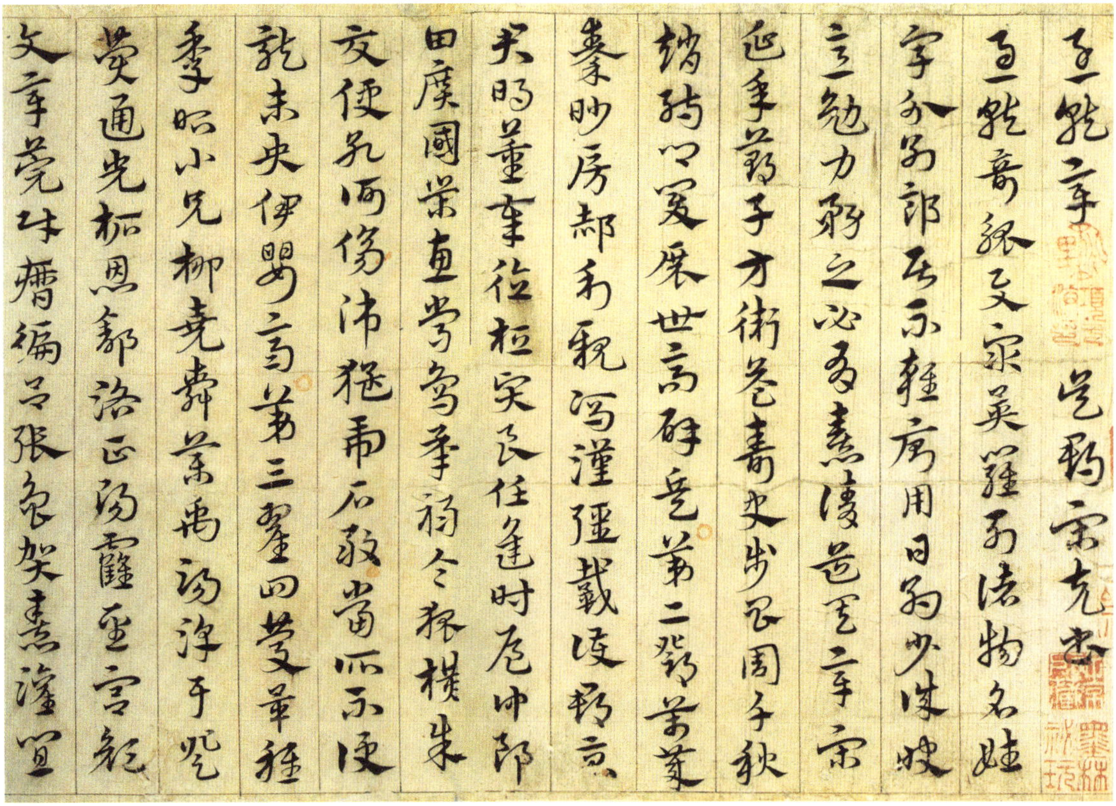

Literacy Textbook in Early Cursive Script (章草急就章 *Zhang Cao Ji Jiu Zhang*)

Song Ke 宋克 (1327-1387, Ming dynasty)
Cursive script (*cao shu*)
20.3 cm × 342.5 cm
Palace Museum, Beijing

Generally speaking, calligraphy of the Ming dynasty put a high premium on visual impact, variation, character postures and personal expression. The most accomplished early Ming calligrapher is arguably Song Ke. This early cursive script scroll by him contains more than one thousand nine hundred meticulously calligraphed ideograms. The hand that holds the brush communicates perfectly with the author's mind to produce a work that vibrates with energy and a quaint simplicity.

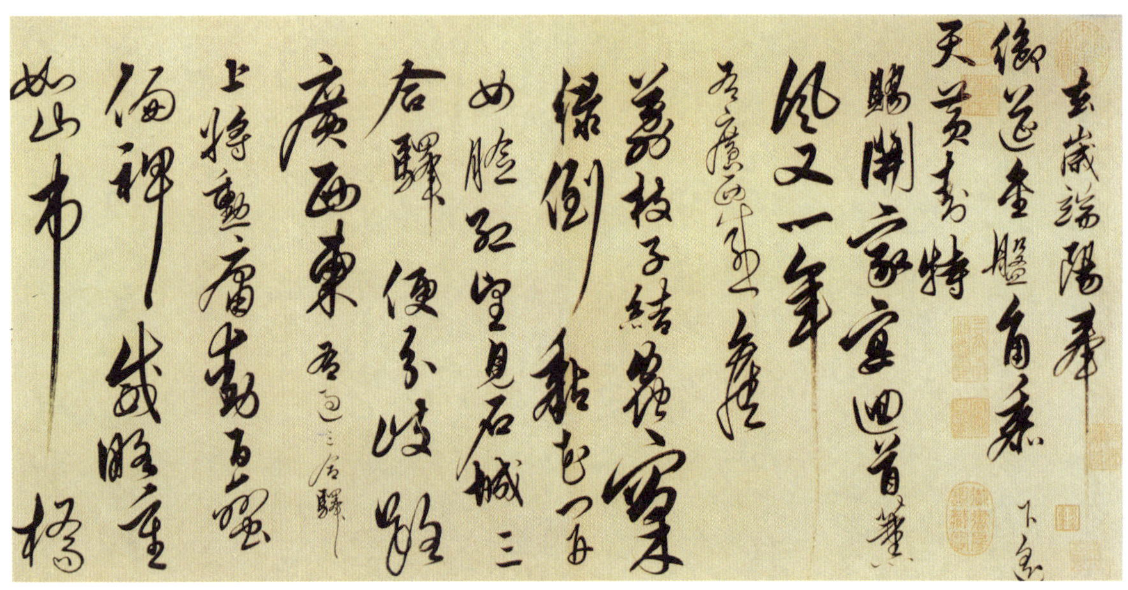

Poems Composed and Calligraphed by the Author in Cursive Script (草书自书诗 *Cao Shu Zi Shu Shi*)

Xie Jin 解缙 (1369-1415, Ming dynasty)
Cursive script (*cao shu*)
34.3 cm × 472 cm
Palace Museum, Beijing

Xie Jin is known for his cursive script calligraphy and this piece is one of the calligrapher's favorites. Xie Jin's style is characterized by the ease and liberty of the strokes, the respect for codes and well thought out use of space. Xie Jin's cursive script style fired the opening salvos for the expressive mad cursive script style that came into its own in the late Ming. There is a mix of arrogance and modesty and plenty of intertwining in the style, which at times could be faulted for its excess slickness.

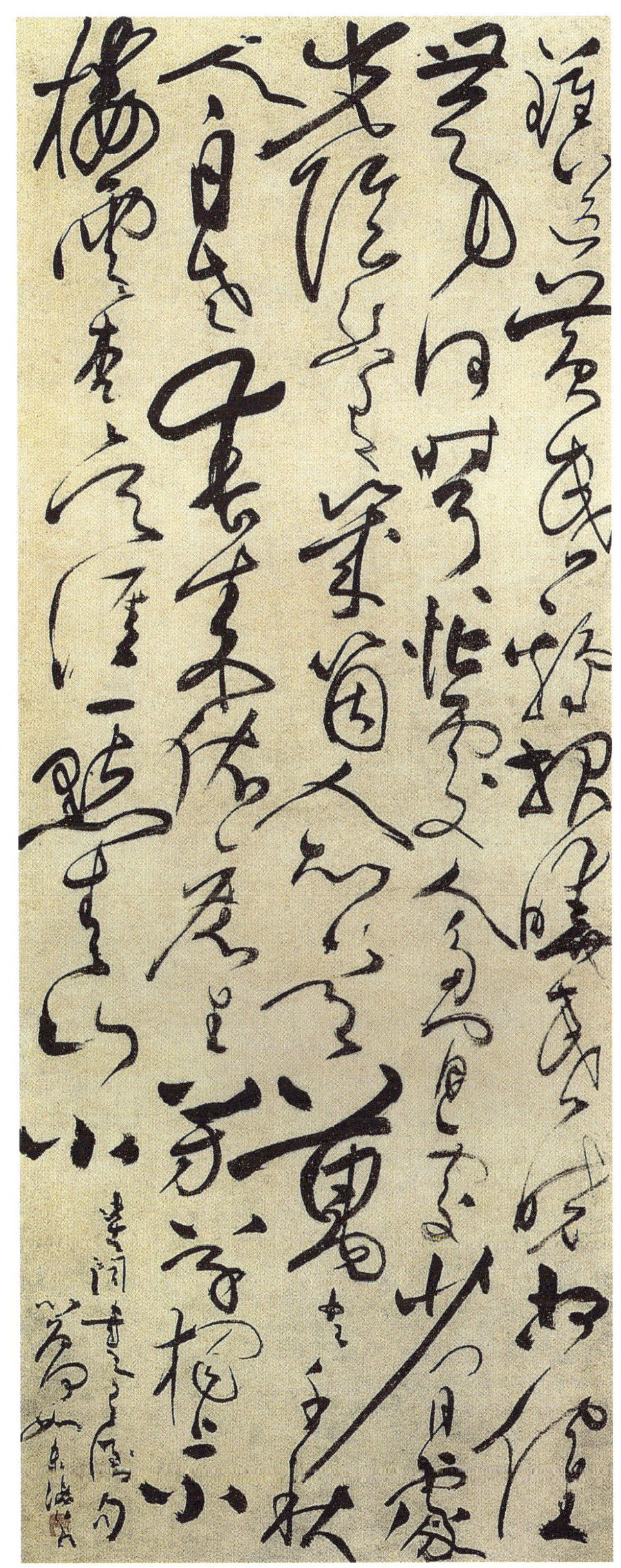

Poem to the Tune "Die Lian Hua" on a Scroll (蝶恋花词轴 *Die Lian Hua Ci Zhou*)

Zhang Bi 张弼 (1425–1487, Ming dynasty)
Cursive script (*cao shu*)
148 cm × 59.4 cm
Palace Museum, Beijing

Zhang Bi, a well known poet, composed and calligraphed his verse directly on paper without going through a draft. When inspiration struck after a few rounds of wine, the poet would let loose his cursive script, which was his forte. *Poem to the Tune "Die Lian Hua" on a Scroll* exhibits speed and movement of the brush, an interesting staggering of the characters and a rich variation in lifting, pressing down and in starting and ending the strokes. The brush is allowed to move in freedom and spontaneity in an open space. The writing is fluid and steady without falling into the pitfall of frivolity.

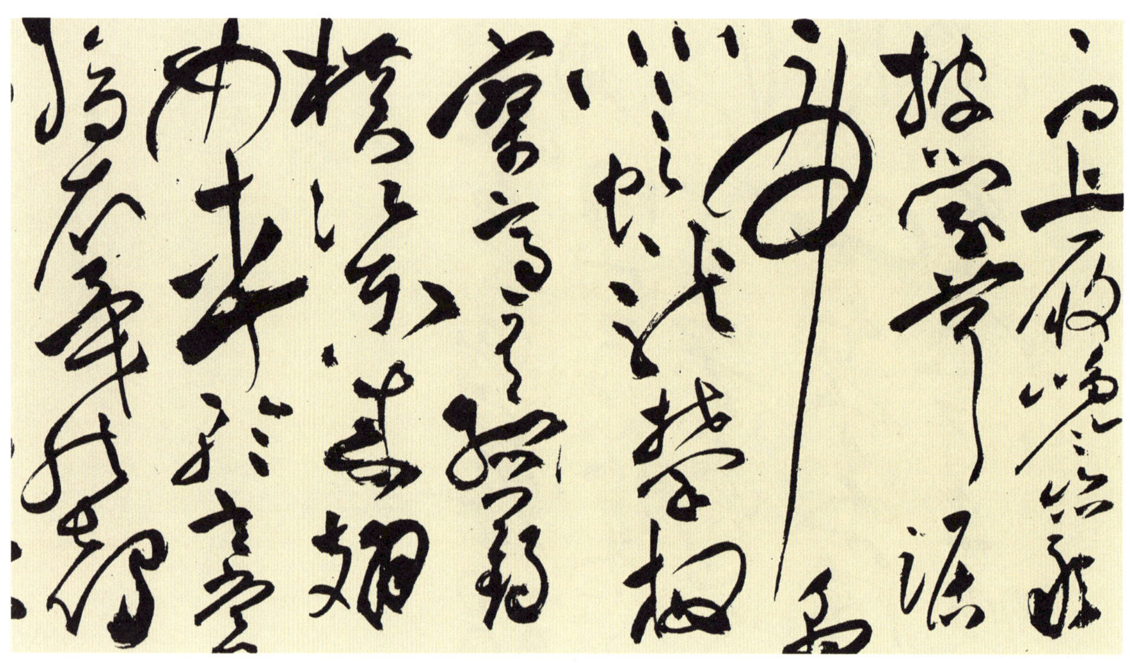

Red Cliff Rhapsody (赤壁赋 *Chi Bi Fu*)

Zhu Yunming 祝允明 (1460-1526, Ming dynasty)
Cursive script (*cao shu*)
Shanghai Museum

In the middle Ming, Suzhou produced a breed of great calligraphers such as Zhu Yunming, Wen Zhengming 文徵明 (1470-1559, Ming dynasty) and Wang Chong 王宠 (1494-1533, Ming dynasty), thus reviving interest in calligraphy and ushering in a calligraphic renaissance in the Ming. For a time conventional wisdom had it that "all calligraphic models are concentrated in Wu country," because all three masters were natives of the Wu region (covering southern Jiangsu and northern Zhejiang). In the cursive script works of Zhu Yunming, the brush is moved by the energy (气 *qi*) and form is derived from momentum. His style incorporates the masculinity of Zhang Xu and the dynamism of Huai Su. Its rhythm brings to mind gale force winds, rain storms, lightning and thunder, evoking the image of a massive army on a triumphant march.

Seclusion (归去来兮辞 *Gui Qu Lai Xi Ci*)

Wen Zhengming 文徵明 (1470-1559, Ming dynasty)
Small regular script (*xiao kai*)
13.7 cm × 16.1 cm
Palace Museum, Beijing

If Wang Xizhi and Zhao Mengfu brought the small regular script style to a peak in calligraphic history, then Wen Zhengming's calligraphic accomplishment was another such peak. His small regular script works are marked by neat writing, finely turned out strokes and even spatial composition in the interior of individual characters, giving them clarity and a graceful strength. He had a preference for starting the strokes with a revealed brush-tip, so the strokes are unambiguous and readily recognizable. Such brush techniques as lifting, pressing, turning, bending, pulling and pushing are all executed with precision.

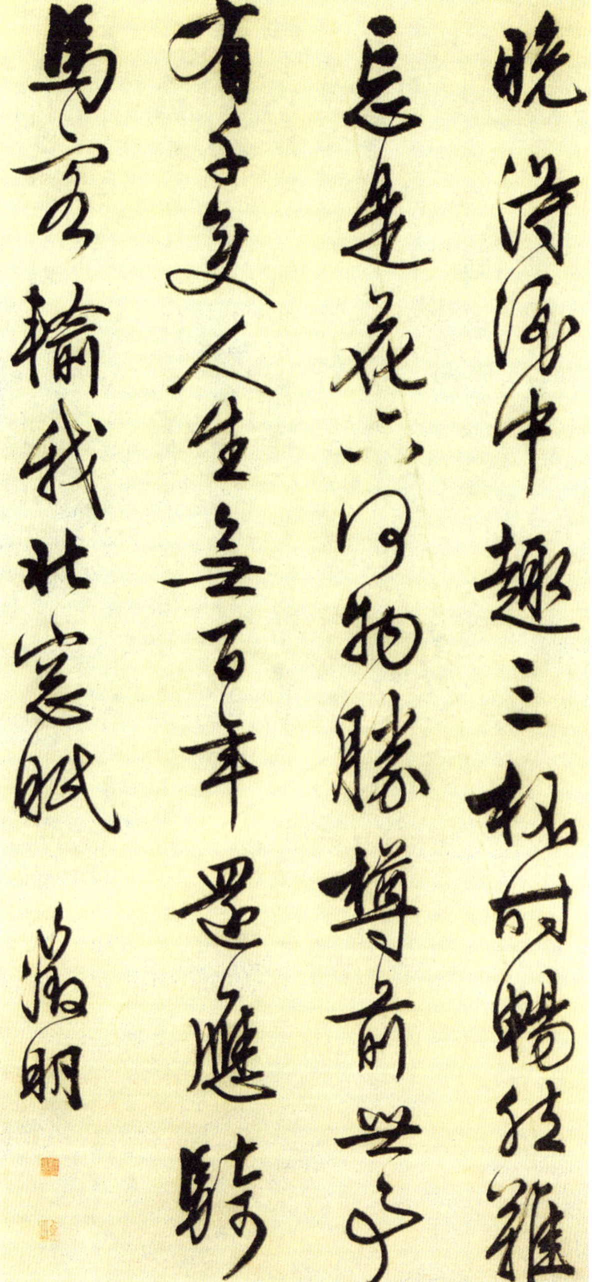

Eight-line Poem in Five-character Meter on a Scroll (五律词轴 *Wu Lü Ci Zhou*)

Wen Zhengming 文徵明 (1470-1559, Ming dynasty)
Running script (*xing shu*)
131.5 cm × 63.5 cm
Palace Museum, Beijing

Wen Zhengming's running script successfully assimilated the styles of Su Shi, Huang Tingjian and Kangli Naonao; it also benefited from Wang Xizhi's *Preface to Buddha's Teachings*. *Eight-line Regular Poem in Five-character Meter on a Scroll* betrays the consideralbe influence of Kangli Naonao in its crisp, clean and swift brushwork. His calligraphic virtuosity allows him to write at a fast speed and yet still be able to show clearly how he begins a stroke, moves the brush and lifts off the paper at the end of the stroke. The switching of the direction of the brush, the transition from one stroke to another and the variation of pressure in lifting and pressing down the brush are accomplished in a speedy but orderly fashion, without compromising fidelity to calligraphic codes.

Poem in Four-character Meter in Seal Script (篆书四言诗卷 *Zhuan Shu Si Yan Shi Juan*)

Xu Lin 徐霖 (1473–1549, Ming dynasty)
Seal script (*zhuan shu*)
29.5 cm × 628 cm
Palace Museum, Beijing

Xu Lin specialized in seal script calligraphy. At an early stage he favored an ornate style but leaned toward a quaint simplicity in later years. The seal script style in this piece is the so-called "jade chopstick seal script" (玉箸篆 *yu zhu zhuan*), marked by an even, unchanging thickness of the lines, the absence of an appended foot (垂脚 *chui jiao*) in vertical strokes and an oblong character structure. The origin of this seal script style can be traced to *Stone Tablet of Mount Yi*. There are few surviving works by Xu Lin but forgeries abound.

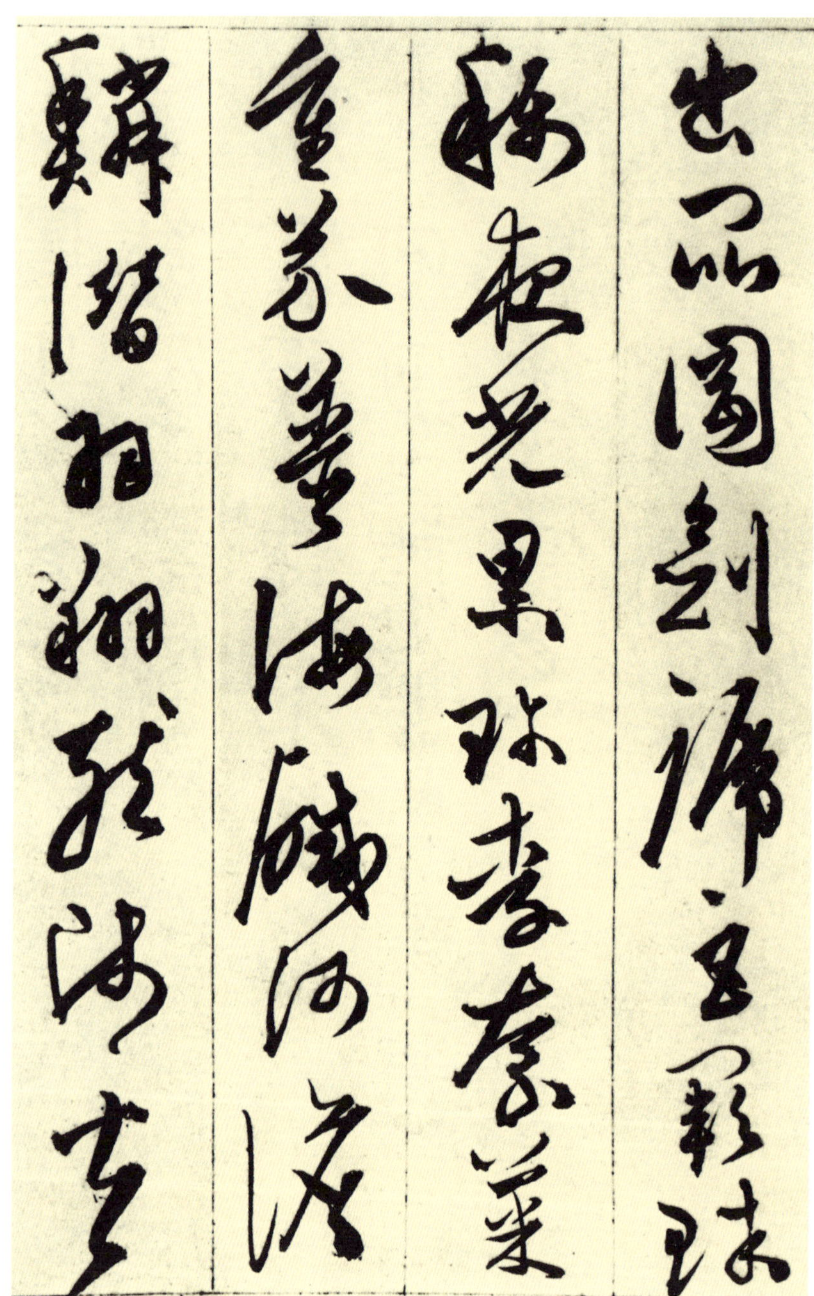

Thousand Character Reader (千字文 *Qian Zi Wen*)

Chen Chun 陈淳 (1483-1544, Ming dynasty)
Cursive script (*cao shu*)

Chen Chun modeled his calligraphy on the style of Wen Zhengming. His works therefore exhibit characteristics of Wen's running cursive script style, with graceful, energetic lines, smooth turnings and an insouciance characteristic of the Wei and Jin dynasties. This vibrant, majestic piece evokes "galloping steeds and phoenixes waltzing in the air."

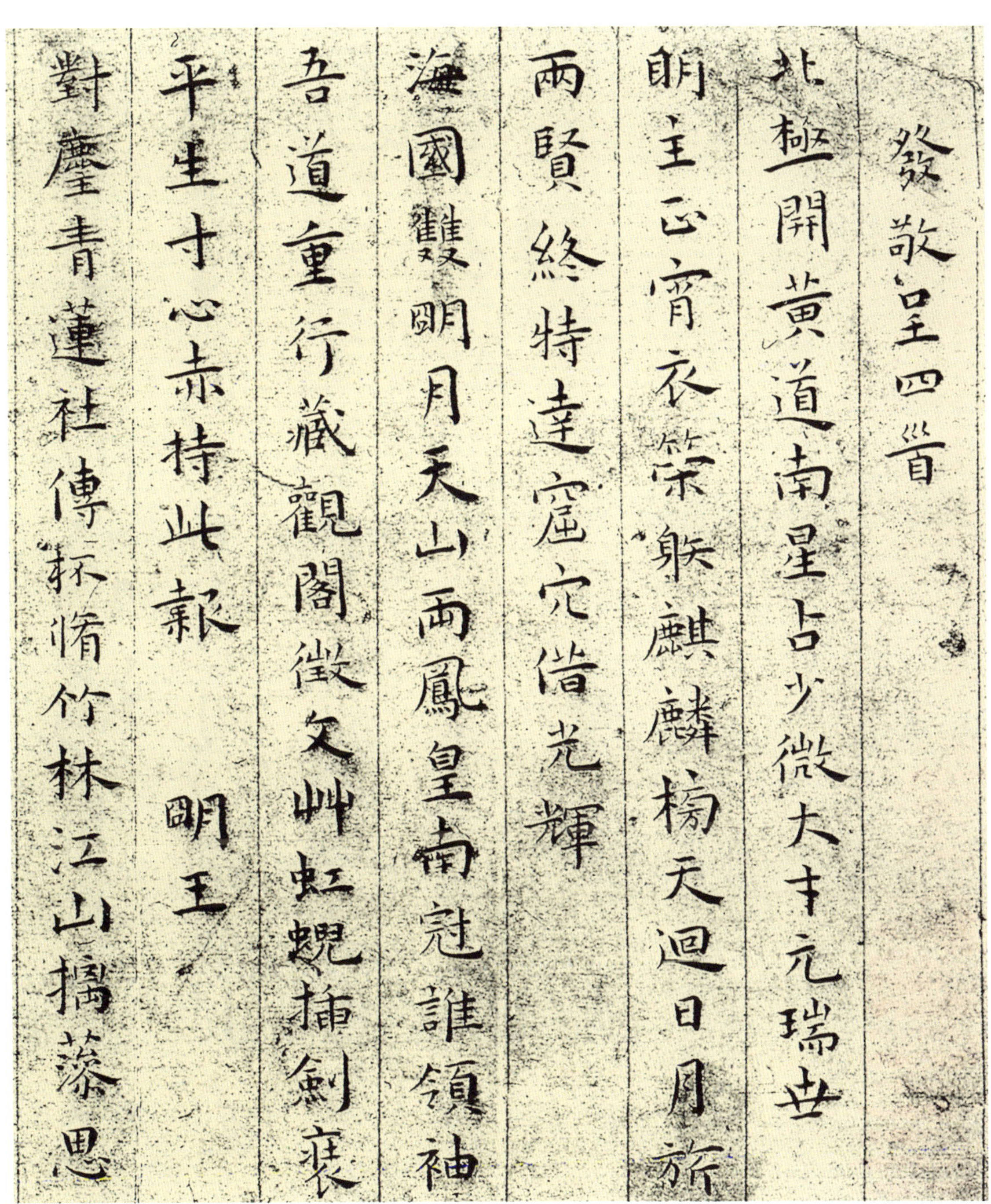

Poem to Honorable Teacher (呈林翁蔡尊师衡山丈诗 *Cheng Lin Weng Cai Zun Shi Heng Shan Zhang Shi*)

Wang Chong 王宠 (1494-1533, Ming dynasty)
Small regular script (*xiao kai*)

Because of its many uses in everyday life, small regular script writing tended to become formulaic as habits formed in long practice hardened into a rut. As a result, many calligraphies in small regular script from the Jin and Tang dynasties on down often lacked artistic merit. This scroll by Wang Chong in small regular script boasts the clarity of Wang Xianzhi, the elegance of Yu Shinan and the breadth and spaciousness of Yan Zhenqing.

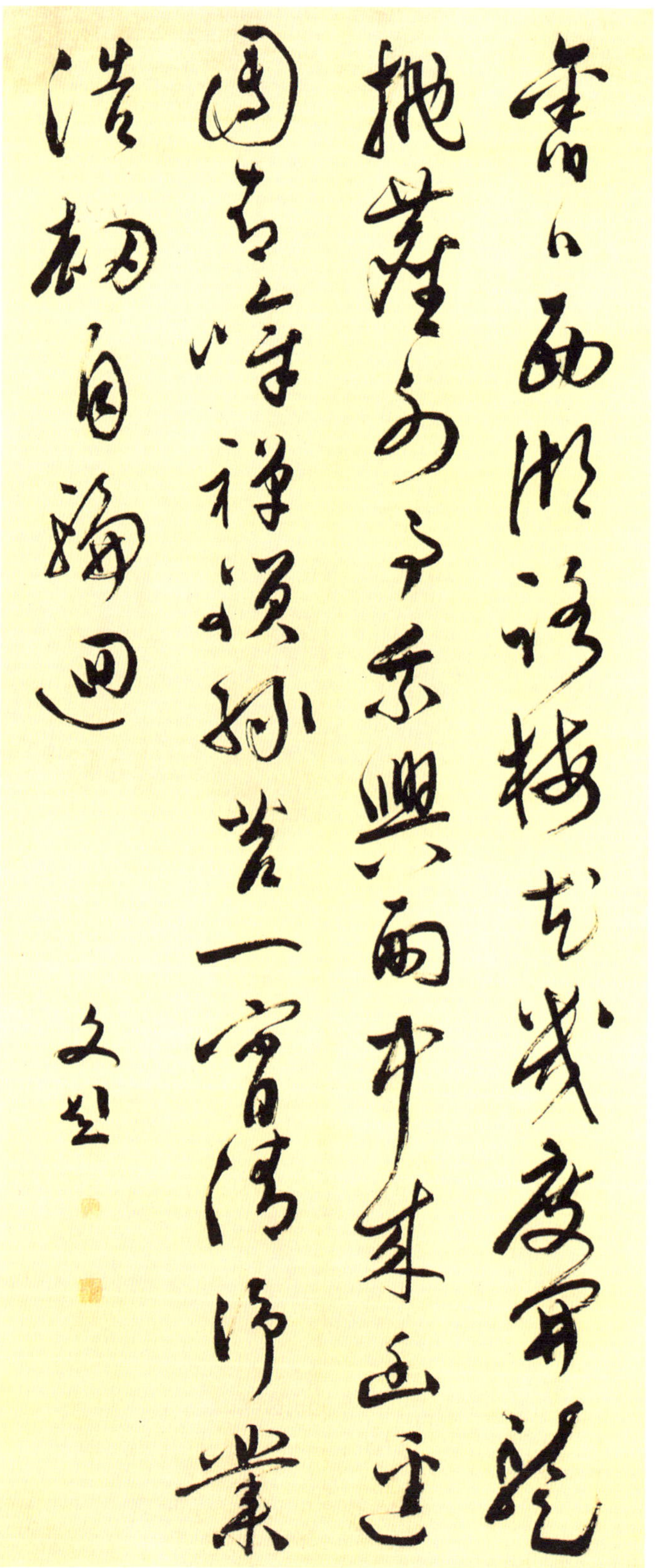

Eight-line Regular Poem in Five-character Meter on a Scroll (五律诗轴 *Wu Lü Shi Zhou*)

Wen Peng 文彭 (1498-1573, Ming dynasty)
Running script (*xing shu*)
148.4 cm × 66 cm
Palace Museum, Beijing

Wen Peng, the eldest son of Wen Zhengming, was known for his cursive script works. In this solid and dynamic piece, one detects no hesitation at the beginning of strokes and no sloppy endings. The author is careful to observe codes and the strokes are round and mellow. Wen Peng combines his father's meticulous, crisp and brisk style with a freedom and fluidity that is distinctly his own.

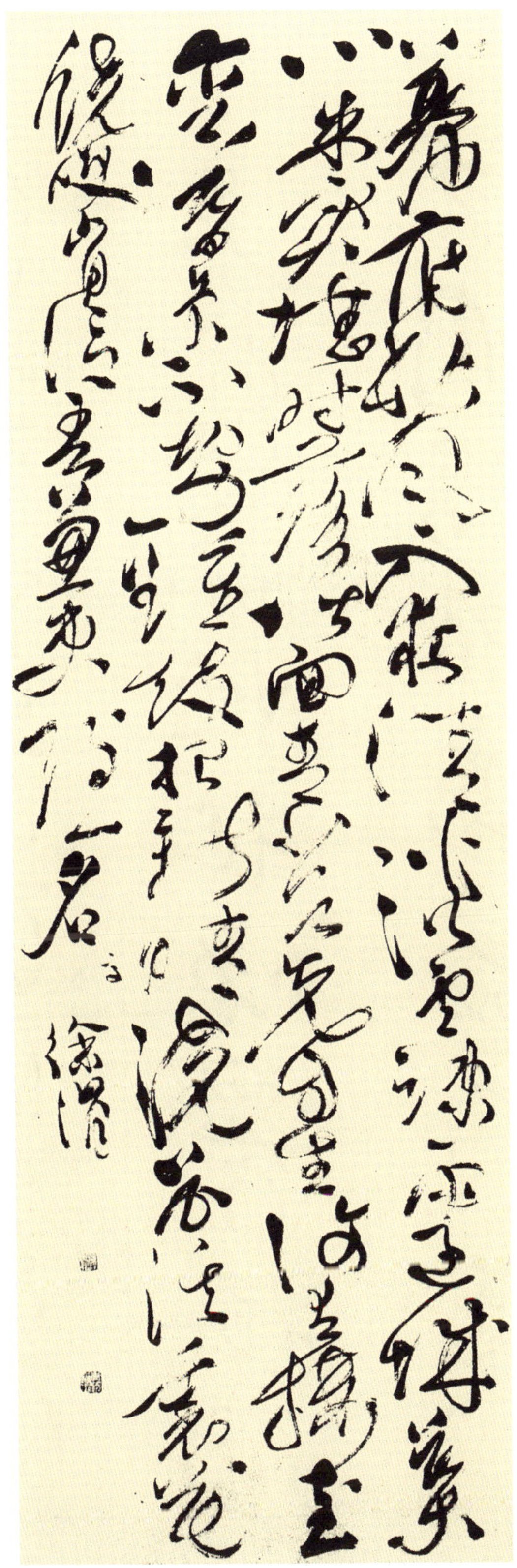

Poem in Cursive Script on a Scroll (草书诗轴 *Cao Shu Shi Zhou*)

Xu Wei 徐渭 (1521-1593, Ming dynasty)
Cursive script (*cao shu*)

Xu Wei, praised as "knight of the calligraphic 'forest', and demigod of the 'eight strokes'," writes an ebullient cursive script with an irrepressible flair. The structure of his characters is broad, open and grotesquely varied, and the spatial composition is a wild patchwork of subspaces of varying sizes and inclinations. The intense passion and striking visual impact of the piece reveal the flamboyant personality and distinctive style of the calligrapher.

Thousand Character Reader (千字文 *Qian Zi Wen*)

Zhan Jingfeng 詹景凤 (1532-1602, Ming dynasty)
Cursive script (*cao shu*)
31.5 cm × 1034 cm
Provincial Museum of Anhui

In this *Thousand Character Reader*, the calligrapher employs a solid, smooth center-brush technique. The entire piece is a continuous whole, written with a natural ink tone and spontaneous turns. The expert brushwork in this mad cursive script work "appears to have a divine hand directing the brush, and is richly varied yet without breaking any convention."

Eight-line Regular Poem in Five-character Meter on a Scroll (五律诗轴 *Wu Lü Shi Zhou*)

Xing Tong 邢侗 **(1551-1612, Ming dynasty)**
Running script (*xing shu*)
142 cm × 33.2 cm
Palace Museum, Beijing

The late Ming produced a talented crop of calligraphers, the best among whom included Xing Tong, Dong Qichang, Mi Wanzhong 米万钟 (1570-1628, Ming dynasty), Zhang Ruitu 张瑞图 (?-1644, Ming dynasty), Huang Daozhou 黄道周 (1585-1646, Ming dynasty), Wang Duo 王铎 (1592-1652, Ming dynasty) and Ni Yuanlu 倪元璐 (1594-1644, Ming dynasty) Extolling Wang Xizhi as "the foremost calligrapher in history," Xing Tong dedicated himself to emulating the Wang style, and in his pursuit of the spirit and technique of Wang Xizhi he has left the world with a rich body of works copying Wang's calligraphies, which account for a large part of his surviving oeuvre. In this piece, the brushwork exhibits a spontaneous simplicity and an unaffected self-expression that successfully marries the spirit of the imitating calligrapher to the graceful, dynamic body of Wang-style calligraphy.

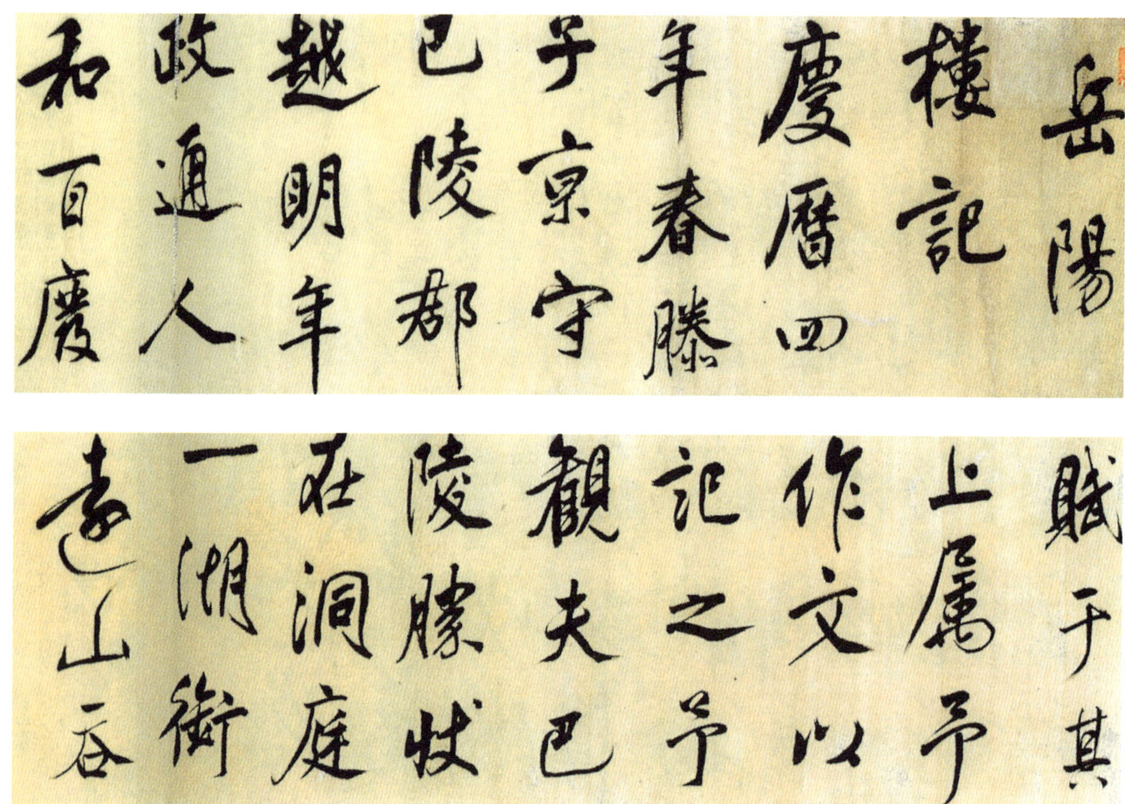

Yueyang Pavilion (岳阳楼记 *Yue Yang Lou Ji*)

Dong Qichang 董其昌 (1555-1636, Ming dynasty)
Running script (*xing shu*)
37.6 cm × 1499.5 cm
Palace Museum, Beijing

Dong Qichang is the most renowned painter-calligrapher of the Ming dynasty and has left a major imprint in the world of Chinese calligraphy. He is known for a quaint, simple style with a smooth purity. The long scroll featuring fist-sized ideograms has the feel of a work completed in one breath. The graceful, energetic, easily flowing brushwork combines the unaffected exuberance "worthy of Yan Zhenqing's 'boniness' and Zhao Mengfu's 'grace'," the breadth and steepness of Mi Fu and the insouciance of Wang Xizhi. The work is redolent of intellect and culture.

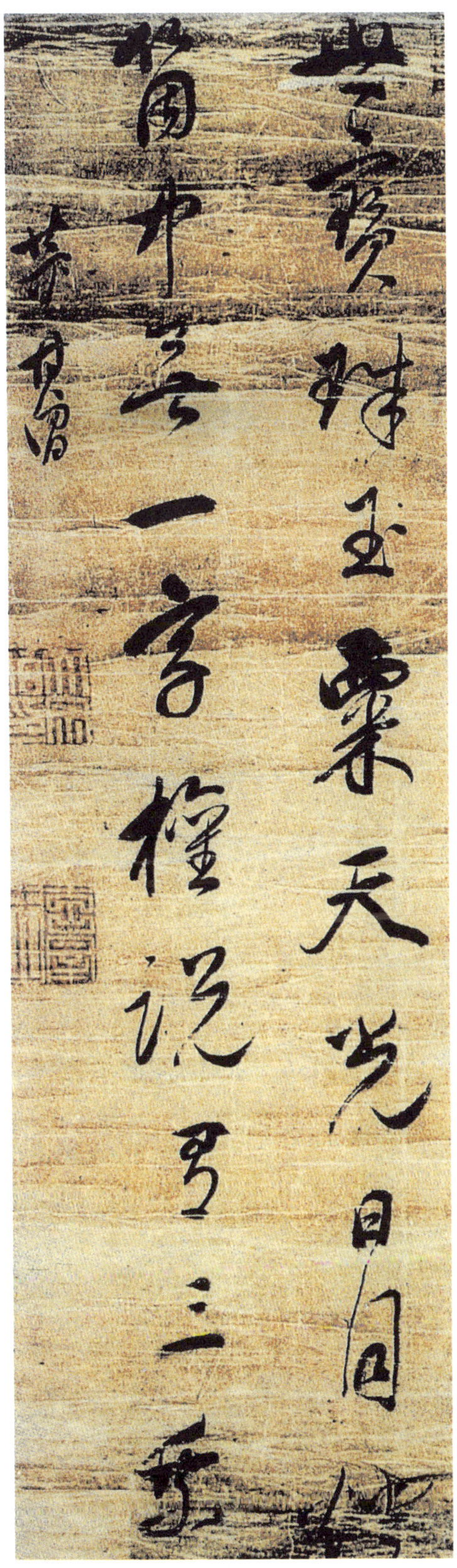

Poem in Five-character Meter on a Scroll (五言诗轴 *Wu Yan Shi Zhou*)

Dong Qichang 董其昌 (1555-1636, Ming dynasty)
Running script (*xing shu*)
96 cm × 28.8 cm
Provincial Museum of Anhui

In this scroll, the spatial composition is modeled on the simple, spare style of Yang Ningshi of the Five dynasties marked by wide spaces between columns and an airy character structure. The spontaneous, deliberately clumsy brushwork gives a sense of the author consciously stopping short of full deployment of the brush or unreserved self-expression. Chinese landscape paintings fall under either the Northern school or the Southern school in Dong Qichang's system of classification. He considered the Southern school the authentic torchbearer of the literati painting tradition. As in his paintings, he sought above all to express the spirit and soul of ink and brush in his calligraphies.

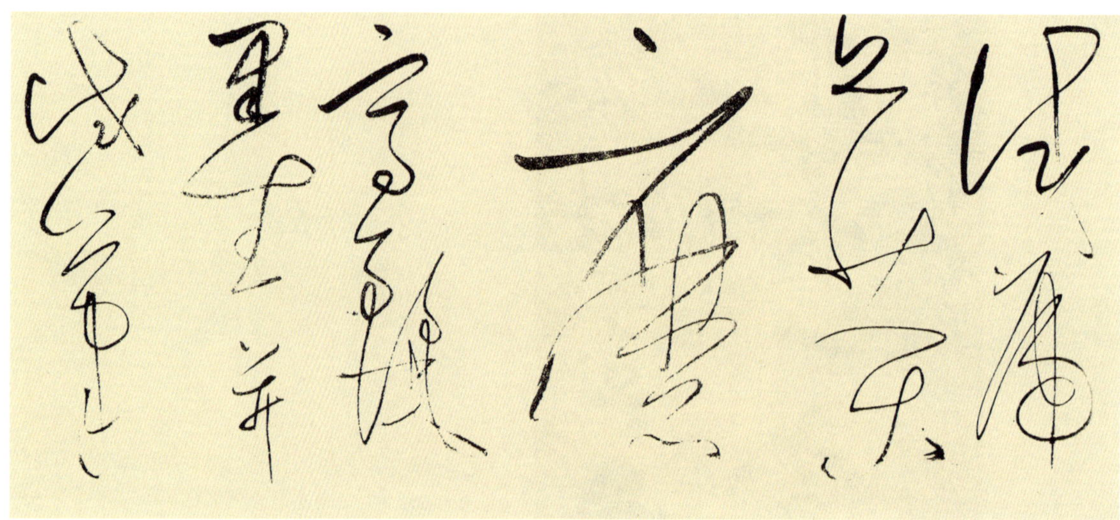

Trial of Writing (试书帖 *Shi Shu Tie*)

Dong Qichang 董其昌 (1555-1636, Ming dynasty)
Cursive script (*cao shu*)

This piece gave an account of the artist's creative process "With rain falling outside the window and no pressing business to occupy myself...Sampling tea from Tiger Hill and grinding an ink stick from Korea, I tried the brush, doodling on the paper." Enjoying a tranquil and leisurely moment, the calligrapher did not particularly fuss with rules for lifting, pressing, pausing and reversing the brush and as a result the thickness of the lines does not vary much and the strokes are smooth and slender. There is a refreshing charm to the work, something akin to the purity and beauty of *si zhu*—a kind of string and woodwind music in the areas south of the lower reaches of the Yangtze River.

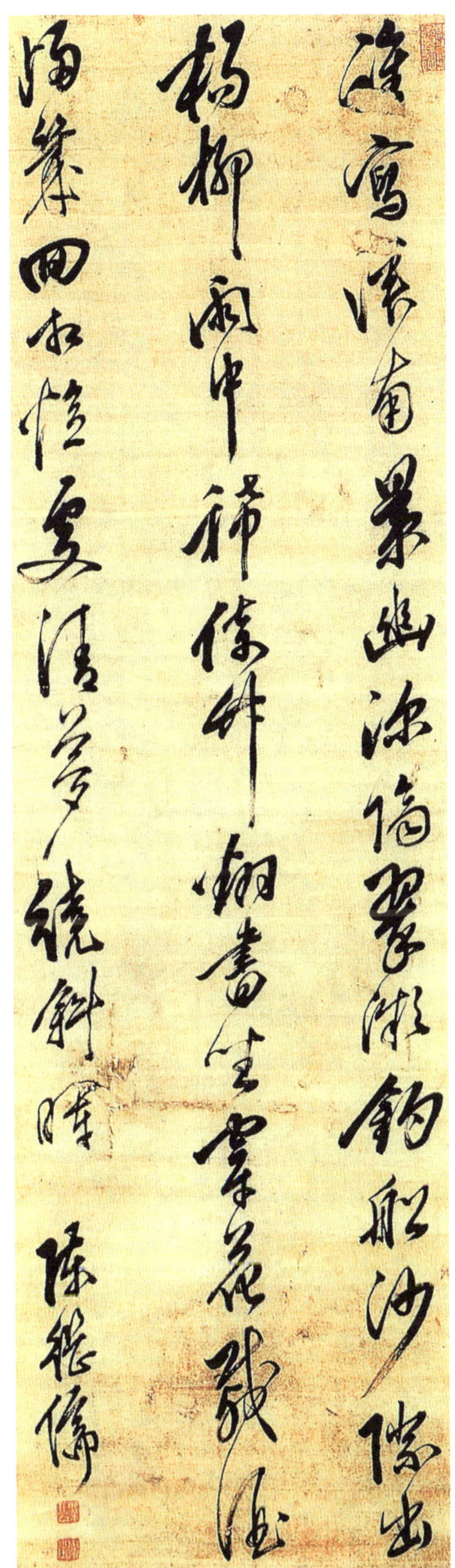

Poem in Five-character Meter in Running Cursive Script (行草书五言诗轴 *Xing Cao Shu Wu Yan Shi Zhou*)

Chen Jiru 陈继儒 (1558-1639, Ming dynasty)
Running cursive script (*xing cao*)
166.8 cm × 49.5 cm
Provincial Museum of Anhui

Chen Jiru shared fame with Dong Qichang in landscape painting. The structure of characters in this piece is a graceful elongated form. The calligrapher neatly spreads his brush as soon as it hits the paper and makes smooth, natural looking turns and transitions between strokes, with delicate links. A cultured look runs through the work.

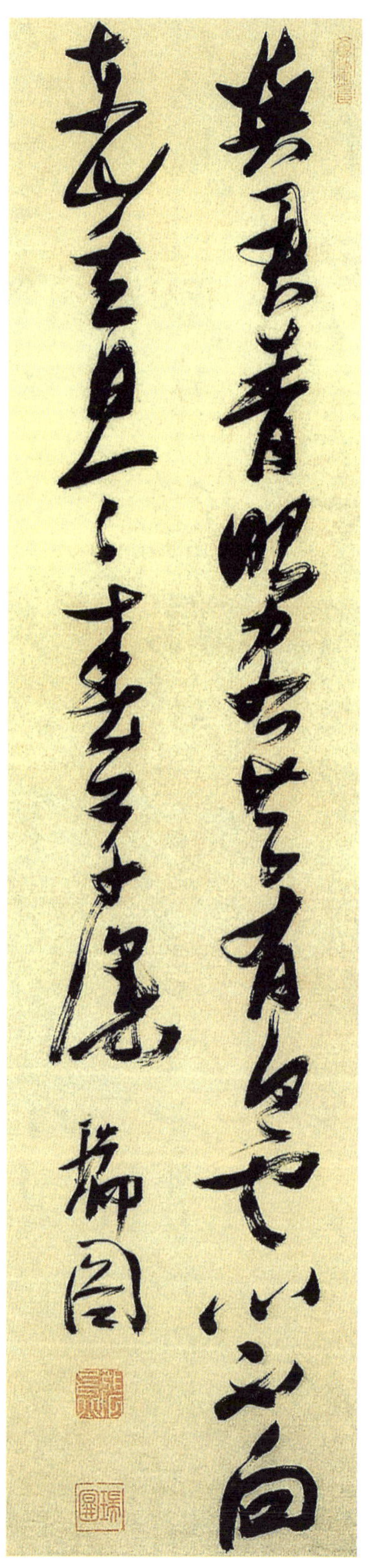

Quatrain in Five-character Meter on a Scroll (五绝诗轴 *Wu Jue Shi Zhou*)

Zhang Ruitu 张瑞图 (?-1644, Ming dynasty)
Running script (*xing shu*)
172.7 cm × 43.5 cm
Palace Museum, Beijing

In Zhang Ruitu's calligraphy, "all round corners are written as sharp turns, in a departure from tradition" (observation of Qing calligrapher Liang Yan). When starting and ending a stroke, he abandons the conventional technique of "hiding" the brush-tip and boldly shows off the tip of the brush even in cursive script to create a sharp, crisp look.

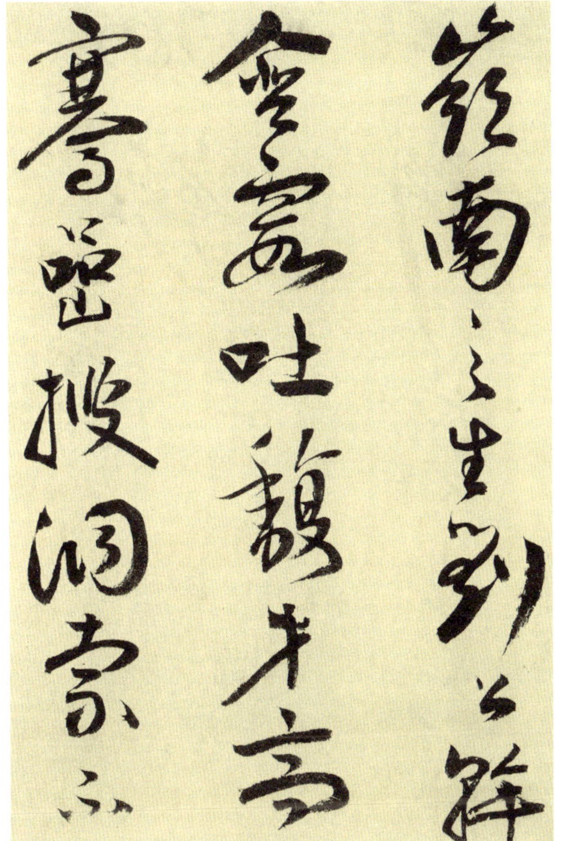

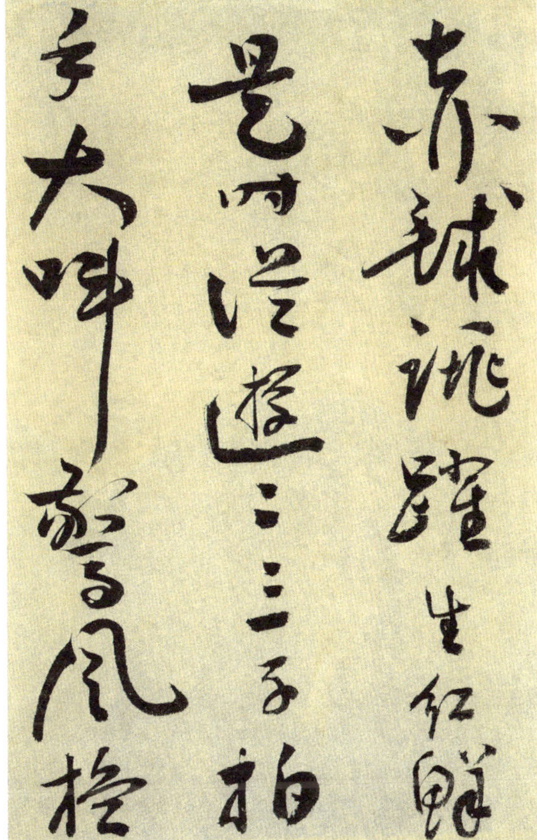

Poem about Climbing Mount Tai (登岱诗 *Deng Dai Shi*)

Jiang Jie 蒋杰 (years of birth/death unknown, Ming dynasty)
Running cursive script (*xing cao*)
20 pages, each 31 cm × 20 cm
Private collection

Jiang Jie's calligraphy had a major following for a time in the late Ming and early Qing. Some calligraphers ranked him among the "Four Calligraphic Greats" of the Qing dynasty, with Dong Qichang, Mi Wanzhong and Huang Daozhou. In this collection of poems, the calligrapher's brush follows the mood changes in the poetry, alternating between virility and tenderness, quickening and slowing, taking off in flight or settling down, switching between running script and a cursive hand and mixing center-brush and side-brush methods. The calligraphy gives expression to the temperament and the temperament suffuses the calligraphy.

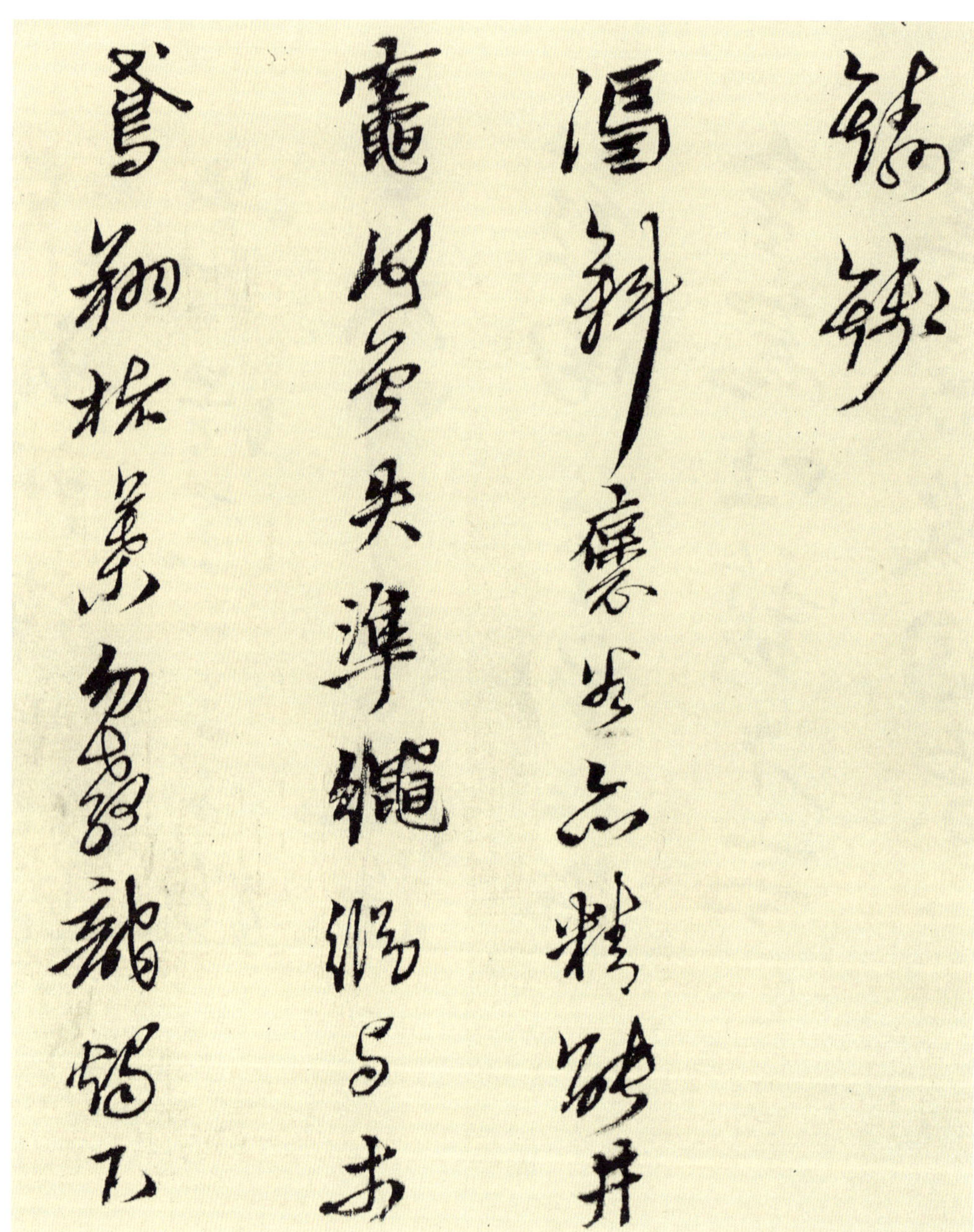

Chanting Poems in the Mountain (山中杂咏 *Shan Zhong Za Yong*)

Huang Daozhou 黄道周 (1585-1646, Ming dynasty)
Cursive script (*cao shu*)
Palace Museum, Taipei

In this elegantly calligraphed poem on a scroll, the columns are compact; the only exceptions are the extended last stroke in the character " 斜 " and the wider space in the character pair " 余闲 ". The sharp contrast between this density and the wide spaces between the columns evokes a venerable elderly Confucian scholar sitting serenely in a mountain woods, physically still but mentally and spiritually active, his thoughts stretching back a millennium.

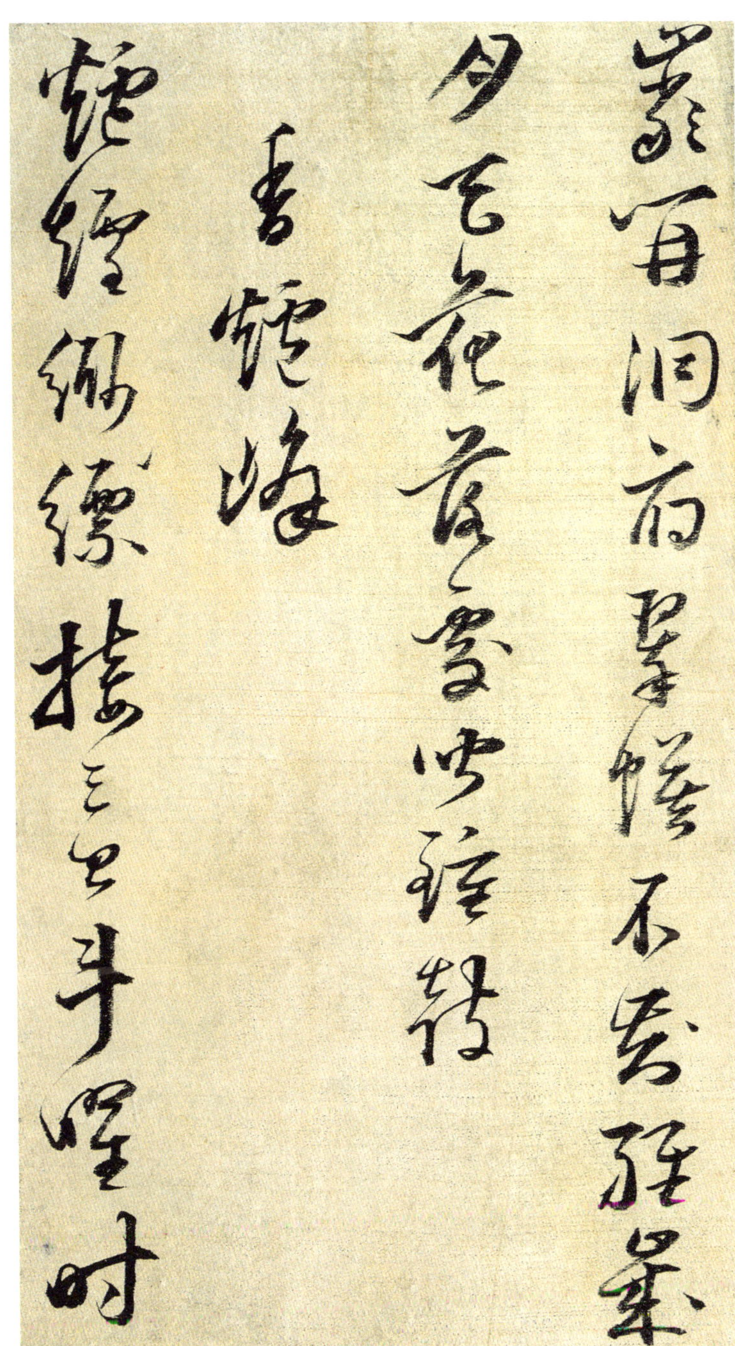

Poems about Travelling (纪游诗册 *Ji You Shi Ce*)

Jiang Fengyuan 姜逢元 (years of birth/death unknown, Ming dynasty)
Cursive script (*cao shu*)
20 pages, each 27.5 cm × 16 cm
Provincial Museum of Anhui

Although this collection of poems is in semi-cursive script, the calligrapher often starts his strokes in regular script, employing the side-brush technique and a sharp brush-tip. After starting a stroke with a sharp tip, the artist would apply downward pressure before lifting it up to create a sharp, crisp clerical script style ending. The strokes are smoothly and expertly executed, with the brush twisting and turning with ease, producing characters with a charming variety of postures. The calligraphy in this piece is marked by an uninterrupted flow of brush movement, a delicate grace and great intellectual depth.

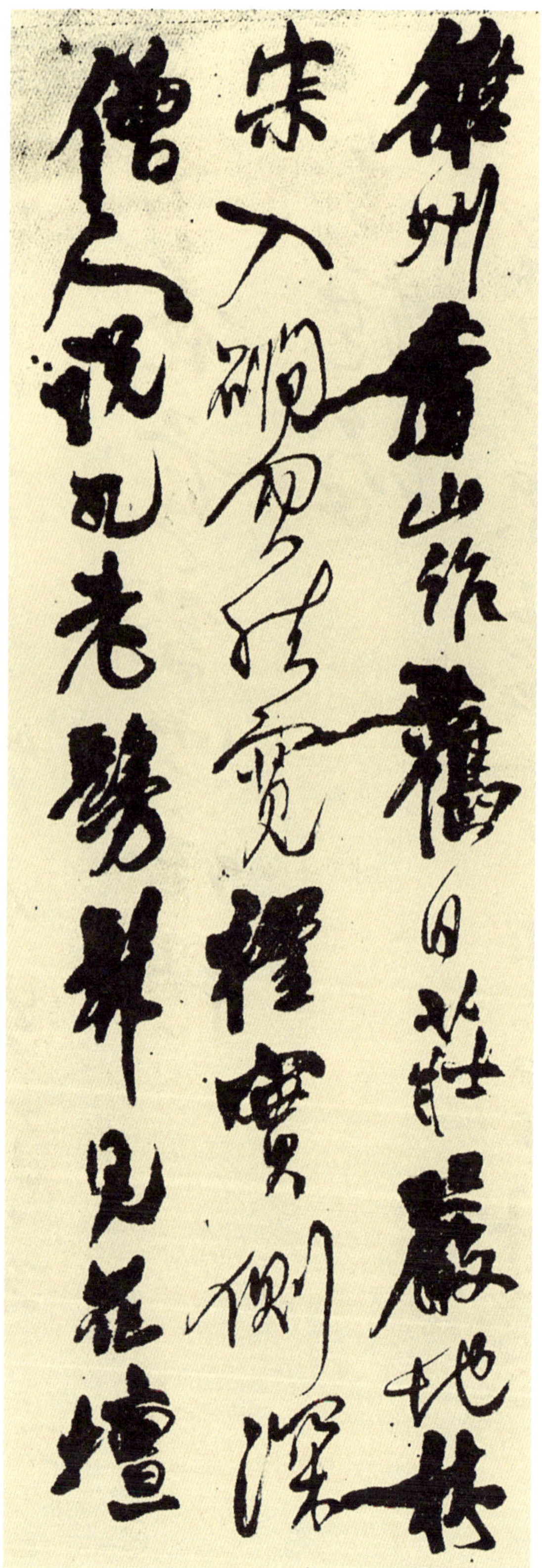

Poem about Mount Xiang (雒州香山作 *Luo Zhou Xiang Shan Zuo*)

Wang Duo 王铎 (1592-1652, Ming dynasty)
Running script (*xing shu*)

Wang Duo, also known under the cognomen Juesi, was with Huang Daozhou and Ni Yuanlu one of the "Three Calligraphic Greats of the Late Ming." But unlike Huang and Ni, who were killed for refusing to serve a new master under the Qing, Wang Duo was rewarded with high office as he switched his loyalty to the Qing court with the overthrow of the Ming by the Qing. Although he was widely scorned for his moral failure, later critics, rightly, did not consider it ground enough for negating his calligraphic achievement, which prompted many to compare him to the great calligraphers of the Northern Song dynasty. His cursive script style is full of energy, boldness and spontaneity. His innovative approach in the use of ink, referred to as the "ink oozing technique," creates a special effect by causing a seepage of the ink across the border of the stroke as the calligrapher lifts, presses and pauses his brush in certain ways.

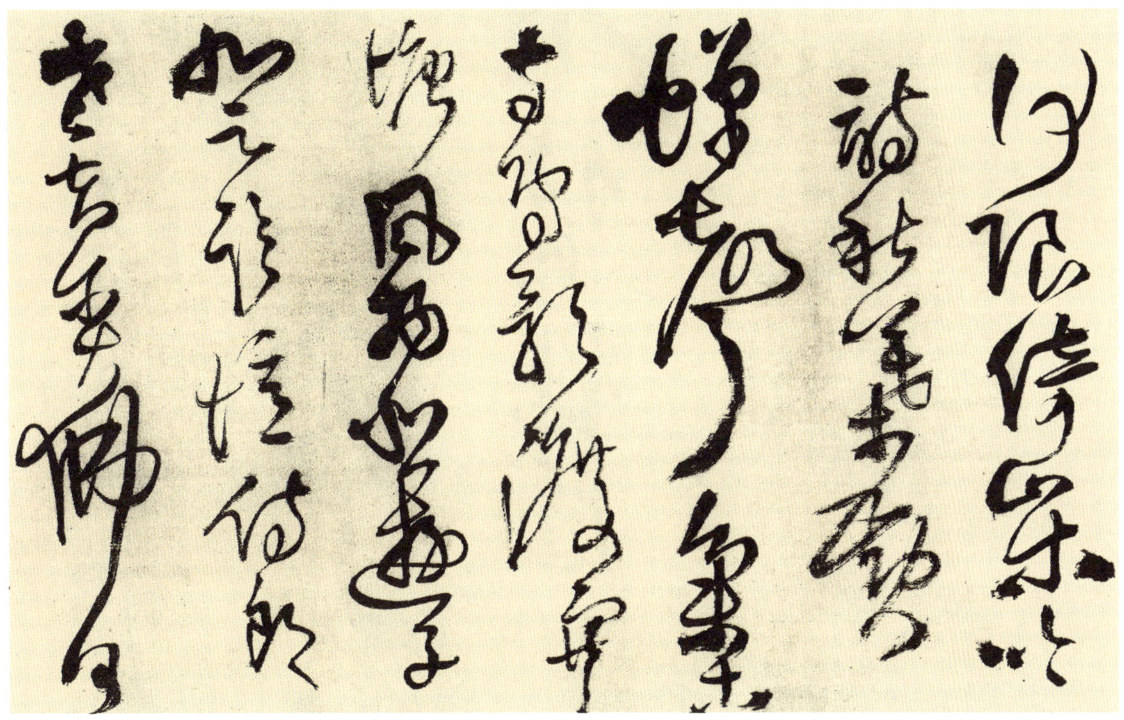

Poems in Cursive Script (草书诗卷 *Cao Shu Shi Juan*)

Wang Duo 王铎 (1592-1652, Ming dynasty)
Cursive script (*cao shu*)

The Ming dynasty was overthrown by the Qing about the time when Wang Duo turned 40. In a reflection of his angst and anguish as he struggled with conflicting, uncertain loyalties, the event marked a turning point in his calligraphic evolution as he moved from a refined style to one characterized by a wild, untrammeled brushwork, daring character shapes, intricate strokes and a crazy-quilt spatial composition. In the words of the Qing calligrapher Fu Shan 傅山 (1607-1684, Qing dynasty), "Before the age of 40, Wang Duo wrote with great contrivance; after 40, he shed all the artifices and as a result became a master."

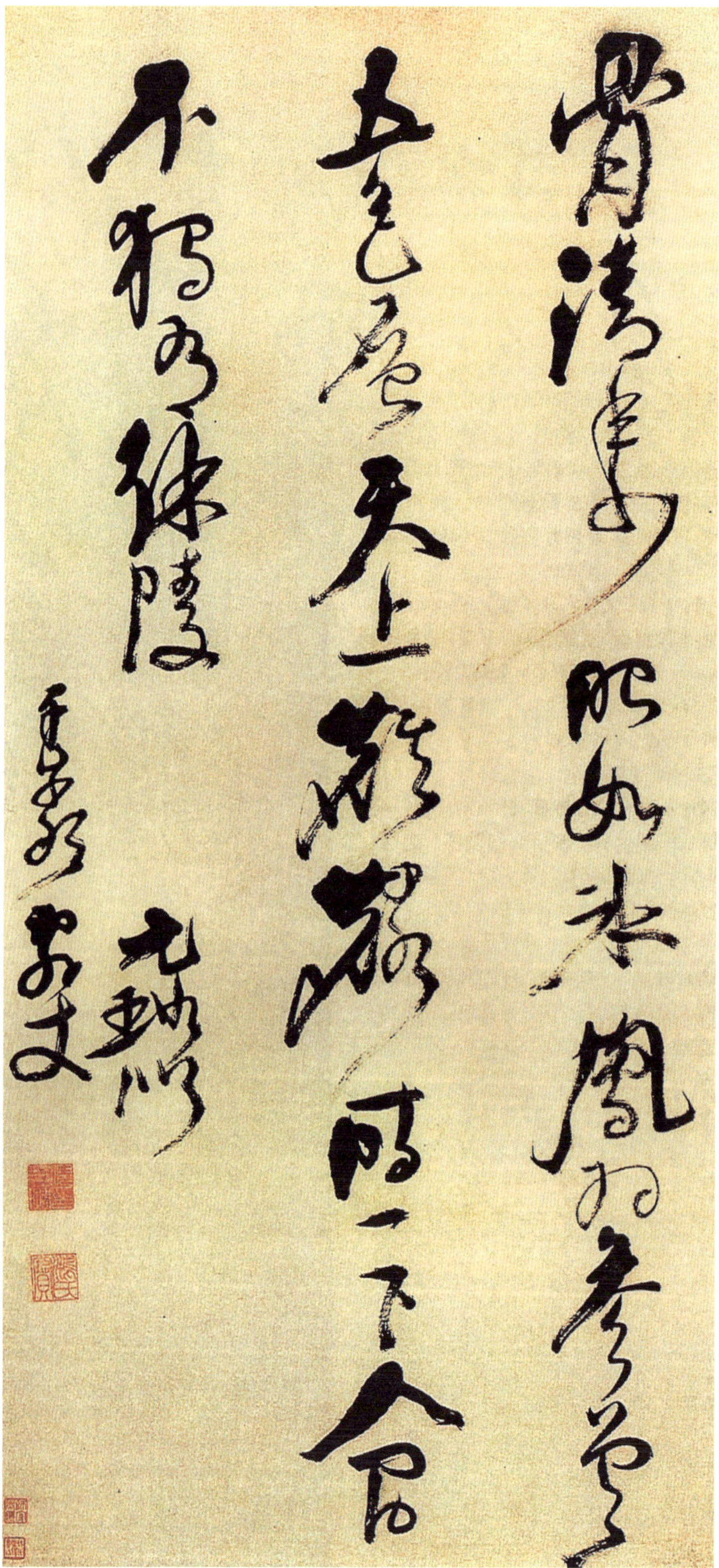

Poem of Du Mu on a Scroll (杜牧诗轴 *Du Mu Shi Zhou*)

Ni Yuanlu 倪元璐 (1594–1644, Ming dynasty)
Running cursive script (*xing cao*)
128.5 cm × 93.1 cm
Palace Museum, Beijing

Ni Yuanlu's running cursive script style adds a heaviness and resistance to pauses, lifts and turns of the brush, which stirs up the composition by "creating divisions and alliances" and alternating between dark and dry ink tones. This magnificent piece evokes the image of a master wielding a pliant brush over the paper creating ideograms that curl and uncurl at whim like mercurial clouds in the sky.

Qing Dynasty

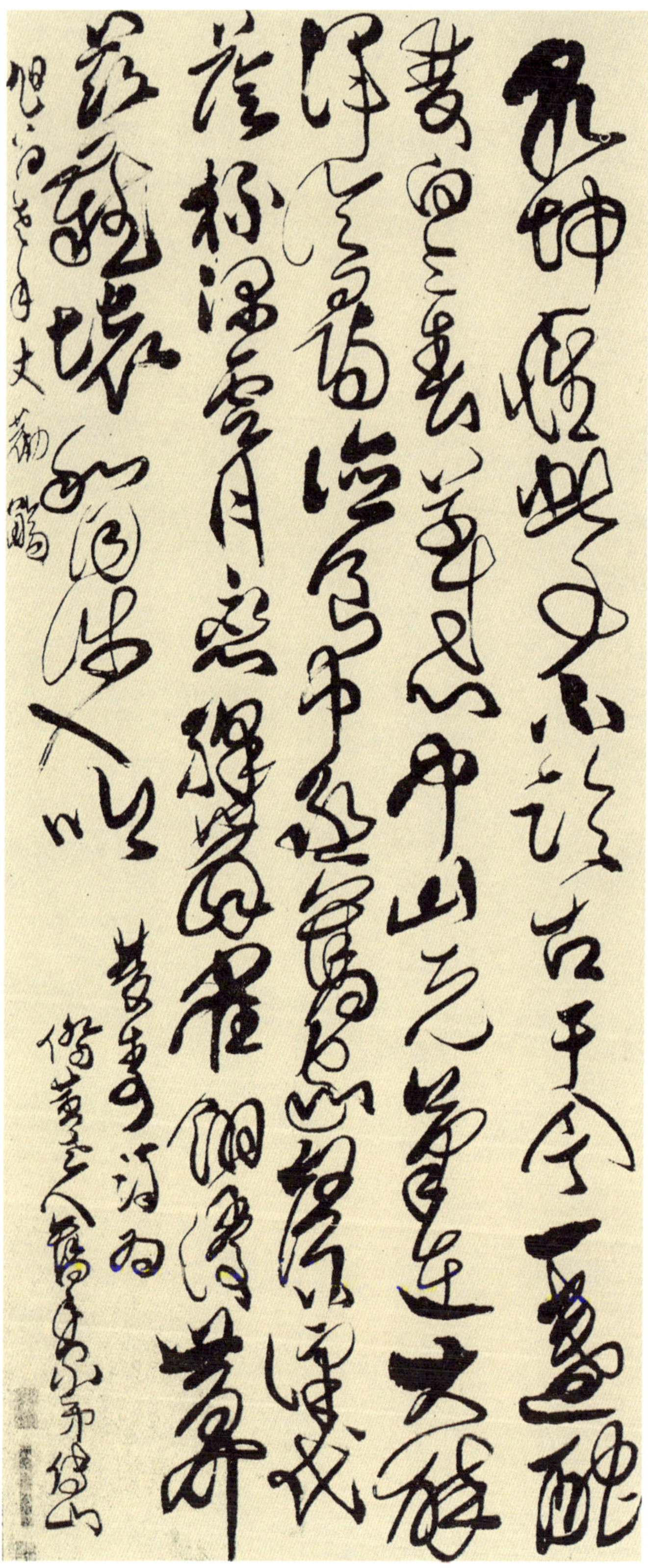

Poems in Cursive Script on a Scroll (草书诗轴 *Cao Shu Shi Zhou*)

Fu Shan 傅山 (1607-1684, Qing dynasty)
Cursive script (*cao shu*)

Fu Shan had a proud, unyielding temperament. He adamantly refused to take the civil service examination administered by the Qing court following the overthrow of the Ming. He was a versatile calligrapher with virtuosity in regular script, cursive script, seal script and clerical script. In calligraphy, he "preferred clumsiness to refinement, plainness to elegance, disjointedness to slickness and spontaneity to contrivance." This iconoclastic view shook the world of calligraphy and had a significant impact on the esthetic perception and artistic creation of later generations. He also provided the intellectual ferment for the founding and evolution of the stele school of calligraphy as he encouraged learning from stone inscriptions to forge a naive calligraphic style.

Poem to the Tune "Huan Xi Sha" (浣溪沙词 *Huan Xi Sha Ci*)

Zheng Fu 郑簠 (1622-1693, Qing dynasty)
Clerical script (*li shu*)
173.6 cm × 89.6 cm
Shanghai Museum

This work clearly took its inspiration from *Cao Quan Tablet*. It combines the roundness of seal script, the spaciousness of clerical script and the clean lines of regular script. Its airy, elegant style and aura show the decided influence of Dong Qichang.

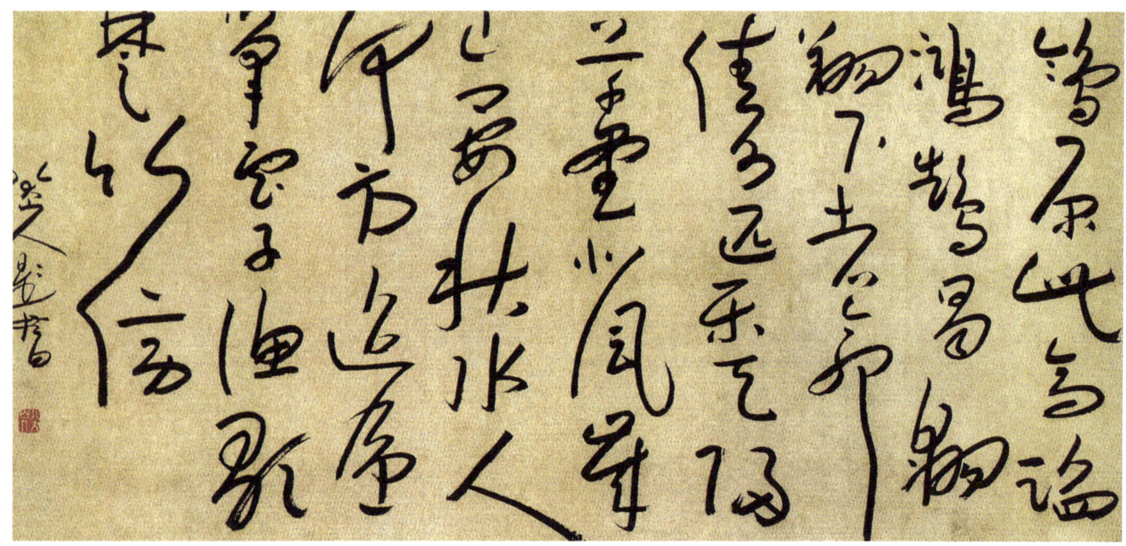

Poem to a Painting (题画诗轴 *Ti Hua Shi Zhou*)

Zhu Da 朱耷 **(1624 or 1626-1705, Qing dynasty)**
Running script (*xing shu*)
77.9 cm × 166.8 cm
Palace Museum, Beijing

Zhu Da, also known under the sobriquet "*Bada Shanren*" (八大山人), became a monk after the fall of the Ming dynasty. He was an accomplished poet and painter-calligrapher and one of the "Four Monks of Early Qing," with Shi Tao 石涛 (1641-c. 1718, Qing dynasty), Hong Ren 弘仁 (1610-1663 or 1664, Qing dynasty) and Kun Can 髡残 (1612-c. 1692, Qing dynasty). He has a unique style marked by even thickness of the lines, round and smooth corners, mixed character sizes, the pursuit of levelness in inclination and a skilled use of the "dry" brush. This scroll employs exclusively the center-brush technique and exhibits a solid brushwork with easy flowing strokes. There is a distinctive mixture of different character sizes, varied compactness of the characters and an airy spatial composition.

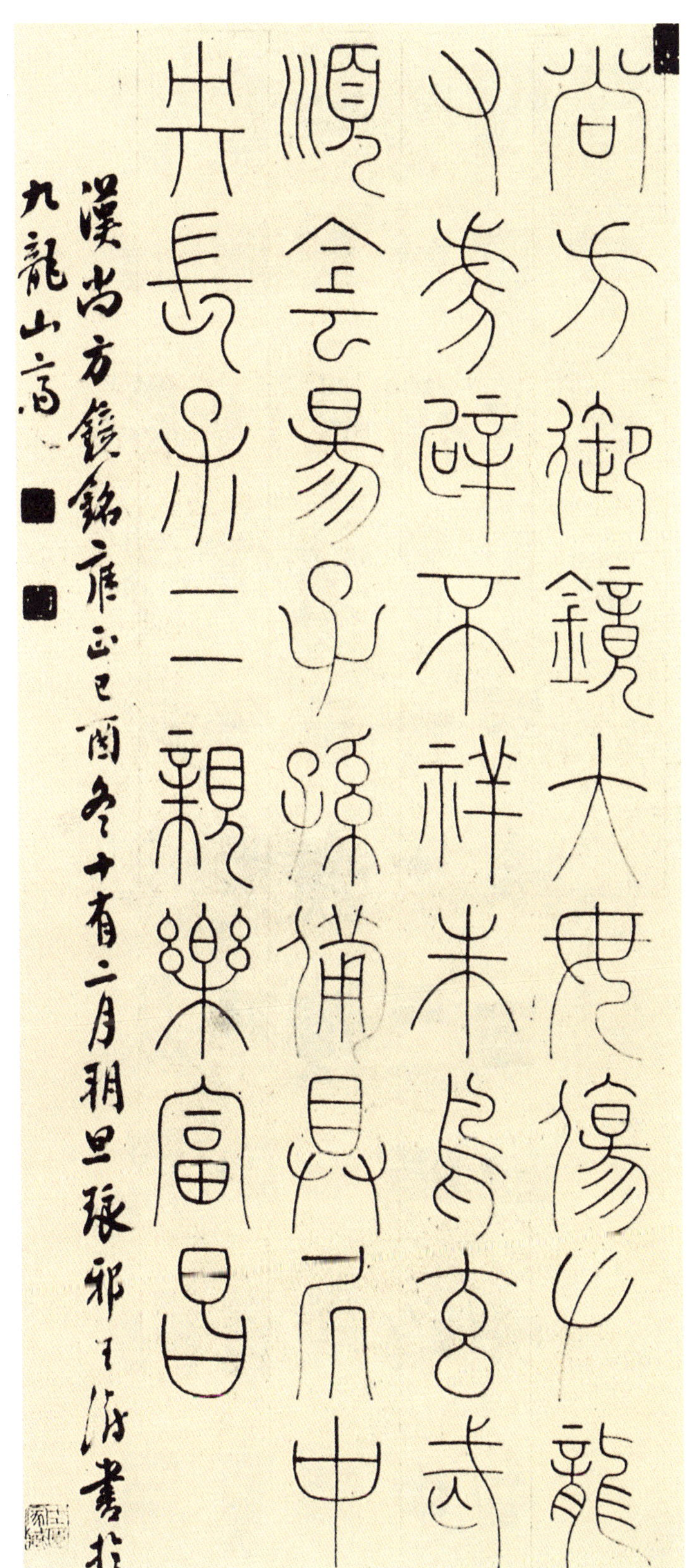

Mirror Inscription (尚方镜铭 *Shang Fang Jing Ming*)

Wang Shu 王澍 **(1668-1739, Qing dynasty)**
Seal script (*zhuan shu*)

The seal script style of Wang Shu employs the center-brush technique; his lines undulate gently and gracefully to create a calligraphy characterized by roundness, smoothness, clarity and energy. This piece is a typical example of "jade chopstick seal script", with a neat character structure, foursquare characters, and well aligned columns and rows comprising equal-sized characters. A varied sense of the compactness of the spatial composition comes about as a natural consequence of the different number of strokes in each character. The entire piece has a feel of uncontrived elegance to it.

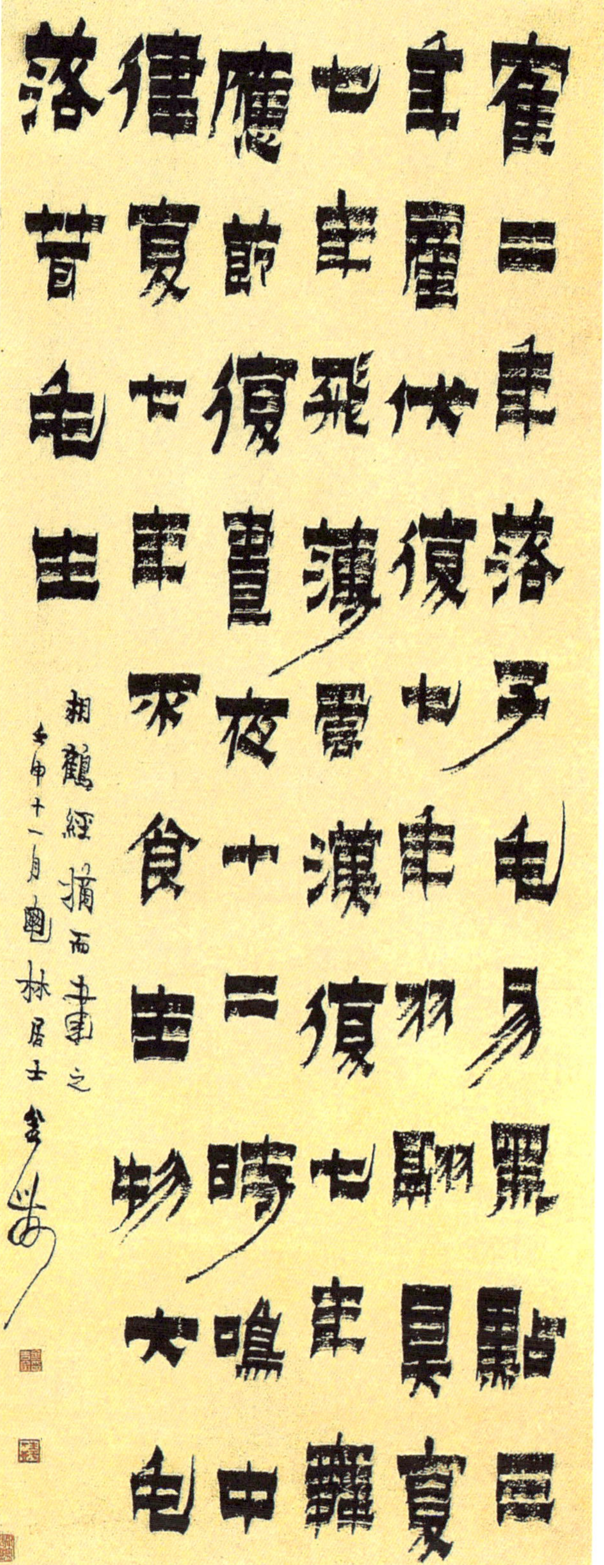

Classic of Crane on a Scroll (相鹤经轴 *Xiang He Jing Zhou*)

Jin Nong 金农 (1687-1763, Qing dynasty)
Clerical script (*li shu*)
278 cm × 50.7 cm
Palace Museum, Beijing

Jin Nong, Zheng Xie 郑燮 (1693-1765, Qing dynasty) and six other painters and calligraphers were known as the "Eight Eccentrics of Yangzhou." In calligraphy, Jin Nong preferred the stele tradition (碑学 *bei xue*) to the model-letters tradition (帖学 *tie xue*). Modeling his calligraphy on the *Mount Hua Tablet* and the *Divine Prophecy Tablet* inscriptions, he created a so-called "paintbrush" style (漆书 *qi shu*), a radically different style marked by thick horizontal strokes made with a deliberate, tension-filled brush movement and a predominantly side-brush technique and delicate, slender upright strokes written without using the back brush-tip method (intended to blunt the hard edges of stroke beginnings and endings), in sharp contrast to the horizontals.

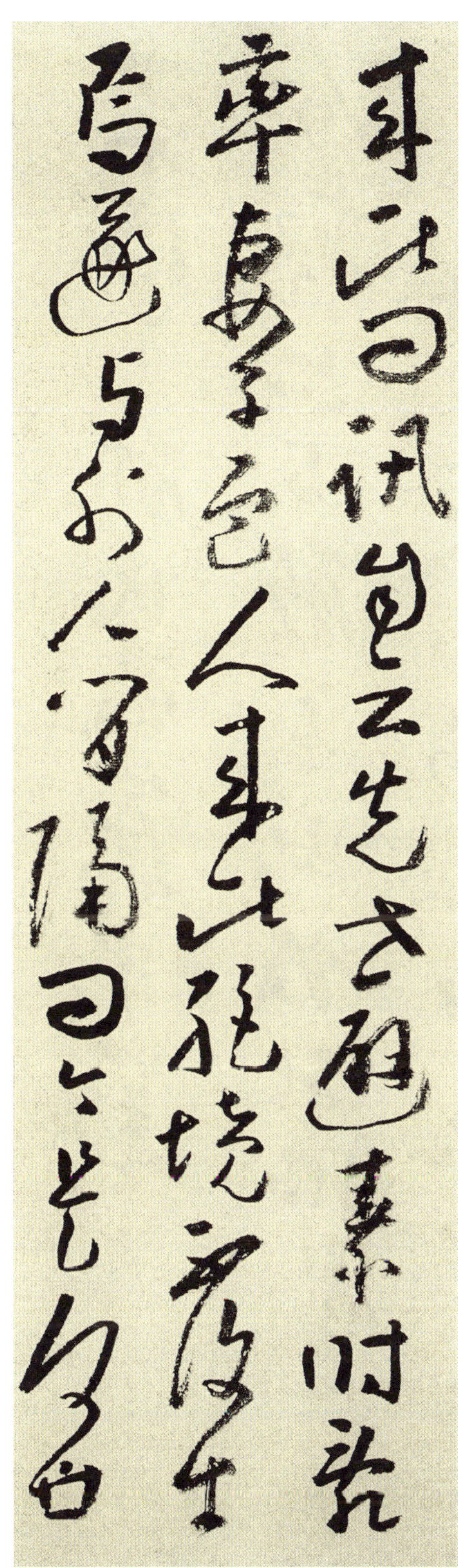

Peach Blossom Shangri-la (桃花源记 *Tao Hua Yuan Ji*)

Huang Shen 黄慎 (1687–after 1768, Qing dynasty)
Cursive script (*cao shu*)
38 cm (length of hand roll)
Palace Museum, Beijing

Huang Shen, one of the "Eight Eccentrics of Yangzhou," took the calligraphy of Huai Su of the distant past as his model and drew inspiration from the Ming masters. He applied his experience in managing the space density of paintings to his calligraphies to create magnificent cursive script works characterized by exuberant movement, disjointed strokes that nevertheless convey continuity, skillful fine tuning of speed, a judicious combination of tension and release, and a kinship to painting.

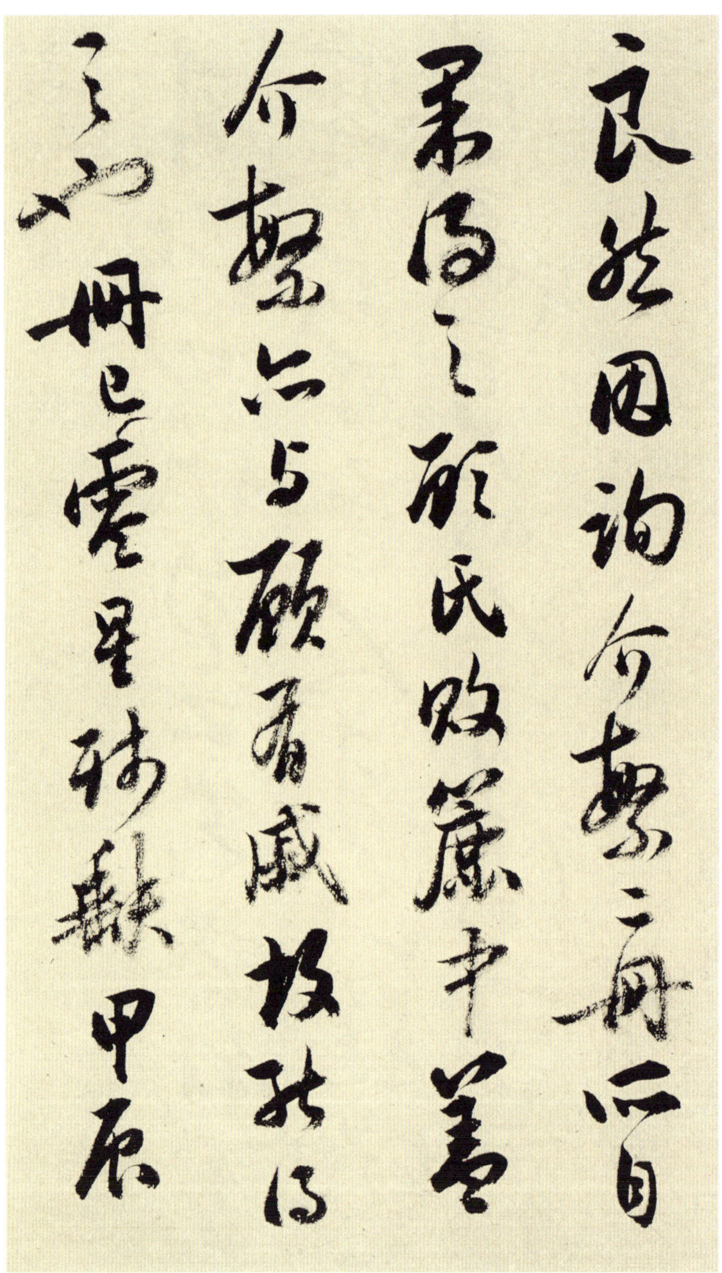

Colophon to a Model-letters Copybook (宝晋斋帖跋 *Bao Jin Zhai Tie Ba*)

Liang Yan 梁巘 (1710-1785, Qing dynasty)
Cursive script (*cao shu*)
20 pages, each 25 cm × 14.8 cm
Provincial Museum of Anhui

While modeling his calligraphy mainly on Li Yong and drawing inspiration from masters like Wang Xizhi and Dong Qichang, Liang Yan was not slavishly beholden to any style. He had the bold, creative idea of employing the running cursive script on stone steles, hundreds of which have survived. His calligraphy is distinguished by a neat, strictly regular character structure, square strokes with a round feel, suppleness and an urbane gentility. His belief that "in calligraphy the Jin dynasty stresses the esthetic, the Tang emphasizes codes, the Song pursues the spirit and the Yuan and Ming dynasties value the beauty of form and posture" aptly sums up calligraphic traditions in China.

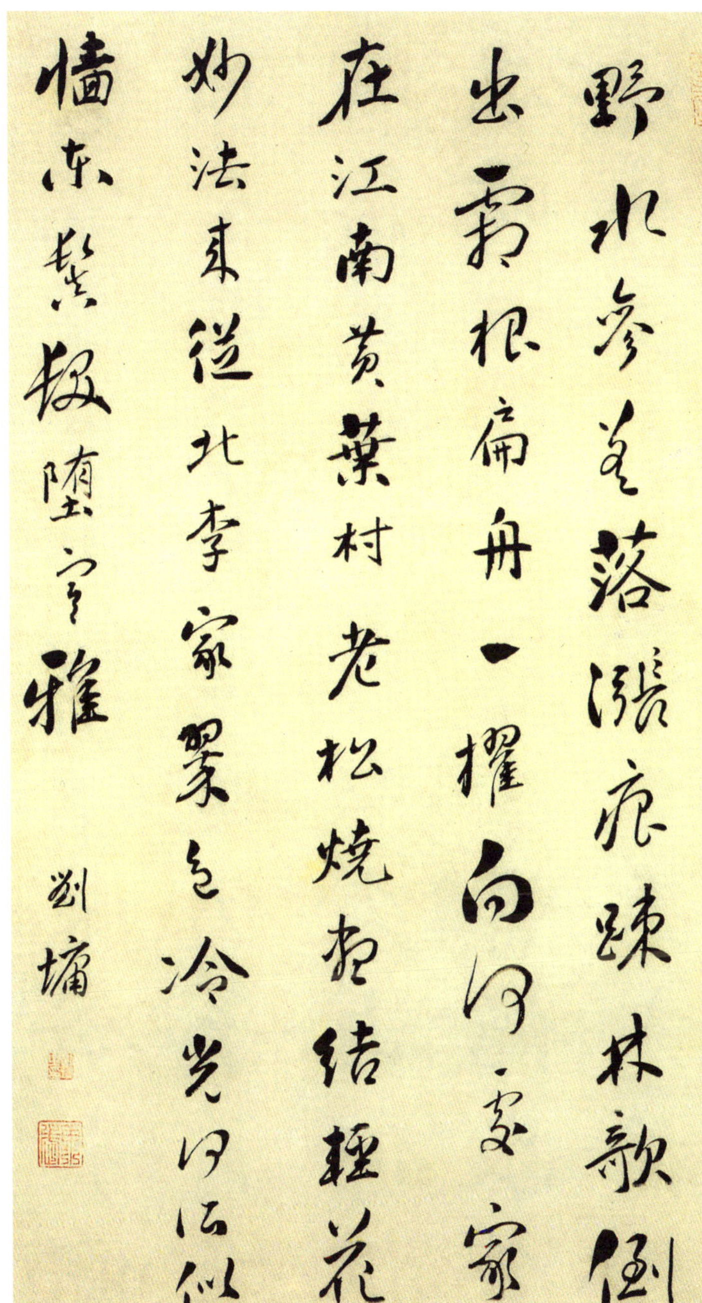

Hanging Scroll Containing Two Quatrains in Seven-character Meter (七绝二首诗轴 *Qi Jue Er Shou Shi Zhou*)

Liu Yong 刘墉 (1719-1804, Qing dynasty)
Running script (*xing shu*)
101.2 cm × 58.5 cm
Palace Museum, Beijing

Liu Yong, Weng Fanggang 翁方纲 (1733-1818, Qing dynasty), Liang Tongshu 梁同书 (1723-1815, Qing dynasty) and Wang Wenzhi 王文治 (1730-1802, Qing dynasty) were considered the "Four Masters of the Qing Dynasty." Liu Yong was often referred to as the "Dark Ink Grand Councilor," because of his penchant for dark ink tones and his rise to the high office of Grand Secretary of *Tiren* Pavilion. He pays a great deal of attention to the construction of the ideograms, and is a stickler for the principle of a staggered, layered organization of space to avoid a mechanical look. The solid, simple style with supple, energetic characters in this scroll, though consisting of few thick, dark-toned strokes, nevertheless exudes a refreshing charm, "like stars scattered in the celestial galaxy."

國家厚恩由渭源縣令十餘年
擢至監司既獲譴仍予湔悔不
遽廢棄中心感激末由仰報涓
埃時方開四庫全書館敬令維
桓具狀于執事 奏充摠校

Epitaph for the Second Son (次男维桓圹铭 *Ci Nan Wei Huan Kuang Ming*)

Wang Wenzhi 王文治 (1730-1802, Qing dynasty)
Regular script (*kai shu*)
11 pages, each 28.2 cm × 13 cm
Provincial Museum of Anhui

Wang Wenzhi's calligraphy places emphasis on flair and elegance of form, and favors the use of a soft, long brush. His contemporaries often compared him to the "Dark Ink Grand Councilor" Liu Yong and referred to him as "Pale Ink *Tanhua*" (淡墨探花 *dan mo tan hua*) because he once passed the court-administered national civil service examination with the third highest marks, hence the title *Tanhua*. His graceful style is shown in this epitaph composed and calligraphed by him.

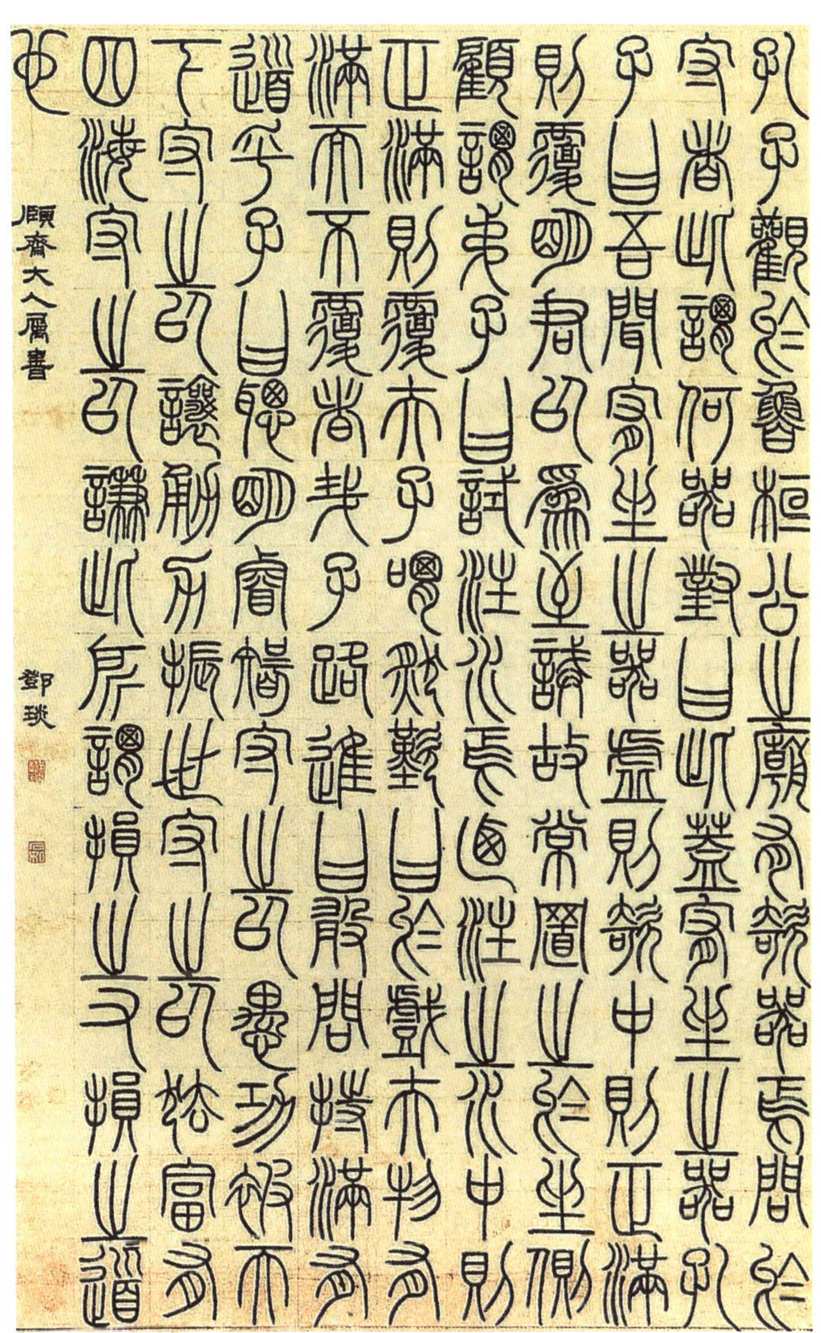

Writings in Seal Script on a Scroll (篆书文轴 *Zhuan Shu Wen Zhou*)

Deng Shiru 邓石如 (1743-1805, Qing dynasty)
Seal script (*zhuan shu*)
117 cm × 74 cm
Palace Museum, Beijing

With the rise of the stele school of calligraphy in the middle Qing, the ancient styles of seal script and clerical script were once again looked upon with favor by the calligraphers. Deng Shiru, equally accomplished in seal script, clerical script, regular script and clerical script calligraphy, was best known for his seal script. He favored the use of long-tip goat hair brushes in his seal script works to create forceful, clean lines and compact characters.

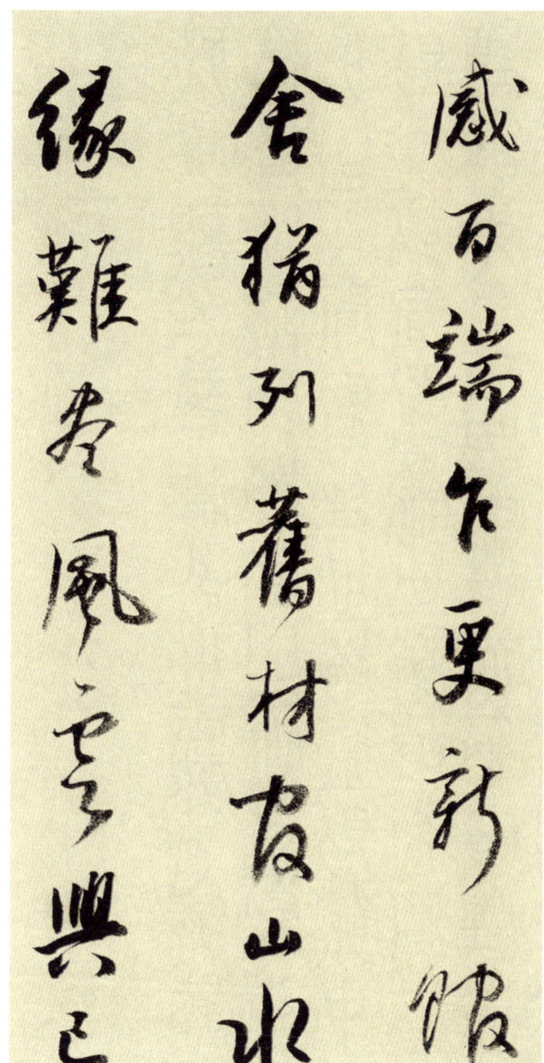

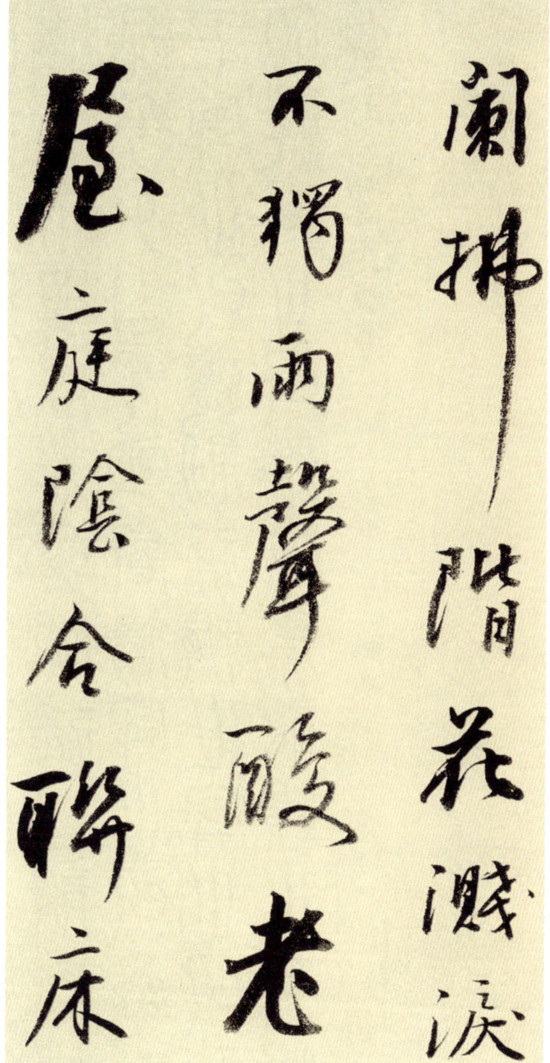

Preface to the Album of Poems (自序诗歌册 *Zi Xu Shi Ge Ce*)

Tie Bao 铁保 (1752-1824, Qing dynasty)
Running script (*xing shu*)
10 pages, each 24.5 cm × 10.5 cm
Provincial Museum of Anhui

This work is notable for the solid and compact structure of the characters, a brush that attacks the paper sideways from the air, full-bodied strokes, a well-defined tempo and an even pace. The balance and the uniform look are belied by variations in the thickness of the lines, ink use and character formation. An esthetic of serenity, mental pacing and airy elegance prevails.

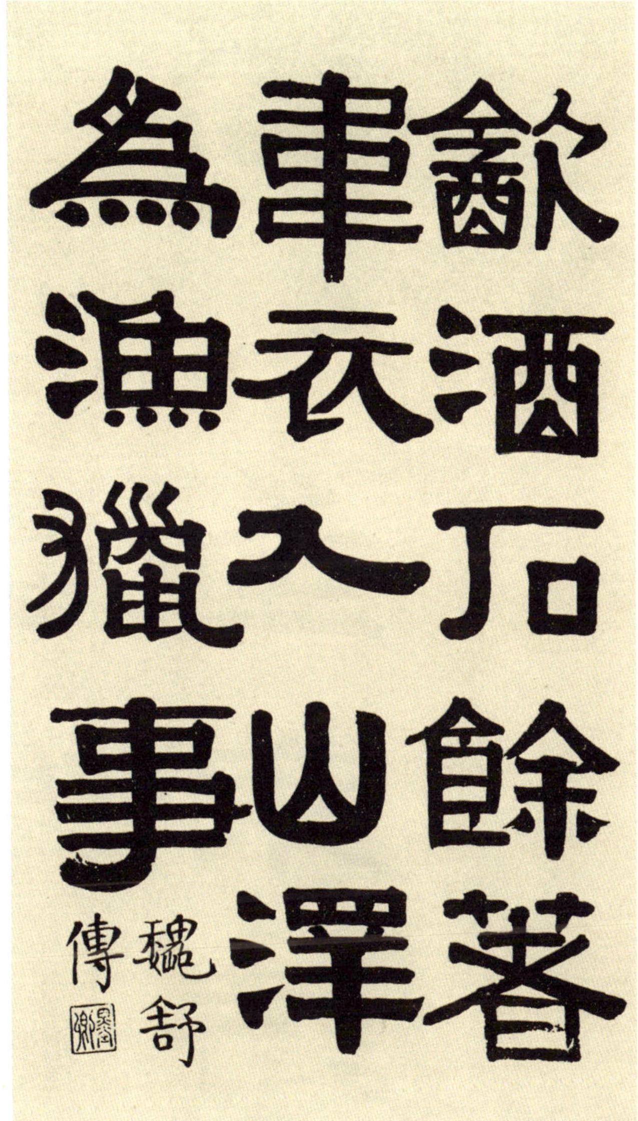

Biography of Wei Shu (魏舒传 *Wei Shu Zhuan*)

Yi Bingshou 伊秉绶 **(1754–1815, Qing dynasty)**
Clerical script (*li shu*)

In Yi Bingshou's clerical script works, the brushwork is solid and smooth, and often stops short of consummation, giving the calligraphy an understated charm. With its square character structure, airy spatial composition and foursquare horizontals and verticals filling the square character grid, the piece is strongly redolent of bronze and stone inscriptions.

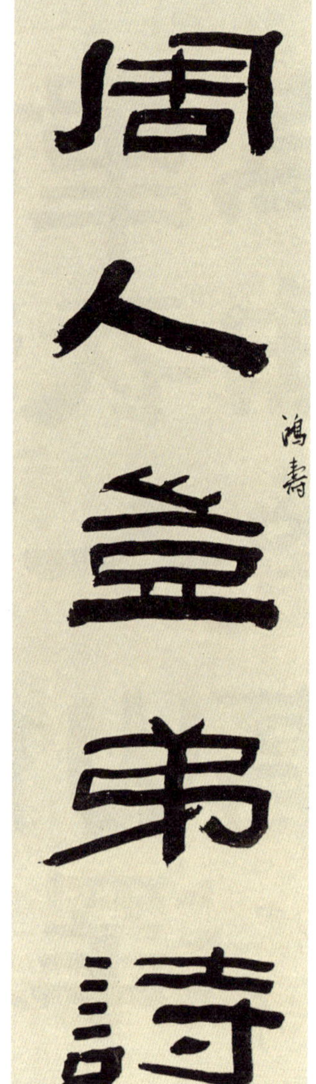

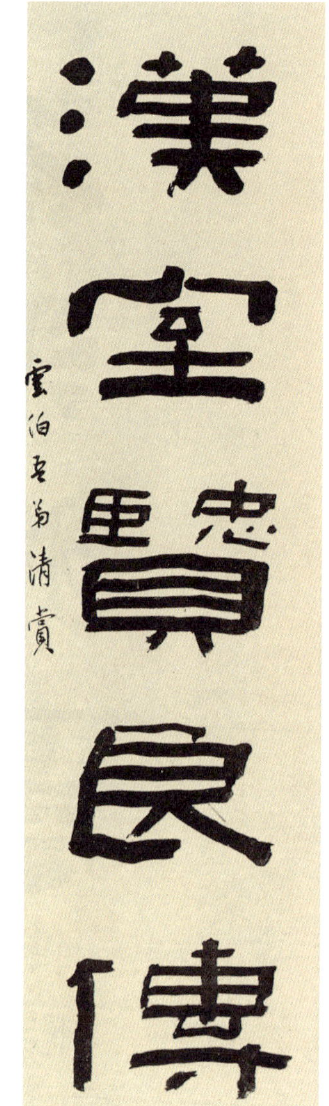

Pair of Matching Couplets Beginning with "Han Shi" and "Zhou Ren" on Each Couplet (汉室周人对联 *Han Shi Zhou Ren Dui Lian*)

Chen Hongshou 陈鸿寿 (1768-1822, Qing dynasty)
Clerical script (*li shu*)

Chen Hongshou's clerical script works have a strong flavor of bronze and stone inscriptions. He believed that "in verse, painting or calligraphy, too much virtuosity is inimical to the creation of a natural charm." Simplicity, spontaneity and genuine feeling were the goals of his artistic pursuit, and a genteel urbanity was his nature. The most notable quality of this pair of matching couplets is the contrast between contraction and distension, as a result of which every character is composed of parts that are alternately very compact or very relaxed.

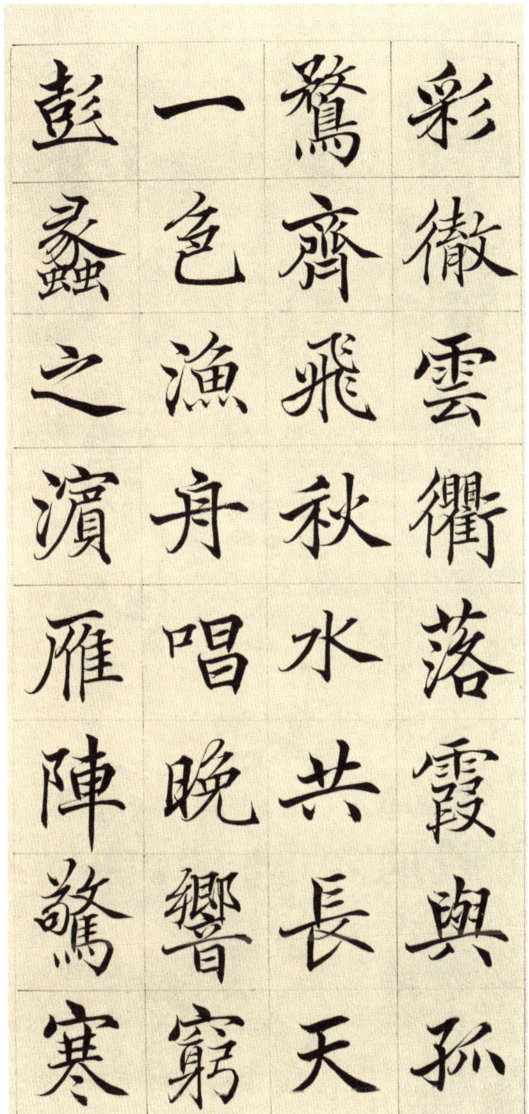

Preface to the Prince Teng Pavilion (滕王阁序 *Teng Wang Ge Xu*)

Gao Kai 高垲 **(1769–1839, Qing dynasty)**
Regular script (*kai shu*)
Private overseas collector of Chinese descent

In this work Gao Kai drew inspiration from several masters: in character structure it approaches the style of Zhao Mengfu; in graceful writing it is closer to Chu Suiliang and the mellowness comes from Yu Shinan. On the other hand, while all past masters had their own distinct regular script styles, Gao Kai was found wanting in this respect and appeared to have a bland, impersonal style. The neat "*Guan Ge Ti*" (馆阁体), a style popular among scholars in the Ming and Qing dynasties, was the ultimate epitome of this flawed approach.

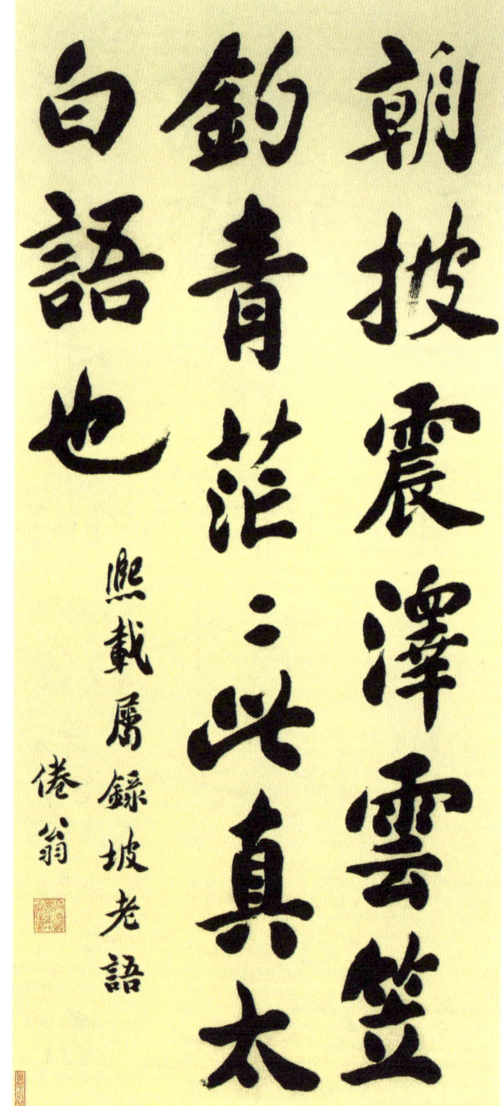

Speech of Po Lao on a Scroll (坡老语轴 *Po Lao Yu Zhou*)

Bao Shichen 包世臣 (1775-1855, Qing dynasty)
Regular script (*kai shu*)
130 cm × 57.7 cm
Palace Museum, Beijing

Bao Shichen was renowned for his theoretical work on calligraphy; his book on calligraphy *Oars for the Boat of Art* (艺舟双楫 *yi zhou shuang ji*) was widely read. This scroll with its solid, stable character forms shows a strong influence of the northern stele tradition and is characterized by a slow speed of brush movement, a generous use of ink and a novel esthetic.

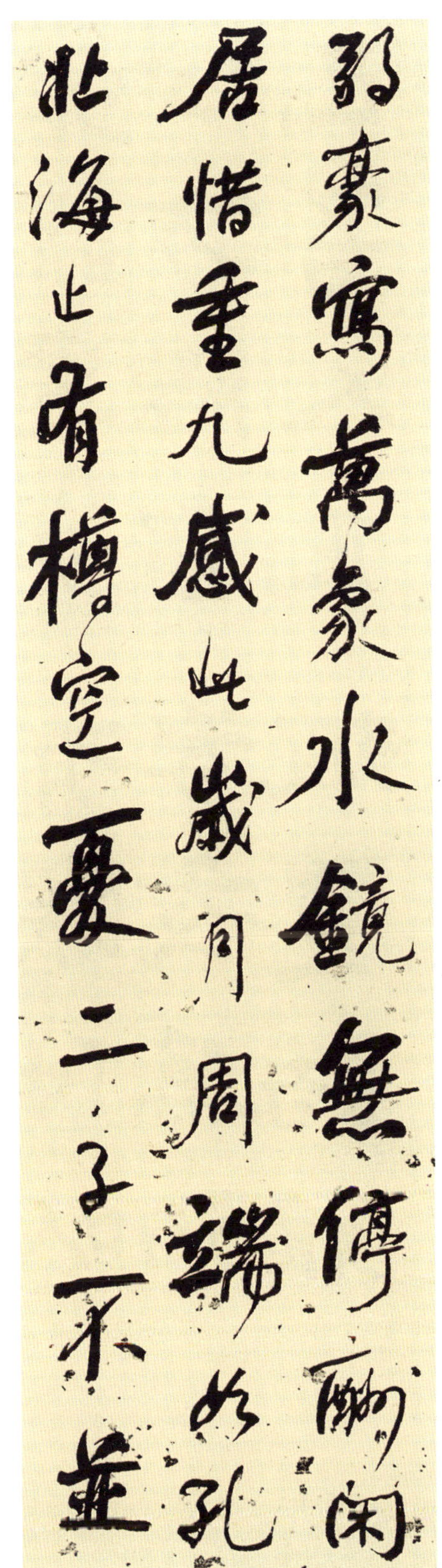

Su Shi's Poems Written in Reply to Tao Yuanming's Poems (东坡和陶诗 *Dong Po He Tao Shi*)

He Shaoji 何绍基 (1799-1873, Qing dynasty)
Running script (*xing shu*)

In the middle and late Qing dynasty, many calligraphers encouraged the study of Tang steles, in the belief that since Ouyang Xun's style showed a clerical script influence and Yan Zhenqing's calligraphy a seal script influence, they should be able to reconnect with the seal script style of the Qin and the clerical script style of the Han through the medium of the Tang steles. He Shaoji was an exponent of this movement. In his calligraphy, he starts a stroke with the reversed brush-tip method, adjusts to center-brush by folding the brush in the opposite direction, moves the brush along, slightly shakes the brush and finally slowly lifts the brush to end the stroke. This technique enables the calligrapher to create plump, undulating lines and to preserve their elegance despite the plumpness.

Copy of "Zhang Qian Tablet" (临张迁碑 *Lin Zhang Qian Bei*)

He Shaoji 何绍基 (1799-1873, Qing dynasty)
Clerical script (*li shu*)

In He Shaoji's own words "I began my study of calligraphy by learning seal script and clerical script and therefore did not miss a single northern stele inscription. I was indifferent to the southern model-letters school of calligraphy." His copies of the *Zhang Qian Tablet* inscription alone exceeded a hundred. But he adopted an interpretative approach to copying canonical works, and as a result evolved an idiosyncratic style uniquely his. As he often said, calligraphers need to strike out on their own in order to achieve self-expression through ink and brush.

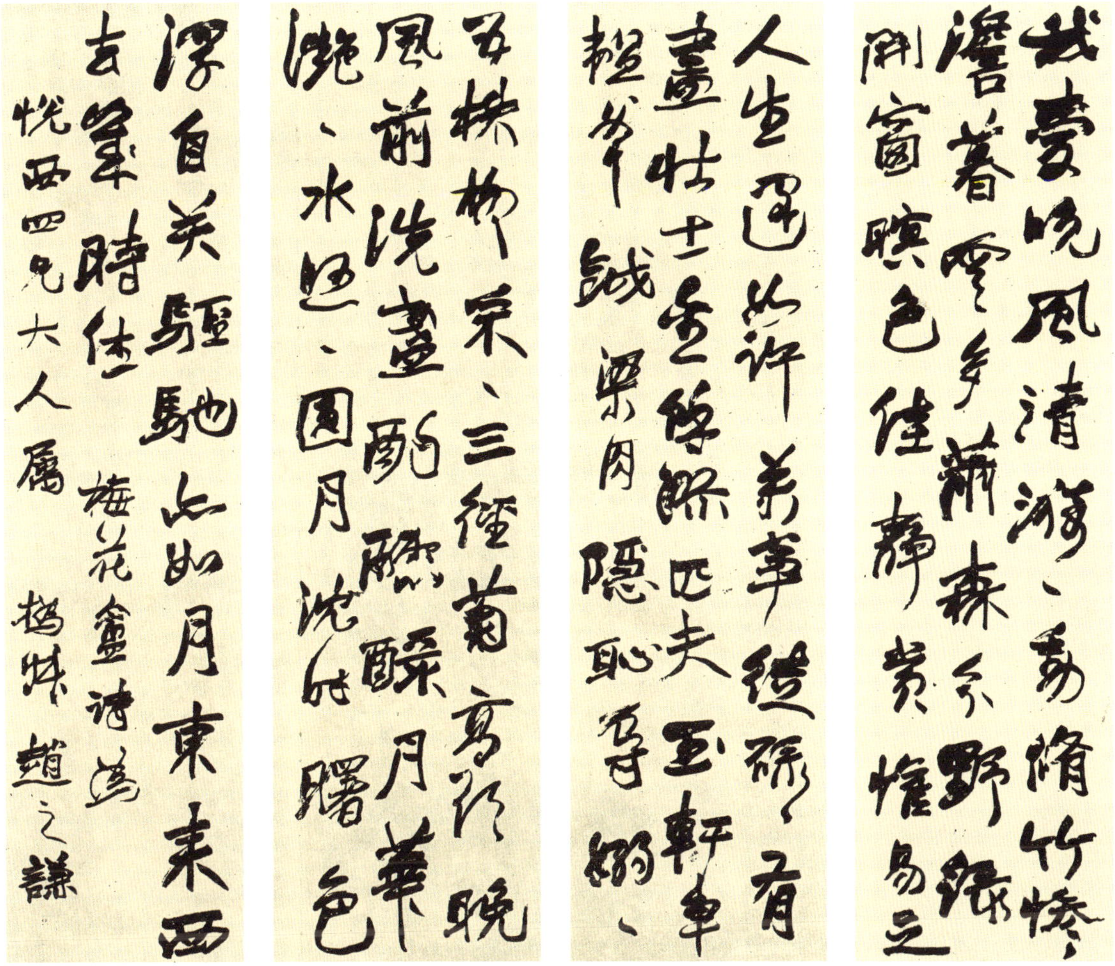

Plum Blossom Hut (梅花庵诗 *Mei Hua An Shi*)

Zhao Zhiqian 赵之谦 (1829-1884,
Qing dynasty)
Running script (*xing shu*)

Zhao Zhiqian's running script blends seal script, clerical script and the northern stele tradition. The calligraphy in this poem is characterized by fluid movement, and an open, expansive character structure. The ease with which the brush changes its pace, the interesting variation in space density and in inclinations and postures combine to make it a remarkable piece of calligraphy.

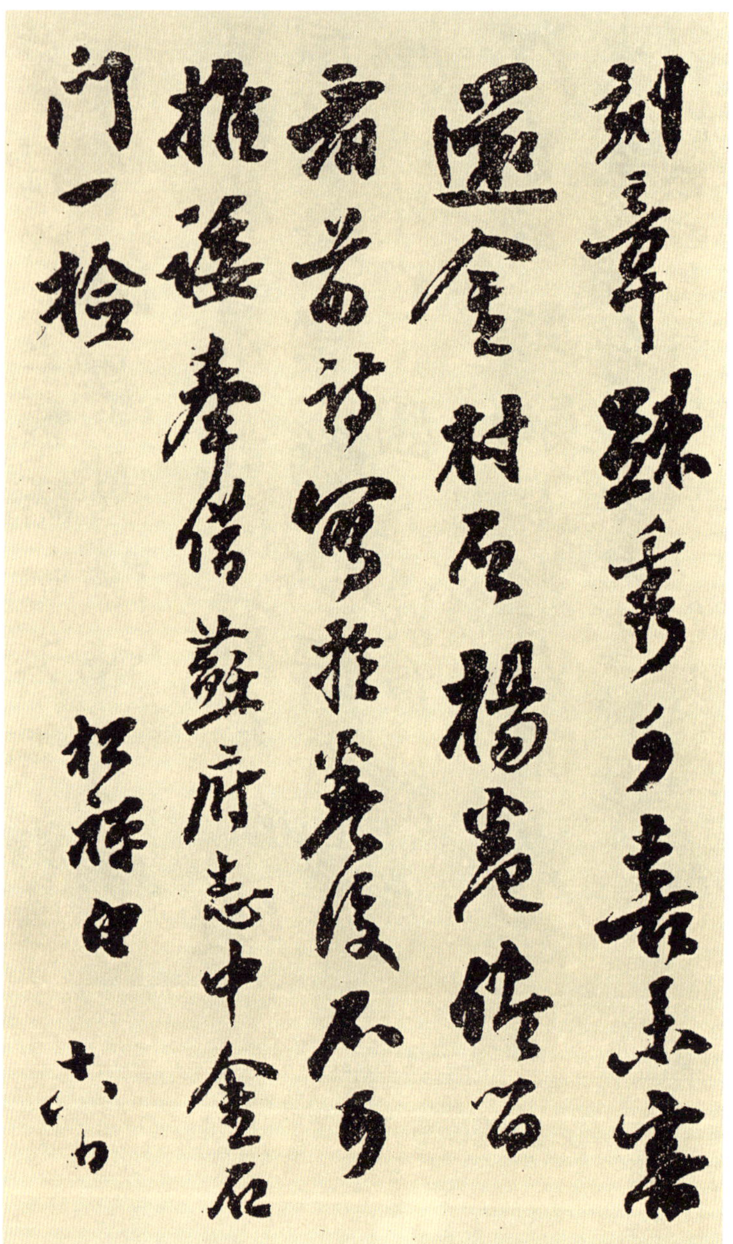

Autograph Letter (手札 *Shou Zha*)

Weng Tonghe 翁同龢 (1830-1904, Qing dynasty)
Running script (*xing shu*)

Weng Tonghe's calligraphy combines the grandness and elegance of Yan Zhenqing, the masculinity of the Han and Wei stone inscriptions and Mi Fu's free spirit to create an individualistic style.

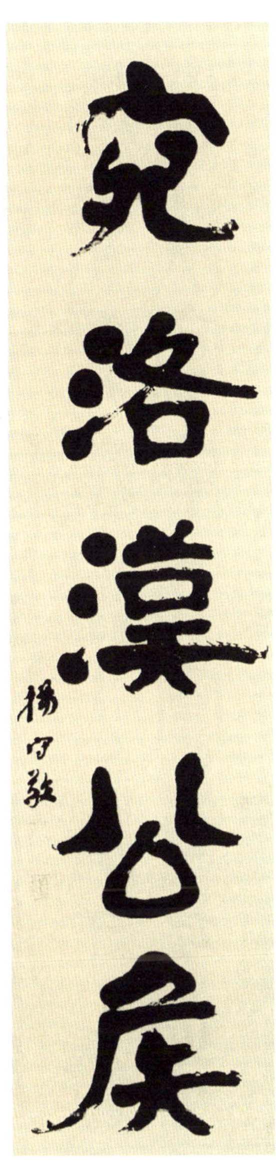

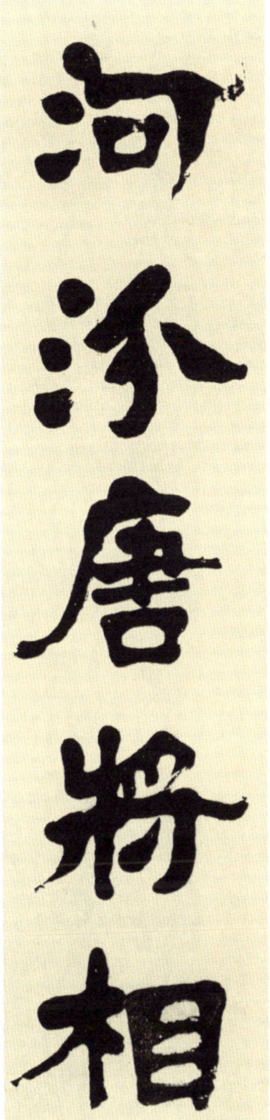

Pair of Matching Couplets Beginning with "He Fen" and "Wan Luo" on Each Couplet (河汾宛洛对联 *He Fen Wan Luo Dui Lian*)

Yang Shoujing 杨守敬 (1839-1915, Qing dynasty)
Clerical script (*li shu*)

During his tenure as a diplomat at the Chinese embassy in Japan, Yang Shoujing actively promoted China's stele school calligraphy in that country and was praised as the "father of calligraphy modernization in Japan." In his answer to a question by a Japanese calligrapher about studying Han stone inscriptions, he pointed out that beginning learners of the clerical script style should not begin with *Cao Quan Tablet* or *Yi Ying Tablet*, to avoid the pitfall of being contaminated by the vulgarity of the Tang clerical script style. This distinctive pair of couplets could be regarded as a demonstration of his point. Although in clerical script, the piece exhibits regular script characteristics in the shapes and forms of its strokes and in their organization.

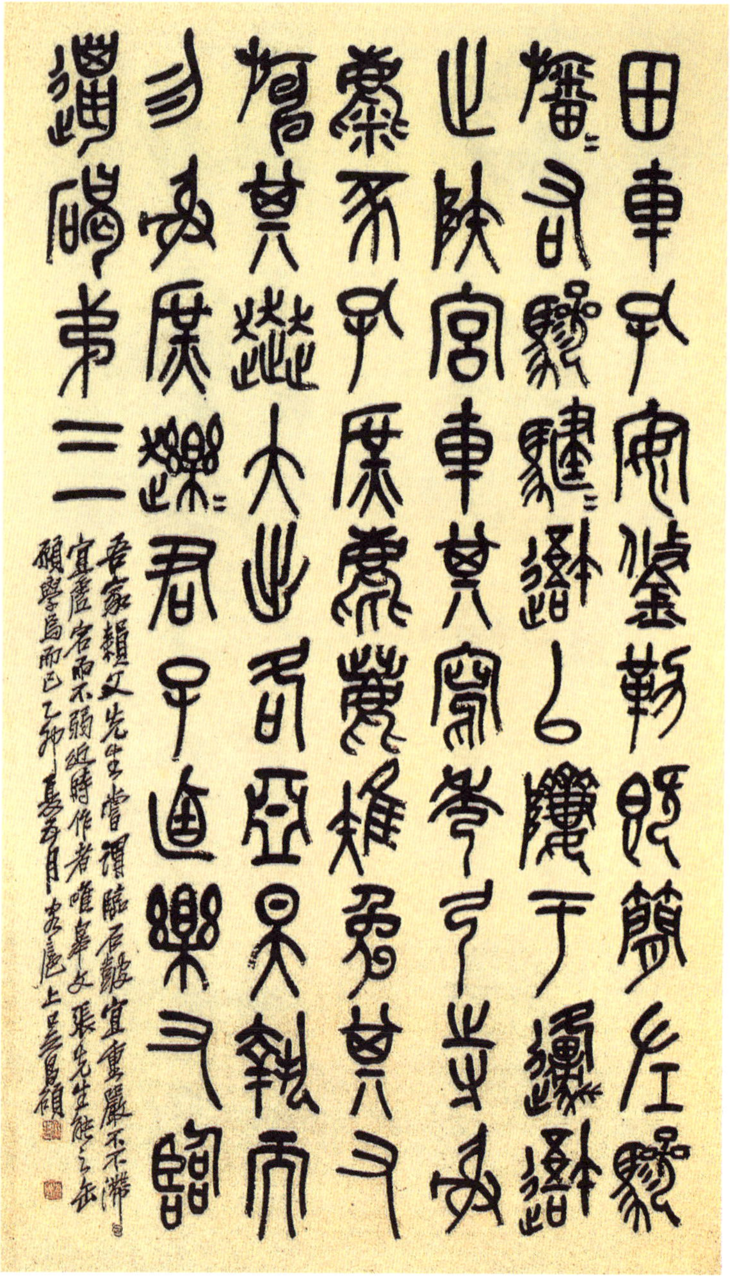

Copy of Stone Drum Inscriptions on a Scroll (临石鼓文轴 *Lin Shi Gu Wen Zhou*)

Wu Changshuo 吴昌硕 (1844-1927, Qing dynasty)
Seal script (*zhuan shu*)
149.5 cm × 82.3 cm
Palace Museum, Beijing

Wu Changshuo disregarded tradition to forge a unique style of his own. He was an excellent imitator of the stone drum inscriptions. He was able to capture the spirit of the original inscriptions and blend his own understanding and style into the copy. The trick was in creating a copy that appeared to resemble the original yet was different. Under his brush, the lines acquire more mass than the original and the structure of the characters is more relaxed. There is a more interesting variation in the organization of space; and the entire piece has a powerful visual impact.

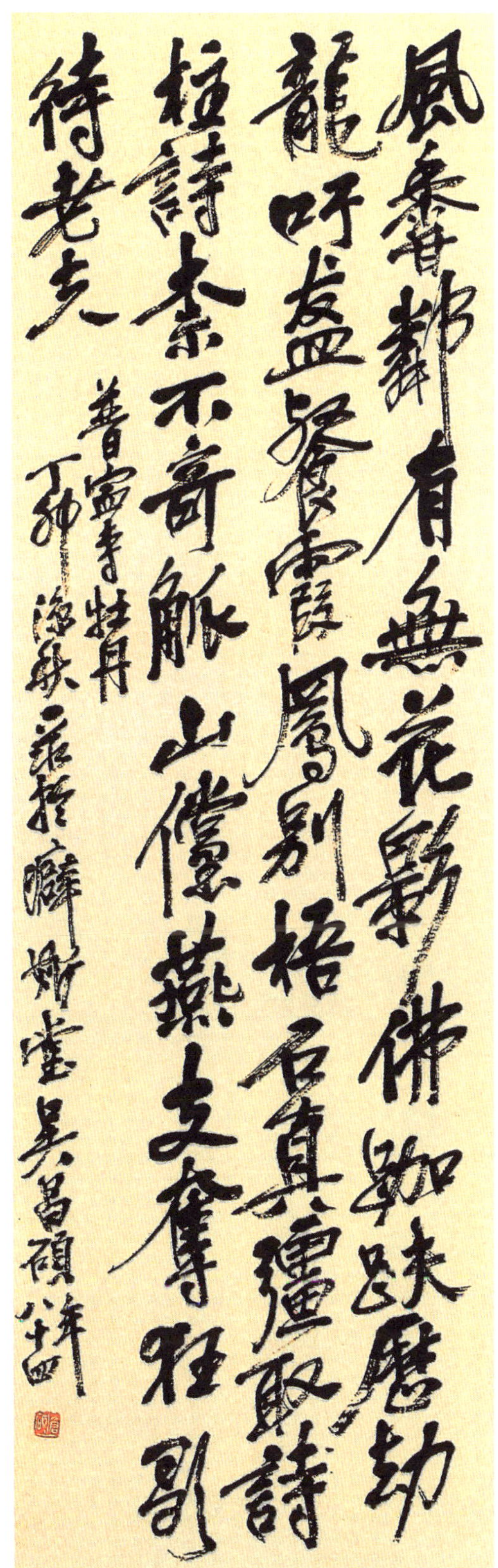

Poem in Five-character Meter on a Scroll (五言诗轴 *Wu Yan Shi Zhou*)

Wu Changshuo 吴昌硕 (1844–1927, Qing dynasty)
Running script (*xing shu*)
136 cm × 47 cm
Palace Museum, Beijing

Wu Changshuo's running script style is characterized by an archaistic clumsiness and robust energy. Its disregard for calligraphic codes gives it a special appeal. The brushwork alternates between heavy and light touches, with heftier beginning strokes and horizontal strokes and thinner left diagonal strokes, as is evident also in his plum paintings. Although characters are inclined, the calligrapher skillfully maintains a stable center of gravity by fine-tuning the thickness of the strokes.

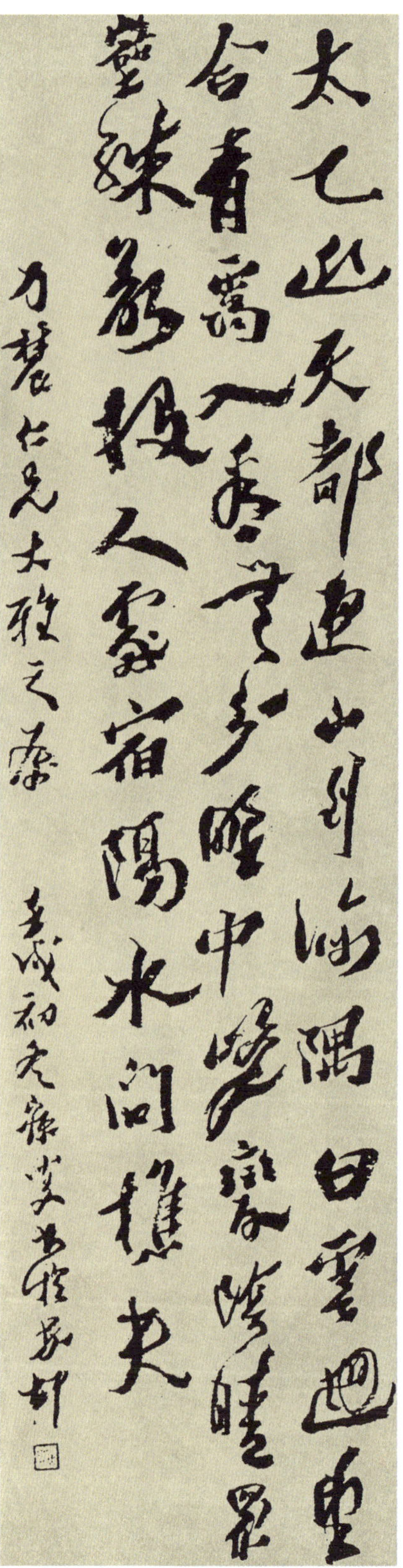

Mount Zhongnan (终南山诗 *Zhong Nan Shan Shi*)

Shen Zengzhi 沈曾植 (1850-1922, Qing dynasty)
Running script (*xing shu*)

Shen Zengzhi, who studied model letters before turning to the stele inscriptions, was eventually able to blend the two traditions to create a distinctly personal style. His contemporary Zeng Xi had this to say about his calligraphic style "his skill shows through an apparent clumsiness; his ingenuity is reflected in his less than fluent brushwork; and his strength lies in instability." The clumsiness and the lack of fluidity come from the brush-tip being moved against the grain of the paper; and the instability results from his giving up the balance in individual characters to seek coordination and balance between characters and columns.

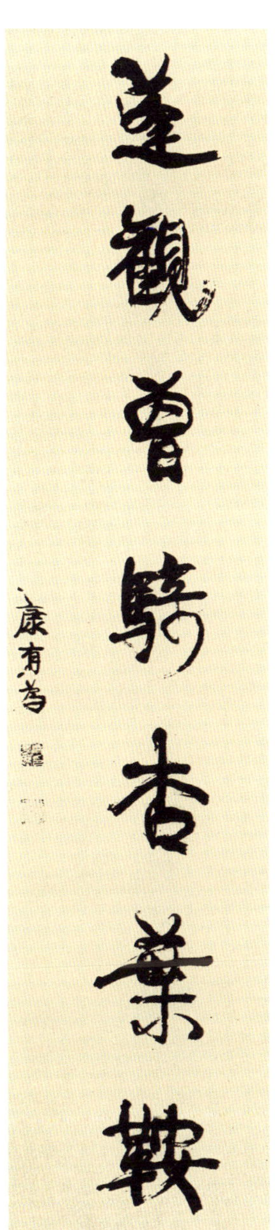

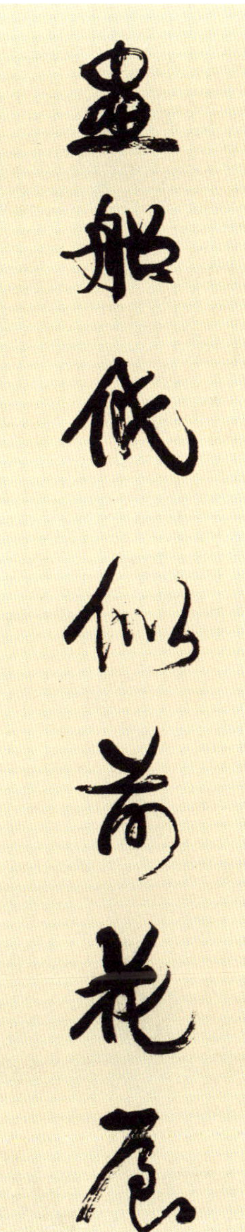

Pair of Matching Couplets Beginning with "Hua Chuan" and "Peng Guan" on Each Couplet 画船蓬观对联 *Hua Chuan Peng Guan Dui Lian*)

Kang Youwei 康有为 (1858-1927, Qing dynasty)

Kang Youwei was a leader of a reform movement in China's modern history. He was also renowned for his theoretical works on calligraphy. In his *Amplification of Oars for the Boat of Art* (广艺舟双楫 *guang yi zhou shuang ji*), he criticized the excessive softness of the model-letter tradition and advocated the virility of the Han and Wei stone inscriptions. His calligraphy is modeled on northern stele inscriptions such as *Inscription on Stone Gate* and *Diamond Sutra of Jingshiyu on Mount Tai*, in a style characterized by freedom of will, a robust brushwork and the absence of links between characters. The free rein given to the brush creates a cohesive whole despite this lack of linkages.

Modern

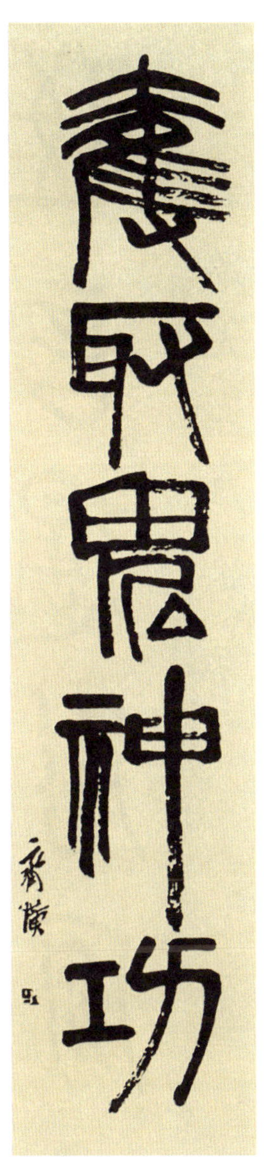

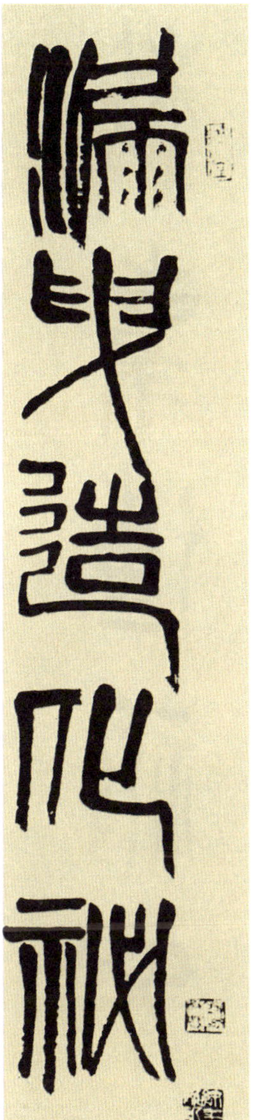

Pair of Matching Couplets Beginning with "Lou Ye" and "Duo Qu" on Each Couplet (漏曳夺取对联 *Lou Ye Duo Qu Dui Lian*)

Qi Baishi 齐白石 (1864-1957)
Seal script (*zhuan shu*)

Drawing nourishment from the stele inscriptions of *Cuan Long Yan Tablet*, *Divine Prophecy Tablet* and *Mount Sangong Tablet* (祀三公山碑 *si san gong shan bei*), Qi Baishi forged a personal style characterized by a solid, energized brushwork, squarish characters, angular corners and swift writing, disregarding the requirements of balance. In his seal script works, he pays great attention to the use of ink and brush. He begins a stroke by applying strong pressure and ends it gently but by no means sloppily. His brushwork is so packed with force that the brush-tip seems almost at risk of penetrating the paper. Just as in his paintings, there is a spontaneity to his use of ink tones and moistness of the brush.

Pair of Matching Couplets Beginning with "Yu Yan" and "Yi Shi" on Each Couplet (语言艺事对联 *Yu Yan Yi Shi Dui Lian*)

Huang Binhong 黄宾虹 **(1865-1955)**
Bronze writing (*jin wen*)

As ancient inscriptions on bronze vessels pass through the rigors of engravings and castings, oxidation and cleanings, the lines become coarse and the ideograms are blurred and illegible, giving them an elegant gravitas of age. How to capture this elegance with the brush was a major concern of calligraphers following the rise of the stele school. Some favorite ideas included "tarry in movement, move while tarrying," and "pause and fold back in increments to avoid too facile a passage" (quoted from Bao Shichen). This pair of matching couplets is marked by a mellow roundness and clean lines, a virility underlying the gracefulness and smoothness despite a conscious effort to write against the grain.

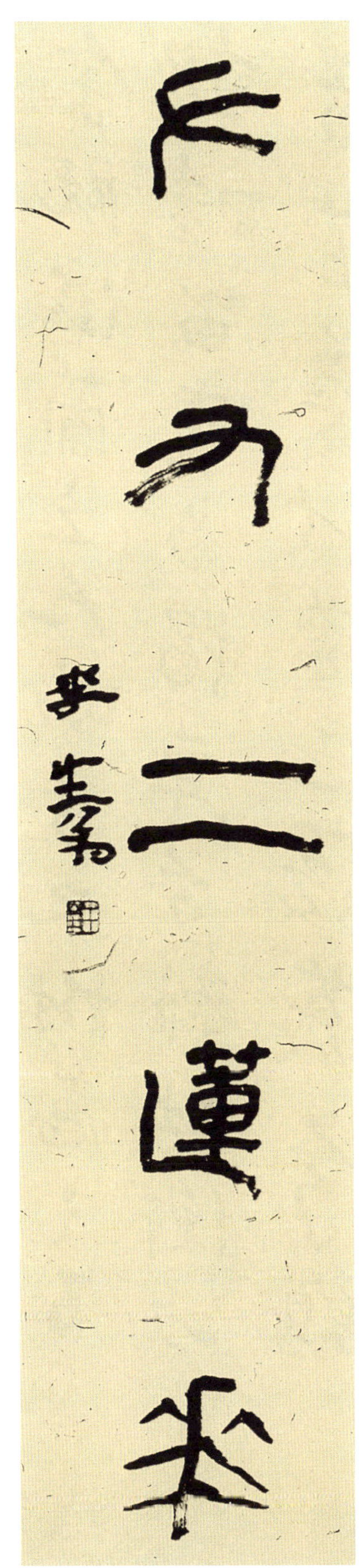

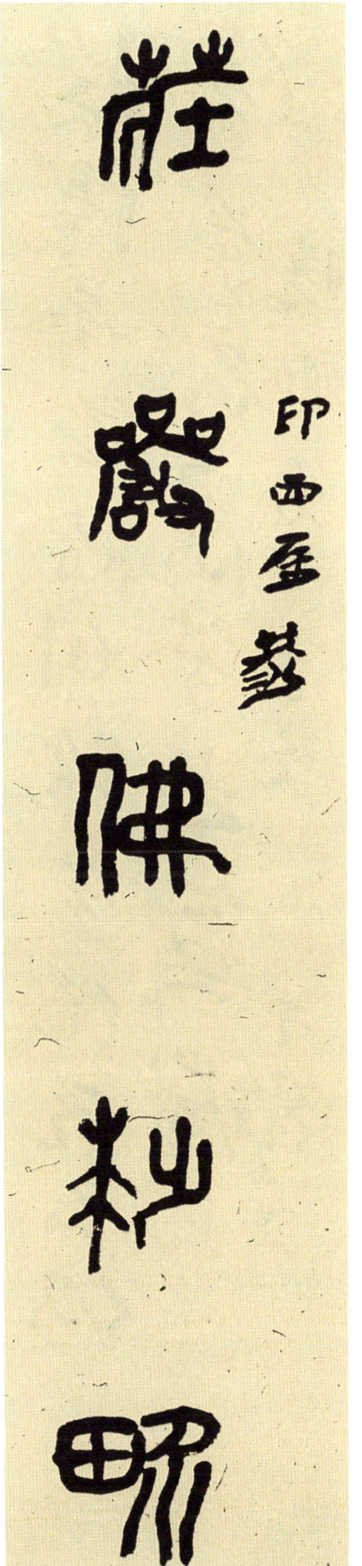

Pair of Matching Couplets Beginning with "Zhuang Yan" and "Zuo You" on Each Couplet (庄严左右对联 *Zhuang Yan Zuo You Dui Lian*)

Xu Shengweng 徐生翁 **(1875–1964)**
Seal script (*zhuan shu*)

With the rise of the stele school in the Qing dynasty, seal script enjoyed a comeback. Wang Shu et al led the way by restoring the original look of the seal script of the Qin dynasty, followed by Zhao Zhiqian and Wu Changshuo, who gave it a running script transformation, and finally Qi Baishi and Xu Shengweng, who further added their bronze writing and clerical script adaptations. In this pair of matching couplets in seal script, the strokes and the structure of the characters show an unmistakable influence of the inscription on *Bronze Plate of the San Tribe* with lines resembling ancient vines chapped by dryness, raspy and unadorned, exuding a naïve charm.

The Lament (离骚 *Li Sao*)

Yu Youren 于右任 (1879–1964)
Running cursive script (*xing cao*)

Yu Youren's calligraphies are marked by a grandeur of spirit and understatement. Not feeling bound by traditional rules, such as the requirement of hiding the brush-tip at the beginning and end of a stroke, he gives free rein to the brush, over which he exercises excellent control. A tough, unconventional personality peeks through an untrammeled style. The structure of the characters is modeled on the squat form of the Northern Wei stone inscriptions. The piece shows lively variation on the basis of a narrow, upright posture of the characters, and is distinguished by cohesion, energy and unconventional construction. He cautioned against excessive "crossing, touching, eye-formation and parallelism" in the construction of cursive writing and favored a clean, unconventional esthetic.

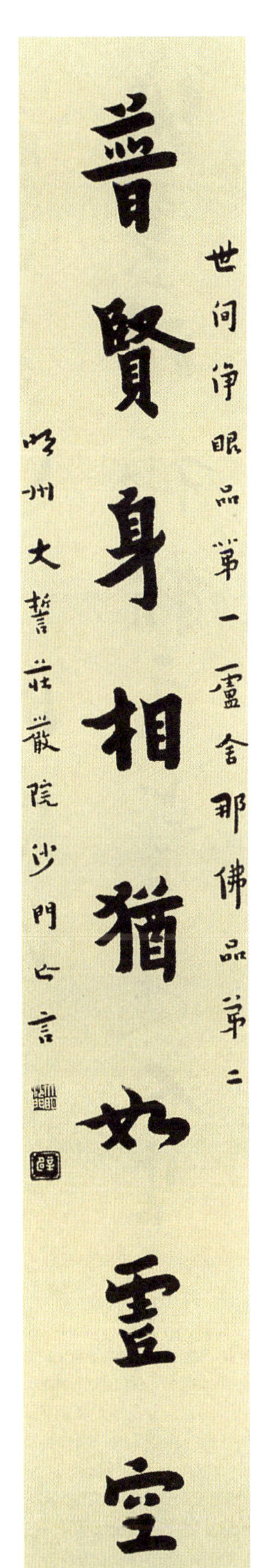

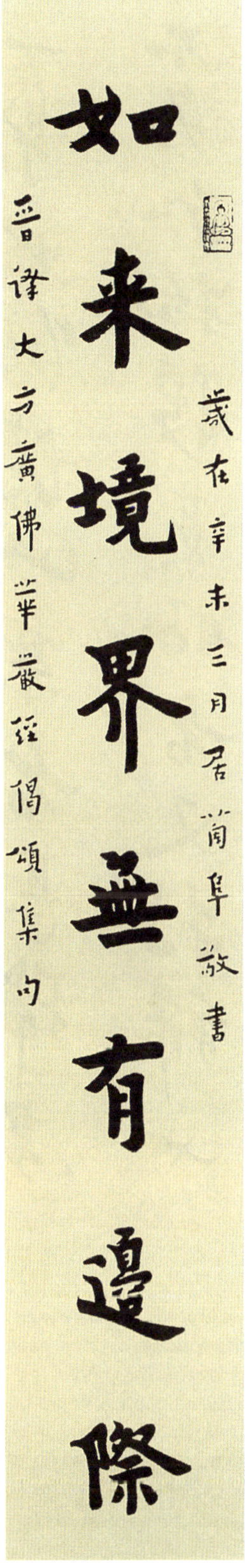

Pair of Matching Couplets Beginning with "Ru Lai" and "Pu Xian" on Each Couplet (如来普贤对联 *Ru Lai Pu Xian Dui Lian*)

Li Shutong 李叔同 **(1880-1942)**
Regular script (*kai shu*)

Li Shutong had a legendary and colorful life, metamorphosing from a well-born young gentleman into the deeply spiritual Buddhist dharmacarya Hongyi. His calligraphic style also evolved from the flamboyant to the plain and simple. His works, unadorned and understated, have an enduring appeal, and evoke, in the words of Ye Shengtao 叶圣陶 (1894-1988), "an urbane gentleman discussing the way of Buddha, in a dispassionate, congenial manner, without conceit or false modesty. His strength is beyond simple ink and brush, and therefore his calligraphy has an enduring appeal and grows on you."

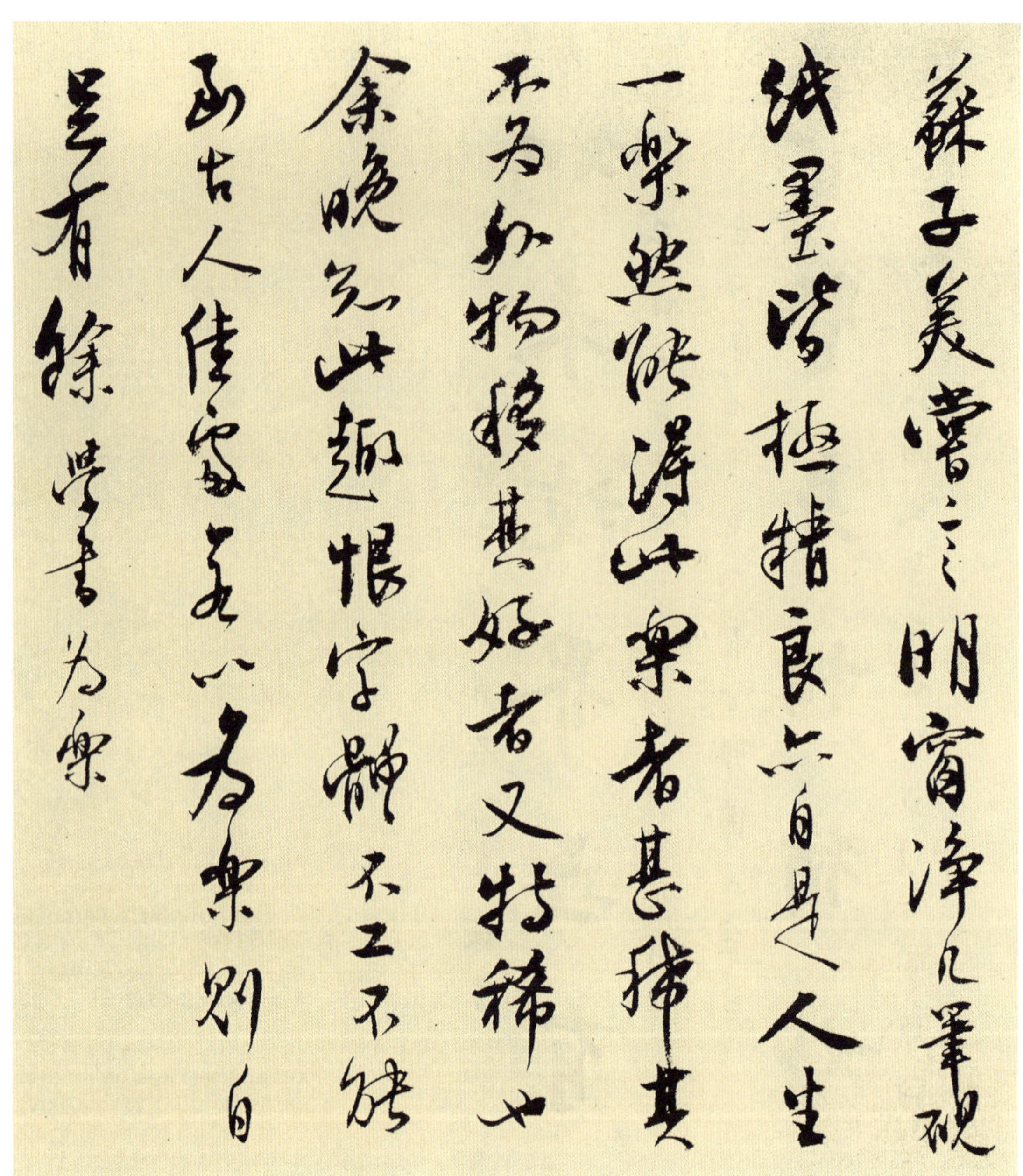

Pleasure of Learning Calligraphy (学书为乐 *Xue Shu Wei Le*)

Shen Yinmo 沈尹默 (1883-1971)
Running script (*xing shu*)

Describing his calligraphic learning experience, Shen Yinmo stated, "I became interested in learning calligraphy at age 12 or 13, beginning with stone inscriptions such as Ouyang Xun's *Sweet Spring at Jiucheng Palace* and *Tablet of Huangfu Dan* (**皇甫诞碑** *huang fu dan bei*), but I had no clue about brush use." When he was 25, he was shaken by Chen Duxiu's harsh criticism of his calligraphy and made a determined effort to copy all stone inscriptions he could find from the Han, Wei and the Six dynasties. This was followed by a running cursive script period during which he studied Mi Nan'gong, Zhi Yong, Yu Shinan, Chu Suiliang and all the way back to Wang Xizhi and Wang Xianzhi, finally synthesizing all those styles into his own graceful and robust style.

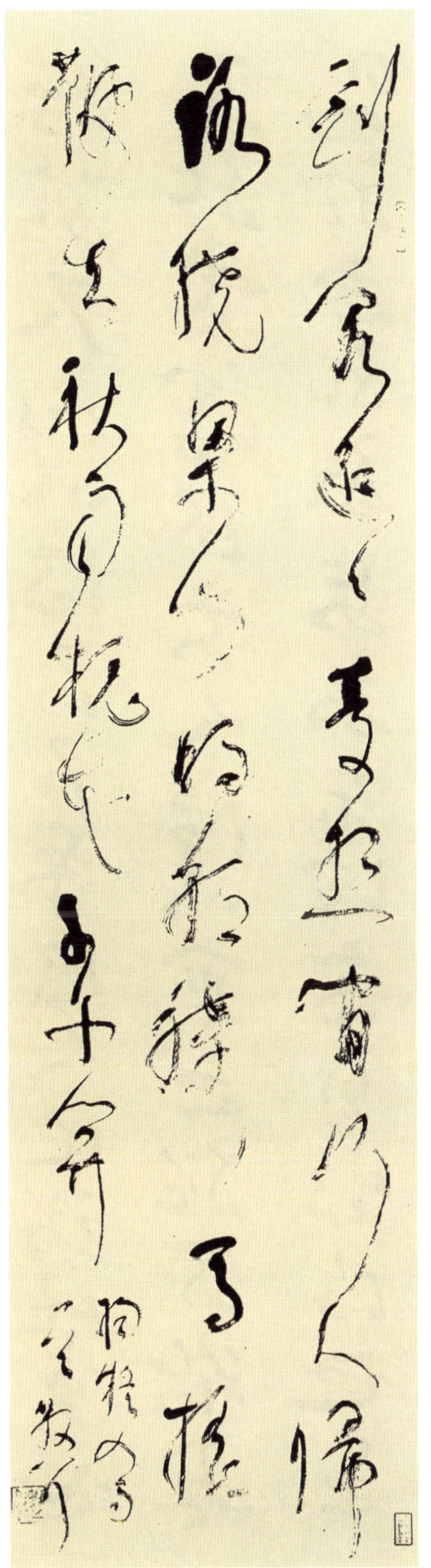

Poem in Cursive Script on a Scroll (草书诗轴 *Cao Shu Shi Zhou*)

Lin Sanzhi 林散之 (1898–1989)
Cursive script (*cao shu*)

Lin Sanzhi had a preference for long-tipped goat-hair brushes, which have the advantage of a large ink-holding capacity and enabled him to write a whole piece with only one dip in the inkstone, until the ink went from wet to moist to dry to drier to driest and finally to exhaustion. This gradual drying of the ink accentuates the rhythm of the calligraphic piece. The contrast between the "lushness of spring grass and dryness of autumn vines" also imparts a sense of painting to the calligraphy.

Colophon in Cursive Script (草书跋 *Cao Shu Ba*)

Wang Juchang 王蘧常 (1900–1989)
Early cursive script (*zhang cao*)

Under the influence of his teacher Shen Zengzhi, Wang Juchang pursued a synthesis of all styles and forms from the past to the present. In his old age, his calligraphy was a blend of stele inscriptions and the writing on wooden slips of the Han dynasty. In his later works, the brush is moved against the grain as in stele inscriptions, and the structure of the characters takes a squat form as on Han wooden slips, giving breadth to his calligraphies.

Works

English	Dynasty	Chinese Pinyin	Chinese	Page
A Gift of Chives	Five dynasties	jiu hua tie	韭花帖	105
A Poem for Zong Dao	Yuan dynasty	dan shi shi	淡室诗	157
A Poem to Chen Zheng	Yuan dynasty	chen jun shi tie	陈君诗帖	143
A Visit to Chengnan	Song dynasty	cheng nan chang he shi	城南唱和诗	136
Altar to an Immortal on Mount Magu	Tang dynasty	ma gu xian tan ji	麻姑仙坛记	8, 90
Amogha Tablet	Tang dynasty	bu kong he shang bei	不空和尚碑	93
Appeal for Funds for True Mirror Temple	Yuan dynasty	zhen jing an mu yuan shu juan	真镜庵募缘疏卷	155
Autobiographical Notes	Tang dynasty	zi xu tie	自叙帖	9, 97, 98
Autograph Letter	Qing dynasty	shou zha	手札	202
Autumn Thoughts (a poem)	Yuan dynasty	qiu xing shi	秋兴诗	145
Autumn Thoughts (a prose poem)	Yuan dynasty	qiu xing fu	秋兴赋	147
Biography of Wei Shu	Qing dynasty	wei shu zhuan	魏舒传	195
Bitter Bamboo Shoot	Tang dynasty	ku sun tie	苦笋帖	95
Bronze Plate of the San Tribe	Western Zhou dynasty	san shi pan	散氏盘	6, 12, 211
Cao Quan Tablet	Han dynasty	cao quan bei	曹全碑	7, 20, 29, 185, 203
Chanting Poems in the Mountain	Ming dynasty	shan zhong za yong	山中杂咏	178
Chronicle of the Building of the Buddha Image by Shi Pinggong	Northern dynasties	shi ping gong zao xiang ji	始平公造像记	54, 56
Chronicle of the Building of the Buddha Image by Yang Dayan	Northern dynasties	yang da yan zao xiang ji	杨大眼造像记	56
Chronicle of the Building of the Buddha Image by Yao Boduo and His Brothers	Northern dynasties	yao bo duo xiong di zao xiang ji	姚伯多兄弟造像记	55
Classic of Crane on a Scroll	Qing dynasty	xiang he jing zhou	相鹤经轴	188
"Classic of Filial Piety" Scroll	Tang dynasty	xiao jing juan	孝经卷	82, 102
Classic of Secret Revelation	Tang dynasty	yin fu jing	阴符经	76
Cliff Carving on Rock Celebrating the Opening of a Suspended Plank Trail in Baocheng	Han dynasty	kai tong bao xie dao ke shi	开通褒斜道刻石	19
Colophon in Cursive Script	Modern	cao shu ba	草书跋	216
Colophon to a Model-letters Copybook	Qing dynasty	bao jin zhai tie ba	宝晋斋帖跋	190
Colophon to Bamboo Painting Guide	Yuan dynasty	ti mo zhu pu zhi shi san	题墨竹谱之十三	152
Colophon to Lu Hong's Painting of Ten Scenic Attractions around His Thatched Hut	Five dynasties	lu hong cao tang shi zhi tu ba	卢鸿草堂十志图跋	107
Confucius Dreams of His Death	Tang dynasty	zhong ni meng dian tie	仲尼梦奠帖	8, 70
Confucius Temple Tablet	Tang dynasty	kong zi miao tang bei	孔子庙堂碑	8, 71, 72
Copy of "on the Seventeenth Day"	Yuan dynasty	lin shi qi tie	临十七帖	154
Copy of Stone Drum Inscriptions on a Scroll	Qing dynasty	lin shi gu wen zhou	临石鼓文轴	204
Copy of "Zhang Qian Tablet"	Qing dynasty	lin zhang qian bei	临张迁碑	200
Cuan Bao Zi Tablet	Eastern Jin dynasty	cuan bao zi bei	爨宝子碑	7, 50
Cuan Long Yan Tablet	Southern dynasties	cuan long yan bei	爨龙颜碑	7, 50, 53, 209
Diamond Sutra of Jingshiyu on Mount Tai	Southern and Northern dynasties	tai shan jing shi yu jin gang jing	泰山经石峪金刚经	64, 207
Discourse on Calligraphy	Tang dynasty	shu pu	书谱	9, 77, 82
Divine Prophecy Tablet	Three Kingdoms	tian fa shen chen bei	天发神谶碑	6, 35, 188, 209
Draft Eulogy for a Nephew	Tang dynasty	ji zhi wen gao	祭侄文稿	8, 89, 119
Eight-line Poem in Five-character Meter on a Scroll	Ming dynasty	wu lü ci zhou	五律词轴	164
Eight-line Regular Poem in Five-character Meter	Yuan dynasty	wu yan lü shi tie	五言律诗帖	151

Works

Works

Works

English	Dynasty	Chinese Pinyin	Chinese	Page
Poem in Cursive Script on a Scroll	Ming dynasty	cao shu shi zhou	草书诗轴	169
Poem in Cursive Script on a Scroll	Modern	cao shu shi zhou	草书诗轴	215
Poem in Five-character Meter in Running Cursive Script	Ming dynasty	xing cao shu wu yan shi zhou	行草书五言诗轴	175
Poem in Five-character Meter on a Scroll	Ming dynasty	wu yan shi zhou	五言诗轴	173
Poem in Five-character Meter on a Scroll	Qing dynasty	wu yan shi zhou	五言诗轴	205
Poem in Four-character Meter in Seal Script	Ming dynasty	zhuan shu si yan shi juan	篆书四言诗卷	165
Poem of Du Mu on a Scroll	Ming dynasty	du mu shi zhou	杜牧诗轴	182
Poem on the Painting "Listening to the Zither"	Song dynasty	ting qin tu ti shi	听琴图题诗	125
Poem on the Painting "Two Pines"	Song dynasty	shuang song tu ge juan	双松图歌卷	139
Poem to a Painting	Qing dynasty	ti hua shi zhou	题画诗轴	186
Poem to Express Melancholy after Demotion	Song dynasty	huang zhou han shi shi juan	黄州寒食诗卷	8, 119
Poem to Honorable Teacher	Ming dynasty	cheng lin weng cai zun shi heng shan zhang shi	呈林翁蔡尊师衡山丈诗	167
Poem to the Tune "Die Lian Hua" on a Scroll	Ming dynasty	die lian hua ci zhou	蝶恋花词轴	161
Poem to the Tune "Huan Xi Sha"	Qing dynasty	huan xi sha ci	浣溪沙词	185
Poems about Travelling	Ming dynasty	ji you shi ce	纪游诗册	179
Poems Composed and Calligraphed by the Author	Song dynasty	zi shu shi	自书诗	140
Poems Composed and Calligraphed by the Author in Cursive Script	Ming dynasty	cao shu zi shu shi	草书自书诗	160
Poems in Cursive Script	Ming dynasty	cao shu shi juan	草书诗卷	181
Poems in Cursive Script on a Scroll	Qing dynasty	cao shu shi zhou	草书诗轴	184
Poems of Han Shan and Pang Yun	Song dynasty	han shan zi pang ju shi shi	寒山子庞居士诗	124
Poems to Share with Friends before Leaving for Tiaoxi	Song dynasty	tiao xi tie	苕溪帖	9, 129
Poems Written on Sichuan Silk	Song dynasty	shu su tie	蜀素帖	9, 126
Prabhutaratna Buddha Pagoda Tablet	Tang dynasty	duo bao ta bei	多宝塔碑	8, 87
Practical Way to Immortality, The	Five dynasties	shen xian qi ju fa	神仙起居法	9, 106
Preface to Buddha's Teachings at Goose Pavilion	Tang dynasty	yan ta sheng jiao xu	雁塔圣教序	8, 75, 76
Preface to Buddha's Teachings Made by Pasting Together Ideograms from Wang Xizhi's Calligraphic Oeuvre	Tang dynasty	ji wang sheng jiao xu	集王圣教序	9, 84
Preface to the Album of Poems	Qing dynasty	zi xu shi ge ce	自序诗歌册	194
Preface to the Collected Writings of Zhang Zongfu	Song dynasty	mu ji ji xu	木鸡集序	141
Preface to the Inscription of Officials' Name	Tang dynasty	lang guan shi zhu ji xu	郎官石柱记序	8, 79
Preface to the Prince Teng Pavilion	Qing dynasty	teng wang ge xu	滕王阁序	197
Quatrain in Five-character Meter on a Scroll	Ming dynasty	wu jue shi zhou	五绝诗轴	176
Quatrain in Seven-character Meter in Running Script	Yuan dynasty	xing shu qi jue	行书七绝	149
Red Cliff Rhapsody	Ming dynasty	chi bi fu	赤壁赋	162
Rhapsody on the Luo River Goddess	Eastern Jin dynasty	luo shen fu	洛神赋	7, 47, 150
Rhapsody on the Luo River Goddess in Small Regular Script	Yuan dynasty	xiao kai luo shen fu	小楷洛神赋	150
Rhyme Prose	Tang dynasty	wen fu	文赋	9, 83
Ritual Vessels Tablet	Han dynasty	li qi bei	礼器碑	7, 20, 21, 22, 26, 29

Works

English	Dynasty	Chinese Pinyin	Chinese	Page
Scroll of Poems Composed and Calligraphed by the Author	Song dynasty	zi shu shi juan	自书诗卷	135
Seclusion	Ming dynasty	gui qu lai xi ci	归去来兮辞	163
Shi Chen Tablet	Han dynasty	shi chen bei	史晨碑	7, 20, 21, 26
Song Gao Ling Miao Tablet	Northern dynasties	song gao ling miao bei	嵩高灵庙碑	52
Speech of Monks with High Moral Integrity	Song dynasty	zhu shang zuo tie	诸上座帖	9, 123
Speech of Po Lao on a Scroll	Qing dynasty	po lao yu zhou	坡老语轴	198
Spring	Tang dynasty	wen quan ming	温泉铭	68
Stone Drum Inscriptions	Warring States period	shi gu wen	石鼓文	6, 13, 57
Stone Inscription of a Biographical Note	Han dynasty	chao hou xiao zi can bei	朝侯小子残碑	18
Stone Tablet of Mount Yi	Qin dynasty	yi shan ke shi	峄山刻石	8, 14, 165
Su Shi's Poems Written in Reply to Tao Yuanming's Poems	Qing dynasty	dong po he tao shi	东坡和陶诗	199
Sweet Spring at Jiucheng Palace	Tang dynasty	jiu cheng gong li quan ming	九成宫醴泉铭	8, 69, 71, 214
Tablet of the Xuanmi Pagoda	Tang dynasty	xuan mi ta bei	玄秘塔碑	8, 100, 101
Taoist Scripture "Ling Fei"	Tang dynasty	ling fei jing	灵飞经	94
Thousand Character Reader	Tang dynasty	qian zi wen	千字文	103
Thousand Character Reader (by Chen Chun)	Ming dynasty	qian zi wen	千字文	166
Thousand Character Reader (by Zhan Jingfeng)	Ming dynasty	qian zi wen	千字文	170
Thousand Character Reader in Cursive Script	Tang dynasty	cao shu duan qian wen	草书断千文	81
Thousand Character Reader in Regular and Cursive Scripts	Tang dynasty	zhen cao qian zi wen	真草千字文	9, 67
Thousand Character Reader in Small Cursive Hand	Tang dynasty	xiao cao qian zi wen	小草千字文	98
Tombs of Ancestors	Tang dynasty	qi xian ying ji	栖先茔记	6, 99
Trial of Writing	Ming dynasty	shi shu tie	试书帖	174
Twelve Tang Poems	Yuan dynasty	tang ren shi shi er shou	唐人诗十二首	144
Wang Hong Fan Tablet	Tang dynasty	wang hong fan bei	王洪范碑	85
Wang Ji Tablet	Three Kingdoms	wang ji bei	王基碑	36
Wooden and Bamboo Slips Bearing Partial Contents of the Confucian Classics on Rites and Etiquette Unearthed in Wuwei	Han dynasty	wu wei li yi jian	武威礼仪简	17
Wooden Tablets of Juyan	Han dynasty	ju yan han jian	居延汉简	16
Writings in Seal Script on a Scroll	Qing dynasty	zhuan shu wen zhou	篆书文轴	193
Xian Yu Huang Tablet	Han dynasty	xian yu huang bei	鲜于璜碑	25
Yi Ying Tablet	Han dynasty	yi ying bei	乙瑛碑	7, 20, 21, 26, 203
Yueyang Pavilion	Ming dynasty	yue yang lou ji	岳阳楼记	172
Yunhui General Li Xiu Tablet	Tang dynasty	yun hui jiang jun li xiu bei	云麾将军李秀碑	9, 86
Zen Master Xinxing Tablet	Tang dynasty	xin xing chan shi bei	信行禅师碑	8, 78
Zhang Meng Long Tablet	Northern dynasties	zhang meng long bei	张猛龙碑	7, 61
Zhang Qian Tablet	Han dynasty	zhang qian bei	张迁碑	7, 20, 25, 30, 200

Scripts

Terms

English	Chinese Pinyin	Chinese	Page
appended foot	chui jiao	垂脚	165
back brush-tip	hui feng	回锋	20, 188
center-brush	zhong feng	中锋	43, 49, 89, 93, 95, 116, 117, 139, 170, 177, 186, 187, 199
contractive	nei ye	内擫	13, 45, 56, 67, 69, 75, 76, 131, 132, 140
diagonal strokes	bo zhe	波磔	5, 21, 22, 24, 28, 29, 34, 70, 101, 117, 205
"dry" brush	tu bi	秃笔	37, 186
expansive	wai tuo	外拓	13, 28, 35, 45, 56, 63, 67, 71, 75, 201
forward brush-tip	da feng	搭锋	139
model-letters tradition	tie xue	帖学	188
no paired swallows	yan bu shuang fei	燕不双飞	18
one wave, three reversals	yi bo san zhe	一波三折	24, 30, 75
"paintbrush" style	qi shu	漆书	188
reversed brush-tip	ni feng	逆锋	124, 139, 199
round stroke	yuan bi	圆笔	18, 27, 43, 55, 72, 77, 155
side-brush	ce feng	侧锋	43, 54, 116, 117, 177, 179, 188
silkworm head and swallow tail	can tou yan wei	蚕头雁尾	21, 24, 30
"slim gold" style	shou jin ti	瘦金体	78, 92
square stroke	fang bi	方笔	17, 25, 43, 50, 55, 62, 137, 139, 190
stele tradition	bei xue	碑学	7, 188, 198, 201
swallow tail	yan wei	燕（雁）尾	18, 22, 28, 34, 50, 52, 117, 155
understated	liu fa	留法	195, 213

Dynasties in Chinese History

Xia Dynasty	c.2070BC - c.1600BC
Shang Dynasty	c.1600BC - c.1046BC
Zhou Dynasty	c.1046BC - c.221BC
Western Zhou Dynasty	c.1046BC - c.771BC
Eastern Zhou Dynasty	770BC - 256BC
Spring and Autumn Period	770BC - 476BC
Warring States Period	475BC - 221BC
Qin Dynasty	221BC - 206BC
Han Dynasty	206BC - 220AD
Western Han Dynasty	206BC - 25AD
Eastern Han Dynasty	25AD - 220AD
Three Kingdoms	220AD - 280AD
Wei	220AD - 265AD
Shu Han	221AD - 263AD
Wu	222AD - 280AD
Jin Dynasty	265AD - 420AD
Western Jin Dynasty	265AD - 316AD
Eastern Jin Dynasty	317AD - 420AD
Northern and Southern Dynasties	420AD - 589AD
Southern Dynasties	420AD - 589AD
Northern Dynasties	439AD - 581AD
Sui Dynasty	581AD - 618AD
Tang Dynasty	618AD - 907AD
Five Dynastives and Ten States	907AD - 960AD
Five Dynasties	907AD - 960AD
Ten States	902AD - 979AD
Song Dynasty	960AD - 1279AD
Northern Song Dynasty	960AD - 1127AD
Southern Song Dynasty	1127AD - 1279AD
Liao Dynasty	907AD - 1125AD
Jin Dynasty	1115AD - 1234AD
Xixia Dynasty	1038AD - 1227AD
Yuan Dynasty	1279AD - 1368AD
Ming Dynasty	1368AD - 1644AD
Qing Dynasty	1644AD - 1911AD